Acclaim for Phillip
Simon Girty Turncoat Hero

"*Simon Girty Turncoat Hero* is a scrupulously researched, fascinating account of the events surrounding the frontier war in general and an exoneration of Simon Girty in particular.

Phillip Hoffman has managed to take a mountain of raw data (battles, treaties made and broken, both sides floundering through the woods with short supplies, runners routinely sent on 100-mile foot-journeys to deliver messages) and turn it into a very readable account of "how the West was lost."

- Review by Susan F. Lum, *Aspen Times*, Aspen, Colorado

"I finished reading the book last night, and to say I am impressed would be an understatement. It belongs on the shelf of every person with an interest in North American frontier history, and it ought to be at the top of libraries' order list."

- Review by author Ed Butts, Guelph, Canada

"I have read almost all of the books and articles about Uncle Simon and I must say this book by Phil Hoffman is the most accurate in-depth account of Simon Girty, his life and the Girty family of the 1700s that I have had the pleasure to read. I highly recommend it to anyone interested in early America and its heroes."

- Kenneth E. Girty, Renfrew, Pennsylvania

"Phil Hoffman brings to light minute details from the life of Canadian folk hero, Simon Girty. In his own style, augmented with multiple source materials, Hoffman provides an unbiased and detailed account of the man, important to his British associates and his native "brothers." Hoffman humanizes the man by revealing details from Girty's private family life.

Simon Girty Turncoat Hero is an authoritative text for scholars at all levels. Descendants may now experience well-deserved pride in their ancestor, Simon Girty. Thank You, Phil!

- As reviewed by author Madeline Malott, Kingsville, Ontario

"This is a much-needed reappraisal of a central figure of the colonial and revolutionary period of American history. As part of a total war against the native peoples, which included biological and ecological warfare, systematic treaty-breaking, and the vilification of any whites who resisted or objected to this policy, Girty was made a scapegoat and object of derision and fear."

- Eric Marchbein, Squirrel Hill, Pittsburgh, Pa.

"After years of anticipation, Phillip Hoffman's book *Simon Girty Turncoat Hero* has finally made it to press and into my hands. Phillip Hoffman has spent 19 years in meticulous research and turned it into a fascinating, and probably the truest account of one of the most 'misunderstood' historical figures on the American frontier, Simon Girty.

Mr. Hoffman gives us great insight into the British, American, and Indian politics, Simon's contemporaries, and life and war on the frontier. Mr. Hoffman's adept writing skills have taken a much vilified and hated individual and given us another side of Simon's complicated personality; a side of Simon Girty that other writers either ignored or never understood."

Stephanie Thalman, Simon Girty's fourth great-granddaughter

"Hoffman gives us a clear and detailed picture of the negotiations, battles, deceptions, Indian alliances and follies during the Indian conflicts with the impla-cable Americans following the Revolution that only many years of research could have attained. 'Thousands of acres,' he wrote, 'were needed to fulfill the enlistment promises of land that had been made to officers and men. If there was no other way, America would clear the Indians off by force.' To do this the Americans had to demonize the Indians. Hoffman gives us the tragic human nature of this struggle for land and power in which Simon Girty played a major role. The book will be a valuable addition to those written on the men and women who shaped this period of our history."

- As reviewed by author David Beasley, United Empire Loyalists of Canada

Simon Girty
TURNCOAT HERO

This book is dedicated with affection
to my brother, Allan W. Eckert.
It was his books *Wilderness Empire* and *The Frontiersmen*
that first brought Simon Girty to my attention.

Simon Girty
TURNCOAT HERO

The Most Hated Man on the
Early American Frontier

PHILLIP W. HOFFMAN

Flying Camp Press

An Imprint of:

American History Imprints
Franklin, Tennessee
(888) 521-1789
www.Americanhistoryimprints.com

ISBN 13: 978-0-9842256-3-7

Library of Congress Control Number: 2009937709

First Paperback Edition November 2009

Book design by Stanford Alan Griffith
Printed in the United States of America on acid-free paper

CONTENTS

PROLOGUE

[Copy on reverse of Indian Gum Card]

—No. 67—

Known as SIMON GIRTY, the Renegade.
Captured as a mere child by the Senecas, he
adopted the ways of the Redskin and was an
illustration of how bad a bad man can be.
He encouraged the raiding of his Indian friends
and was himself the spectator of the burning
at the stake of Colonel William Crawford. He
died in 1818 an outcast, alone, without friends,
as is the just deserts of every bad man Red or white.

This is one of a series of ninety-six cards. More
cards illustrating romantic America to Follow.

INDIAN GUM

The World's Greatest Penny Value
[Goudey Gum Co., Boston, Mass., c. 1930]

DANIEL BOONE AND SIMON GIRTY were both born in Colonial Pennsylvania within fifty miles of each other, and just three years apart. Both became legends in their own time. Boone ended up one of America's greatest pioneer heroes, and Girty became its most infamous frontier traitor and outlaw renegade. Their legends muddle history.

Thanks to an ever-expanding list of books, articles, films and TV shows that pay homage to his real and imagined exploits, Daniel Boone has been popularized as the quintessential American pioneer. He is Boone, the establisher and protector of numerous settlements in the western wilderness of North Carolina, Kentucky, Virginia and Missouri; Dan'l Boone, the rescuer of helpless young white women who were captured by savages, Captain Boone, then Major Boone, then Colonel Boone, Judge Boone, Assemblyman Boone, and Syndic Boone. Mostly, we remember him as an early leader of the great effort to "civilize" America's once-savage wilderness. Reflecting on the outcome of his pioneering, the aged Boone told interviewer John Shaw that he had been "the instrument by which they [the Indians] lost their hunting grounds."

Boone's identity as a popular frontier folk hero was launched in 1784 when writer John Filson's exploitive *The Adventures of Col. Daniel Boone* was first published. From that foundation Boone's legend has been steadily reinforced.

Less remembered today, but better known than even Boone to the settlers of the American frontier at the conclusion of the Revolutionary War, and the Indian Wars that followed, Simon Girty is served to us as a bloodthirsty white frontiersman-renegade, a traitor who turned against both his race and his nation. We are assured of this in numerous books, articles, official military correspondence, congressional records, essays, poems, plays, films and even songs.

It's the job of the historical biographer to reveal the truth about the characters they choose to study. Fortunately, from thoughtful, well-researched and illuminating works like John Mack Faragher's *Daniel Boone, The Life and Legend of an American Pioneer* (Henry Holt and Company, New York, 1992), we learn that the real stories of American icons are frequently not the ones we have come to expect or believe.

Although he was indeed a noted frontier explorer, the real Boone did not discover Kentucky and, as a woodsman, his skills were no better than many of the noted frontiersmen of his day. A good shot, Boone's marksmanship did not measure up to the likes of a Michael Stoner, or several other sharpshooters of his era. Although renowned as a great Indian fighter, when he was interviewed as an old man Boone admitted to having killed only three men (all Indians) in his whole life. As a frontier military leader, Boone's achievements pale in comparison to those of men like George Rogers Clark. Boone's deeds as a scout, spy and Indian fighter were exceeded by such men as his friend Simon Kenton, who, coincidentally, was also a close friend of Simon Girty. Avoiding conflict whenever he could, Boone did not possess the aggressive nature of Simon Kenton or Simon Girty. Unlike the mythic pioneer hero he became, the real Daniel Boone was not compelled to draw settlers to the west by any noble, civilizing urge, but because he needed money and craved recognition. As a businessman, he tried his hand at trading, tavern keeping, surveying and land dealing, but under his direction these enterprises inevitably failed. Over the course of his life, Boone lost tens of thousands of acres of valuable land to harder-edged businessmen and his final years were spent in poverty.

Cursed by a sensitive ego, Boone's judgment was often overpowered by his emotions. In 1782, during the Revolutionary War, just before the battle of Blue Licks, Boone warned a company of avenging Kentuckians to go no further; that he had seen from the signs that a strong force of British-allied Indians was waiting ahead in ambush. In response, a hot-head accused Boone of being yellow, after which the fool-hearty man wheeled his horse and charged across the Licking River, daring the rest of the company to follow him. To avoid being labeled a coward, Boone joined the others in crossing the river. A few minutes later, his son Israel was among the dozens of Kentuckians who were slaughtered in one of early America's most disastrous frontier defeats. Fighting with the Indians at Blue Licks was Simon Girty, whom the Americans later erroneously credited with commanding the British-Indian forces at that bloody event.

The elderly Boone chose to live in isolation rather than at a settlement, and he was befriended by his former Shawnee captors. Boone cherished their visits and admired their "honest" friendship. "His Shawnee captors had become his second family," Faragher wrote. "… following his remove to Missouri, he reestablished his relations with the Indians who also emigrated westward, and during the last two decades of his life they paid frequent visits to each other's homes and camps, hunting together and talking over old times." A woman who knew Boone revealed to historian Lyman Draper that, regarding the Indians, Boone once confessed to her, "I am very sorry to say that I ever killed any, for they have always been kinder to me than the whites."

A writer-historian should avoid choosing facts that fit the story he wants to tell, and simply do his best to get the story right. John Filson's *The Adventures of Colonel Daniel Boone* was meant to create and enshrine a frontier hero. Some two hundred years later, John Mack Faragher gave us the real Daniel Boone. In 1890, exploiting Girty's notorious image, Consul Wilshire Butterfield's heavily slanted *History of the Girtys* cemented Simon's infamy.

The best source of material about Simon Girty's life lies within the mammoth collection of articles, interviews, notes, letters, journals and newspaper clippings collected by historian Lyman Copeland Draper in the mid-19th century. Today, Draper's manuscript collection resides amid the archives of the Wisconsin Historical Society. Reproduced on microfilm, it has become an enormously important resource of frontier fact and lore for researchers from all over the world (American frontier history has large numbers of fans in Germany and Poland).

Like Boone, Girty was exploited by journalists, historians and novelists, and his exploits, real and supposed, are recounted in dozens of early frontier publications. Thankfully, British and Canadian archives containing early civil and military records help illuminate the truth. Take away their mythical status and Boone and Girty still remain as bold, larger-than-life characters.

There are many books that present Revolutionary War history as though the American rebels and British forces were the sole participants in that conflict, but in truth there were two wars on two fronts: the battles of General Washington and his opponents which took place primarily on the eastern seaboard, and the other bloody war that raged on the western frontier, in which North American woodland Indians played a vital role. Nearly forgotten, Simon Girty's adventures serving American, British and Native American interests from 1764 through 1794 provide a rare and important glimpse into the chaotic dynamics of early American frontier conflict. In order to understand America's true beginnings, it's a story we all should know.

Note to the reader: Excerpts from personal diaries, letters, correspondence and other original documents quoted in this book retain their original spelling and punctuation.

Chapter One

BETWEEN TWO WORLDS

LATE IN THE MORNING of 16 June 1744, a large Iroquois delegation on its way to treaty meetings at Easton, Pennsylvania halted to rest on the road beside the farm owned by Simon Girty, Sr. The procession was piloted by Conrad Weiser. The day before, Weiser had purchased and "killed a stier for them, and bought 200 weight of flower." Some 245 men, women and children were traveling with him. The day was warm and sunny and the travelers were in no hurry after feasting and drinking rum most of the preceding night. Weiser stopped the procession at a shady, comfortable spot beside a farm where he knew the Indians would be welcomed. Then he went to find Girty, Sr. to buy "5 shillings worth of Bread and Milk." It was a sizeable order. Simon looked to his cows and his wife Mary tended her oven.[1]

The Iroquois delegation included twenty-four chiefs and sachems, all adorned in their finest clothing. Their attire was decorated with elaborate quill and bead embroidery, and their hats and shirts bore shiny silver ornaments which dazzled in the sunlight. The men, who were traveling on foot, wore tomahawks and knives in their belts, and carried muskets or bows. Many of the women, particularly those with babies, rode horses that were also decorated with colorful blankets and tack. The assembly presented a spectacularly exciting and inviting scene to five-year-old Thomas Girty and his younger brother, three-year-old Simon, Jr. who hurried into the throng. Their parents had no reservations whatever in allowing their youngsters to wander among such a crowd.

After the bread and milk had been delivered, Mary and Simon

Girty mingled among the Indians, greeting and welcoming them as courtesy and diplomacy required.

That evening, after the Iroquois contingent had moved on, Simon, Sr. might have felt some sense of satisfaction. Since his arrival in the New World, he had acquired a young wife, three sons, a home, a productive farm, cattle and horses, and a successful trading business. He was known and respected by such notable men as Conrad Weiser and Thomas McKee, and his future seemed bright. Simon had a credit line above £300 for trade goods from his wholesaler, at a time when a live steer could be purchased for £4, one hundred acres of farmland could be had for £15, and a two-year contract for an indentured servant's labor could be acquired for £5. While Girty was not as important or successful a trader as Conrad Weiser or Thomas McKee, he was, nevertheless, better off than most, if not all, of the German farmers of Lancaster.

When he arrived in North America in about 1730, Simon Girty, Sr. was middle-aged and single. Neither of these circumstances made him the least extraordinary. Like many of his countrymen, he came to colonial America to escape from poverty so extreme that he had forsaken having a wife and children. Unlike the majority of Europeans who emigrated to America in the early 1700s, few of Girty's peers would have described themselves as farmers. They were rough laborers, fence-builders, carpenters, masons, scavengers, poachers, and opportunists. Competitive, ambitious and energetic, they had become clever in the arts of survival; and for those who were soon to choose life on the frontier, these were vital qualities.

There is nothing to indicate where in Ireland Girty, Sr. came from, but his descendents say he was Protestant and probably from the north. His name first appears in the records of Lancaster, Pennsylvania in 1736. He was illiterate, and the accepted spelling of his name is most likely a colonial derivation of McGearty, Gearty, Garrity or Garrarghty. On some early documents the name appears as Girtee.

Based upon his route to the frontier, Simon Sr. most likely first set foot on American soil at Philadelphia, and soon after his arrival made his way to Pennsylvania's western frontier, established himself at Chambers' Mill at Paxtang, six miles north of John Harris' ferry on the Susquehanna River, in Lancaster County. Currently the location of the state capital at Harrisburg, at that time the area was dominated by German farmers and was also an important hub for the fur trade. Seeking employment, Simon rejected the life of a farm laborer and went looking for a job in the Indian trade. A local trader hired him on as a packhorse man.

A number of western and northern trade routes led from Paxtang, piercing the country of the Allegheny and Ohio River valleys where resident Indians harvested deerskins—the primary commodity of the fur trade. Coursing the wilderness over these ancient trails, Scots-Irish traders traversed hundreds of miles of rugged territory, favoring their pack trains as strongly as their French competitors—the *coureurs-de-bois* or "Bush Rangers" who followed the rivers south from Canada and the Great Lakes—preferred their canoes.

A horse train rarely consisted of more than twenty animals. Tied head to tail, they walked in single file, led by one man and trailed by another. Their packs held rum, guns, gunpowder, lead, flints, tomahawks and vermilion, plus strouds, blanketing, matchcoating (a type of cloth), linen and calicoes of the brightest colors. There were also supplies of wampum (glass beads), lace, thread, gartering, ribbons, women's stockings and all kinds of ready-made clothing, as well as knives, brass and tin kettles, traps, axes, hoes, whistles, looking glasses, silver rings and jewelry. The horses cost anywhere from £7 to £25 per animal, and each of them carried about 150 pounds of goods. In addition to the cost of the animal and the cargo it carried, each horse had to be outfitted with a packsaddle, tack and the all important bells—which were fastened to them every night when they were turned out to forage. Thus the traders had a sizeable investment in each pack train. Workers like Simon Girty, who managed the freight and the horses twenty-four hours a day, seven days a week, earned £2 per month.

As a rule, the eastern woodland Indians preferred the company of the more congenial *coureurs-de-bois*. The French traders wore Indian clothing, learned the Indian languages and customs, married Indian women, and wintered in their villages. By comparison, the English traders often seemed haughty and overbearing. Nevertheless, English traders were readily welcomed, for they presented a wider variety of goods, of better quality, and priced well below what the French demanded. Aided by liberal business policies, which included the extension of credit to their Indian customers, many traders from Pennsylvania and Virginia did very well. The traders received their goods on credit from local suppliers who had secured their inventories on credit from Philadelphia companies who, in turn, had been extended credit by English manufacturers.

Conrad Weiser and Thomas McKee were the two most successful traders in Lancaster. Weiser was a German immigrant who came to New York as a child. Recognizing opportunity, his clever father arranged for his son to spend his teenage years among the Mohawks, in order for him to learn their customs and language. As a result, Conrad's knowledge of the culture of the Six Nations (Iroquois Confederation), of which the Mohawks were a member, was without peer, and his financial achievements matched his diplomatic successes.

Equally as knowledgeable about Indian culture, as a young man Thomas McKee was captured by Shawnees and was condemned to death. At the risk of her own life, a Shawnee girl in her teens saved him. McKee married her and over the years he became one of the most popular traders serving the western tribes. His trading post and home were located at McKee's Half Falls on the Susquehanna River at Dalmatia, about sixty miles north of Paxtang. It was either Weiser or McKee (most likely the latter) from whom Simon Girty secured the credit and initial inventory that enabled him to launch his own business.

While the Indian trade offered appealing financial opportunities to enterprising men, the liabilities were considerable. Once a trader entered the wilderness, he put everything he owned at risk—including his own life. By the time Girty took up this business, substantial conflict was taking place among the tribes as they competed with one another for control over the most productive hunting grounds.

Simultaneously, tensions between the English and the French for jurisdiction over the Ohio and Allegheny valleys were also accelerating. White or red, the politics of the region were in turmoil. An Indian nation allied to the French might suddenly reverse its position and seek alliance with the British, or vice versa. Such an event would instantly affect that nation's relations with its neighbors. Accordingly, as a trader journeyed from one region to another, he had to be in constant contact with the Indians, visiting with them, trading news, and collecting the information that could help him avoid political or physical catastrophe on the trail ahead. As it was with his fellow traders, Girty's survival depended on not only remaining on good credit terms with his suppliers, but also upon the strength of his friendships with the various Indian nations he dealt with during the conduct of his business. It was smart to be popular with Indians. By choice, Girty concentrated on the Delawares, and the degree of his acceptance was attested to when one of their war chiefs, a man called Killackchckr, honored him by taking the name "Simon Girty" for his own—to be proudly used whenever he dealt with whites. At the time, such an honorary practice was common.[2]

Compared to his life in Ireland, Girty may as well have landed on another planet. The difficulty of his adjustment was compounded because his new profession demanded that he learn the protocols of two worlds—native and colonial. Apparently, Girty, Sr. succeeded, for in a relatively short span of time he acquired 300 acres of rich bottom land located on the east bank of the Susquehanna River near Chambers' Mill at Paxtang. There, after building a home, he sucessfully courted and married a young English woman.

His bride, the former Mary Newton, was considerably younger than her enterprising husband and appears to have had strong religious convictions. The birth of their first son, Thomas, in 1739, came at a particularly difficult and precarious time for Simon and Mary. Warlike Shawnees had recently relocated to the Ohio Valley and were busy strengthening their ties to the French. To counter this threatening alliance, English authorities asked the Six Nations to pressure the Shawnees into returning to their former villages along the

Susquehanna River, where they might be better controlled. Obstinate and unpredictable, the Shawnees stood fast, declaring in simple terms their mandate: they would not go anywhere they did not want to go, and they were prepared to die to defend that premise. However, despite their apparent rigidity, the Shawnees were not averse to meeting with English representatives to discuss the situation. As it turned out, the English defused the crisis by submitting to Shawnee demands that traders be prohibited from bringing rum, whisky, brandy or wine into their villages. In return, the Shawnees promised to detach themselves from their recent alliances with the French.

The Shawnee promises were short-lived. Before the end of the year, their warriors joined a French-led thrust down the Mississippi, attacking British-allied Chickasaws and Catawbas. Then, in 1740, the Shawnees turned on the French, attacking one of their fortified posts on the Ohio. After this, the Shawnees once again made friendly overtures to the English. Some historians have suggested that this came about because throughout the Ohio Country, Pennsylvania traders—like Simon Girty—were winning the battle for control of the fur trade.

One great advantage that Girty and his fellow traders had over their French competitors was the proximity of their home bases to the Indian villages they served. The northern winter closed the St. Lawrence for nine months of the year; and due to the rapids, it took French traders anywhere from three to five weeks to get from Montreal to the Niagara portage. By comparison, traders leaving from the Susquehanna could reach the Ohio River in just fourteen days. Thus, while the winter trapped the *coureurs-de-bois* in the North Country, Girty and his peers were already on the trail doing business.

On 14 November 1741, well after the first snow had fallen, the Girty family was blessed with another son. He was a broad-chested, stout-legged boy with jet-black hair and eyes so dark they appeared to be black. He was named after his father. Fifteen months later, in February of 1743, James Girty was born. Unlike his brothers, this Girty child was slender and lanky, with light hair and blue eyes.

The Girty boys were raised in the shadow of the Indian trade. Their father maintained a warehouse stocked with trade goods on his property, and there were frequent visits by the local natives. Fond of children, the Indians lavished attention on the Girty brood and often brought presents for the boys. In contrast to the majority of colonial children who lived on frontier farms (and whose parents feared and hated Indians), the Girty boys matured in an environment where natives came and went, and where they were always welcome. Because the Girtys were Irish and because of their open affiliations and dealings with the Indians, they were unlike the majority of German immigrants who farmed the neighboring lands. The social stigma attached by the majority of settlers to anyone who associated with Indians was something Simon, James and George Girty would have to live with throughout their lives. As boys and men they would be referred to as "Injun lovers," a badge the three "Injun Girtys"—like their father—chose to wear openly. Men in the Indian trade were universally shunned and distrusted by the majority of frontier inhabitants. It came with the profession.

Lancaster County was no more than a scattered collection of tiny enclaves whose westernmost settlements were all east of the Susquehanna River. Settlers near the frontier lived each day with a visceral fear, for across the river, or perhaps just beyond the nearest tree line, there were hordes of sub-human savages who celebrated war, and who enthusiastically inflicted unspeakable cruelties upon their enemies. Despite their fear, there was no doubt among the European immigrants that it was their Christian duty, as expressed in the Old Testament, to "go and subdue the land." Fervent sermons at their churches encouraged the taming of the wilderness. Despite their fear of the savages, there was little doubt that it was their righteous Christian duty to tame the wilderness. Surely, God had not created such vast forests and prairies to be wasted! A minority of them believed that the Indians were also God's children, and that they could be converted to Christian civilization. The vast majority, however, passionately advocated for the extermination of the heathen, whom they referred to as the spawn of the anti-Christ. The term "red-devil" was rooted in Calvinism and predestination. Those who were not of the elect—chosen by God to be saved—would be barred from entering the gates of heaven. If the savages were not for God, they must be against God. And who is against God? Satan, of course.

Because their father was an Indian trader and not a farmer, the Girty brothers were considered outcasts. This situation toughened them and drove them to independent thinking. They learned to decide what was right or wrong for themselves. Aggressive, tough, clever and adventurous, the Girty brothers were learning to survive in a world that could in a moment's notice turn violent and cruel.

There are no records to show the role that religion played in the life of Simon, Sr., but he was standing beside his wife at a German Lutheran Church in Lancaster on 11 October 1746, when his fourth son George (born at Paxtang on 8 March) was baptized. The godfather was Girty's neighbor Andrew Sanderson. Church records do not indicate whether any of their other sons were present, but the Girtys now had an indentured servant named Honour Edwards, and she could have managed their place and tended their children whenever they were away.[3]

As the Girty family had grown so had the colony of Pennsylvania, which in 1748 was populated by 110,000 English subjects. The city of Philadelphia contained 1,500 houses and over 13,000 people. Lancaster County had more than 1,000 homes. The distant New York colony boasted 61,589 non-Indian residents, of which almost 10,000 were black slaves. By 1763, 50% of Virginia's non-Indian population were African slaves.

In the wilderness, the most productive hunting grounds for furs and deerskins moved steadily westward; and thus, the distances Girty had to travel in order to reach his Delaware customers increased accordingly. Leaving Paxtang, he led his pack trains over the Great Allegheny Path, which carried him to Irish George Croghan's plantation at Silver Springs, some five miles west of Harris' Ferry. Born in Dublin, Croghan was one of the most influential men in the region. Although he had a meager education, his adventurous personality made him perfect for his time and place. His estate was located on a large tract adjacent to the convergence of all the major trade routes to the west and northwest. He employed twenty-five men as agents, and he owned more than one hundred packhorses. His headquarters had become a popular place where travelers—including Indians—were welcome to rest, drink and trade news.

Six miles north of Croghan's, the trail Girty followed dropped down into the Sherman Valley and crossed Sherman's Creek. This hilly country was overgrown with pines, red and white oaks, and hickory. Each time he made this journey and halted to let his horses drink from Sherman's Creek, the practicality of building a station there must have tantalized and frustrated him. With a cabin, corrals and warehouse there, he could shorten his travel time to the trading opportunities on the Allegheny and gain a one or two day advantage over most of his competitors. However, the Pennsylvania lawmakers had not yet acquired any of the land north of the Blue Mountains and, in turn, no patents had been granted to any land companies. Thus, not a single acre could be legally acquired. Despite this legal hurdle, there were a few daring squatters scattered throughout the area, and their presence was a continual provocation to the Delawares who repeatedly complained to their Six Nation overlords. As a result, Six Nation sachems frequently raised the issue with Pennsylvania authorities, but nothing of substance had come of it, and the squatters remained. Everyone more or less believed that it was only a matter of time before the governor of Pennsylvania acquired the lands and made them available.

In 1747, Thomas Lee of Virginia and veteran Maryland trader Thomas Cresap organized the Ohio Company, whose objective was to push the Virginia frontier northwestward to the Ohio River. Among the principal investors were Lawrence and Augustine Washington— half-brothers to sixteen-year-old George. In 1748, the Ohio Company petitioned the English king and Privy Council for 200,000 prime acres located near the Forks of the Ohio River (the confluence of the Ohio, Allegheny and Monongahela Rivers, where present-day Pittsburgh is located). A year later, the Ohio Company's petition was granted, with the condition that they establish a fort and settle no less than one hundred families on the site within a time frame of seven years. The investors were delighted to obtain such an astounding prize.

Quick to recognize this new British threat to gain control of the Ohio Valley, the Governor General of New France ordered an expedition to explore the region, and to claim all of the Ohio River drainage for King Louis XV.

Based on such developments, there were many reasons for Girty Sr. to suspect that Pennsylvania might soon purchase tracts on the Juniata River and along Sherman Creek. Girty knew that once such a purchase was announced, immigrants would flood into the country to stake quick claims. He and several of his fellow traders had already explored and decided upon the lands that they wanted, and they were not about to risk losing everything to newcomers. Quietly, Girty and a few companions crossed the Susquehanna, chose the lands they wanted, axe-blazed the trees bordering them, and then began constructing cabins and corrals.

Responding to this new invasion, a delegation of angry Senecas, Onondagas, Tutelos, Nanticokes and Conoys met on 1 July 1749 with Pennsylvania Governor James Hamilton at Philadelphia, and delivered their ultimatum. Fearing a bloody Indian war, the governor promised to have the squatters removed.

It is not known whether the Girty family wintered at their old home east of the Susquehanna or at their new residence on Sherman's Creek in 1750. But in May of that year, a sheriff arrested them at the latter location. Other nearby squatters were also taken into custody, and their buildings and corrals were set afire. Made to post bonds of £500 each, the offenders were bound over for trial at Cumberland County Court. Girty was later found guilty by a magistrate and fined.

Although Girty's losses were steep, they were not insurmountable. He still had his trading business, his home and property in Lancaster, his servants, horses, cattle and other assets. But for a fateful meeting with a stranger named Samuel Saunders (or Sanders) in November, Simon Sr. would have swiftly recovered from the Sherman Creek setback.

According to an 1847 letter sent to the historian Lyman Copeland Draper by Joseph Munger, Jr., a great-grandson of Simon Girty,

Sr., "the trader met his fate when: [Simon, Sr.] ... had a difficulty with one Samuel Sanders, Girty challenged him; they met and both missed, they then took their swords, Girty made a miss step and fell. Sanders treacherously run him through with his sword, which caused his death."[4]

In 1893, the granddaughter of Simon Girty, Jr., Nancy Ann Sanford, stated in a legal affidavit that her grandfather, Girty, Sr., "was killed in fighting a duel with a British officer."[5]

The last date any civil records indicate that Simon Sr. was still alive was 6 November 1750. Depending on the source, Sanders (or Saunders) was a convict, an escaped bond servant, a soldier, or a rival trader who competed with Girty and murdered him to steal his trade goods. While Sanders' status is clouded, there is no question that he was arrested and brought to trial at Philadelphia for the murder of Girty, and that he was convicted of manslaughter and sent to prison.

The conviction of Samuel Sanders for Girty, Sr.'s death followed another more covert crime perpetrated against the Girty family. In February 1751, only some three months after Simon's murder, Indian trader Thomas McKee, and tavern owner George Gibson, appeared together before William Plumsted, Registrar General for the Probate of Wills, in Lancaster County. McKee and Gibson persuaded Plumsted to backdate by a full year their application to act as sole administers in the estate of the deceased, who died intestate. McKee claimed he was owed £300 for trade goods he had supplied to Girty on credit. This clever, but illegal, back-dating strategy allowed him to gain rapid access to Girty's major assets—namely his property on the Susquehanna—without having to worry about competing claims by other claimants. There is no evidence, however, that either McKee or Gibson put any immediate pressure on Mary Girty to vacate the premises.[6]

At the time of their father's death, Thomas was eleven, Simon Jr. was nine, James was seven, and George was only four. The widow Girty confronted her situation with determination. Together, she and her sons planted and harvested a thirty acre plot and managed to survive. It was common for frontier boys of Thomas's and Simon's age to have acquired basic skills with muskets and traps, and they no doubt provided small game for the pot—rabbits, woodchucks, pigeons, ducks, geese, and swans. Simon, Sr. had white and red friends, and surely some of them visited his widow and children to help with their harvesting, or by donating gifts of salt, provisions, game, or other necessities.

Two years after her husband's death, Mary was being courted by a young man named John Turner, who may have at one time worked for Simon Sr. Pleasant, easy-going and even-handed, Turner was a hard worker and a man whom the Girty sons readily accepted. Turner called on her regularly for over a year and, near the end of 1753, she accepted his marriage proposal. Turner owned land on Penn's Creek in the Buffalo Valley (present Union County), and he moved his new family there. As soon as the former Girty farm was vacated Thomas McKee took possession.

About the same time that John Turner married the widow Girty, Governor Robert Dinwiddie of Virginia sent off twenty-one-year-old George Washington to gather intelligence on French activities at the Forks of the Ohio. Specifically, Washington was to seek out the French authorities and advise them that they were trespassing on British soil. He was also to attempt to tighten British alliances with resident tribes.

Since Washington had virtually no military training, Governor Dinwiddie's decision to have him lead such an important military and diplomatic mission might appear odd in retrospect. Indeed, Major Washington was only awarded his commission on October 30th, the same day that he departed on his assignment. Dinwiddie had received disturbing news about French patrols nosing about the Forks, where the Ohio Company's land patent required the construction and maintenance of a fort. If the French managed to take possession of this strategic location, the Ohio Company would be unable to validate its grant. Governor Dinwiddie's interests are better understood when one realizes that he had accepted a substantial gift of shares in this company on the day that he took office. So, while Washington's mission had all the earmarks of a noble, patriotic and brave endeavor conducted on behalf of His Majesty's interests, it was more accurately the response of powerful men who feared their personal fortunes were in jeopardy.

When it came to acquiring or protecting raw land, Washington's qualifications were unsurpassed: he was energetic, aggressive and unrelenting in pursuit of his objectives. For generations, land speculation had been the principal source of his family's wealth. Due to the recent death of his half-brother Lawrence, in July 1752, George inherited half of his Mount Vernon estate, as well as his shares in the Ohio Company. These riches made young George the Ohio Company's most conspicuous and powerful member.

Mary Girty-Turner was carrying John Turner's first child when, in the summer of 1754, it was announced that the colonial government of Pennsylvania had purchased the entire Juniata River Valley and everything south of it from the Six Nations, all the way to the Maryland border. The purchase included Sherman's Valley, exactly as Simon, Sr. had predicted. Mary's late husband had simply made the right move at the wrong time.

John Turner, Jr. was born in February 1755, about the same date as General Edward Braddock's arrival in Virginia from London. Braddock immediately began to assemble an army of British regulars and colonial militia to invade the Ohio Country. Within a few months the general had assembled a force of some 1,400 officers and men, plus cooks, kitchen workers, camp followers, and long trains of baggage wagons. Starting from Fort Cumberland, Maryland, Braddock's ponderous army crawled along established trading routes towards Fort Duquesne, as the new French fort was called, at the Forks of the Ohio.

In July, still some ten miles below Fort Duquesne, Braddock was ambushed by a force of about one hundred French soldiers, one hundred Canadian volunteers, and perhaps a thousand Indians. During the ensuing battle, Braddock maintained his troops in rigid formations, requiring them to stand in an open roadway and receive withering fire from the French and Indians who used trees and rocks for cover. British losses exceeded 900 casualties, including Braddock, who was fatally wounded. The general was later discredited for the most crushing defeat ever administered to a British army on American soil. Following the battle, most of the English prisoners were tomahawked, tortured to death or burned at the stake. Among some twenty-six officers who survived the battle and escaped torture was George Washington, who had fought courageously and had argued without success for Braddock to allow his infantry to follow the Virginians who, at the onset of the battle, took to the woods to fight the Indians on their own terms.

On 16 October 1755, the French and Indian War came to Penn's Creek in the Buffalo Valley. Delaware warriors killed and scalped members of six German and Dutch families, and some twenty-eight men, women and children were missing. The raiders came from the Delaware village of Kittanning, on the Allegheny River, some forty miles north of the Forks of the Ohio (present Armstrong County, Pa.). Fearing for the safety of his family at their sparsely populated locale, John Turner sold his land and moved to Indian Old Town, on the Juniata River (present site of Lewistown, Pa.), where a rapidly growing settlement was being established.

In December, the construction of Fort Granville began on the banks of the Juniata River at the mouth of Kishacoquillas Creek, not far from the new Turner homestead. Turner, who had enlisted as a militiaman, helped build the stronghold.

The new fort was designed to have stockades "fifty feet square, with a Block-house on two of the Corners, and a Barrack within, capable of Lodging Fifty Men." It was to be one of three new installations that would constitute a hurried line of defense west of the Susquehanna River. Deputy Governor Robert Hunter Morris described it in a February 1756 letter to General William Shirley:

... 15 miles northeast of Fort Shirley, near the mouth of a branch of the Juniata called Kishequokilis, a third fort is erected, which I have called Fort Granville. This fort commands a narrow pass where the Juniata falls through the mountains which is so circumstanced that a few men can maintain it against a much greater number, as the rocks are very High on each side, not above

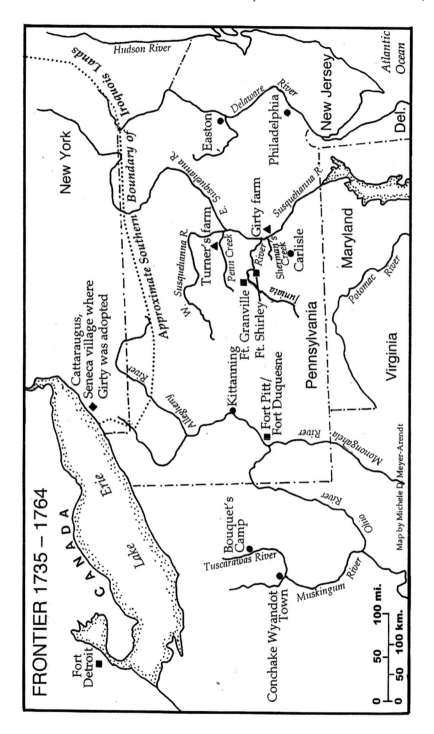

FRONTIER 1735–1764

Map by Michele D. Meyer-Arendt

a gun shot asunder, and thus extended for six miles, and leads to a
considerable settlement upon the Juniata, between Fort Granville
and where the river falls into the Susquehanna.[7]

Deputy Governor Morris failed to mention the existence of a ragged
little ravine that led from the north bank of the Juniata to within
an arm's throw of the fort's south palisade. The depression was deep
enough to allow a man to crawl its length unexposed to anyone
within or on top of the fort's outer walls, and although its presence
had been noted and there had been some talk about filling it in, it was
an unpleasant secondary chore that somehow got put aside.

In March 1756, settlers along the Juniata were kept on edge by a
series of small but deadly Indian raids. On the 25th, due to a lack of
supplies and the need to shift soldiers to other outposts, the garrison
at Fort Granville was reduced to 60 men. Six days later, scouts from
the fort spotted a party of four hostile warriors only a mile away. It
was assumed that these warriors were spying to learn the strengths
of the place. With only three rounds allotted per man with which to
defend the fort, it was decided not to risk sending a squad after the
intruders.

The frontier garrison suffered more than a shortage of ammunition; they also suffered from a shift in command at an inopportune
time. On 22 May, their commander, James Burd, was promoted to
major and reassigned. Burd was replaced by Lieutenant Edward Ward,
who was promoted to captain. Second-in-command fell to Lieutenant
Edward Armstrong, whose older brother Lt. Colonel John Armstrong
commanded British forces west of the Susquehanna from his base at
Carlisle.

By July, Indian raids forced Turner and his family to flee with their
neighbors to Fort Granville for safety. On 22 July, one of Captain
Ward's men was fired upon and wounded by Indians as he made
his way back to the fort and safety. Shortly thereafter, sixty warriors
appeared before the fort and challenged the defenders to come out
and fight. Ward ignored their challenge. The Indians lingered outside

the fort for a short time and then left and began to shoot all the cattle they could find.

The next day, Captain Ward sent patrols out to search for the raiders, without success. Even so, Ward wanted to keep everyone inside the stockade, but it was harvest time for the early wheat and oats, and many of the farmers urged Ward to provide them with protection while they took in their crops. At first, the captain declined; but on the 30th, just eight days after the initial Indian challenge, Ward's scouting patrols once again found no fresh sign, and he relented. The farmers and their families who wished to leave returned to their homesteads, and Ward sent out patrols to protect them. John Turner elected to remain inside the fort with his family. What happened in the following hours and days is best captured by a report in the 19 August 1756 edition of the *Pennsylvania Gazette*. The article reads:

Captain Ward Marched from the Fort with his Ensign, and all the men that belonged to it, except 24, under the Command of Lieutenant Armstrong, to guard some Reapers in Shearman's Valley; That soon after he left the Fort, it was attacked by 100 French and Indians, who were bravely kept at a Distance all that Afternoon and Night by our People: That the next Morning the Enemy took Juniata Creek, and came under its Bank to a Gutt [said to be about 12 feet deep] and crept up till they came within about 30 or 40 feet of the Fort, where the Shot from our Men could not hurt them: That into that gutt they carried a Quantity of Pine Knots, and other combustible matter, which they threw against the Fort, till they made a Pile and Train from the Fort to the Gutt, to which they set Fire, and by that means the Logs of the Stockade catched, and a Hole was made, through which the Lieutenant [Armstrong] and a Soldier were shot, and three others wounded, while they were endeavoring to extinguish the Flames: That the Enemy then called to the Besieged, and told them, that they should have Quarter, if they would surrender; upon which, it is said, one John Turner immediately opened the Gates, and they took possession of the Fort; That they made

*Prisoners 22 soldiers, 3 women, and 5 or 6 children of which the
French took the Young Men and Women, and the Indians the
older Men and Children, and having loaded them with Flour
"etc." they set off, after setting up French Colours near the Fort, on
which they left a Shot Pouch, with a written paper in it: That
when they had marched a little Way from the Fort, the French
Commander (Captain Louis Coulon de Villiers) ordered Captain
Jacobs (a Delaware war chief) back to burn the fort, which he did;
That the Prisoners traveled five days with them, till they came to
the place where they had left their Baggage and Horses, where
they found ten Indians, and some white Prisoners, and heard that
a number of Indians, with more Prisoners, had left that Place the
Day before they got there; that one of our Soldiers growing weak,
and not able to keep up with them, they killed and scalped on the
Top of a high hill; and that another Man, named Barnhold being
wounded in the Arm, they did not tie him in the night, by which
he made his escape, after being Six days with them, and brought
us the above Intelligence. It is said one of the Indians is slightly
wounded.*

---

*Loaded with plunder, the captives who had been taken at
Fort Granville were marched to Fort Duquesne, and then on to
the Delaware village of Kittanning on the Allegheny River. Upon
their arrival there, John Turner was removed from the other
prisoners, confronted with accusations, condemned, and then
tortured to death in view of all the captives, including his wife
and family.*[8]

It was later claimed that Turner—loving stepfather to the Girty
boys—had been put to death by order of a Delaware war chief known
as Toweah or Chief Jacobs. The gruesome details revealed how he was
tortured with repeated applications of red-hot gun barrels, some of
which were pushed completely through parts of his body. Apparently
this was all done very systematically, so that only pain (and not death)

would result. Turner's awful agony lasted some three hours, ending when he was tomahawked.

Not long after the death of her second husband, a war party of Shawnees took Mary Girty-Turner and her eighteen-month-old son, John, Jr., to Fort Duquesne. Her other sons remained at Kittanning. At the time, Thomas was eighteen, Simon was fifteen, James was twelve, and George was ten. Having witnessed the gruesome death of their stepfather, their emotional state can only be imagined. As the days passed, the Indians put to death a number of their captives, but most of these victims were tomahawked and their deaths were mercifully quick.

Why the Indians selected John Turner, Sr. for torture remained a mystery. The real causes are revealed in a French military report written at Fort Duquesne after the event. The document summarizes the debriefing of Captain Louis Coulon de Villiers, the French officer in command at the fall of Fort Granville:

REPORT OF CAPTAIN LOUIS COULON DE VILLIERS

… he [de Villiers] had dry wood cut up and hauled near one of the bastions, taking advantage of a gully 15 paces from the fort, which provided cover from the enemy. At sunrise he kindled a fire which was so fanned by the wind that after Mr. Braford [French for Bras Fort or Strong Arm, i.e., Lt. Armstrong] the lieutenant in temporary command of the fort, had been killed, the gates of the fort were opened to him…. This fort was a square flanked by 4 bastions, the sides measuring 83 paces. Captain E. Ward, who commanded there, had left two hours before the attack for Carlisele (sic) to get money for the garrison, which had gone 6 months unpaid. It was composed of 64 men and the storekeeper, who was also captured. The captured Sergeant, who had surrendered after the death of the Lieutenant, was recognized on the 12th at Fort Duquesne by the Delaware Indians, who were often among the English during peacetime, for having killed one of his comrades in order to marry his wife. They reproached him for this

crime; he gave his reasons and excuses/explanations, which were absolutely not listened to or accepted on examination, and with few formalities, he was condemned to the fire by the Indian Grand Council and commenced to be grilled with red-hot gun barrels.[9]

Girty, Sr. had been a popular trader among the Delawares, and a number of the Kittanning Indians would have been familiar with his home on the Susquehanna and with the appearances of his wife and children. Any of these people could have recognized Mary Girty or her boys. Apparently, the Delawares had correctly heard that their old friend, the trader Simon Girty, had been killed in a fight with another white man. But they were not aware that Girty's murderer had been arrested, tried, convicted and imprisoned. The Indians convinced themselves that Turner was guilty of Simon Girty's murder, and he was made to pay a terrible price.

Following the killing of their stepfather, the Girty brothers were well treated by the Delawares. As candidates for adoption, resocialization would have already begun.

At Carlisle, Lt. Colonel John Armstrong carefully reviewed news of the recent disaster. Stung by the death of his younger brother who was in command at Fort Granville, Armstrong was grimly determined to demonstrate to the enemy that their villages—including their own women and children—were no longer safe. The attack he planned to lead against Kittanning would be the first long range British sortie directed against French-allied natives. His force would consist of seven companies (almost 300 men), mostly militia.

When the Shawnees who brought Mary Girty-Turner and her infant son to Fort Duquesne arrived, they were interviewed and scolded by French officers for their mean and deplorable treatment of the Fort Granville prisoners. Angered by these accusations, the Indians sold one of their English captives to the French for nine kegs of brandy and then departed to a nearby village where they drank until late in the evening. Before dawn, while the Indians were in a deep sleep, three of the Fort Granville captives still under their control slipped away. These escapees, all soldiers, walked for three weeks straight and made it to the Potomac and safety. Their reports were of intense interest to Lieutenant Colonel Armstrong.

On 18 August, a party of Shawnees again took Mary Girty-Turner and her son John to Fort Duquesne, where she was allowed to visit the chapel and meet with the chaplain, Friar Denys Baron. Mary was greatly concerned that her son might be taken away from her and perhaps killed before he had been baptized. Baron agreed to perform the ceremony, and John Hannigan and a woman named Sarah Foissey were summoned to witness the event and serve as godfather and godmother. For the official chapel records, Mary declared that she was English, that she had been lawfully married to John Turner at the time her infant was conceived, and that her maiden name was Newton. Following John Turner's baptism, the Shawnees took Mary and her son to one of their towns on the Scioto.

On the morning of the 30th, Colonel Armstrong rode out from Fort Shirley (present Shirleysboro, Huntingdon County, Pa.) with seven companies made up mostly of Scots-Irish settlers from the Cumberland Valley. His officer staff included Captain Edward Ward. On 3 September, the force arrived at the Beaver Dam country near Hollidaysburg, where they joined an advance party of scouts. Two days later the men were within fifty miles of Kittanning, and thus far they believed they had not been discovered. Learning from the mistakes of Braddock, Armstrong sent spies ahead to scout the best approaches to the Delaware town.

By 7 September, the captive Girty boys had been at Kittanning for thirty days. Although he was still at the village, Thomas had been separated from his three younger brothers. That evening, most of the inhabitants—including the younger captives—were outdoors watching or participating in an annual harvest celebration. Dancing and singing continued until the early hours the next morning.

Not more than ten miles away, one of Armstrong's spies reported that he had seen a few Indians sitting by a fire on the road about six miles from the town. Armstrong sent a small detachment of thirteen men and a lieutenant to keep these warriors under observation until first light, when they were to be killed.

Avoiding the main trail, Armstrong and his army slipped through the forest and arrived at the banks of the Allegheny River about three o'clock in the morning, just before the setting of the moon. Disoriented, the militia did not know for certain in which direction—up river or down river—the Indian town of Kittanning lay. While Armstrong pondered this predicament with his chief of scouts, someone nearby thought he had heard something. Everyone listened. The faint pounding of distant drums and cadence of ritual singing was unmistakable and it came from downstream. Armstrong later wrote:

JOURNAL OF LT. COLONEL JOHN ARMSTRONG

… after ascertaining the location of the town, it became us to make the best of the remaining Moon Light, but ere we were aware, an Indian whistled in a very singular manner, about thirty perches from our front in the foot of a Corn Field; upon which we immediately sat down, and after passing Silence to the rear, I asked one Baker, a Soldier who was our best assistant, whether that was not a Signal to the Warriors of our approach. He answered no, and said it was the manner of a Young fellow's calling a Squaw after he had done his dance, who accordingly kindled a Fire, cleaned his Gun and shot it off before he went to Sleep. All this time we were obliged to lie quiet and hush, till the moon was fairly set. Immediately after, a Number of Fires appeared in different places in the Corn Field by which Baker said the Indians lay, the night being warm, and that these fires would immediately be out, as they were designed to disperse the Gnats.[10]

The majority of houses at Kittanning were situated on the east bank of the Allegheny where, at dawn, Armstrong launched his attack.

The three younger Girty boys were being held in a house directly across the river from the initial firing. At the first sounds of gunfire, their guards forced them out of bed and rushed the boys inland, keeping the brothers on the move.

On the east bank of the river, a majority of the Kittanning warriors took up positions in some of the houses bordering the main path, where they came under assault. There was considerable confusion while the warriors attempted to defend the village perimeter, and their women and children fled into a nearby wood.

Armstrong's men soon surrounded the houses that were held by warriors, and the battle stalemated. Both sides continued to fire at each other sporadically. Although trapped, the warriors kept the English at bay. Armstrong ordered a squad to set fire to the adjacent buildings; a few moments later he received a musket ball in his shoulder.

The fire spread rapidly from building to building, and soon threatened the houses occupied by Chief Jacobs and his warriors. Armstrong's men called for the Indians to surrender. The warriors responded with insults. According to Armstrong's journal, as the occupied buildings caught fire:

... one of the Indian Fellows, to show his manhood, began to sing. A Squaw in the same House, and at the same time, was heard to cry and make Noise, but for so doing was severely rebuked by the Men; but by and by the Fire being too hot for them, two Indian Fellows and a Squaw sprung out and made for the Corn Field who were immediately shot down.[11]

A few moments later, Chief Jacobs was shot as he attempted to scramble out a small opening near the roofline of his burning house. Then an adjacent building exploded with a roar as its entire roof was blown off when a keg of gunpowder stored inside ignited. Ejected by the blast, an Indian's leg and thigh sailed to a great height and then fell into an adjacent cornfield within sight of several Pennsylvanians.

Armstrong had no idea how many enemy warriors had been across the river when he began his attack, and now he worried that the unseen Indians might outflank his troops. The town was in flames, and at least 30 to 40 warriors had been killed along with an unknown number of women and children. His troops had freed eleven people— including Thomas Girty. Prudently, Armstrong decided to withdraw his forces. Captured Indian horses were utilized to carry the wounded. As the English raiders departed, a few white captives who had hidden themselves in the cornfields attempted to follow after them. All of these people were caught by the Indians and put to death.

Exactly what Simon, James and George Girty experienced following the attack on Kittanning is lost. However, the testimonies of other captives offer insight, including the published accounts of Swiss-born Marie Le Roy and German-born Barbara Leininger. These two women had been held prisoners at the village of Kittanning for ten months at the time of Armstrong's attack. Recalling their ordeal, the two women related:

MARIE LE ROY AND BARBARA LEININGER

After the English had withdrawn we were again brought back to Kittanny, which town had been burned to the ground. There We had the mournful oppor-tunity of witnessing the cruel end of an English woman who had attempted to flee out of her captivity and return to the settlements with Col. Armstrong. Hav-ing been recaptured by the savages, and brought back to Kittanny, she was put to death in an unheard of way. First, they scalped her; next, they laid burning splinters of wood, here and there, upon her body; and then they cut off her ears and fingers, forcing them into her mouth so that she had to swallow them. Amidst such torments, this woman lived from nine o'clock in the morning until toward sunset, when a French officer took compassion on her, and put her out of her misery.

Three days later an Englishman was brought in, who had, likewise attempted to escape with Col. Armstrong, and he was burned alive in the same village. His torments continued only about three hours; but his screams were frightful to listen to.[12]

By the end of September the Indians were abandoning the ruins of Kittanning and all three of the captive Girty brothers had been dispersed. Simon had been given away to a small party of Western Senecas who took him north towards Lake Erie, James had gone to the Shawnees, and George remained with the Delawares. The boys were in terrible danger, and they doubted they would ever see each other again.

Simon's captors took him to one of their villages in upstate New York, near the shores of Lake Erie. After a few weeks of testing and orientation (Simon later claimed he had been made to run a gauntlet), he was adopted and became a member of the Western Senecas (also known as "Mingoes"). The world he had entered was that of the most populous and politically powerful nation of the unvanquished, confederated Iroquois tribes. Comprised of no less than four thousand people, the Senecas were the western-most members of the Iroquois League. Their territory extended eastward from Lake Erie all the way to Seneca Lake, beyond which the Cayugas lived. East of the Cayugas were the Onondagas, and beyond them were the Oneidas, the Tuscaroras, and finally, the Mohawks, whose easternmost villages stood on the banks of the Hudson River.

Simon would have learned how the land of the Iroquois League figuratively represented a longhouse, compartmented by the Six Nations. As an adopted child within the Seneca nation, Simon was taught that his new people were "the keepers of the western door." As such, they protected the interior of the longhouse by blocking any invaders from that direction. They also controlled the Great Path, over which Iroquois League warriors traditionally traveled to attack their enemies to the west or south. For centuries the Seneca nation had fought and hunted from the shores of the Atlantic to the Mississippi, as far south as the Carolinas, and as far north as Hudson's Bay. They had fought both the English and the French at various times; and by 1756, their chiefs had sat in councils with Europeans for more than a hundred years. Both the French and English courted the Seneca leaders. And the tribes of the northeast, who lived outside the longhouse of the Six Nations, considered the Seneca to be the most feared and yet the most respected of peoples. Simon was in the hands of one of the biggest and most powerful of Indian nations.

Fortunately, accounts of white hostages taken by the Indians in the same region and about the same time as Simon help to describe what he and his brothers most likely encountered. Writing about his own introduction to Indian life, former hostage James Smith recalled:

The day after my arrival at the aforesaid town, a number of Indians collected about me, and one of them began to pull the hair out of my head. He had some ashes on a piece of bark, in which he frequently dipped his fingers in order to take the firmer hold, and so he went on, as if he had been plucking a turkey, until he had all the hair clean out of my head, except a small spot about three or four inches square on my crown; this they cut off with a pair of scissors, excepting three locks, which they dressed up in their own mode. Two of these they wrapped round with a narrow beaded garter made by themselves for that purpose, and the other they platted at full length, and then stuck it full of silver brooches.[13]

Entering his first Six Nation village, young Simon Girty would have seen a few dozen bark houses scattered across meadows. Still within the memory of the oldest inhabitants were orderly towns with streets, surrounded by moats and palisaded walls. The empty remnants of some of these ancient places still stood amongst the newer and smaller villages. Vulnerable to the white man's artillery, such fortified towns had been difficult to build and maintain; and thus, they were no longer viable. Instead of that former grandeur, the active villages that Simon Girty saw were sprawling settlements of bark-covered houses and cabins built by families and kin groups who frequently abandoned their homes, only to move on and build again whenever the idea suited them.

As it was with all the woodland Indian nations, in order to quickly re-socialize white captives, the Seneca people had perfected a process that cleverly communicated the seductive draw of Indian life. Simon was exposed to it long before he reached the town where he was finally adopted into a family. In some ways the transition was subtle—such as the replacement of hard-heeled European shoes with soft moccasins. On the trail, the captives ate the warriors' fare: nuts, dried fruits, berries, and parched corn meal mixed with maple sugar, plus smoked or dried game or fish. The food was compact and light to carry, and highly nourishing in small amounts. Everything to eat or drink was equally shared between captor and captive. Warmth, shelter and sleep were similarly shared. The message to the captives was clear: the warriors were not only guarding them but also taking care of them as best as they could. From the beginning, a captive like Simon was encouraged to learn the language of his captors, and to learn and do what was proper. Mistakes were never laughed at, but successes were quickly rewarded with compliments and smiles. Female prisoners were not molested sexually. The fundamental reason for taking captives was to secure new members for their families and clans, and accordingly, no warrior would attempt to violate a future sister or cousin at the risk of breaking the incest taboo. Although it was not uncommon to torture and kill women prisoners, there were severe penalties for the warrior who sexually forced himself upon one. Murder was a crime to be revenged by the victim's family, while rape was the only capital offense to be punished by the tribe as a whole.

The captive narrative of Isaac Webster provides a fascinating glimpse into Indian psychology:

We continued our march toward Canada on the west side of Lake George, until dark. The Indians then made a halt, and concluded to rest during the night. Here they sat down around a small fire, which they struck up for the purpose of lighting their pipes, and after smoking out two or three pipes apiece, they begun to think about securing us for the night. They requested us, however, to make oath that we would not attempt to escape from them, promising us at the same time, as a reward for our fidelity, that we should be free from bonds, should fare as they fared, and be treated like brethren. Canfield complied with their request, and had the liberty to sleep unbound; but I refused to comply, choosing rather to be secured than to be guilty of perjury, as I was determined to escape from them, if providence favored me with an opportunity. A very distressing scene ensued, upon my deciding not to swear to them. They ordered me to lie down on my back, which having done, they took a small cord, put it round my neck,

*and fastened it to a stake, which they had driven into the ground
for that purpose. They then caused me to extend my arms, as far
as I could, and fastened them by the wrists, as they had done my
head, to stakes driven into the ground. Two of the Indians then
lay down, one on each side of me, with their tomahawks in their
hands, and their bodies across my arms.*[14]

Webster's treatment was not uncommon. On the other hand, as
insinuated in his narrative, if captives gave their word not to escape,
they were often let loose from their bonds and allowed to move about
freely after the Indian party made their nightly camp. For those who
violated their oaths (most of whom were quickly tracked down and
recaptured), the punishments were harsh. Male or female, these
unfortunates were usually tortured to death, and often other captives
were collected so they could witness these events.

Once a captive like Simon was formally adopted, his transition
was total. Individuals who were adopted instantly attained color-
blind social status within their families, within their clans, and within
the entire Iroquois Confederation. To the Indian mind, an adopted
member of a family was simply, family—regardless of the color of the
skin, the hair or the eyes. Indeed, some former captives later became
important civil or war chiefs. Adoption was an honor, and any captive
who did not reach this status was almost always put to death. When
an Indian from the Six Nations went to war, he was aware that if he
fell into his enemy's hands he would either be adopted or tortured to
death—one or the other. Either way, he would be lost to his former
nation forever. The decision to adopt or to kill a captive was made
almost immediately upon the prisoner's arrival at the home village
of his captors. The first and often the most crucial test a captive faced
upon entering his captor's home village was to be paraded for inspec-
tion by the mourning women, all of whom had recently lost a loved
one. As the heads of their families, these women were encouraged to
inspect the captives and appease their loss by making a selection. For
the captives, however, being chosen for adoption was still no guarantee of escaping an agonizing death, for all the men selected by the

mourning women had yet to run a gauntlet designed to test both their courage and their endurance.

In his 1851 book *League of the Iroquois* nineteenth-century ethnologist and historian Lewis Henry Morgan described the initiation process:

At the time appointed, which was usually three or four days after the return of the band, the women and children of the village arranged themselves in two parallel rows just without the place, each one having a whip (clubs or sticks) with which to lash the captives as they passed between the lines.[15]

At the start of the gauntlet run, captives being tested were shown a goal or objective they must run to which would serve as the finish line and refuge; then they were led back to the starting place and compelled to run for their lives. The practice was to immediately dispatch those who fell from weakness or exhaustion, while those who emerged in safety were treated with affection and kindness. The severity of the beating a prisoner received in a gauntlet was dictated by two factors: 1) how many of the people wielding whips were filled with hate over the recent death of a loved one, or 2) the age of the prisoner making the run. Very young prisoners—those who could be most easily resocialized as Indians—were seldom forced to make such a run, and those who did were seldom seriously harmed.

The more friends a prisoner was able to make among his captors, the better were his chances for survival. Apparently, Simon had a warm, likable personality and a quick, easy smile. Many who knew him as an adult remembered him as a "charmer" and a man who loved jokes and laughter. But now his ability to make friends was hindered by his inability to express himself in the Seneca language. Having just witnessed the terrible death of his stepfather and the torture of other captives, Girty had considerable motivation.

Up to the time of his capture, Simon's family and his father's trading business had been the nucleus around which his life revolved. Simon's father had no relatives in the New World, and it appears that only one member of Mary Girty's family resided in Lancaster County. While there may have been limited socialization with neighbors at harvest time, for the most part the Girty family functioned as an independent unit. There had been no schools at Paxtang, nor any churches offering regularly scheduled services. Now, most likely for the first time, Simon was being intimately exposed to a close-knit society in which the people of an entire village behaved as though they were an extended family. He was now in a situation where people seemed to care deeply for one another, and often spent their evenings visiting from one house to another—a place where hospitality was an art. In *League of the Iroquois* Lewis Henry Morgan discussed the socialization of a woodland Indian village:

> *Their houses were not only open to each other at all hours of the day, and of the night, but also to the wayfarer, and the stranger. Such entertainment as their means afforded was freely spread before him, with words of kindness and of welcome. The Indian had no regular meal after the morning repast, but he allayed his appetite whenever the occasion offered. The care of the appetite was left entirely with the women, as the Indian (man) never asked for food. Whenever the husband returned, at any hour of the day, it was the duty and the custom of the wife to set food before him. If a neighbor or a stranger entered her dwelling, a dish of hominy, or whatever else she had prepared, was immediately placed before him, with an invitation to partake. It made no difference at what hour of the day, or how numerous the calls, this courtesy was extended to every comer, and was the first act of attention bestowed. A neighbor or a stranger calling from house to house, through an Indian village, would be thus entertained at every dwelling he entered.*[16]

Besides being exposed to collective hospitality, Simon was also being introduced to a world where it appeared that the Seneca women had considerably more respect and power than their white sisters. Under English law, any property a woman brought to a marriage became the property of her husband and any income she generated after marriage belonged to her husband. Legally, a woman in English society had no property or monetary rights within the confines of marriage. But within the woodland Indian community, a woman's role and rights enjoyed an elevated status, since the tribal economy and nearly all its social institutions were matriarchal. Men were responsible for hunting, warfare and diplomacy; accordingly, their activities might keep them away from their families for long periods of time. While their men were absent, the women remained at home living in bark houses, which for generations had been located near the same cornfields, vegetable gardens and orchards. Each female head of a family planted, tended and harvested crops from her own private lot in the cornfields that surrounded the village, or from her rows of fruit trees in the town's orchards. How such crops were to be used, traded or given away was entirely her decision. Seneca women were self-sufficient, and while their implements may have been primitive compared to those of the colonists, their knowledge of horticulture and the hybridization of corn was advanced. Indian women harvested a million bushels of corn each year, and the cornfields surrounding an Iroquois village might stretch for miles. Influenced by the colonists, by 1750 the raising of livestock—poultry, hogs and cattle—was popular among the Indians. Simon was maturing in this new social environment, and there can be no question that his perspectives were strongly impacted by his experiences. The world he was being exposed to was far more sophisticated than what he, or any colonial, might have imagined.

The native way of farming, both in spirit and pace, was unlike anything Simon had known. On the Pennsylvania frontier, colonial farmers labored hard from sunrise to sunset, exerting themselves to the very limits of their strength and endurance. Unless their sons were of an age to help, the men generally worked in the fields by themselves. At harvest time, neighbors might join to share the work, but these were hardly bright affairs. The mood was solemn and conversation was kept to a minimum. "Proper" work meant *hard* work.

By contrast, in Simon's new world, Seneca women, from young girls to grandmothers, shared the labor of agriculture as a pleasurable social enterprise. Small children were carried on the backs of their mothers, aunts or sisters, or were allowed to play close by. Chatter and joking among the women was almost nonstop. Meals were lengthy, usually taken under shade trees or in meadows near a creek or river, with women from each household contributing a dish or two. Seneca women were unburdened by religious or social ethics demanding that life was be to be endured rather than enjoyed. While men defended the society, caught meat, built the homes, cleared trees, moved rocks, and broke rough ground, women were the contented machine of Seneca agriculture.

Back in Lancaster County, where Simon and his brothers had been raised, rules came from the top down, and the colonial civil government consisted almost entirely of men who had been appointed by superiors. Furthermore, if they did not fear it outright, the people of the frontier were unquestionably wary of authority. From Simon's perspective, governors, soldiers, regulations, licenses, taxes, sheriffs and magistrates symbolized British colonial government. By comparison, the Senecas had a sophisticated, functional form of democracy in which adult women exercised extraordinary power. When one of the fifty hereditary sachems of the Iroquois League died, it was the senior women of his lineage who nominated his successor. Although only men were allowed to make speeches during council, both sexes attended the meetings with the women conspiring behind the scenes, arguing issues, lobbying and influencing their spokesmen.

Each of the six Iroquois nations contained eight tribes or clans: Wolf, Bear, Beaver, Turtle, Deer, Snipe, Heron and Hawk. A Mohawk of the Wolf tribe recognized a Seneca of the Wolf tribe as his brother and so on. To individuals in the Iroquois League, every member of their own tribe (or clan) was as much his brother or sister as if they had been born of the same mother.

The government was structured in three levels. Local issues were decided at the town or village level where the chief's council (numbering up to 20 men) was comprised of delegates for each tribe (clan). At the next level were the councils of the nation. At the time of Girty's capture, the Senecas were divided into two political factions: one pro-French, the other pro-English. The Seneca national council—comprised of all the chiefs of the village councils—met only occasionally, when issues arose that required the attention of its members.

At the third and highest level of government was the Grand Council that assembled each autumn at Onondaga. The Grand Council consisted of fifty sachems (chief statesmen) with representation from each member nation. The distribution had nothing to do with national populations and the sachems were allotted as follows: Onondaga 14, Mohawk 9, Seneca 8, Oneida 9 and Cayuga 10. The Tuscaroras, who had only recently been admitted to the League, had no representatives but spoke through the Cayugas. All the nations were equal when it came to deciding an issue, and before any proposition could be effected, unanimity had to be achieved. The concept of majorities and minorities was unknown.

As it was with most Indian nations, personal freedom was at the heart of the Iroquois government. Decisions of the Grand Council were not laws that had to be obeyed. They did not supersede private judgment or free will.

In Simon's new world, except for the few communal structures like ceremonial or council lodges, all the longhouses that comprised a village were owned by women who were the heads of their families. Constructed of poles and bark, the average home was about twenty by fifteen feet in size and about the same height. The frames were five or six upright forked poles set firmly into the ground along the longest walls. There were four poles at each end. Each pole stood about ten feet above the ground,, and at their apex cross poles were secured horizontally. Poles that served as rafters were similarly affixed, and the roof was rounded and arched. The frame was sided and roofed with red elm or ash bark, rough side out. There was a smoke hole at the center of the roof directly over a fire pit that had been dug in the dirt floor. Some of the houses were built to accommodate two, three or even four compatible families, each with their own fire. There were entry doors at opposite ends of the structures, and conspicuously displayed over one of them would be the tribal device or sign of the owner. Inside, located against the long walls, were benches of poles and bark running the full length of the house. The benches were covered with mats of skins or blankets and, about five feet above them, berths were affixed to the side frames to serve as beds. Weapons, hunting gear, snowshoes, domestic utensils, clothing and other items were hung from the rafters.

From the start, Simon demonstrated a natural gift for acquiring language. The majority of Senecas could speak elementary English and there were also adopted whites who could help him learn. As he became more skilled in their language, Girty would have discovered that the Senecas held two callings in high esteem for their young men: oratory or arms. Indeed, the Senecas had a quick and enthusiastic appreciation for eloquence. As one historian explains so well, "The chief or warrior gifted with its magical power could elevate himself as rapidly as he who gained renown upon the warpath."[17]

In addition to being powerfully persuasive, sachems were required to recite from memory numerous complex and specific historical accounts involving individuals, villages, tribes and nations. In a society without a written language, all oral history resided within the memories of the sachems and other familial storytellers. To imprint the stories and histories indelibly upon the collective memory of the people, the message had to be eloquent and engraved over and over through powerful oratory skills. What seemed to Europeans an endless repetition of traditional phrases was in fact a basic necessity to the preservation of Indian history.

Considering the prominence Girty later achieved as an interpreter, with command of no less than nine Indian languages (and perhaps as many as eleven), there should be little doubt that even as a young man he had an extraordinary appreciation for communication. His ability to listen, memorize, translate, and accurately repeat a complex speech hours, days, or even weeks later, is attested to by the many social groups (red and white) who later relied upon him as their chosen inter- preter. Living in a multilingual environment, the Indians honored and respected men who served as interpreters, and there is good reason to believe that they carefully groomed Simon for such a role.

At the time of Simon Girty's capture, one of the two most sig- nificant Seneca war chiefs was a pleasant looking thirty-six-year-old native called Guyasuta (also known as Kiasutha, or Kayashota). A member of the Wolf Clan, Guyasuta was a "Mingo," one of a loose confederation of Six Nation Indians who had immigrated to the Ohio Country, the majority of whom were Western Senecas. They identified more closely with the Shawnees and Delawares living in the same region than with the Iroquois Confederacy that stretched far to the east, into upper New York. Literally, Guyasuta's name meant "crosses standing in a row." He was not a hereditary chief but had earned his rank. Famous as an orator, it was Guyasuta who had accompanied George Washington in 1753, when the young Virginian was on his first military mission carrying Governor Dinwiddie's protests up to the French commander at Fort Le Bouef. As a principal war chief, Guyasuta was interested in the development of all the young Western Seneca men coming of warrior age, native-born or adopted. There is little doubt that the two first met when Girty began his life among the Senecas, and there is some evidence that Guyasuta may have been Girty's adoptive Seneca father. However, it is far more likely that Guyasuta served as Girty's village uncle, his mentor, and later as his patron.

Whatever their viewpoint, most of Girty's biographers agree that his blunt honesty, fierce independence, and his predilection for making up his own mind all stemmed from his early years living among the Senecas. It is equally apparent that Girty's disregard for materialism, as well as his intense loyalty to friends—white, red, old and new—came from his experiences as an Indian. Throughout his life, Simon related better to people rather than to property or politics.

Girty's sexuality may also have been influenced by the Seneca culture, in which there was very little premarital interplay between males and females. Formal visiting or courting between the sexes was virtually unknown. When an unmarried man and woman were casually brought together in a social situation, there was little or no conversation between them. Among the Senecas, marriage wasn't based upon the affections of a couple, but upon an arrangement or a contract between the mothers of the parties involved, although matrons and wise men of the tribes to which the parties respectively belonged did offer suggestions to the respective women—just as the women of the village offered suggestions to the men regarding village and tribal manners. As part of this intricate system of courting and marriage, young men were not urged to marry before the age of twenty-five, and then they were almost always encouraged to unite with a woman several years their senior, on the supposition that they needed companions who were experienced in the affairs of life. As early historian Lewis Henry Morgan explained: "Thus, it often happened that the young warrior at twenty-five was married to a woman of forty, and oftentimes a widow; while the widower at sixty was joined to the maiden at twenty."[18]

By the age of seventeen, Girty would have learned that the Seneca ideal of manhood was a complicated role. He had to be a good hunter; in addition, he had to demonstrate self-discipline, autonomy and responsibility. A Seneca man provided for his family, his village and his nation, and he remained steadfastly loyal to his friends. When necessary, a Seneca man was obliged to transform himself into a stern and ruthless warrior who avenged any injury done to those under his care. In that role, he was expected to remain indifferent to privation, pain, or even death. Once a decision had been made to go to war, any warrior was free to form a war party. One simply announced the intention, and other warriors either joined him or signaled their rejection by ignoring his call.

Although they did not fight as warriors, women nevertheless had great influence in the assembly of war parties and could make or break them by their support or disapproval—just as in matters of village and national politics. It was the women who provided the moccasins and the dried foods that the men would take on their journey, and a woman could indirectly express her veto of a war declaration by simply withholding these supplies.

According to captive James Smith, war was the main topic of discussion among the young men:

[We heard that] some time in July 1758, the Ottowas, Jibewas, Potowatomies, and Wiandots, rendezvoused at Detroit, and marched off to Fort DuQuesne, to prepare for the encounter of General Forbes. The common report was, that they would serve him as they did General Braddock, and obtain much plunder.

From this time, until fall, we had frequent account of Forbes's
army, by Indian runners that were sent out to watch their motion.
They spied them frequently from the mountains ever after they
left Fort Loudon. Notwithstanding their vigilance, colonel Grant
with his Highlanders stole a march upon them, and in the night
took possession of a hill about eighty rods from Fort DuQuesne;
this hill is on that account called Grant's hill to this day. The
French and Indians knew not that Grant and his men were there
until they beat the drum and played upon the bagpipes, just at
day-light. They then flew to arms, and the Indians ran up under
covert of the banks of Allegheny and Monongahela, for some
distance, and then sallied out from the banks of the rivers, and
took possession of the hill above Grant; and as he was on the point
of it in sight of the fort, they immediately surrounded him, and as
he had his Highlanders in ranks, and in very close order, and the
Indians scattered, and concealed behind trees, they defeated him
with the loss only of a few warriors: most of the Highlanders were
killed or taken prisoners.[19]

It was Guyasuta who had led the Indian forces that defeated
Colonel Grant. During the fight, the English suffered 270 killed,
42 wounded, and several taken prisoner—including Grant himself.
After their victory, the Indians held a council with their French allies,
and although the French urged them to stay and help defend Fort
DuQuesne, most of the warriors opted to return to their home villages, and only some 200 elected to stay and fight. Led by Guyasuta,
the remaining warriors marched off with French forces to confront
General Forbes. Once again, according to James Smith:

They met his army [Forbes] near Fort Ligoneer, and attacked
them, but were frustrated in their design. They said that Forbes's
men were beginning to learn the art of war, and that there were a
great number of American riflemen along with the redcoats, who
scattered out, took trees, and were good marks-men; therefore they
found they could not accomplish their design, and were obliged

> *to retreat. When they returned from the battle to Fort DuQuesne,*
> *the Indians concluded that they would go to their hunting. The*
> *French endeavored to persuade them to stay and try another*
> *battle. The Indians said if it was only the red-coats they had to do*
> *with, they could soon subdue them, but they could not withstand*
> *Ashalecoa or the Great Knife, which was the name they gave the*
> *Virginians. They then returned home to their hunting, and the*
> *French evacuated the fort which General Forbes came and took*
> *possession of without further opposition, late in the year 1758, at*
> *this time began to build Fort Pitt.*[20]

With the British conquest of Fort Duquesne, the tide of war turned and the northern and western tribes abandoned their former allies, who, on 8 September 1760, surrendered all of Canada. Simon was nineteen years old then, and still living with the Senecas at a village near the eastern shores of Lake Erie.

Having expended most of their gunpowder, and greatly in need of other supplies which they could only obtain from Europeans, the Indians attempted to make peace with the British in order to re-establish trade. As gestures of their good will, they began delivering up white captives. Between June 1759 and October 1761, George Croghan, Deputy Indian Agent at Fort Pitt, received a total of no less than 338 English captives turned over to him by Delawares and Shawnees.

Although her name does not appear on any of the Croghan captive lists, Mary Girty-Turner had nevertheless returned to white society by 1761, and was then living on Squirrel Hill near Fort Pitt. Her young son, John Turner, Jr., was still in the hands of the Shawnees.

Indian aspirations for achieving a genuine peace began to fade when, after taking possession of the French forts, the English refused to leave. This made it clear to the western nations that their former enemies had no intention of abandoning the Allegheny and Ohio Valleys as they had promised. Confirming this suspicion, white settlers began to swarm into the region, and because of the commercialization of hunting, game populations rapidly diminished. The few deer that remained were uncommonly wary, and bows and arrows were no longer practical weapons for subsistence hunting. The Indians of the region were by now completely dependent upon the English for powder, lead, firearms and gun repair. Compounding their plight, when the English finally did decide to resume trade, they refused to extend credit to the Indians, as had been their former practice.

Afraid of re-igniting the recent conflict, the Privy Council in London quickly issued orders to the governors forbidding them to grant lands or to create settlements "which may interfere with the Indians bordering on those colonies." By the spring of 1763 "the ministry was committed to an imperial policy of conciliation on matters of land and trade with Indian tribes."[21]

Events were now unfolding which would lead directly to the return of Simon and his two brothers. The principal reason for England's involvement in the New World was the pursuit of economic gain, yet after more than a century of endeavor the costs of providing military protection to the colonists were draining the British treasury. As the colonies had grown so had the need for more forts and soldiers. After nine years of almost continuous warfare with the Indians, it appeared that unless there were major changes to British statesmanship, such increasingly expensive and bloody conflicts would continue.

In an attempt to formulate new policies to appease the Indians and keep the cost of maintaining the frontier at a minimum, colonial governments formed committees and began investigations. Philadelphia Quaker Charles Thomson's book *An Enquiry into the Alienation of the Delaware and Shawanese Indians from the British Interest,* published in London in 1759, had a profound impact. Thomson was sure that it was their steady loss of lands to the English that had turned the Indians' affection. He claimed that it did not matter whether Indian lands were seized or purchased, the result was always the same: the displaced Indians were forced to subsist upon the hunting grounds of their former neighbors and, as a result, game populations quickly depleted. Discontent among the Indians was almost immediate, and these conditions invariably prompted them to make war against the English, whom they blamed for all their problems. The only way to reduce colonial military expenditures was to make friends of the Indians, and the best way to accomplish this was to prevent further white settlement of their homelands.

The result was the Royal or King's Proclamation of October 1763, which, since it ultimately motivated the richest, most influential men in the colonies to foment revolution, may well be the most important document in American history. Essentially, the new royal proclamation declared that all the lands that drained north or west from the crest of the Allegheny Mountains to the Ohio River were property of the king, to be reserved as hunting grounds for the Indians. There was to be no further direct acquisition of Indian lands by British subjects in the American colonies, and colonists were not to move beyond the Proclamation Line, its boundary. Hence forth the only way Indian lands could be acquired was through and with permission of the English crown. These restrictions instantly thwarted the operations of George Washington, Ben Franklin, Patrick Henry, Henry Lee, and other wealthy property owners, and the land speculation companies they either controlled or in which they were heavily invested.[22]

Attempting to enforce the King's Proclamation, the British commander at Fort Pitt did all he could to maintain the fragile peace. Aware that illegal settlers might ignite a new war, Colonel Henry Bouquet (a Swiss mercenary), issued his own proclamation, making it illegal for any English subjects to settle, hunt, or trespass on Indian hunting grounds without having first obtaining written permission from him, or from appropriate colonial governors. Violators were to be arrested, sent to Fort Pitt for trial, and punished "according to the nature of their offence, by the sentence of a court martial."[23]

Although tenuous, the peace held for a short time and the Indians brought in an ever-increasing number of captives to be repatriated. Most of these captives begged to remain among the Indians, and British soldiers had to tie and carefully guard them.

Despite the English government's best efforts to control the settlers and to conciliate the tribes, by 1763 it was too late to avoid conflict. Indian nations living north of the Ohio River and up to the Great Lakes grew restless. The charismatic and passionate oratory of an Ottawa called Pontiac, and cries for warfare from Guyasuta, gave the concerns of several Indian nations the power of a united voice. Within two years of the end of the French and Indian War, Ottawas, Shawnees, Senecas, Delawares, Ojibwas, Miamis and Mississaugas picked up the hatchet. The bloody conflict that ensued became known as Pontiac's Rebellion, or the Pontiac-Guyasuta War. Simon Girty was now age twenty-two, and his brother James Girty was twenty. Seven years after their capture at the surrender of Fort Granville, they were still living as Indians.

It is highly unlikely that either Simon or James participated in any fighting during the French and Indian War or the Pontiac-Guyasuta War, as it was unacceptable for an adopted warrior to join a war party aimed against his former people. Such a taboo assured that the adopted subject would never have to face combat with blood relatives, or encounter a situation where he might be recognized and then claimed.

By the middle of 1764, a string of Indian victories occurred that resulted in the fall of every English outpost in the Ohio and Great Lakes regions except for Forts Pitt and Detroit, which the Indians finally recognized were undefeatable. The will of the Indian masses to continue the war broke, and in June, General Bradstreet and Sir William Johnson hosted a Grand Council, during which some twenty or more tribes sued for peace. The treaty that was achieved declared:

1. *All prisoners in the hands of the Indians were to be repatriated.*
2. *All claims to the posts and forts of the English in the west were to be abandoned, and leave given to the British to erect such other forts as might be needed to protect traders, "etc." Around each fort as much land was ceded as a "cannon shot" would fly over.*
3. *If any Indian killed an Englishman he was to be tried by English law: the jury one-half Indians.*
4. *Six hostages were given by the Indians for the true fulfillment of the conditions of the treaty.*[24]

Two months later, Colonel Henry Bouquet left Fort Pitt with 1500 men to subdue the Mingoes, Delawares, and Shawnees in Ohio, and to bring back prisoners of war. Serving under him as an interpreter and as an Assistant Deputy Agent for the British Indian Department was twenty-nine-year-old Lieutenant Alexander McKee (whose father Thomas, in Lancaster, Pennsylvania, was still trying to acquire the former Girty farm on the Susquehanna River).

Colonel Bouquet had achieved a remarkable string of victories. Delawares, Senecas and Shawnees met with him on the Tuscarawas

River at the former Wyandot town of Conchake, and Guyasuta was one of the principal delegates.

Addressing the Indians, Bouquet stated:

If we choose, we can exterminate you from the earth. I give you twelve days from this date to deliver into my hands all the prisoners in your possession without exception: Englishmen, Frenchmen, women, and children; whether adopted into your tribes, married, or living among you under any other denomination or pretense whatsoever. And you are to furnish these prisoners with clothing, provisions, and horses to carry them to Fort Pitt. When you have fully complied with these conditions, you shall then know on what terms you may obtain the peace you sue for.[25]

Oddly, among the hostages presented to Bouquet to stand as assurance that the terms of the treaty would be faithfully carried out was the Delaware chief Killackchckr (called *Simon Girty*), who had honored Girty Sr. by taking his name as his own for use in dealing with the whites.

Following the treaty talks, which concluded on 12 November, the Indians began to deliver their prisoners. In his 1929 book *Indian Wars of Pennsylvania*, C. Hale Sipe wrote:

No pen can describe the scenes when the captives were brought to Bouquet's camp during those October and November days of 1764. Husbands met their captured wives. Long lost children were restored to their parents. Sisters and brothers met, after long separation, in many cases since the autumn of 1755. Many captured when children, were unable to understand a word of their mother tongue. Many had married among the Indians and had Indian children dear to their hearts. Indian fathers shed torrents of tears over the surrender of their children, and pitifully recommended them to the care and protection of the humane commander. Many of the captives had to be bound when delivered to Bouquet, to keep them from returning to their Indian relatives and friends.[26]

Two days later, on 14 November, Lieutenant Alexander McKee worked on a document he was preparing for Sir William Johnson, the Superintendent of Indian Affairs. His record listed 206 white captives who had just been returned. Included were "Simon" and "Jammy," along with 47 other names that McKee had just scripted in a neat column titled: Males taken in Pennsylvania, 1756.[27]

Twenty-three years of age, about five foot nine inches tall, stocky and muscular, no doubt wearing his raven-black hair in the scalp lock of a Seneca warrior, dark-eyed Simon Girty would have been clad in his finest set of clothes—decorated shirt, breechcloth, beaded leggings, and quilled moccasins. Amidst the confusion of the moment, he may not have recognized his light-haired younger brother James, who, like him, had been living among the Shawnees. They had not seen each other after their departures from Kittanning, some eight years earlier. James was now twenty-one years old, "tall and slim, fully six feet high—a very long neck—a long flat, nose—blue eyes and not having the least resemblance to Simon."[28]

After praising Simon's character and lingual skills, Guyasuta handed him over to McKee, who may have remembered him from his own boyhood at Lancaster. Later, McKee brought Simon and James together and most likely informed them that their mother and two of their brothers (Thomas and George) were all living on Squirrel Hill, near Pittsburgh. Simon and James were exciting prospects for McKee, and he carefully began the business of recruiting them as interpreters for the new Colonial Indian Department offices at Fort Pitt. They were by McKee's side four days later when Bouquet's army decamped to facilitate their return to Fort Pitt.

The Mingo-Seneca Simon Girty, who could speak nine Indian languages and was now transitioning back to colonial life, was vastly different from the teenager who had been captured at the fall of Fort Granville eight years earlier. For now and forever Simon's world would consist of things Indian and things English, and he would have friends and relations in both spheres. McKee found him a cheerful, energetic and perceptive companion who understood not only the various languages, but also the cultural nuances, political structure, religious rituals, personal values and familial network of most of the woodland

Indian nations strung between the waters above Fort Pitt all the way to Fort Detroit. Whether or not McKee fully trusted Simon Girty at this time is unknown, but the Deputy Agent for Indian Affairs was no fool. He must have recognized that the crafty Guyasuta may have steered Simon to him in order to plant a Seneca spy inside the British Indian Department.

CHAPTER TWO

INTERPRETER, INTERMEDIARY AND FRONTIER SPY

UPON THEIR ARRIVAL at Pittsburgh, Simon and James were reunited with their mother and brothers Thomas and George. Except for John Turner, Jr. who was still with the Shawnees, all of Mary Girty's sons were now home again. The three repatriated brothers—soon to be referred to as the "Indian Girtys"—blazed a claim to several hundred acres on the hill and began to erect a large log house.

Having matured among the Senecas, Delawares and Shawnees, Simon, George and James Girty had much to share, but their elder brother was often shut out. Thomas had no affection for Indians. He was nineteen-years old when Fort Granville was surrendered, and the warriors had treated him harshly as an adult. Made to carry a heavy load of plunder during the captives' march to Kittanning, he was then forced to witness a series of horrific acts, beginning with the torture and killing of his own stepfather. Thomas's stay at Kittanning was hateful and brief, for he was one of the eleven white captives liberated during Colonel Armstrong's raid. Brought to Carlisle, Pennsylvania, he was taken to Armstrong's home and business. In January 1758, the Clerk of the Court of Cumberland County recorded that the then twenty-one-year-old Thomas had been formally bound as an agricultural apprentice to John Armstrong for six years. The arrangement was a success; Thomas liked farming and Armstrong taught him the latest agricultural techniques. At the time of his brothers' return from life among the Indians, Thomas was courting a young woman and it is likely his forthcoming marriage to her is what had prompted Simon, George and James to build a home for themselves and their mother.[1]

Despite their differences, the "Indian Girtys" and Thomas were brothers and they cared for each other. Leaving their lands to be cleared, farmed and managed by their elder brother, Simon, James and George spent most of their time at or near Fort Pitt.

Simon enjoyed working with McKee. Blessed with extraordinary lingual skills and possessing an easy familiarity with Indians, Girty was in the right place at the right time. The end of the French and Indian War had ushered in a new age for British-Indian relations, and Fort Pitt, at the headwaters of the Ohio, was ideally located to launch trading operations that the British hoped would bring them control as far west as the upper Mississippi River. The installation was in serious disrepair due to heavy flooding and neglect. Six years earlier, when the English had wrested control over the Forks of the Ohio area from the French, Fort Duquesne's capture signaled the virtual end of French military operations in the Ohio valley. Now, in 1765, the place no longer had much military value. Colonel Bouquet was opposed to rebuilding the fort, advocating instead that it would better serve British interests as a commercial trade center.

Although the war with the Indians was over, English relations with the western and northern tribes were strained. The Shawnees urgently wanted the British to send out traders but, pending the achievement of a formal peace with the recalcitrant Pontiac, Henry Bouquet had restricted English trade to only a few official stores located at selected forts. At these posts, inventories were limited, prices were rigidly fixed, and they were only open infrequently for business. Essentials that the Indians needed—including gunsmithing, firearms, powder and lead—were for the most part unavailable.

Simon had been at Pittsburgh only a few months when, in May 1765, Guyasuta came to Fort Pitt to represent the Senecas at council meetings hosted by McKee's immediate superior, George Croghan, Deputy Superintendent for Indian Affairs. In addition to Guyasuta, some 500 Seneca, Shawnee, Delaware and Wyandot ambassadors and warriors were also there to press for the resumption of full and open trade. Simon and his brother James worked the meetings as translators.

Without improved trade, the Shawnees argued, there could be no real peace. With the majority of their villages situated farther to the west than the Delaware or the Western Senecas, they complained that it was impractical and dangerous for them to travel so far from their hunting grounds to trade; they did not relish exposing themselves to hostile settlers living near Pittsburgh.

Croghan's position was that until a genuine peace had been achieved with all of the formerly hostile tribes, it was impossible for the English to resume full scale trading. In an effort to bridge the impasse, the Deputy Superintendent invited the Shawnees to join him on an expedition to the Mississippi to meet and hopefully make peace with Pontiac. The Shawnees agreed, and on 10 May 1765, in a gesture of good faith, they brought in and turned over to Croghan a group of forty-four white captives. Twenty-one were females ranging in age from five to thirty, the youngest male was five, and the oldest was twenty-five. The Indians thought that all of them had been captured in Virginia. Among the captives were two women brought in by Muncie Indians (Delawares), and a young male whom the Shawnees claimed they abducted at Cove, Pennsylvania, ten years ago. Taken as an infant, the boy could not speak any English and his white name was unknown. The Shawnees guessed him to be eleven years of age. Creating the official returning captive list, McKee penned his Shawnee name: "Theecheapei."[2]

Thin and tall for his age, the boy had a dark complexion, dark brown eyes, and long, straight black hair. His appearance, coloring and manners might have deceived others into believing him to be a full-blooded Shawnee, but the look of his eyes and hair caught the attention of the Girtys. Mary Girty-Turner was summoned and, after studying him closely, she confirmed through her tears that it was her son. Although John Turner, Jr. had no memories of her, he did not resist being taken to Squirrel Hill. Dining together again for the first time in more than a decade, it was a very special night for the Girty family. Unlike almost all of the other young white captives whom the Shawnees had just returned, John was not being held against his will, nor surrounded by a crowd of mystifying strangers with whom it was impossible to communicate. The Girty family included three white warriors and two of them spoke the Shawnee tongue fluently. Simon genuinely liked the boy and during the ensuing summer he served as one of John's mentors. His fondness for John was enthusiastically returned, and a special bond developed between them.

On 18 July, several hundred miles west of Fort Pitt, George Croghan and his Shawnee escorts met with Pontiac. The Ottawa war chief realized that continued struggle against the English was senseless. With his acceptance of peace, the door to the Mississippi and the Illinois Country was opened. The success of Croghan's diplomatic expedition dramatically increased Fort Pitt's value as a trading center. Hearing the news, ambitious traders hurried there from Philadelphia. Among them was twenty-two-year-old George Morgan, who came to establish a western office for his firm, Baynton, Wharton and Morgan. Morgan knew what he wanted. Immediately after his arrival he arranged for twenty wagons to haul his company's goods from Philadelphia to Fort Pitt. For their return to Philadelphia, he planned to load the wagons with skins and furs he would acquire from Indians in the Illinois Country. Morgan was a visionary merchant whose plans for his company's expansion were in three phases: the moving of trade goods from Philadelphia to Fort Pitt; the storage of trade goods and acquired hides and skins at Pittsburgh; and thirdly, the methodical distribution of goods via shipments down the Ohio River to the Mississippi and upstream to the Illinois settlements.

Because of their knowledge of the terrain and the Indians, Morgan actively sought the advice of men like Simon and James Girty. One of Morgan's newest employees was a young, black-haired, dark-skinned, dark-eyed, pug-nosed immigrant named Matthew Elliott. After arriving from Ireland in 1761, Elliott had successfully established himself as a trader serving the Shawnees and Delawares of the Scioto River region. During the late Indian war, Elliott served with McKee under Bouquet. Both men had close ties to the Shawnees: McKee's mother was either a Shawnee or a former white captive who had been adopted and raised by Shawnees, and Elliott had married a Shawnee woman.

Through Morgan and other merchants, Simon and James Girty became familiar with a growing number of long hunters, river men, traders and interpreters who were assembling at Pittsburgh. Almost all of them had at one time or another lived comfortably among the Indians. These men readily accepted Simon and James.

The frontiersmen drawn to Fort Pitt were among the first to embrace the benefits of a remarkable firearm that had originated in Europe but had only recently reached the colonial frontier. Called a "rifle," because of spiraled or rifled grooves cut into the bore of its long barrel, the weapon was now being manufactured by German gunsmiths in Lancaster, and its performance in range and accuracy was a dramatic improvement over the common, smoothbore musket. Carefully loaded, aimed and fired by a competent marksman, the spinning bullet from one of these deadly new guns could consistently hit a man-sized target out to two hundred yards. By comparison, the musket possessed by both the Indians and British soldiers was only accurate to some seventy-five yards. Given an open field of fire, a few sharpshooters armed with these new rifles could eliminate large numbers of opponents with deadly impunity. Understandably, rifles also improved the harvesting of animals for the hide trade. Acquiring their own Lancaster rifles, Simon and James Girty would have soon learned the ballistic advantages of careful bullet casting and more consistent loading and shooting techniques. On the Pennsylvania frontier, where sharpshooting was both a survival skill as well as a source of pride, competitive shooting matches became increasingly popular. Morgan sponsored a number of such contests and bet heavily on his favorites. Although they were never champions, both Simon and James Girty were good enough to compete in contests involving the finest shots in colonial America.

Utilizing the services of such skilled individuals—men who could shoot, hunt, communicate, and if need be, fight with Indians—businessmen like Morgan and Croghan concentrated on establishing trade in the Illinois Country where the most productive fur harvesting could take place.

Simon Girty's new world was one in which the fur traders required vast areas of wilderness habitat to supply the basic commodity of their enterprise, while their opponents, the land speculators, were equally determined to convert the same wilderness to farmland; pushing the wild game and the Indians ever westward.

Composed of many of the richest and most influential men in colonial America, the land dealers had been forced out of business by the King's Proclamation of 1763. Frustrated, many of them were now conspiring to circumvent and, if need be, to gain independence from the king who had curtailed their most lucrative sources of income. Indeed, thirst for Indian land and dissatisfaction with the Proclamation Line, was the biggest single factor behind the War of Independence. In a 1767 letter to William Crawford, an old friend and one of his favorite surveyors, George Washington wrote:

Mount Vernon, September 21, 1767

Dear Sir:—From a sudden hint of your brother's [here Washington is referring to Crawford's brother Valentine Crawford] I wrote to you a few days ago in a hurry. Having since had more time for reflection, I now write deliberately, and with greater precision, on the subject of my last letter.

I then desired the favor of you (as I understand rights might now be had for the lands which have fallen within the Pennsylvania line,) to look me out a tract of about fifteen hundred, two thousand or more acres somewhere in your neighborhood, meaning only this, that it may be as contiguous to your own settlement as such a body of good land can be found.

... a tract to please me must be rich (of which no person can be a better judge than yourself), and, if possible, level.

... I offered in my last to join you in attempting to secure some of the most valuable lands in the King's part, which I think may be accomplished after awhile, notwithstanding the proclamation that restrains it at present, and prohibits the settling of them at all; for I can never look upon that proclamation in any other light (but this I say between ourselves) than as a temporary expedient to quiet the minds of the Indians. It must fall, of course, in a few years, especially when those Indians consent to our occupying the lands. Any person therefore, who neglects the present

opportunity of hunting out good lands, and in some measure marking and distinguishing them for his own, in order to keep others from settling them, will never regain it.

... By this time it may be easy for you to discover that my plan is to secure good deal of land ... I would choose, if it were practicable, to get large tracts together; and it might be desirable to have them as near your settlement of Fort Pitt as they can be obtained of good quality.

... I recommend that you keep this whole matter a secret, or trust it only to those in whom you can confide, and who can assist you in bringing it to bear by their discoveries of land. This advice proceeds from several very good reasons, and, in the first place, because I might be censured for the opinion I have given in respect to the King's proclamation, and then, if the scheme I am now proposing to you were known, it might give the alarm to others, and, by putting them upon a plan of the same nature, before we could lay a proper foundation for success ourselves, set the different interests clashing, and, probably, in the end, overturn the whole. All this may be avoided by a silent management, and the operation carried on by you under the guise of hunting game, which you may, I presume, effectually do, at the same time you are in pursuit of land ...[3]

About the same time that Washington was instructing his friend Crawford to find and illegally survey forbidden lands on his behalf, the trading firm of Baynton, Wharton and Morgan was petitioning the government to occupy former French forts in the Illinois Country, in order to better protect English trade and to offset continuing ambitions of the French and Spanish. Morgan offered to supply all the provisions required for these garrisons by obtaining sufficient grain and flour, produce, and hogs from local French farmers, and by acquiring meat—deer and buffalo—through large, commercial hunting operations. Morgan figured to build boats and then hire dozens of hunters whom he could send down the Ohio River and then east into the rich buffalo grounds of Kentucky, via the Cumberland, Tennessee, and

Kentucky Rivers. Harvesting the meat, his crews would salt and pack it into sealed barrels—an improved process on an old idea which Morgan himself had helped to develop. He was convinced that if it was salted properly, buffalo meat would remain fresh for a year or more as long as the barrels remained well-sealed. A convincing salesman, Morgan won a contract. In the summer of 1767, he sent a trial crew down into Kentucky. Working only from August through the end of September, they killed more than 700 buffalo and rendered their tallow. In the winter of the same year, Morgan's second expedition brought back an astounding 18,000 pounds of buffalo beef, 60 venison hams, 55 buffalo tongues, and many barrels of tallow. From these results, Morgan knew his hunters were capable of not only meeting but exceeding the requirements of the British garrisons in the Illinois Country. Shrewdly, he found a ready market for the surplus in the West Indies, where salted buffalo meat was welcomed as a new, cheap source of food to feed black slaves who worked the English sugar plantations. Morgan arranged to send the meat south to New Orleans for trans-shipment to the Caribbean.

Early in the summer of 1768, Morgan began the business in earnest. He made ready to send sixty hunters aboard four boats some three hundred miles up the Cumberland River, to hunt the salt licks and cane fields that attracted the great buffalo herds. Tantalized by the nature of such an adventurous enterprise, Simon Girty took leave from McKee and went to see Joseph Hollingshead, the Philadelphian whom Morgan had put in charge of his hunting operations.

With Morgan's approval, Hollingshead signed Girty on as a foreman. In June, two boats with twenty-man crews were readied and the first, with Girty in command, departed from Kaskaskia. Hollingshead was to follow after in the second boat, a few days later. There was a plan for the two boats to eventually rendezvous at a point much further up the Cumberland River.

From men who had hunted buffalo, everyone on Girty's boat knew the dangers. Once provoked, a buffalo could charge as fast as a running horse and it often took several well-placed shots to bring it down. Like the buffalo that foraged the Kentucky cane fields, the

Shawnees, Cherokees and Chickasaw warriors who regularly hunted there were equally unpredictable and dangerous. Despite the inherent risks, once they were on their way, the crews were jovial and good natured. Things went well until the first week of July when a war party of some thirty Shawnees ambushed Girty's boat while it was beached on the shores of the Cumberland River, near the present site of Carthage, Tennessee. Recognizing that their position was untenable, Simon and a few of his men made a run for it, and then, in a desperate attempt to throw off the Indians, they split up. Girty was pursued by a group of warriors, but he was fast and had great stamina, and he slowly outdistanced them. It would have been logical for anyone in his situation to just keep going until he had lost his pursuers. But Simon was more angry than afraid. Crossing a meadow, he chose a tree to use for cover; he then rested his rifle over a limb, watched his back trail and waited with a cold, deadly purpose.

When the foremost of his pursuers presented himself, Simon took careful aim and brought him down. As far as is known, this was Girty's first killing. Reloading quickly, he turned and hurried on. Encountering a rock outcropping, he scrambled to the top, found a comfortable place to sit, and once again watched his back trail. Simon's actions—speeding off to prepare an ambush—were a typical warrior tactic of the Senecas. Girty waited for over an hour, but no one appeared. Apparently, after discovering the body of their fallen comrade, the other warriors had prudently decided that their quarry was too swift and too deadly to continue their chase.

Evaluating his next move, Simon chose between making his way west to the Ohio River or going back to the hunting camp to see if any of his men had survived. He went back to the hunting camp, but when he reached the boat, all he found were mutilated bodies. The boat's hull was stove-in, and the Shawnees had smashed open the barrels of meat and tallow and tossed them into the river, along with all the hides. It was unsafe for Girty to linger, so there was no time to bury his comrades. He could follow the Cumberland River westward and look for Hollingshead's boat, which he knew was somewhere downstream between his own position and the Ohio River, or he could travel north to the Kentucky River, and follow it westward out to the Ohio. Once there, he could wait and hail a passing boat to take him to Fort Pitt. Girty chose to warn Hollingshead and then hurry back to Morgan in the Illinois Country.

On 20 July, writing from his office at Kaskaskia, Morgan sent the following to his partners at Philadelphia:

> *… I was going on with the forgoing When Simon Girty one of our Hunters, came in from the Shawana River & informed me that about thirty Indians had attackd our Boat & that no body had made their Escape but himself that he knew of. He is a Lad Who is particularly attach'd to me otherwise he would not have come here to give me this Intelligence but would have immediately proceeded to Fort Pitt. Mr. Hollingshead will give you his Character … Had not this disaster happened, we should have collected more Skins from that Quarter by Decr next than we trade for here in twelve months…. Besides the skins, they would have rendered about 20M Wt of Tallow & Brought in Meat sufficient for the Garrison all next year. They had agreed to remove about 15 or twenty miles higher up the River that very Day. The same Party of Indians a very few days after attackd six Virginia Men Who were hunting with six Horses on one of the branches of the Green river—They killd one Man named [the name is illegible]—took one Joseph Blankenship prisoner, with all the horses. The other four men made their Escape which Blankenship also did after they had crossed the Ohio.*
>
> *… On Saturday evening following, being the 16th   … Blankenship arrived here. On Sunday Morning I sent out Simon Girty with three other good woodsmen to seek for Cope and his partner [Galloway]. As they did not return that Day, Lt. Ancram, my Chickasaw Indian & myself went out on Monday morning. About $1 $1iles off we fired several Guns & were answered by Girty, Who the evening before had found Cope & Galloway strolling up & down the Woods they knew not Where.*[4]

Simon had made it back to Kaskaskia—a distance in excess of three hundred miles—in less than fifteen days. Then, without having giving him time to recover, Morgan had sent him off to search for the two lost hunters. Stories of Girty's remarkable performance in these events spread across the frontier.

After suffering the loss of so many hunters, and facing the threat of more Indian attacks, Morgan rethought his plan and opted to curtail his Kentucky buffalo-meat operations. Let go, Girty made his way back to Pittsburgh where McKee was happy to re-employ him.

The Indian Department Girty returned to was facing increased hostility from the western tribes for, despite promises made to Pontiac and Guyasuta, English authorities were simply unable to control or curtail the illegal migration of settlers. Hoping for a solution, Sir William Johnson scheduled peace talks to be held at Fort Stanwix, New York. Johnson hoped to defuse the situation by convincing the Indians to let the King purchase new lands that would allow for increased migration.

Some 3,000 Indians, primarily from the Six Nations, attended the meetings in the Fall of 1768. Girty was there with McKee, translating and distributing food and other supplies. When the talks concluded, the boundary for colonial expansion (as established in the King's Proclamation of 1763) had been moved north to the Ohio River, and as far south as that river's junction with the Tennessee—only thirty miles from the Mississippi. Sold to the English by the Six Nations, these new lands were suddenly opened to settlement. The purchase included a corner of present-day northern Alabama, most of West Virginia, much of Tennessee, and all of Kentucky. The lands that had been sold to the English by the Six Nations were hunting grounds of the Shawnees and Delawares, who were naturally outraged by the transaction. Defending their right of sale, the Six Nations told the English that, since they had defeated the Shawnees and Delawares, those people were now their subjects, and they had no say or rights in the matter. The English were made to understand that if necessary, the Six Nations would help enforce the sale.

The sum paid to the Six Nations exceeded £13,000 in silver, but the real purpose of the Iroquois League was not to acquire money, but to deflect new white immigration to the south, away from their home-lands. The chiefs of the Six Nations had shrewdly manipulated the English for their own benefit, and there can be little doubt that Girty was aware of what was going on. There was plenty of time for him and Guyasuta to renew their friendship and discuss everything, including Iroquois objectives.

After the Fort Stanwix talks, much of the silver paid to the Six Nations was squandered for trade goods and rum, and feasts, gam-bling and drunkenness went on for weeks.

Prior to the Fort Stanwix Treaty, the land that the Girtys had squat-ted on at Pittsburgh could not be legally acquired. After the treaty a land office was opened near Fort Pitt, in April 1769, and the place was immediately overwhelmed with more than 2,700 applications. Among the filings were petitions from Thomas, Simon and George Girty. Thomas had just married his bride Ann, and each of the three brothers applied for separate 300 acre tracts on Squirrel Hill (part of which included their mother's claim).[5] The cost of the land was fixed at £5 per 100 acres, plus one penny per acre quit rent. As James Girty's name is conspicuously absent from the 1769 deed filings, most likely he was out trading in the Ohio Valley.

Having their hunting grounds sold from beneath their feet by the Six Nations, large numbers of protesting Shawnees came to Fort Pitt to complain. This proved awkward for McKee, who had just married a Shawnee woman. Thus, while his sympathies were surely with the Shawnees, his position as an officer of the British Indian Department required him to defend English policy. The best he could do to assuage the Shawnees was promise them that he would quickly transmit their complaints to George Croghan and Sir William Johnson.

The situation continued to simmer. In the Fall of 1769, in hopes of resolving the problem, English authorities summoned representatives from the Six Nations to Fort Pitt. During these meetings Simon served as the principal interpreter. The work was demanding; he had to listen carefully to speeches from one side or the other, accurately remember every word and every nuance, and then correctly voice the speakers' positions, questions or answers in proper sequence. Although nothing substantial was accomplished by the councils, Girty's performance helped to reinforce his reputation as a talented, reliable intermediary and interpreter—to Indians and colonial authorities alike.

Simon's life required him to play a number of diverse roles as he danced from one involvement to another, from one culture to the other. His time with his family and neighbors on Squirrel Hill was in stark contrast to his time working for the Indian Department, and the time he spent with fur traders and businessmen was markedly different from the time he spent with Indians or frontiersmen. He was energetic and perceptive, and was honing his natural ability to acquire, evaluate, utilize and debate information on a variety of subjects, as sharply as he would have been had he been attending a good university.

Because of Girty's reliability and his maturing social and political skills, McKee frequently asked Simon to deliver official messages and diplomatic invitations to Indians residing in distant villages. After concluding official business, Simon often enjoyed the privileges due an honored, diplomatic guest. Seated inside a bark house, partaking of his host's best food, he could spend hours sharing news and gossip.

Although many repatriated former white captives suffered difficult social readjustments after returning from years of life among the Indians, Girty had no such trouble. Unlike his contemporaries, who almost always favored residing in either the Indian or the white worlds, Girty thoroughly enjoyed living in both. Sparked by diversity, he found it boring if he remained too long in a single lifestyle or routine. People who knew him at the time recalled him as an active, jocular and outspoken man, rough but popular. Some called him "important," and a few pointed out that although he was generally good-natured, he could quickly become antagonistic and aggressive to people he did not care for, especially if he was drinking. A few women remembered him being dark, stout and good-looking, a "commanding" man.[6] Some people recalled that he was an inveterate prankster. Clearly, Girty was larger-than-life. Whether they were praising or cursing him, nobody seems to have remembered him in vague or lifeless terms.

Simon savored early Pittsburgh. At the edge of the frontier, located at the confluence of the region's three greatest rivers, it was the terminus for all the major roads and trails heading west, north and south. Directly across the Monongahela from Fort Pitt rose a great mountain whose peak contained a mammoth deposit of coal that often caught fire and burned for years. Known today as Mt. Washington, in Girty's time it was called by its Indian name: Hill-That-Burns. Although in disrepair, the fort itself was still impressive. With all its outworks, the fortress occupied over seventeen acres, and its walls encompassed two full acres upon which stood barracks, magazines, guardhouses and other buildings.

If Girty departed from Fort Pitt to follow the Allegheny River northward four miles, it would have led him to George Croghan's estate. Further upriver were the desolate ruins of Kittanning. Continuing up the Allegheny, Simon would have eventually reached the Seneca villages where he grew to manhood.

Downstream from Fort Pitt, Girty could see where the muddy current of the Monongahela pressed up against the green waters of the Allegheny, and the great Ohio River was born. Rejecting each other at first, a distinct brown-green line ran for a mile or so down the center of the river. Four miles downstream was the mouth of Chartier's Creek, where Girty's friend Alexander McKee lived on a 1,400 acre tract. Ten miles beyond McKee's place was Logstown, where "Horseface" John Gibson had a trading post. Like the Girty brothers, Gibson had also been born in Lancaster and he was only a year older than Simon. Following the death of Girty, Sr., Gibson's father had joined Thomas McKee in the scheme to secure the Girty farm on the Susquehanna. In 1763, John Gibson was captured by Indians and condemned to death. He owed his life to a young Indian woman who saved him from the stake. Gibson was among the 209 white captives, who, along with Simon and James Girty, were released in 1764 by the Indians. John Gibson married the Mingo woman who had saved him, a younger sister of Chief John Logan.

If Girty chose to follow the Monongahela upstream from Fort Pitt, he would soon reach the Youghiogheny River, where, following its course another twenty-five miles, he would reach Stewart's Crossing

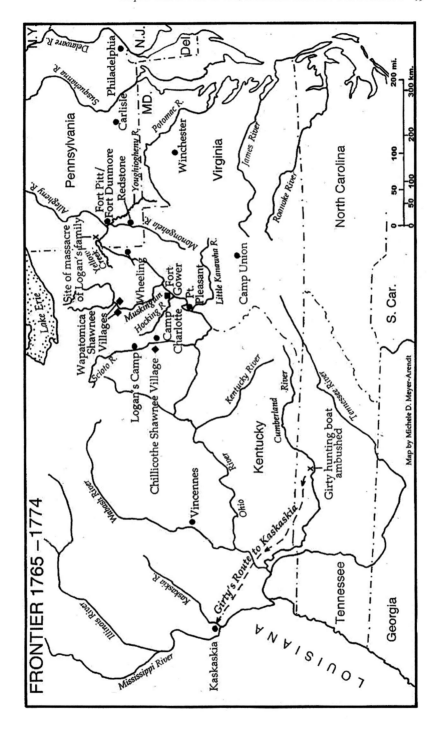

and the estate of the surveyor, William Crawford. Crawford had soldiered with George Washington during the French and Indian War, and the two men had been close friends since childhood. Girty knew Crawford, although they were not close friends. It's likely that if Simon was out that way, he would have stopped to pay his respects and swap news.

At Pittsburgh, in addition to the bigger warehouses maintained by the major trading firms, there were a number of smaller buildings, usually no more than dirt-floored log cabins, that often served independent traders both as stores and living quarters. By 1770, Simon Girty was supplementing his income with a little trading, and he had rented one of these. In January of that year he went to Philadelphia to collect some money owed to him by Baynton, Wharton and Morgan. While he was there, John Baynton tried to hire Simon to carry some letters up to George Croghan in New York, but Girty rejected the offer. Baynton next attempted to talk him into working for George Morgan again out in the Illinois Country, but Simon wanted more money than Baynton was willing to pay. Following their meeting, Baynton wrote to George Croghan:

10 JANUARY 1770

Under cover you have a few lines that I intended to send you of Girty, who has declined going to New York—his business was with you—I believe the poor fellow is in a great want of money....
... I would willingly have [Girty] go down with Mr. Morgan—I have a high opinion of him in every respect, according to his situation save that the rogue is unconscionable in his demands for his services.
... if any person can induce him to go you can.[7]

Considering that Girty was apparently in great need of cash, it is difficult to understand why he refused to hire himself out to carry Baynton's letters to Croghan, or why he rejected the offer to work for Morgan again. The answer may partially lie in the fact that at this time Girty was infatuated by a tall, dark-haired, half-Indian beauty named Elizabeth Lowrey. The lady was the eldest daughter of Colonel

Alexander Lowrey, a prominent fur trader who lived on Montour Creek, six miles downstream from Fort Pitt. Although there was no official marriage, Elizabeth came to live with Girty at Pittsburgh where she was frequently seen on his arm or by his side. After a few months, she was generally accepted as his wife. Simon's involvement with Elizabeth and with growing social and business activities would no doubt have increased his need for money.

Girty loved the nightlife of Pittsburgh, and one of his favorite spots was a noisy tavern owned by Samuel Semple. Popular with both traders and land jobbers, it was at Semple's Tavern where Simon first met and struck up a friendship with Dr. John Connolly, a freewheeling Irish businessman and an enterprising Virginia land speculator. Married to Samuel Semple's daughter, Connolly was George Croghan's nephew, and he had just returned to Pittsburgh from a tour of the Illinois Country.

Simon's work associated him with officers of the Indian Department and other members of the colonial government—and with the Indian statesmen who were their counterparts. Accordingly, men like John Connolly frequently sought his advice. At twenty-nine-years of age, Simon had established himself as a gifted interpreter, a man with a unique knowledge of Indians, and as a crafty backwoodsman who had traversed the country from upper New York to the Kentucky lands. Few men on the frontier would have been able to provide more accurate insights into prevailing native attitudes. Simon had a good reputation. He had acquired a beautiful young wife, he operated his own modest trading business, he had respectable land holdings on Squirrel Hill, and he was known for scrupulously keeping his word and paying his debts. Lacking a formal education, he nonetheless had an excellent vocabulary and was politically astute. He was considerably more sophisticated about business and frontier politics (red and white) than the majority of his rough-hewn contemporaries, such as Simon Kenton or Daniel Boone. While the latter two were hunting and exploring the wilderness, Girty was involved with the highest and most critical levels of frontier decision making, red or white, civil or commercial.

West of the Allegheny Mountains, the boundary between

Pennsylvania and Virginia was still unsettled, and squabbles between the two colonies for possession of the western lands intensified—particularly in the region around Fort Pitt. Girty tightened his relationship with the Virginia faction. He was still strongly connected to the Senecas and probably agreed with their objectives to deflect white immigration. The Fort Stanwix Treaty of 1768 had opened the gates to new settlements, and whether the Shawnees, Mingoes or Delawares liked it or not, immigrants were already infiltrating the Kentucky lands. Virginia's leaders were unconcerned. If war came, they expected the Six Nations to take part as English allies or to remain out of the fray altogether. Either way, considering the prize, the Virginians were ready to fight. Things were moving fast for Simon—perhaps too fast.

In 1771, to further Pennsylvania's claims to the western lands, John Penn created a new county he named Bedford, which included the entire Pittsburgh region. Girty was among those who voted in Bedford's first election, perhaps in support of McKee and William Crawford who, after the votes were tallied, were sworn in as Justices of the Peace.

The creation of Bedford County outraged George Croghan and other Virginians, who protested vehemently. Fortunately, their cause was about to acquire an important ally in the person of John Murray, Fourth Earl of Dunmore. Lord Dunmore had served as governor of New York in 1770, and now, in October of 1771, he was seated as the new Royal Governor of Virginia. Hoping to acquire western estates of his own, Dunmore found congenial associates and advisors among the land speculators of Virginia, including both George Washington and Andrew Lewis.

Soon after Lord Dunmore's arrival at Wheeling, John Connolly presented him a petition bearing over six hundred signatures from citizens of Pittsburgh who wanted Virginia to take control of their city. Although the idea caught his interest, Virginia's governor was not yet ready for such an overt act. However, he gave John Connolly his support and backing, and when Connolly returned from Wheeling, he was the undisputed leader of the Virginia faction at Pittsburgh, with Simon Girty as one of his right-hand men.

In order to focus his attention on personal business and land interests, George Croghan resigned his position as Deputy Superintendent of Indian Affairs. Although a number of men coveted the commission, Sir William Johnson knew that during the preceding two years Alexander McKee had more or less managed the Fort Pitt office, and he gave the job to him. The role of Deputy Superintendent of Indian Affairs was non-partisan, and Johnson felt secure that McKee would not favor the interests of Virginia over those of Pennsylvania.

In the summer of 1772, McKee assigned Girty to escort Chief Guyasuta from Fort Pitt to New York. Simon welcomed the opportunity to travel and spend time with his old friend. At the time, Guyasuta was serving as the "Half-King" or deputy of the Iroquois League for the entire Allegheny-Ohio region. His office required him to be the voice of the Six Nations to all the Delawares, Shawnees and Cherokees living in the Ohio Valley. Sir William Johnson summoned Guyasuta to Johnson Hall (on the Mohawk River in upstate New York), to discuss the Shawnee crisis. While they were en route to New York Girty and Guyasuta encountered Reverend David McClure, who, with his interpreter, was traveling on the same trail, in the opposite direction. Girty was familiar with McClure's interpreter, and both parties halted to exchange greetings and news. McClure was headed west to minister to the Indians of the Ohio Country. After meeting the Mingo-Seneca leader, the missionary asked for Guyasuta's appraisal of his chances.

Wearing a scarlet shirt trimmed with lace, and a gold-laced hat, Guyasuta delivered a thoughtful answer which the reverend later noted in his journal:

[Guyasuta was afraid that McClure's stated mission] would not succeed; for the Indians are a roving people and they will not attend to your instructions; but take courage and make trial. The King of the Delawares (meaning the Delaware chief Teedyskung) and his warriors are now at home and you will see them.

… Guyasuta also mentioned that there already was a minister at the town of Kuskuskoong, on Beaver Creek, and that one

half of the Indians were offended with the other for hearkening to him.[8]

Concluding their conversation, Girty and Guyasuta continued on to Johnson Hall. After Guyasuta's meeting with Sir William, Girty accompanied the chief back to Pittsburgh, arriving there in the fall of the year. Guyasuta oversaw several meetings during which Indian delegates voiced complaints about the encroachment of settlers and surveyors upon hunting grounds located along the lower Ohio River. Guyasuta decided he needed to see Sir William again, and once more, Girty was happy to travel with him. For this assignment, which took place between September 1773 and March 1774, Simon earned five shillings a day.

There are no records that mention how or where Elizabeth Lowrey spent that winter, but when Girty returned from New York she was no longer his woman.

Virginia's determination to settle the disputed western lands was headed towards all-out war against the Shawnees and any Pennsylvanians who stood in the way, and Simon Girty knew which side to support.

CHAPTER THREE
DUNMORE'S WAR

WHILE SIMON WAS AWAY IN NEW YORK with Guyasuta, charges were filed against him in an October 1773 session of the Westmoreland County court held at Hanna's Town, and a warrant was issued for his arrest. The charges stemmed from Girty's participation with other Connolly supporters in harassing their opposition at Pittsburgh.

In the Spring of 1774 when Simon returned from his second trip to New York with Guyasuta, Fort Pitt had been renamed Fort Dunmore and it was no longer in the state of Pennsylvania. Six months earlier, wanting the fort for a base from which he could launch military operations against the Shawnees, Lord Dunmore's council approved his request to create a new county to be called West Augusta, Virginia. Its environs would include Pittsburgh and nearly all of southwestern Pennsylvania. Virginia's governor then sent John Connolly and enough armed men to guarantee the capture and conquest of Fort Pitt, which was quickly renamed. There was little that John Penn could do to respond to Virginia's invasion, since Pennsylvania's Quaker-inspired charter left him without any authority to raise troops. In the face of such blatant, back-handed political actions, the Westmoreland warrant for Girty's arrest no longer had teeth.

After his return, Girty spent more and more of his time helping Connolly and the Virginians. Simon was transitioning from the role of peacemaker to warrior, and in this he had Guyasuta's blessing. The reason for Simon's commitment to the Virginia cause is an enigma only if he is viewed as a stereotypical English colonist. Such a viewpoint denies that he was every inch an adopted Seneca, that he was maintaining close ties to that nation, and that he had spent the previous two years as the almost constant companion of his patron, Chief Guyasuta. Thinking as a Western Seneca, it was as easy for Simon to be pro-Iroquois and anti-Shawnee as it was for colonists living along the western frontier to be pro-Virginian or pro-Pennsylvanian.

As an important member of Connolly's gang, Simon got into several scrapes. One incident is described in a deposition taken from Samuel St. Clair, who swore that he was present at the Pittsburgh house of a trader named Aeneas Mackay when George Aston, Simon Girty, and a Connolly sheriff arrived, accompanied by several armed men. Mr. Mackay was not at home. Apparently, after insulting Mrs. Mackay, Asten ordered some of his men to force their way into the Mackay yard to pull down a sheep shed and stable. The Virginians were in the process of demolishing these structures when Mr. Mackay returned home. Harsh words were exchanged and, according to St. Clair, he saw Asten level a rifle at Mackay, who instantly rushed his opponent, grabbed at the weapon and began to wrestle him for it. During their struggle, the sheriff seized Mackay. Next, according to St. Clair:

> ... he saw one of the Crowd strike at the said Mackay with either a stick or a Whip, said Mackay being carried to the fort by said Sheriff, in the meantime, this deponent deposeth, that he saw the aforesaid Asten strike at Mrs. Mackay's Head with the Barrel of his Gun, with great violence, but Simon Girty, who stood by, parried off the Stroke with his hand.[1]

Two days later, Simon was with 180 Virginia supporters escorting John Connolly to the Westmoreland County courthouse, where he had been summoned to answer charges. Outgunning his opposition, Connolly insulted the court in his opening address and then withdrew without even waiting for its response, making it clear that he had no fear of the Pennsylvanians or their laws. Even if he were to be convicted, there was no way—short of war—that they would be able to collect a fine from Connolly or arrest and jail him. During

Connolly's boisterous return to Fort Dunmore, his mob jeered and taunted any members of the opposition they met along the way.

Girty's life at Fort Dunmore had become bizarre. The offices of the colonial Indian Department were situated side-by-side in adjacent buildings with the headquarters of Connolly's Virginia militia. In his offices, Alexander McKee worked feverishly to preserve a fragile peace with the Shawnees while, a few feet away, John Connolly and his companions plotted to provoke a war with the same Indians. Despite their conflict, Girty somehow managed to maintain amicable working relationships with both men.

McKee's position required him to remain accessible to tribal representatives. To thwart him, one afternoon several of Connolly's men fired their rifles across the river in the general direction of a nearby Indian encampment. The joke was anything but funny at the receiving end. After abandoning the campground, the Indians sent complaints to McKee and claimed that they were now afraid to come over to the fort. McKee responded by arranging clandestine meetings with Indian leaders at his own home, at George Croghan's estate, or at other safe houses. Despite Girty's membership in Connolly's gang, McKee had no problem trusting Simon to deliver such invitations, nor did he have any qualms about relying upon Girty to safely escort and protect the Indian delegates.

By then it had become obvious that Lord Dunmore was determined to make war against the Shawnees. Realizing that their efforts to offset the forthcoming conflict were no longer productive, the officers at the Indian Department began to isolate the Shawnees by working to prevent other nations from joining their cause. Among his many concerns, McKee knew that James Girty and Matthew Elliott were still out trading across the Ohio River deep inside Shawnee country and they had large quantities of guns and powder in their trade goods. McKee rightly worried that these armaments would fall into hostile hands.

Needing overt hostile actions from the Shawnees to justify sending Virginia forces against them, the governor and John Connolly were frustrated by Shawnee leaders who, not yet ready for war, were successfully restraining their warriors. Dunmore and Connolly began to manufacture provocations. One of their schemes was to send surveyors out ranging over the disputed country along the Ohio River between the mouths of the Kanawha and Kentucky rivers. Piloted by George Rogers Clark, a party of these surveyors made their way north to Michael Cresap's trading post at Redstone [present Brownsville, Pa.]. Upon his arrival there, Clark wanted to know if war against the Shawnees had yet been declared, and if so, what were his orders? Cresap sent a rider on to John Connolly at Fort Dunmore for answers. Connolly's written response was cryptic. He answered that he had just sent men to the Shawnees asking them whether they wanted war or peace, "and that war was inevitable." Connolly asked Clark to form his party of surveyors into a militia unit, take command, and then scout the country around Wheeling, providing cover to the inhabitants as they fortified themselves.[2]

On 26 April, a wounded trader named Stephens was brought to Fort Dunmore. The man claimed that he and his two Indian companions had been paddling a canoe down the Ohio River when they were fired upon by men who remained hidden in reeds at the river's edge. Stephens said that the first volley from shore killed a Shawnee in his canoe and a moment later, a second salvo took the life of the other Indian with him, a Delaware. Stephens surmised that the killers were a party of men led by Michael Cresap, and he believed that they were on their way to attack a small village of Indians somewhere on Yellow Creek.

In an effort to keep a lid on the powder keg, McKee sent Girty and other agents to bring in chiefs from the nearest towns for clandestine discussions. While Girty and his fellow agents collected the Indian representatives, Lord Dunmore ordered Connolly to call up and assemble the militia at Pittsburgh. Dunmore wanted a hundred men sent at once to Wheeling under captains William Crawford, Angus McDonald and Dorsey Pentecost. As soon as they arrived there, they were to erect a fort. For the moment, George Rogers Clark and his armed surveyors were the settlers' only protection.

William Crawford told a startling story upon his arrival at Pittsburgh. Crawford had heard that the band of surveyors led by Michael Cresap and George Rogers Clark had encountered some

Indians in canoes, and had chased them fifteen miles downstream before driving them to shore. In the skirmish that followed, a few men were wounded on both sides, and one Indian was captured. Soon after, Cresap and his men made up their minds to attack the camp of the Mingo chief John Logan, which was located on Yellow Creek. Although Crawford's account of that attack would have been sketchy, it provides basic details of what took place. The morning after they had decided to raid Chief Logan's camp, during a break following a rapid march of some five miles, Cresap and George Rogers Clark discussed recent personal experiences they had had with Logan. The preceding month both men had independently visited the Mingo's camp and had been afforded the utmost hospitality. Thinking it over, Cresap and Clark agreed to abandon their planned attack on Logan and return to Redstone. However, not all of their men were so inclined, including Daniel Greathouse and some twenty others, who went off to act on their own.

On the morning of 30 April (at which time Chief Logan himself was away hunting), Daniel Greathouse and his men murdered several Mingoes at his camp. The victims included Logan's mother, his brother, and a younger sister—the wife of John Gibson. Reputedly, Gibson's wife died begging for her life, with Gibson's infant strapped to her back.

Chief Logan was popular at Pittsburgh, where he was well known as an advocate for peace. After the treacherous murder of his relatives, the enraged Mingo chief swore that he would not lower his hatchet until he had taken ten lives for every one of his family who had been butchered. Thus the manipulations of Lord Dunmore and John Connolly had borne fruit. Logan and the Mingoes who followed him were now on the warpath.

Just three days after the murders at Logan's camp, Girty escorted a trio of well-known Delaware chiefs who had been invited to Fort Dunmore by the Indian Department, in an effort to limit the spread of the coming war. Simon delivered White Eyes, Captain Pipe and Samuel Compass to Croghan's home, where Guyasuta and several other Six Nation chiefs had been waiting. A spirited meeting took place; and a few hours later, Guyasuta smugly informed Croghan through Girty that if the Shawnees went to war against the Virginians, the Six Nations and the Delawares would not lift a finger to help them. He also warned Croghan that if the Shawnees attacked anyone living in Pennsylvania, both the Six Nations and the Delawares would "resent it." Croghan rushed Guyasuta's message to John Connolly, who in turn expressed the information to Lord Dunmore. It was news Dunmore had been waiting for and he made the decision to go to war—although a few months would pass before any battles were actually fought.

Dunmore's plans hinged upon the building of a fort at the mouth of the Kanawha River (Point Pleasant), and on 24 July, he notified fifty-four-year-old Colonel Andrew Lewis to marshal his forces. As soon as he could, Dunmore wanted Lewis to march the Southern Army to Point Pleasant.

As news of the impending Indian war quickly spread, fighting men from Kentucky and Virginia volunteered in great numbers at Pittsburgh. Among these adventurers was a tall, blue-eyed, rough-featured, auburn-haired, nineteen-year-old frontiersman who went by the name of Simon Butler. The young man's real name was Simon Kenton, but he had been using the Butler alias for almost three years, following a fist fight with a man he believed he had killed. Kenton and Girty met and took an immediate liking to each other. Each of them had heard of the other's exploits (although at this time, thirty-three-year-old Girty was notably more famous). Commenting on their first meeting, an elderly Kenton recalled that he had seen Girty about Fort Pitt and out at Crawford's home the year before, "only he had not had a chance then to sit with him."[3]

As they waited for Dunmore's army to assemble, Girty and Kenton swapped stories. Girty told Kenton how he and his family had been captured during the French and Indian War, and how he had fared living with the Senecas for eight years. Simon also gave Kenton details of his buffalo hunting adventure on the Cumberland River, while he had been working for George Morgan. Kenton responded with stories of his own exploits. The young Kentuckian hoped to enlist as a scout, or what colonials called a "spy," with one of the militia outfits that were forming-up. Girty promised to help him get the job.

From the start, there was powerful chemistry between the two Simons. Both were self-sufficient men of action who shared a love for adventure, hunting and exploration. They cared deeply about friendship and loyalty and were known to be utterly reliable. What makes their relationship so unique is not what they had in common, but how they could become the best of friends despite enormous differences. When interviewed in his elderly years, Kenton referred to Girty as "one of the three best friends of his entire life," and the "bravest looking man he ever saw."[4] Loud, lusty, colorful, outgoing and sociable, Girty was a man of appetites—a schemer who enjoyed city life, politics and manipulating white or red bureaucracies. Kenton, on the other hand, was a quiet, shy man who did not drink, and who fidgeted in a crowded room. Unlike Girty, Kenton was out of his element negotiating a business deal and he disliked such confrontations. While Girty had a natural predilection for Indians, until late in his life Kenton, by choice, had few dealings with them. Like Boone, at the time when he first met Girty, Kenton was essentially a pioneer. It is interesting to note that later in their lives, both Boone and Kenton developed and enjoyed close relationships with Indians who had formerly been their enemies.

In early June, Kenton left Pittsburgh to spy for Major Angus McDonald's 400-man force at Wheeling. He was in good company. McDonald's "spies" included George Rogers Clark, Jacob Drennon, Peter Parchment, Jonathan Zane, Thomas Nicholson and Tady Kelly, all of whom were famous frontiersmen.

Simon Girty remained by John Connolly's side at Fort Dunmore, waiting for orders to carry communications between Pittsburgh and Wheeling. While Girty waited, word came that Sir William Johnson, the Superintendent of Indian Affairs, had suffered a fatal stroke during a conference with Six Nation sachems at his home in New York. With his passing, two decades of Iroquois-English relations ended. In an effort to keep the bond intact, Guy Johnson, Sir William's nephew and son-in-law, was "raised up in his place and given a new Indian name."[5]

In early August 1774, Connolly sent Girty out to find McDonald's army and then return as quickly as possible to report on their progress.

Simon trailed McDonald's troops along Captina Creek and finally met up with a dozen of his volunteers twenty miles below Wheeling, They told Girty that after abandoning their boats at the mouth of Captina Creek the army had struck out overland for the Shawnee town of Wapatomica, almost sixty miles to the northwest (present sight of Dresden, Ohio). Some minor skirmishing took place at Wapatomica and both sides suffered losses. Leaving men behind to guard their wounded, McDonald and the rest of his army pursued the retreating Indians to "the Snake's Town." Having reached a position just across the river from that place, Joseph Nicholson had called over to the Indians, hollering that he was one of the Six Nations. They answered back, wondering, "If he was Simon Girty?"

According to the story, Nicholson yelled back that he 'was not Simon Girty... that [Girty] was at Fort Pitt,' upon which four of the Indians came over." Obviously, Girty was important enough for the Shawnees to know about him, and apparently, they had been informed that he was helping the Virginians. Later, McDonald's men crossed the river, attacked the town and destroyed all the corn they found standing, as well as some three or four hundred more bushels of harvested corn. Then they marched on through many of the upper Shawnee towns.[6]

Girty hurried back to Fort Dunmore, and on 11 August he delivered his report to John Connolly. By the end of the month, the 1,000-man southern division of the Virginia Army had formed up at White Sulphur Springs (now in West Virginia), and Colonel Andrew Lewis was ready to march for Point Pleasant. Simultaneously, Dunmore, with his Northern Army, was prepared to start for Pittsburgh from Winchester.

About this time, nineteen-year-old John Turner, Jr. visited Simon and asked to go to war by his side. Tall, slim, with dark eyes, and black hair, years of farm labor under Thomas Girty had toughened him. Both men understood there would be dreadful consequences if John was captured, for he would be going into combat against the tribe who had adopted him. Even so, it is doubtful that Girty tried to dissuade him. The boy was old enough to make up his own mind. On the plus side, John knew and understood the Shawnees and their language, and he could recall the terrain. Simon took him to Connolly, who enlisted him and placed him into his brother's care. As for the other Girty brothers, George was carefully avoiding involvement in this war, Thomas was preoccupied with farming, and James was still out trading somewhere in Shawnee country and no one had heard from him in weeks.

In the last week of September, Girty, Turner and Simon Kenton watched Major William Crawford (who had just been promoted) depart for Wheeling with five hundred troops, fifty packhorses and two hundred cattle. A few days later, on 30 September, Lord Dunmore arrived at Pittsburgh with an army of 700 men who were quickly joined by Connolly's 200-man West Augusta Battalion, which included Simon Girty, John Turner Jr. and Simon Kenton. Boarding hundreds of riverboats, canoes and pirogues, the Northern Army sailed down the Ohio.

When Dunmore reached Wheeling, he again sent William Crawford ahead with all the cattle and supplies for the army. Marching overland, Crawford had orders to remain on the Virginia side of the river until he reached a point opposite the mouth of the "Big Hockhocking" (present Hocking River), where he was to cross over and build a blockhouse and stockade. Dunmore and the rest of the Northern Army were to arrive there by boat, a few days later.

When Dunmore's fleet reached the Little Kanawha River, about ten miles upriver from the Hockhocking where Crawford and all their supplies were waiting, the governor halted the army and wrote a dispatch for Colonel Lewis, whom he presumed was now waiting for him at Point Pleasant with the Southern Army. The original battle plan had called for the two armies to combine there, and then cross the Ohio River to march against the Shawnee towns scattered all along the Scioto River. Now, deep into the campaign, Dunmore changed the plan. He ordered Lewis to leave Point Pleasant, hurry upriver and join him at the mouth of the Hocking. Everything would hinge upon Lewis's quick receipt of the new orders, which someone would have to carry by canoe through sixty-five miles of hostile country. Dunmore knew he had to choose the correct man for the job and he carefully evaluated his collection of frontier "spies," who included some of the most audacious woodsmen in colonial America. The majority of Lord

Dunmore's Virginia militia were tradesmen and farmers who, plagued by nightmares of being captured by savages, held in awe the frontiersmen who were willing and able to travel on their own hook. So did Lord Dunmore. When he made up his mind he summoned Simon Girty and asked him to carry his vital dispatch to Lewis at Point Pleasant.

It was the greatest honor Girty had yet received and he went off to choose a crew. Silence and stealth were the main requirements and he asked Simon Kenton and twenty-three-year-old Peter Parchment to accompany him. The canoes that they had journeyed in from the Forks of the Ohio were big boats, built to carry twenty or more men. What Simon and his two companions needed was a smaller, faster craft. Finding a sleek little canoe, they set off that afternoon believing that if they pushed hard all night down the Ohio, they might be able to cover the sixty-five miles and reach Point Pleasant by first light. It had rained steadily for a full day and night just three days earlier, yet the river was still low and the current was gentle. There was no moon that night and for the most part, the river was between 600 and 700 yards wide with dense stands of hardwoods lining both banks.[7]

It took no more than an hour for Girty and his companions to reach Crawford and the men who were bivouacked at the mouth of the Hocking. There, Simon and his crew waited for the sky to darken before continuing. When the trio departed, Girty steered the boat out to the center of the river and kept the canoe some 300 yards from either bank. That far from shore there was very little chance for any Indians to see or hear them. All three men knew how to paddle quietly without banging the side of the boat or splashing needlessly; but even so, whatever sounds they did make must have seemed deafening. Racing against the coming dawn the three men pushed hard. Their tensions did not ease as they approached Point Pleasant, for there was a very good chance that some of Lewis' sentries would see them and start firing. However, just before dawn, when they finally pulled their canoe ashore, Point Pleasant was dead quiet. There was not a trace of Colonel Lewis, his army, or anyone else.

After scouting the area it was clear that they would have to make their way back to Lord Dunmore as fast as possible to advise him that Lewis' army was not where it was supposed to be. After a quick discussion Girty and his companions decided to hide Dunmore's letter inside a hollow tree. Some distance from the hollow tree they peeled bark from another, and using a bit of charcoal Peter Parchment (the only one of them who could write) scrawled on the bare trunk where the hidden letter was to be found. This was not as risky as it might seem, for Girty and his two partners had undoubtedly concluded that by then, the Shawnees, with spies trailing both of the Virginia armies, must surely know their locations.

Waiting for nightfall before risking their return voyage, Girty and his companions slept away the daylight hours of 5 October and started out at sundown. Paddling against the current all night, it was well after daybreak when they reached the mouth of the Hocking. Exhausted, Girty reported to Dunmore that Lewis and the Southern Army were missing. Then Girty joined his exhausted companions and found a place to sleep.

The stockade that Crawford had built at the mouth of the Hocking had been named Fort Gower. Reinforced at Wheeling by an additional 100 volunteers (Cresap's militia, including George Rogers Clark), Dunmore's army now numbered some 1,300 men, with almost 200 cattle, 200 pack horses, and some 125 tons of flour.

On the night of 7 October, sent to Lord Dunmore by Colonel Lewis, Captain Andrew Lockridge, William Sharp and William Mann arrived and told Dunmore that the Southern Army's forward elements had finally reached Point Pleasant without making contact with the enemy. Colonel Lewis had found Dunmore's dispatch, and he wished to inform the Governor that he wouldn't be able to move upriver until the remainder of his army arrived, and not before he had established good defensive positions.

Dunmore was frustrated at Lewis' answer. Dashing off another dispatch, he gave it to Girty and again sent him down river. This time, Girty took Simon Kenton and William McCulloch with him. McCulloch was a trader and an experienced frontiersman. Girty and his companions arrived at Lewis' camp on the morning of the 8th and delivered Dunmore's orders.

Once again, Lewis refused to move, this time replying to Dunmore that he would join him there [at the mouth of the Hocking] as soon as the troops, food supply and powder had all reached Point Pleasant.

Waiting for nightfall before starting their return voyage, Girty, Kenton and McCulloch ate and rested. When asked by one of Lewis' troopers whether he thought the Indians would attack soon, McCulloch answered affirmatively. Once again, after paddling hard upriver all night, Girty and his companions arrived at the mouth of the Hocking at first light.

Having paddled back and forth, up and down the Ohio River four times, covering about 380 meandering miles in total, Girty was finally able to rest a full day. Late in the morning of 10 October, Dunmore and a few of his men thought they could hear faint sounds of musket fire, coming from the direction of Point Pleasant—which was only about 25 miles away as the crow flies. Deducing that Andrew Lewis was now engaged by the Shawnees, Dunmore decided to act. He issued orders to make ready to depart the following morning and march inland to attack the undefended Shawnee towns. He was going to put his army between the Shawnee villages and the warriors whom he presumed were now fighting Lewis. By first light of 11 October, the Northern Army was up and moving. Among Dunmore's scouts were Girty, the Cresap brothers, George Rogers Clark, the Nicholson brothers, Jake Drennon, Peter Parchment, Tady Kelly, Jonathan Zane, Simon Kenton, and William McCulloch. Collectively, these were the most capable and experienced bush-fighters on the frontier. Dunmore chose Girty and two trusted Delaware chiefs, White Eyes and John Montour, to pilot his army. Moving ghost-like, all the other scouts were ahead of and off to both sides of the advancing army. With Girty and the two Delaware chiefs, and with the protection of his sharp-eyed scouts serving in the vanguard, Dunmore felt secure that his army could avoid Shawnee traps.

According to Samuel Murphy (who served in Dunmore's army), it was during the march from the Ohio River when Simon Girty spotted, shot at, and wounded an enemy Indian. Years later, Murphy claimed he heard the gunshot and saw the blood that proved "the Indian had been hit." There are no other details or accounts to corroborate the incident.[8]

On the afternoon of the 13th, Dunmore's army was at its third over-night camp north of the Ohio River (near present Nelsonville, Athens County, Ohio), when a trio of messengers from Andrew Lewis arrived. They confirmed that on the morning of 10 October a major battle with the Shawnees erupted at Point Pleasant. The night before the fight, Cornstalk and at least a thousand warriors had quietly rafted across the Ohio in the darkness and slipped up close to Lewis' positions. At dawn the next morning, two of Lewis' men had gone out to hunt meat and they blundered into approaching formations of Cornstalk's warriors. One of the two hunters was killed on the spot, but the other man made it back to the main camp. Aroused, Lewis' troops sprang to action, and were immediately engaged by the Shawnees. The fight-ing went on all day, with neither side winning a decisive victory. At sundown, Cornstalk began to withdraw his warriors back across the Ohio. The Virginians had suffered at least 75 men killed and about 140 wounded. The Indians removed all of their wounded and most of their dead. According to Lewis' messengers, the Virginians found the remains of seventy-eight rafts that the Shawnees had used to cross back over the Ohio (indicating that perhaps as many as seventy-eight Shawnee warriors had been killed).

Dunmore sent Lewis' scouts back to him with a congratulatory note for his victory. When he was ready to do so, Dunmore wanted Lewis to lead his army across the Ohio and march directly for the Shawnee towns, joining with the Northern Army at a designated rendezvous.

Dunmore's men reached a position about fifteen miles from the Scioto River and were preparing their evening camp when Matthew Elliott shouted a "hallow" and approached, carrying a white flag. Elliott was closely followed by some Shawnee chiefs whom Cornstalk had sent to discuss peace. Lord Dunmore learned from them that once Cornstalk had realized it was impossible for his warriors to dis-lodge Lewis' army at Point Pleasant, he had ordered a withdrawal. Masking their retreat with rear guard actions, the Shawnees then crossed back over the Ohio and hurried to defend their homes on the Pickaway Plains—ahead of Dunmore's forces. Aware that Dunmore was coming, Cornstalk had met in council with his subordinates and urged them to make peace. According to Matthew Elliott, what Cornstalk wanted was for Dunmore to immediately withdraw his army from their country, "and then appoint commissioners to meet their chiefs at Pittsburgh to confer about the terms of a treaty."[9]

Dunmore responded that he, too, was inclined to make peace; but as he was so near their towns and since the chiefs from many different nations were already there, it was more convenient to negotiate now than at some future date. With the authority of a conqueror, Dunmore named a place where he intended to make camp, and where he intended to hear their proposals. Then he dispatched a courier to Lewis, with orders for him to turn back the Southern Army and return to Point Pleasant.

The Shawnees asked Dunmore for an interpreter whom they could take back to Cornstalk to help with their communications and the drafting of their terms for peace. Dunmore assigned the task to John Gibson, who was commanding a company in the West Augusta Battalion (the same Gibson whose Mingo wife—the sister of Chief Logan—had been murdered by Daniel Greathouse). Dunmore was unsure whether Cornstalk was sincere about making peace, or whether he was stalling to gain time and strengthen his forces. He sent for Girty and explained the situation, before asking him to accompany Gibson and Elliott back to Cornstalk's village where he was to spy out all he could.

The next morning the Northern Army moved to a site about eight miles east of the big Shawnee town of Chillicothe, where Dunmore fixed his encampment in the center of a twelve-acre meadow on the northern bank of Scippo Creek. He named the place "Camp Charlotte," in honor of his wife. The very same day, not yet having received Dunmore's request for him to stay, and unaware that the Shawnees were talking peace, Colonel Lewis led his army out from Point Pleasant and marched to join Dunmore.

On the 17th or 18th, Girty and Gibson returned to Camp Charlotte. They reported to Lord Dunmore that they had met with Cornstalk and that they were both convinced he was sincere about wanting to make peace. A few minutes later, some anxious Shawnees arrived to complain that Cornstalk had received word that Lewis' army was still coming on.

Dunmore assured them that he had dispatched a messenger to Lewis ordering him to turn back, and that he was certain he would do so. A few hours later, Cornstalk arrived to meet with Dunmore. Among the many issues the two leaders discussed was Cornstalk's concern over Chief Logan having declined his invitations to attend the forthcoming peace talks. Cornstalk feared that no worthwhile peace was possible without the Mingo chief's participation and support. Dunmore promised to send two of his best men off to locate Logan and to try to persuade him to change his mind and play an active role in the peace talks. Then he asked Cornstalk to gather as many chiefs as he could and bring them immediately to Camp Charlotte, as he was anxious to close the war at once; and that if this could not be affected peaceably, he would be forced to resume hostilities.

Dunmore knew that Logan was a Mingo and that Girty had known the chief while he had been living among the Western Senecas. Thus far, Girty had performed brilliantly and the governor was ready again to rely upon his skills and audacity. Accepting the peace mission, Girty later confided to another officer on Dunmore's staff that he believed the task was exceedingly dangerous and that it was an assignment he did not relish. First, there was the challenge of locating Chief Logan, which required travel through areas that hostile Mingoes controlled. Then, when and if Girty was able to find him, there was the problem of convincing him to come to Camp Charlotte to talk peace. Since the murder of his relatives, Logan and his band had taken some thirty white scalps.

Girty trusted two men to accompany him: Simon Kenton and Joseph Nicholson. Although Kenton could not speak an Indian language, he was a superb frontiersman and a man upon whom Girty could rely. Joseph Nicholson was the veteran whom, while spying during McDonald's campaign, had been mistaken for Simon Girty by the Shawnees. Like Girty, Nicholson had lived for years among the Indians and he was fluent in several of their languages. The need for diverse lingual skills was essential to help Girty and his accomplices locate Logan—and to assist them in explaining their peace mission if and when they encountered other Indians. Once they found Logan, however, language would not be a problem, for the Mingo could speak fluent English (and he had done so at many of the conferences held at Fort Pitt).

Two days later, Girty and his companions found Logan at a camp situated on the south bank of present Congo Creek, about three-and-a-half miles upstream from its mouth at Scippo Creek, located in present Pickaway County, Ohio. Claiming he was a warrior and not a counselor, the Mingo chief flatly declined Dunmore's invitation to come to Camp Charlotte. However, Logan said he had important words on the matter that he wanted Girty to carry back to Lord Dunmore and Cornstalk. Logan phrased his sentences slowly and deliberately:

LOGAN'S LAMENT

I appeal to any white man to say if ever he entered Logan's cabin hungry, and I gave him not meat; if ever he came cold or naked, and I gave him not clothing.

During the course of the last long and bloody war, Logan remained idle in his tent, an advocate for peace. Nay, such was my love for the whites, that those of my own country pointed at me as they passed, and said, 'Logan is the friend of white men.' I had even thought to live with you, but for the injuries of one man. Colonel Cresap the last spring, in cold blood, and unprovoked, cut off all the relatives of Logan; not sparing even my women and children. There runs not a drop of my blood in the veins of any human creature. This called on me for revenge. I have sought it. I have killed many. I have fully glutted my vengeance. For my country, I rejoice at the beams of peace. Yet, do not harbor the thought that mine is the joy of fear. Logan never felt fear. He will not turn on his heel to save his life. Who is there to morn for Logan? Not one.[10]

Dunmore's officer staff knew the nature of Girty's mission to Logan and when he returned to Camp Charlotte, he was mobbed. John Gibson quickly pulled him aside and led him into his tent. When Gibson reappeared, he held aloft a paper upon which he had penned Logan's speech as told to him by Girty. Dunmore asked Gibson to read it aloud, and he and the crowd who had gathered were so moved by the Mingo's words that he had Gibson read the speech two more times. Arousing powerful sympathetic emotions, Logan's speech (which later became known as "Logan's Lament") was destined to become one of America's most famous examples of frontier rhetoric.

In the peace that was subsequently arranged between the Virginians and the Shawnees, Cornstalk and his chiefs agreed to meet with Dunmore again at Pittsburgh the following summer, at which time an official treaty was to be formalized. As a gesture of his good intentions, Cornstalk and his sister (a tall, elegant woman commonly referred to as "The Grenadier Squaw") rode alongside Governor Dunmore on the return march to the mouth of the Hocking. The journey back to the Ohio River was relaxed and graced with happy moments. Delighted with the achievements of his spies, Dunmore recalled that Girty and John Turner, as well as the Nicholson brothers, had all spent years living among the Indians. One night, on the spur of the moment, he asked them to entertain him and his officers with an impromptu Indian dance. In good spirits, they accommodated him, kicking firebrands, adding Indian songs and yells—all done with exhibited enthusiasm. When it was over, the governor expressed his pleasure.

If Girty felt elated, he had good reason. Among the Virginians, he was a popular hero, and Lord Dunmore had promised him a promotion. Moreover, in concert with the objectives of the Six Nations, Girty had contributed greatly to the effort that forced the Shawnees to give up their rights to all their hunting grounds east of the Ohio River. Girty had won affirmation in the two worlds that he enjoyed equally. Unfortunately, within months, Virginia's governor would be forced to flee his office in the face of angry colonials, and Girty's close association with him and John Connolly and other Loyalists would bring him serious problems.

Having emerged a hero from his first war, Simon was about to be tested in a much larger and more convoluted conflict.

CHAPTER FOUR
THE PATRIOT

REACHING THE MOUTH of the Hocking River, Girty and the returning Virginia army heard of the decisions of the First Continental
Congress, which had convened in Philadelphia on September 5, 1774.
Dunmore's officers responded by passing a resolution praising their
commander "who, we are confident, underwent the great fatigue of
this singular campaign from no other motive than the true interest
of this country." Then the same officers reaffirmed their allegiance to
the king and crown—being careful to add that "their devotion would
only last while the king deigned to reign over a free people, for their
love of liberty for America outweighed all other considerations, and
they would exert every power for its defense when called forth by the
voice of their countrymen."[1]

Any expectations Simon may have had of basking in the warmth of
his recent achievements were dashed by the threat of impending revolution. Much of the frontier was in chaos. While some men chose to
remain silent to mask their positions, others scrambled to declare their
allegiance with one side or the other. Emotions were running high,
but even so, at the onset there was considerable latitude. Virginia's
revolutionaries were willing to tolerate Lord Dunmore because he
had just led them to victory against the Shawnees, and even though
John Connolly was an outspoken Loyalist, the rebels were content
to let him remain in command at Fort Dunmore. Another Loyalist
allowed to remain on the job was Alexander McKee, who was inter-
vening with tribal representatives who anxiously sought information
about the growing conflict between the whites. To the Indians the

ramifications of a war between colonials and king were deadly serious. Trade had only just resumed, and the chiefs feared that if the whites went to war their vital supplies would be cut off. They debated which alliances might bring them continued access to gunpowder, lead and other essentials. When the war was over there would be but one source for trading and those nations who had allied themselves to the vanquished would be greatly disadvantaged.

While the Indians considered the ramifications of a major war breaking out between the whites, English and rebel military leaders worried about them. It was feared that if the Indian nations unified they could field a force of some 35–50,000 veteran warriors, almost all of them armed with muskets. Both sides understood that the entry of such a force into the war could quickly determine its outcome. The English began to recruit Indians as combat allies while their rebel opponents remained undecided on this issue. Although George Washington advocated enlisting the warriors as allied soldiers, other men of influence, like trader George Morgan, argued vehemently for keeping the Indians out of the war. Months would go by before the question was finally resolved.

Ensign Simon Girty of the Virginia militia was still under the command of John Connolly at Fort Dunmore where, in addition to the intrigues of the smoldering revolution, the older conflict between the Pennsylvanians and the Virginians still flared up from time to time. During a bloody brawl between two mobs in which Girty participated, one man was killed and several were wounded. On the morning of 24 December 1774, Simon Girty and William Christy led a mob of Virginians to the jail at Hanna's Town, where they demanded that the sheriff turn loose a prisoner named William Thomas, a comrade of Connolly whom the Westmorelanders had recently arrested.

Speaking from behind the locked door at the main entrance, Sheriff Samuel Whiteside refused to comply. Grinning, Girty and Christy began to argue loudly as to what method would be the most effective in tearing the building down. They were involved in this boisterous discussion when John Connolly arrived. After a few words with his two officers, Connolly moved to the closed door and threatened to have the sheriff tied and carried away.

Sheriff Whiteside's version appears in a deposition he gave following the incident:

> *... being afraid of ill consequences, both to his Person and Property, this deponent [Whiteside] did open the Door to allow the Prisoner to speak to the Party, and one of them rushed in, seized him, and dragged him out, and also turned out a certain William Dawson, who was likewise in his Custody on Execution, and that it was Conolly himself who laid Hands on (William) Thomas and dragged him out.*[2]

A prankster at heart, Girty must have thoroughly enjoyed the event. In January 1775, aware that his promotion to lieutenant was to be confirmed the following month, Girty spent £1 10s for a new pair of breeches for his officer's uniform. On 23 February, surrounded by other officers who were being promoted, Simon stood in formation on the parade ground at Fort Dunmore, where he was certified as a lieutenant of Virginia militia, Pittsburgh Region. During the ceremony Simon swore the standard oath of allegiance to King George III without hesitation.

Girty was unaware that he was one of several men whose names had been placed on a secret list prepared by Lord Dunmore. The men who were listed were people whom the governor believed would remain loyal to the king and could be relied upon, if war broke out:

> *At Fort Pitt:*
> *Alexander McKee, deputy agent of Indian affairs; James McKee, brother to Alexander; Alexander Ross, a Scotchman; John Campbell; Captain George Aston; Lieutenant Simon Girty; Lieutenant William Christy; Lieutenant Jacob Bousman.*[3]

Unfortunately for Girty, Lord Dunmore's situation rapidly deteriorated, and he was soon forced to take refuge aboard an English warship anchored out in the James River—far from the headwaters of the Ohio. Then, in early June, the "Invasion Law" by which the Virginians had garrisoned Fort Dunmore expired, and John Connolly had no choice but to disband the troops. After serving only five months as a lieutenant of the Virginia militia, Girty was being discharged, and there was nothing he could do about it. To the delight of the Westmorelanders, Fort Dunmore's name was quickly changed back to Fort Pitt.

Re-affirming their friendship, Alexander McKee was happy to reinstate Girty with the Indian Department. At the time, numbers of Delaware and Mingo leaders were gathering at Pittsburgh to attend the peace talks which John Connolly had previously scheduled. Simon was kept busy distributing food and gifts, while helping delegates establish themselves at the campground across the river from the fort. The day before the peace talks were to start, twenty Pennsylvania partisans led by the sheriff of Westmoreland County raided Fort Pitt, seized John Connolly and carried him off to the town of Ligonier. As soon as Girty heard what had happened, he and several of his Virginia associates kidnapped three Westmoreland magistrates. The Pennsylvanians immediately backed down and traded Connolly for the hostage magistrates. As soon as he returned to Pittsburgh, John Connolly began to orchestrate clandestine meetings with Indians during which he blatantly solicited their support for the king. Apparently, Simon's stable world—the one that had allowed him to maintain trusting relationships with most of the factions on the frontier—was swiftly unraveling.

Despite his connections to Connolly and McKee, at his core Girty favored independence. How he came to that decision becomes clouded when one recalls that on the frontier the primary pair of economic forces—land speculators and fur traders—were clearly opposed. The land jobbers needed raw Indian lands and the king was in the way. Conversely, the fur traders knew that development would simultaneously destroy the wilderness and their industry. Although they were driven by economic ambitions and not humanitarian concerns, they at least favored a policy of co-existence with the Indians who were their intended source of labor. It would seem that Girty had far more advantage in keeping with the fur traders than with the developers. However, early in 1775, the issues which were just starting to unfold were not so clearly defined. There were a few influential men on the frontier, like George Morgan, who argued both for independence and for maintaining a strong fur trade once it had been achieved. Girty admired Morgan and there should be little doubt he agreed with his position. Simon had a pressing need to know what the Indian nations were going to do. If the Six Nations picked up the English hatchet, where would that leave him? For eighteen years, the Senecas had been his own people, as much as any of his white countrymen. Only a few months earlier, the idea that he and the Senecas might someday be enemies would have been inconceivable. Except for the Mohawks, who were currently allied to the king, the rest of the Six Nations favored neutrality; however, the situation was volatile and could change at any moment. If war did come, one thing Simon and the rebels would have in common would be a strong desire to keep the Six Nations neutral.

To the Indians attending the Pittsburgh talks, ratification of the Camp Charlotte treaty was a secondary issue. Far more important was the opportunity the proceedings afforded for Indian leaders to meet with people from both sides of the growing white conflict: to question, to listen, to sift for truth, and to carefully measure which opponent had the greater strength. Privy to new developments, men like Girty and McKee were valuable resources. Their Indian supporters wasted no time maneuvering to enhance and nourish their positions. Early in July, a Six Nations delegate delivered the following address at Fort Pitt:

Brethren,

    As we cannot well do without a person who understands the language of the Six Nations, We therefore desire that Simon Girty should be appointed to interpret any matters we may have to say to you hereafter upon Public Business; and if it is agreeable to you, we desire that your String may accompany ours to the Six Nations upon this Subject to let them know of such agreement.[4]

If granted, this request by the Iroquois would guarantee that Girty would stay where he was and, presumably, on their behalf, he could continue to gather information on new policies and developments—

from both the English and the rebels. McKee approved the Iroquois request.

Recognizing the devastation that might occur if a majority of the Indian nations allied themselves to the King, the Continental Congress evaluated its relations with the western and northern tribes and divided the frontier into three districts, each one to have its own Commissioner for Indian Affairs. The first commissioners were to be Patrick Henry, Benjamin Franklin and James Wilson. It would be their responsibility to recruit agents to be sent to the tribes across the Ohio River to try and convince the Indians to stay out of the war. However, Henry, Franklin and Wilson were far too involved with other matters to accept, and they were quickly replaced. Initially, John Gibson was appointed as Indian agent to the Ohio tribes, but his assignment was only temporary and Richard Butler, a well-known Pennsylvania fur trader, succeeded Gibson. Butler's selection was bad news for Girty. A staunch Westmoreland partisan, Butler hated Dunmore, Connolly and all their supporters. With him as Commissioner for Indian Affairs, Middle District, Girty's opportunities for employment were greatly diminished.

On 24 June 1775, the Virginia Assembly appointed six of their own commissioners to go to Pittsburgh to meet with the Indians. After deliberating, the commissioners decided it would be advantageous to send a responsible officer to tour the Indian towns north of the Ohio River, deliver peace messages, and take the pulse of the western and northern tribes. Several men were evaluated and Captain James Wood, a veteran who had served during McDonald's campaign and later on Dunmore's officer staff during the Shawnee war, was offered the mission. Wood accepted. Then the commissioners summoned Girty. Because of his lingual skills and his reputation as a capable guide and frontier spy, they wanted him to serve as Wood's guide, interpreter and bodyguard.

Simon knew James Wood as a brave, serious young man, well educated and direct. The proposed mission would allow Girty to escape from the confusing situation at Pittsburgh and allow him a good opportunity to reinforce his credibility with the rebels. In addition, the promised compensation was significant. Girty was happy to accept the offer.

Girty and Wood's adventure began on the afternoon of 18 July, when they left Fort Pitt and rode south on good horses along a trail that followed along the banks of the Ohio River. After traveling ten miles, they stopped to make camp for the night. At first light they were riding again and before the day was done, they had gone another forty-five miles. On the morning of the 20th they met a Kentucky settler named Garret Pendergrass traveling in the opposite direction on the same trail. Pendergrass told them he had departed from the Delaware Towns only two days prior, and that while he had been there, a large number of warriors had returned from a great council held at some Wyandot town to the north. These Indians had informed Pendergrass that a French trader named Duperon Bâby [pronounced Bau-bee] and an unnamed English officer had delivered strong warnings that the rebels were making ready to strike the Indians very soon.

The next morning, Girty and Wood bid goodbye to Pendergrass and continued their journey. By one o'clock in the afternoon they reached their first objective, a Moravian Indian mission called Gnadenhutten (on the current site bearing that name in Tuscarawas County, Ohio). Indian converts had built the place three years earlier, and like many Moravian missions, it had a chapel with a bell tower, a school, and tidy streets lined by small cabins surrounded by picket fencing. Wearing European clothing, over 130 Delaware converts were in residence, and behind every cabin there was a small, well-tended vegetable garden. In a communal effort, the Delaware converts raised hogs and poultry in abundance, and hundreds of acres had been cleared and planted. By any standards, Gnadenhutten was a successful farming operation, evidenced by large barns and buildings for grain storage. Gnadenhutten also had a number of workshops where converts manufactured commercial products including canoes and brooms—the latter of which were sold in large numbers at the Moravian headquarters in Bethlehem, Pennsylvania.

As Girty and Wood witnessed, life at the Moravian missions was highly regimented. Days began before sunrise with assemblies at the chapel, where prayers and hymns were vocalized in both Delaware and German. As long as they were not trying to sell liquor, travelers of any flag or nation arriving at a Moravian mission could expect extraordinary hospitality. Reverend David Zeisberger had warmly welcomed Wood and Girty and saw that they were promptly provided a hot meal. After they had eaten, Wood explained the nature of their mission, and Zeisberger patiently endured his questions. Zeisberger's answers confirmed what Pendergrass had told them. English officers were indeed touring the Indian towns and attempting to turn the tribes against the rebel Americans. Zeisberger demonstrated a dislike for the English which may have seemed contrived to Wood and Girty. Nevertheless, the next day they thanked their host and departed for Goschachgunk (later called Coshocton), the Delaware's capital town. They had traveled only a few miles and were passing a small Delaware village when a friendly warrior approached them on horseback, asking if he could ride with them. Wood agreed, and the three men camped together that night on the north bank of the Tuscarawas River. They reached the Delaware capital late in the afternoon of the following day.

Goschachgunk lay inside the forks of the Muskingum and Tuscarawas rivers, on the north side of the latter stream. Upon their arrival, Wood and Girty were led to a large council house where they were confronted by a number of drunken Indians. Among the inebriated was the elderly chief King Newcomer (a.k.a. Netawatwes), who had passed out. It was dark before the chief had recovered his senses and was able to speak. While he slept, many warriors and lesser chiefs gathered, including Wingenund and Young John Killbuck. With Girty translating, Captain Wood addressed the crowd:

FROM THE JOURNAL OF JAMES WOOD

Brothers the Delawares:

Your elder brothers in Virginia in their great council have appointed me to come to this place in order to assure you that their hearts are good towards you, that they are desirous of brightening the ancient chain of friendship between you and them, and for which they have appointed commissioners to meet you and the other nations in a general council at Fort Pitt on the 10th

of September next, when they will be glad to meet the chiefs of
your nation and will use their best endeavors to give you a hearty
welcome.

Brothers:
 I have heard with great concern that you have lately been in
council with the French and Wyandots and that you have received
a speech from the French and a belt and string of black wampum.
As there has long subsisted the greatest friendship between you
and us I desire and insist that you will make me acquainted with
anything which may have been said to you by the French or any
others to the prejudice of your elder brothers of Virginia.[5]

Concluding, Wood formally presented King Newcomer a large
string of white wampum, signifying America's desire for peace. Then
he and Girty were taken to a home where they were fed, entertained
and spent the night. While they slept, the chiefs at the council house
debated the issues. The next morning, the two Americans were summoned to hear King Newcomer deliver his peoples' answer:

FROM THE REPORT OF JAMES WOOD

Brothers the Bigknife:
 Your brothers the Delawares are very thankful to you for
your good talk to them yesterday, and are glad to find their broth-
ers' hearts are good towards them and that they will be joyful in
meeting them at the time and place you mention brother, in order
to convince our elder brothers of Virginia, that we desire to live
in friendship with them. I now deliver you this belt and string
that were sent to us by an English man and a Frenchman at Fort
Detroit, with a message that the people of Virginia were deter-
mined to strike us. That they would come upon us two different
ways, the one by the way of the lakes, and the other by the Ohio
and that the Virginians were determined to drive us off and take
our lands—that we must be constantly on our guard, and not to
give any credit to whatever you said as you were a people not to be
depended upon—that the Virginians would invite us to a treaty,

*but we must not go at any rate, and to take particular notice of
the advice they gave which proceeded from motives of real friendship and nothing else.*[6]

As a final gesture, Newcomer presented Wood a white wampum
belt and a string (symbolically transferring and recording his Delaware
speech to the Americans). While Girty and Wood were pleased to
hear that the Delawares were committed to peace, it was disconcert-
ing for them to learn that their English opponents had anticipated
their mission, in detail. They were also aware that the next leg of their
tour would put them among Indians who viewed the American cause
with dark suspicion.

Departing, Girty and Wood made for some Seneca towns located
near Upper Sandusky. Sometime during that ride, Wood met and
hired a Delaware to accompany them. The weather turned bad, and
they suffered under heavy rains. On the afternoon of 25 July, the trio
arrived at a Mingo town where they were met by an angry group of
leaders, including Logan, The Snake, The Big Appletree, and others.
Until recently, most of these men had been held prisoner at Fort Pitt.

Once more, Girty and Wood had arrived at a village when most
of the warriors were drunk, and there was nothing they could do but
wait. After the Mingoes had sobered they were very much interested
in what Girty and Wood had to say. With Girty translating, Wood
delivered the same address he had given to the Delawares and it
brought the same response. The Indians said they would take time
to discuss the issue in private, and when they had come to a decision, they would summon the two Americans to give them an answer.
However, unlike the Delawares who had treated Wood and Girty
with hospitably, the Mingoes were markedly cold to them. No invitation was extended for them to be fed or entertained, and they had no
choice but to make camp outside the town. Wood noted ominously
that a few of the warriors had already painted themselves black.

It had been a long and tiring day for the two travelers, and even
though the Mingoes had been unfriendly, Girty guessed there would
be no serious trouble from them; as such actions would have con-
stituted a major breach of Indian diplomatic protocol. He guessed

incorrectly. About ten o'clock that evening, when both men were sound asleep, they were visited by a party of warriors. Wood was awakened by someone stamping on his head. Girty was also rudely awakened. Standing over them, the warriors hurled insults and threats. It was a hopeless situation. Coolly, Simon and Wood maintained their composure and did not respond. Failing to get a reaction after delivering their tirade, the warriors departed into the night. Although it had been a tense and precarious situation, no real damage had been done. The two peace envoys remained awake the rest of the night. About an hour after the warriors had departed, a Mingo woman slipped up to their camp and whispered that the hotheads who had visited them earlier intended to return some time before dawn to murder them. She advised Girty and Wood to hide in the forest until morning, which they did.

At daybreak, Girty and Wood warily made their way to the council house, where Logan was waiting for them. His mood seemed sour. Speaking English, he commenced to tell Wood how the people of Virginia had killed his mother, his sister, and all his relations. During a long and emotional recitation, he both wept and sang. When he was finished, he confided to Wood that he knew that there were several Mingoes in the village—all of whom had recently been held hostage at Fort Pitt—who wanted to kill him. Then Logan asked if Wood was afraid.

Wood replied that he was not, adding calmly, "we [he and Girty] were two lone men who were sent to deliver a message to them, which we had done, that we were in their power and had no way to defend ourselves, that they must kill us if they thought proper."[7]

Evidently the tough Virginian passed the Mingo chief's test. Logan smiled and then assured him that neither he nor Girty would be hurt. After their meeting with Logan, the Mingoes treated the two American emissaries quite hospitably. The next morning, they bought fresh horses from their hosts and started for the Wyandot towns along the Upper Sandusky. According to Wood's report:

We rode fast and constant, till 7 o'clock in the Evening when we arrived at the Town [this would have been Upper Sandusky], sent off runners for the chiefs who were distant about twenty Miles.[8]

Following diplomatic protocol, Girty and Wood made camp well outside the town and waited patiently to be greeted. At one o'clock in the afternoon of the next day, a party of warriors came to summon them to the village council house where they were met by a number of Wyandots and two Ottawas waiting to hear what they had to say. With Girty translating, Wood addressed the assembly. When he concluded, a chief named War Post requested that they wait for an answer while the issues were discussed in private. Wood and Girty returned to their camp just outside the town.

Later the same afternoon, accompanied by five or six of his warriors, War Post came to visit Girty and Wood. He seemed amicable, admitting that that he and his companions wanted to speak with Girty and Wood "as friends." According to Wood's report:

[War Post said:] ... that they [the Wyandots] always Understood the English had but one King who lived over the Great Water, that they were much Surprized to hear that we were at War with ourselves, and that there had been several Engagements at Boston in which a great number of Men were killed on both sides, that as he had been told many different Stories they would be glad to know the Cause of the dispute, or whether we Expected or desired their Assistance.[9]

Through Girty, Wood answered that his country "did not stand in need of or desire any assistance from them or any other nation, but that we wished them to continue in peace and friendliness with us by observing a strict neutrality, as we had not the least doubt that all differences between ourselves would be soon accommodated." Then he pointed out that there was "great unanimity among the Americans, and that they were now become so strong as not to fear any power on the face of the earth." Later, in his report to the Commissioners, Wood wrote:

> *... In this conversation, I discovered that the Huron Indians had been led to believe that the people of Virginia were a different and distinct nation from the other Colonies, and that by going to War with us they need not fear the Interposition of the other Colonies. This, I think, I effectually removed by making them Acquainted with the Proceedings of the Continental Congress and that the Colonies were bound and obliged to defend each other against attacks from Whatever Quarter they might come. These Questions were likewise put to me at other times by the Shawanese, Delawares, Mingoes and Tawaas and Answered in the same manner.*[10]

By now it was apparent to Girty and Wood that their English counterparts had done a good job turning the Indians against them. The farther north they traveled, the greater hostility the two Americans faced. There was little doubt that the kegs of rum the Indians were drinking had been distributed by the British agents as gestures of good will and friendship. The morning after War Post visited their camp, Girty and Wood were summoned back to the Wyandot council house. War Post told them he had heard that the people of Virginia were at that very moment building a big fort on the Kentucky River, from which they intended to drive off all the Indians to take their lands.

There could be little doubt that War Post's provocative challenge was fueled by English propaganda. Wood answered calmly that he knew nothing about any new fort being built in Kentucky, but that it was true that white settlers were quickly establishing themselves in the whole country eastward of the Ohio, as low down as the Cherokee River. Wood claimed they had the right to do so, since it had all been purchased from the Six Nations in the Fort Stanwix Treaty. He told them "they might rest assured that we had no thoughts of encroaching any farther than we had already purchased and honestly paid for."[11]

War Post asked whether the Americans intended to take Fort

Detroit from the British regulars who were garrisoned there. Wood said he didn't know, but that he believed the Americans looked upon it "to be a place of little or no consequence." Then he added that his nation had already taken Ticonderoga and Crown Point, and that they had beaten the Regulars in every engagement "with considerable loss on their side, and very inconsiderable on ours."[12]

Although they had been treated with respect, by the end of their visit there was no indication to Girty and Wood whether they had won over the Wyandots. The only good sign was that when Wood invited their chiefs to attend peace talks at Fort Pitt, the Wyandots promised to consider it. Girty and Wood departed from War Post's village on the morning of the 29th and rode fast and hard for eight hours, camping that night near the banks of the Scioto River. Their next destination was a band of undisciplined Mohawks who had migrated westward about 1772, and who had settled at the present site of Delaware, Ohio. Their town was named after its leader, an obstreperous warrior called "Pluggy." In his journal, Wood wrote that he and Girty arrived at Pluggy's Town at noon:

. . . when we arrived at the town we found that Pluggy was away from home and all the Indians drunk and very troublesome. Left a String of Wampum and Speech for Pluggy, purchased some dried Meat from an Indian, and then set off for the big salt licks.[13]

The "big salt licks" that Wood referred to was the site of the Mingo town of Seekonk (or Seekunk), and it was after nightfall when he and Girty arrived. The only inhabitants were five hunters and an old woman, all of whom were sharing a cabin. They invited Girty and Wood to join them for the night. Girty may have known all or some of them, and he and Wood accepted the invitation. The next morning, one of the men and the old woman revealed that they too were traveling to the Shawnee Towns, and they asked if they could join Girty and Wood for the journey. Wood agreed. At mid-afternoon on 31 July, the little party reached a cluster of Shawnee villages in the Scioto Valley, not far from where Girty had found Chief Logan during Dunmore's War. They halted and waited for a response. Both men were tense. Girty knew that the Shawnees regarded him as an enemy. Wood must also have been apprehensive. Both men understood that they could not successfully conclude their mission without meeting the Shawnees. They did not have long to wait. It was the Shawnee chief named The Hard Man who came to meet them. Through Girty, Wood explained their mission and requested that representatives from nearby towns be summoned, whom he could later address.

Pointedly, The Hard Man ignored Wood's request, responding in angry tones that a warrior named Chenusaw had returned home only the night before, claiming that the people of Virginia:

FROM THE JOURNAL OF JAMES WOOD

... were all determined upon making war with the Indians except the Governor [Dunmore], who was for peace but was obliged to fly on board of a ship to save his own life. That the Shawnee hostages found they were to be made Slaves of and sent to some other country, that the white people were all preparing for war, and that they showed him many Indian scalps among which Cuttemwha recognized his Brothers'. That the hostages determined if possible to make their escape and accordingly set off in the night, all of them together. That the next day, he being behind the other two at some distance, he was seized by three men, that he heard them determine to kill him, on which one of them proceeded to load his gun while the other two held him by the arms, that before the man loaded the gun he found means to disengage himself and made his escape, leaving his gun and everything, also, that he soon after heard several guns and was positive that Cuttemwha and Neawau were both killed as he had been sixty days traveling and had heard nothing of them.[14]

Wood told The Hard Man that most of what Chenusaw had told him was false, and that he would be glad to confront the man. The Shawnee chief agreed. Chenusaw was summoned and soon arrived with a number of his friends. It was a tense situation.

According to Wood's report of the incident:

> *I explained the whole Matter to him and a number of other*
> *Indians. I informed them that Cuttemwha and Nimwah were*
> *both well and on the Road and that they were bringing his cloaths*
> *[sic] and everything which he had left behind him, and that it*
> *was very unlucky for him he did not turn back as the others had*
> *done to have got a horse and saddle to ride home, as they had.*[15]

The tension eased, and Wood and Girty were allowed to make camp outside the town. That night at their village, several Shawnees enacted a spiritual ceremony and howled like wolves until daylight.

On the morning of 2 August, Girty and Wood were summoned to the council house where Wood presented his final address, inviting the Indians to attend peace talks at Fort Pitt and attempting once again to offset their apprehensions of the Virginians.

In response, The Hard Man thanked Wood for the invitation, which he acknowledged his brothers would gladly accept, and in cordial tones he apologized for the claims made against the Virginians by Chenusaw, whom he surmised had made his mistake due perhaps to a poor understanding of the English language. Next, the chief wanted to know whether a great many of the young men of Virginia were not going to Boston to make war against the English red coats, and if it was true that there had already been several engagements?

Wood answered that only a few men were being sent north, because there already were sufficient soldiers in New England to take care of all the British regulars who were there. He admitted there had indeed been several engagements, saying, "In all of which we had beaten them with great loss on their side and very small on ours, but that we were in daily expectation of all differences being settled between the two countries, to the satisfaction of both."[16]

Then a warrior named The Shade told Wood that he had met some Delawares on the Ohio River who had in their possession many things they had stolen from white settlers on the Great Kanawha River, and he wanted Wood to make it known that the Shawnees were not guilty of these crimes. The conversation continued for several hours, and resolved without any major surprises. Before departing, Wood and

Girty had a chance to speak with James Bavard, a trader who was living among the Shawnees. Bavard told them that the Shawnee women seemed uneasy, as though they expected there would soon be a big war.

Girty and Wood left before sunrise the next morning and, after halting briefly at another Shawnee town, they rode until seven o'clock that evening. It started to rain as they were preparing their evening camp and the downpour continued throughout the night. The following day they rode forty miles before stopping at the cabin of a friendly Delaware woman, where they took shelter for the night. The poor woman had no meat or corn, and could offer them nothing to eat but blueberries. The next morning, just after they started out it again began to rain. They endured a long and miserable ride to White Eyes' village, where, at last, they were able to purchase a little dried meat. Famished, they quickly devoured the food and rode on, reaching Gnadenhutten after sundown. After what they had been through, arriving at the Moravian mission was like stepping into paradise. Warmly received, they were provided with dry clothing, food and drink. They slept the whole night through and attended services conducted by Reverend Johann Schmidt on Sunday, 6 August.

The Gnadenhutten church was a large, square building with a cupola and bell. Inside, planked floors were covered by heavy wooden benches, upon which some 150 pious Delaware converts were seated. Men, women and children were sitting in separate sections, all wearing European-style clothing. The walls of the chapel were decorated with numerous German scripture paintings. Reverend Schmidt, who had lived among the Indians for years, prayed in the Delaware language, preached in English, and sang Psalms in German. When called upon, the Indians participated with enthusiasm in all three languages. It was as if Girty and Wood had entered another world.

The duo returned to Fort Pitt on the afternoon of 11 August. Having faced considerable danger and hardship, they had traversed the Ohio Country from one end to the other, successfully completing a daring and difficult diplomatic mission. Wood's subsequent report to the Virginia commissioners provided an accurate appraisal of their current political situation. In addition to reinforcing his credibility as a loyal and trustworthy patriot, Girty's stalwart performance as Wood's guide and interpreter amplified his image as a skilled frontiersman and intermediary.

While Simon and Captain Wood were touring the Ohio Valley, a number of important changes had taken place at Pittsburgh. For one thing, John Connolly was gone. Ten days after Girty and Wood had departed on their tour, Connolly had left with White Eyes and two other Delaware chiefs to meet with the Virginia Committee for Indian Affairs at Winchester. Two days later, Connolly departed without explanation and made his way to Lord Dunmore, who was then living aboard the British war ship *Prince William,* anchored in Norfolk harbor. There he and Lord Dunmore spent the following two weeks planning future operations against the rebels, after which the governor put Connolly aboard the tender *Arundell* to sail to Boston to meet with General Thomas Gage.

Something else that had changed in Pittsburgh during Girty's absence was that the local land speculators no longer concerned themselves about violating the restrictions of the King's Proclamation of 1763. Under rebel control it was possible, once again, to get new claims quickly surveyed. Ironically, while Girty and Wood had been risking their lives promising the Indians of the Ohio Valley that America had no wish to acquire their lands, George Croghan had initiated a purchase of some six million acres from the Six Nations, the location of which was just across the Ohio River from Fort Pitt.

In August, Samuel Wharton wrote to his brother Thomas, urging him to become actively involved in land purchases with members of the Continental Congress. He told his brother it was imperative that the Continental Congress hurriedly pass a resolution validating purchases made directly from the natives. He also believed that if the right palms were greased, such a resolution would be approved and he suggested that half-shares in their company be given to eight members of Congress, in addition to a share that had been already set aside for Patrick Henry.

Thus, while some men hurried to acquire Indian land, others were increasingly concerned that disgruntled warriors would soon become the greatest threat to the American frontier. Concluding his formal report to the Virginia Commissioners, Wood warned:

> *. . . from every discovery I was able to make, the Indians are form-*
> *ing a General Confederacy against the Colony having been led*
> *to believe that we are a people quite different and distinct from*
> *the other colonies. I intend myself the Honor of Waiting on the*
> *Convention if they should not rise before the 25th in order to give*
> *them every Information in my power, I wou'd beg leave to make*
> *an Observation that there is no Garrison at Fort Pitt that the*
> *Inhabitants in the Neighbourhood of it are in the most defenceless*
> *situation and that there will be in my opinion at least 500 Indians*
> *at the treaty.*[17]

Wood's warning was taken seriously. Captain John Neville (acting under Virginia orders and commanding one hundred Virginia militiamen) was given orders to take immediate possession of Fort Pitt. On 12 September, the day after Captain Neville's arrival, commissioners from Virginia and from the Continental Congress met at the fort to discuss the forthcoming talks with the Indians. Patrick Henry and Benjamin Franklin had already resigned their commissions; Dr. Thomas Walker of Virginia and Lewis Morris of New York were appointed to serve in their place. Both were prominent land speculators.

Just before the Indian delegates were to arrive, James Wood restated to the commissioners that he and Girty had found that British authorities were busy riling the Indians across the Ohio, and that he had done his best to explain that the United Colonies desired only the neutrality of the natives. He had also reaffirmed to the Indians that the Americans did not intend to cross the Ohio River to attack them if, in return, they would agree not to molest any of our settlements south of that stream, and that this was the policy of Congress. Then he delivered the speech to the commissioners that had been given to him by the Seneca chief, White Mingo, who, at that moment, was hiding at George Croghan's house after having been shot at by two unknown white assailants. The Seneca had no idea why an attempt had been made against his life, and he was demanding an explanation from the commissioners.

It was decided to send out a party that included Captain Wood, John Walker, George Morgan and Louis Morris, with Simon Girty and John Montour along as interpreters. Their task was to find White Mingo, placate him, and investigate the incident. The delegation returned to Fort Pitt the next day. They reported they had found the chief, and claimed that they had convinced him that if the guilty men were ever caught, they would be sent to prison (although none ever were).

A month later, on the night of 20 September, nine members of the Indiana Land Company met clandestinely at Pittsburgh, to further schemes for their eventual acquisition of Indian lands across the Ohio River. Notably, one of the leaders was none other than George Morgan. Apparently, Girty, who had complete faith in Morgan's integrity, knew nothing of the secret meeting or of Morgan's duplicity.

By 7 October, delegates of the Delawares, Shawnees, Mingoes, Wyandots, Ottawas and Senecas were all present at Fort Pitt, and the talks got underway. The principal spokesman for the Indians was Guyasuta, with Simon acting as his interpreter. The Virginia commissioners opened the talks by explaining how all thirteen colonies were now of one family, with a great fire at Philadelphia, and that they wished to resolve the situation with the Shawnees in conformance to Dunmore's original treaty, drafted at Camp Charlotte. These discussions did not conclude until the nineteenth of the month, at which time presents from Virginia and from the Continental Congress were handed out. Both sides clearly understood that in return for the Indians' promise to remain neutral, the Americans had vowed to observe the Ohio River as a boundary.

Within days, to further the American cause, John Gibson was sent to tour the Ohio Country with the great white wampum "Congress Peace Belt," a symbol of American friendship which was six feet long and more than six inches wide.

The American presence at Fort Pitt, and the British garrison at Fort Detroit were now the two centers of white influence on the frontier. At Detroit, less than a hundred British soldiers commanded by Lt. Governor Henry Hamilton occupied the base. It was under

Hamilton's direction that English agents were aggressively inciting the western tribes to take up the hatchet against the "United American States," and it was these men who had made things uncommonly dangerous for Girty and Wood.

To gain the support of the Indian nations, the British continually reaffirmed that the King's Proclamation of 1763 prohibited the colonists from acquiring any more Indian lands, and that the King had no design on Indian lands situated north or west of the Ohio. But, the British warned, if the rebels won their independence, no such restrictions would apply, and they would surely cross the Ohio River, destroy the Indians, and take everything.

The rebels hoped to counter this threat by convincing the western and northern tribes that the British were lying to them: that the people of the United American States had no designs on their homelands, and that they would surely win their fight for independence. Once the war was over, they promised, they would remember who had been their friends. These were powerful and convincing arguments, but they were worthless unless they could be carried to distant villages and articulated by men who understood the Indians and their languages, had their respect, and who were willing to risk their own necks for the American cause.

In mid-January, 1776, the Colony of Virginia paid Girty the handsome sum of £113, 8s for his tour with James Wood through the Ohio Country. While Simon's credibility as a patriot had been strengthened by his performance as Wood's guide and interpreter, his former association with John Connolly fueled suspicion. Only two months earlier, Connolly had been arrested for treason and was captured carrying documents that revealed a plan for a combined English-Indian attack on Fort Pitt. Soon after Connolly and some of his accomplices were thrown into jail at Frederick, Maryland, orders came for him to be transported to Philadelphia. The day before the scheduled move, Connolly wrote some secret letters, gave them to one of his men, and then helped the fellow to escape. On 12 January, Connolly's man was recaptured while still carrying all the letters. One of his seized documents was addressed to Alexander McKee. In it, Connolly asked him "to provide for Mrs. Connolly and to tell Captain Lord at Vincennes, to push down the Mississippi and join Lord Dunmore." Connolly also advised McKee that he had recommended him to General Gage. Already suspected of disloyalty, McKee was seriously damaged by these new revelations. His response was to remain at home and to try and maintain a low profile. Rumors soon circulated that Loyalists were using his house for secret meetings.

Because of his association with Connolly and McKee, there was no way for Girty to avoid being smeared. However, the situation apparently had little or no impact upon his activities. Being mistrusted by the public-in-general was nothing new to Girty. Due to their long and obvious associations with Indians, the three "Injun' Girtys" had never been afforded much trust or good will by the majority of the people at Pittsburgh. What had far more relevance to Girty was how the rebel leaders viewed him, and in their eyes, he was still a reliable agent; someone whose unique expertise, contacts and skills made him a valuable intelligence asset.

Girty could have easily improved his credibility by simply divorcing himself from McKee, but with Simon, personal relationships transcended materialism, politics, and oftentimes, even good sense. Thumbing his nose at his critics, he continued to visit his old friend whenever it suited him; and all the while McKee's predicament slid from bad to worse.

In February, Colonel John Butler, commanding the English fort at Niagara, addressed a secret letter to "Captain McKee," inviting him to attend Indian councils that were scheduled to take place there. Unfortunately for McKee, American agents at Niagara intercepted and read the letter, and then sent it on. Before the document reached McKee, an American officer arrived at his home to inform him that a letter was on its way to him from Canada, and that he would be "required to reveal any of the contents that pertained to the United Colonies."[18]

A few days later, the West Augusta Committee of Safety gathered at McKee's home and required him to read aloud the letter that Colonel Butler had sent to him. Although there was no proof that McKee had committed any disloyal acts against the patriots or their cause, it was plain that Colonel John Butler regarded him an active and faithful Loyalist, and McKee was offered the choice of either putting his signature to the following parole or being placed under arrest for treason:

SWORN STATEMENT OF ALEXANDER MCKEE

I, Alexander McKee, Deputy Agent for the Indian Affairs for the District of Fort Pitt, do hereby promise and engage that I will not transact any business with the Indians on behalf of the Crown or Ministry; that I will not directly or indirectly correspond with any of the Crown or Ministerial officers, nor leave the neighborhood of Fort Pitt, without the consent of the committee of West Augusta.
Given under my hand, at Pittsburg, this ninth day of April, 1776.[19]

McKee signed the document and agreed to a demand that he remain at his estate. Under such circumstances, Girty's continued visits to his old friend were bold, daring and obstinate.

It was also in April that the Continental Congress arrived at the conclusion that the state of Indian relations was too important a matter to leave in the hands of colonial committees or local agents. Things began to look up for Girty when the decision was made for a congressional appointee to take over as the new Commissioner for Indian Affairs, Middle District, at Fort Pitt. George Morgan, who, it was generally believed, had a superior understanding of the region and its peoples, replaced Richard Butler. Morgan had not prospered recently, and he had lobbied hard for the new position. Advised he had won the appointment, Morgan departed at once from Philadelphia for Pittsburgh. His new office required him to quickly enlist highly qualified special agents whom he could send out in an orchestrated effort to persuade the Indian nations to keep out of the war. The 13-diamond Great Congressional Peace Belt (which had been presented to the Indians the previous fall at Fort Pitt), was to be carried to all the important outlying villages, and the Indians were to be instructed that Congress was importing foreign goods for them, to make certain their trade was uninterrupted by the war. Adding to his burden, Morgan's orders also required him "to prevent impositions upon the Indians by the whites, to inspire within the natives a love of justice and humanity, and to dispose them toward adopting the arts of civilized life."[20]

As soon as he arrived at Fort Pitt, Morgan hired Simon Girty, his favorite company hunter from the Kaskaskia days. Then Morgan recruited Joseph Nicholson, Peter Long and William Wilson. All four of these frontiersmen had lived for years among the Indians and each of them had worked for Morgan at one time or another in the fur trade. The contract Morgan offered to Girty was specific:

Pittsburgh May 1st, 1776
To Simon Girty,

The Public Service requiring an Interpreter for the Six Nations at this place, you are hereby appointed to that Employement at the rate of five eights of a Dollar per diem during good Behaviour or the pleasure of the Hon'ble Continental Congress or their Commissioners or Agents for the Middle Department.

You are upon all occasions to use your utmost endeavours to promote the Public Tranquility & maintain a good understanding between the United Colonies and the Indians; and inform me of all Intelligence which may come to your knowledge. You are to obey all my lawful & reasonable orders during my Agency & faithfully to keep secret all private Councils between the Commissioners, Agents, Indians & yourself, so far as the Public Good shall require it.

You are to visit & confer with all Indians who shall come to this Post so early after their arrival as possible—to learn their Business here, & immediately to acquaint me therewith.

In case of any Discontent among the Indians you are immediately to inform me thereof—and you will take care that none of them, on any Account be insulted or injured by the Inhabitants, & be equally cautious to prevent any of them injuring the Inhabitants.

You are upon no account to be concerned in Trade or be assistant therein unless when call'd upon to see Justice done between the Traders and Indians.

For extraordinary Services you shall be entitled to further
reasonable allowance as the case may be.
   Given under my hand at Pittsburgh this first day of May 1776.
   sign'd Geo. Morgan
               Agent for the United Colonies[21]

What was unstated in their contracts, but which was well understood by Girty and his fellow agents, was that if they were to fall into
the hands of the British they would be hanged or shot as spies.

On 15 May, Morgan entrusted the Great Congressional Peace Belt
of the United Colonies to Girty and sent him to the Grand Council of
the Six Nations, which convened annually at Onondaga, New York.
Acting as the formal ambassador of his fledgling country, Simon's
challenge was to present its message for peace and to ask for the same
in return, from what was at that time the most powerful of Indian
political confederations. This was the most difficult and significant
mission Girty would ever conduct while serving under the American
flag. The odds against his success were considerable, for the Mohawks
were already raiding for the English, and his own people—the
Senecas—were preparing to join them.

Simon arrived at Onondaga on 14 or 15 June, by which time
the majority of sachems and matrons of the Iroquois League had
assembled (except for any Mohawk delegates, whose absence was
conspicuous). At the appointed moment he rose, faced the huge
gathering, and delivered his greetings and address, as well as some
carefully prepared American speeches and peace messages. Although
the Iroquois delegates had no history by which they could measure
the validity or strength of American promises, they had great respect
for the man who stood before them, and they listened intently. When
he had finished, Girty solemnly presented his hosts with the Great
Congressional Peace Belt, and then withdrew to await the result of
their deliberations.

At the time, Girty could not have known that only two weeks
earlier, Guyasuta and other representatives from the Six Nations had
met with Colonel John Butler at Fort Niagara. Butler strenuously
attempted to enlist their active support against the "United Colonies,"

but his efforts failed to break the Iroquois League from its position of neutrality. Fuming over the American treaty of friendship that had been concluded at Fort Pitt the preceding fall, the English colonel had fired the following broadside:

COLONEL JOHN BUTLER TO INDIANS AT FORT NIAGARA

Your Father the Great King has taken pity on you and is deter-mined not to let the Americans deceive you any longer—tho' you have been so foolish as to listen to them last year and to believe all their wicked stories—they mean to cheat you and should you be so silly as to take their advice and they should conquer the King's Army, their intention is to take all your Lands from you and destroy your people, for they are all mad, foolish, crazy and full of deceit. They told you last Fall at Pittsburgh that they took the Tom Hawk out of your hands and buried it deep and trans-planted the Tree of Peace over it. I therefore now pluck up that Tree, dig up the Tom Hawk, and replace it in your hands with the edge toward them—that you may treat them as Enemies.[22]

But the majority of the Iroquois leaders did not trust Colonel Butler, and his efforts resulted in only some thirty Senecas, and a few Chippewas and Ottawas, embarking for Canada to make war on the Americans.

When the Grand Council at Onondaga concluded their delib-erations, they summoned Girty to present himself before them again, and then they gave him everything that he, George Morgan and the United States had hoped for—the Six Nations solemnly re-commit-ted their nation to a policy of neutrality for the duration of the war. To underscore their firm commitment to neutrality, Simon was given the following message to carry back to Morgan:

You know that among all People there are evil-minded persons who try to spoil good agreements and good resolutions but they cannot turn the minds of the Chief Men and Warriors of this Council for we look on Peace and want to enjoy it.[23]

The Grand Council informed Girty that it had also decided that Kayingwaurto (a.k.a. Sakayengwalaghton or "Old Smoke," the principal war chief of the Eastern Senecas) was to travel at once to Fort Niagara with an escort of six warriors. Upon his arrival, he would demand from Colonel Butler that all the Six Nations warriors who had been persuaded to strike the Americans be recalled. In the event that Butler refused, Kayingwaurto's companions were prepared to personally find and retrieve the warriors. Girty was also given the following proposition to carry back to Fort Pitt, created to persuade the southern and western tribes who were then in alliance with the Iroquois League to remain unified and neutral.

Brothers and Nephews,
We desire you to continue to sit still and preserve the peace and Friendship with all your Neighbors—remain firm and united with each other so as to be like one Man—We desire you to be strong and keep your Country in Peace.[24]

Except for lack of a Mohawk endorsement, Girty's mission was a virtual triumph. The significance and importance of his accomplishment could not be overestimated by the colonial leadership, for without having to face a major threat along its western and northern frontiers, the military leaders of the United Colonies could concentrate their efforts against British forces in the east.

Elated, Simon hurried home with the good news, arriving at Pittsburgh on 1 July 1776. Three days later, the Continental Congress declared:

DECLARATION OF INDEPENDENCE

...That these united Colonies are, and of Right ought to be Free and Independent States, that they are Absolved from all Allegiance to the British Crown, and that all political connection between them and the State of Great Britain, is and ought to be totally dissolved....[25]

On 6 July, Shawnee, Delaware and Iroquois delegates met with Morgan at Fort Pitt to reaffirm their desire to remain neutral. Girty's achievement had surpassed his exploits in Dunmore's War, yet his glory was short-lived, for on August 1st, Morgan fired him as interpreter and agent to the Six Nations. Like a bolt of lightning, some cataclysmic conflict had occurred between Morgan and Girty; an explosive and irreconcilable difference. Something sharp enough to disembowel a long and mutually rewarding relationship. Morgan's momentous decision is explained in his journal by a single, mysterious statement, saying only that he "had discharged Girty for ill-behavior."[26]

Girty's "ill-behavior" had nothing to do with drunkenness. Morgan himself was no teetotaler. He had traded in rum and spirits for years (and had even initiated plans for a whisky distillery in Illinois in 1770–71, which was stymied by British authorities), and as Indian agent at Fort Pitt he had often authorized rum to be given to the Indians. Morgan often surrounded himself with teamsters, boatmen, frontiersmen, traders and other rough types who participated with gusto in hard-drinking revelry. At the time of their break-up, the Morgan-Girty relationship was more than ten years old. During that decade several of Morgan's letters and journal entries attest to the respect and affection he had for Girty. While Simon may indeed have been drunk when their explosive final confrontation occurred, it must have been something much more significant than an outburst of drunken behavior that destroyed their relationship.

In order to keep the Indians out of the war, it was vital for Morgan's agents to convince the northern and western tribes that the United American Colonies had no desire to acquire their lands. When Girty was voicing these promises to the Great Council at Onondaga, he was advising people he cared about on issues that affected their very survival. Considering his background, there can be little doubt *that he believed what he was telling them.* Girty thought of Morgan as a leader of the Indian-trade and he was unaware that the Commissioner for Indian Affairs, Middle District, was secretly invested in companies whose only hope for profits were in acquiring, subdividing, and selling Indian lands that were located across the Ohio River. Morgan was also involved in a scheme to create a new state once the war for independence was won, which was to include all of the Pennsylvania land claims lying west of the Fort Stanwix line.

Having great affection for the trader, the Delawares had named Morgan *Tamanend,* or "The Great Peace Maker." If the Delawares, Shawnees, Wyandots and Mingoes were to discover that Commissioner Morgan was involved in schemes designed to take possession of and to exploit their homelands, repercussions for the patriots might have been catastrophic. Morgan's betrayal would have ignited an already volatile frontier. Once Girty was aware of Morgan's duplicity, it was no longer in his own best interest to continue carrying the commissioner's voice to the western and northern tribes. Considering what Simon's brief tour as ambassador to the Six Nations had accomplished for the fledgling United American Colonies, the implications of the loss of his services are profound. It appears, however, that no one above Morgan was ready to challenge the trader's decision in the matter.

If anything, Girty was resilient, and a few weeks after his dismissal he was once again busy. The governor of Virginia wanted to raise a new regiment for the Continental Army comprised of men from Virginia and southwestern Pennsylvania, and Girty had volunteered to be one of its recruiters. He was given a quota and there was some promise that if he achieved it, he would be rewarded with a captaincy and would command a company. At the time, Girty was described as being dark-skinned, straight, and heavy, middle sized or a little above, and as a good-looking man. When he was with the Indians he dressed as they did, but when in town, he donned the clothing of a businessman.

Despite their promise of neutrality, the Iroquois Confederacy continued to debate its stance as political fires heated the issues. One strident voice against neutrality was that of Joseph Brant, a fiery young Mohawk chief who had been raised and educated by Sir William Johnson (and whose sister Molly had been Sir William's mistress). Brant pounded at the Senecas to reconsider their position and pick up the English hatchet. The times were chaotic and Indian loyalties were volatile. For the moment, it appeared that the Lakes Indians were allied to the English, while the Shawnees and Mingoes were vacillating. Only the Delawares were committed to helping the Americans, and, because of this, the Wyandots were pressuring them to change their minds. By mid-August, the Iroquois promise of peace which Girty had brought back from Onondaga was slipping almost as fast as Simon's credibility. There was some good news on the 26th of the month, when White Mingo arrived at Fort Pitt to reassure Morgan and the other congressional commissioners that:

ADDRESS OF WHITE MINGO TO GEORGE MORGAN,
FORT PITT, 26 AUGUST 1776

Brothers the Big Knife [Virginia] and Onas [Pennsylvania], listen to me—

Sometime ago we received your good speech, which was sent up the Allegheny River by Simon Girty, which we looked upon to be very good and do now return you thanks for it. We had some uneasiness of mind until we received it. We have likewise heard your good talk since then: and do much approve of it, you have never said anything to us but what was good, & have constantly recommended what would be for our own advantage. We and all the warriors on the Allegheny River are very glad that you sent your talk to Guianguahtah [Kayingwaurto], he has made fast of the old Chain of Friendship & I am sure will never part with it, except it be wrested out of his hands.[27]

However, any relief that resulted from White Mingo's peace promises was offset a few days later, when Matthew Elliot returned from his tour of the Ohio Country with bad news. Sent by Morgan to visit the Shawnees and Delawares, Elliott's assignment had been to distribute gifts, gather intelligence, promote neutrality, and to extend invitations for forthcoming peace talks. From all that he had seen and heard, Elliott claimed he was convinced that war with the western tribes was inevitable. He suspected that if the Indians whom he had been inviting actually came to Fort Pitt, they would not be there to talk peace, but to destroy the place.

Alarmed by Elliott's news, Morgan asked Congress to quickly send supplies to key frontier outposts and prepare them to withstand sieges. He also urgently requested that a general officer be sent to Fort Pitt, to take charge of the frontier war.

Early in September, there were reports that a large force of warriors led by British officers was coming to attack Fort Pitt. Girty was asked to set aside his recruiting duties, and rush a warning to the people at Carlisle. He did so, but the expected enemy attack failed to materialize.

Pittsburgh's land speculators were undeterred by the promise of impending war, and they continued their surveying operations. Due to conflicting claims over some tracts that had recently been purchased directly from Indians, an investigating committee convened at Pittsburgh in the spring of 1777. The dispute involved Kittanning, and in March, when both Simon and his brother Thomas were summoned to testify, they related their experiences as hostages at Kittanning.

As the weather turned warm, raids by British-allied Indians against American outposts and remote settlements steadily increased. Riled by these bloody incidents, frontier residents were ready to attack any Indians on sight.

Morgan complained bitterly to Congress that: "Parties of white men [had] formed around Pittsburgh with the express purpose of murdering friendly savages." Recognizing that the situation on the frontier was rapidly deteriorating, Congress (with George Washington's endorsement) promoted Lieutenant Colonel Edward Hand to Brigadier General and rushed him to Fort Pitt to take command of the western war.[28]

Girty had met Edward Hand back in 1765 when the then British officer had first come to serve at Fort Pitt. A congenial and popular man, Hand joined the rebels at the outbreak of the revolution and was given command of the 1st Battalion of Pennsylvania riflemen. Joining with Washington before the siege of Boston, he afterwards made a name for himself in the battles of Long Island, Trenton and Princeton. While highly regarded as a field officer, Hand had no experience facing Indians in the wilderness, and instead of bringing an army with him, he came to Fort Pitt on 1 June with only a few subordinate officers. He faced the daunting task of defending Pittsburgh while also conducting the western war of the United States with only two companies of the 13th Virginia Regiment, which he inherited.

By July, recruiter Girty exceeded all expectations and jubilantly achieved his enlistment quota of 150 men. Unfortunately for Simon, there were too many officers who were still uncertain of his loyalty, and instead of granting him the captain's commission that he had worked for, he was only awarded a lieutenancy. The command he wanted went instead to John Stephenson (half-brother of Col. William Crawford). Although he must have been bitterly stung, Girty apparently made no protest. Then, a few weeks later, when his regiment shipped out to fight at Charleston, Simon was left behind to serve at Fort Pitt on detached duty. Simon had had enough. He resigned his commission and went to see General Hand. Hand hired him at once to serve as an interpreter, agent and spy.

The general was determined to take the war to the Indians, but had been unable to raise enough men for the job. His recruiting difficulties had been exacerbated by rumors of outrageous Loyalist conspiracies. In one such alleged scheme, patriots at Pittsburgh were to be murdered, after which the fort itself was to be handed over to General Hamilton, Captain Alexander McKee and Simon Girty. George Morgan and General Hand himself were named as co-conspirators. Taking control of the volatile situation, Hand had all of the accused conspirators arrested, pending investigation. A squad of soldiers took Girty to the guardhouse at Fort Pitt. George Morgan and Alexander McKee were confined to their homes. Colonel John Campbell was arrested and then paroled in order to remain at Hand's side during the investigations. Hand made certain that Congress was advised in detail. After preliminary interrogations, he and Colonel Campbell traveled south to Fort Randolph to confront their principal accusers. While they were away, Girty escaped.

Having bragged that nobody could hold him against his will, and that he could free himself from the fort's guardhouse anytime he pleased, Girty made good his boast and vanished from his cell one Sunday evening. He spent the night sleeping in an apple tree in the

King's Orchard on the square adjacent to the fort. The next morning, he presented himself at the main gate, and wearing a broad grin, announced that he was there to turn himself back in.

While his stunt may have been a prank, it demonstrated that if Simon had been guilty of treason, he could have easily made good his escape. Soon after, a civil magistrate examined his case and found him innocent of all charges. Despite their enmity, Girty testified on George Morgan's behalf, claiming that he was a loyal patriot. Morgan, John Campbell, and Alexander McKee were all cleared, but in the latter's case there were additional charges, and Hand paroled him to his house, pending Congressional instructions.

Hand's problems were exacerbated when Fort Henry at Wheeling came under attack. Led by the Wyandot chief known as The Half King, a hundred or so warriors briefly besieged the installation and then withdrew. Very little damage was done. Nevertheless, the incident exasperated General Hand, who was fiercely determined to strike back, but could not do so for lack of troops. Too many borderers had already left to fight with General Washington. Hoping to raise at least 500 volunteers from Westmoreland and Bedford Counties, and another 1,500 from Virginia, Hand's expectations went unfulfilled. The largest force he was able to put together was only one hundred men.

By the fall of 1777, reports reached Fort Pitt indicating that Senecas and other Six Nation warriors were raiding for the British. General Hand sent for Girty. Hand wanted Simon to go to the Senecas and ask them to formally declare whether the Six Nations were, or were not, at war with the United States. Simultaneously, Girty was to also collect as much military intelligence as possible about the activities of the British and their Indian allies. Hand dangled the promise of a captaincy over Girty if he accepted the mission.

Whether it was for the promised commission, or to serve Hand and the rebel cause, or, simply because of the nature and dimension of the challenge, Girty agreed. Riding over familiar terrain, he made good time and arrived at the Seneca town of Connewago on 14 November. He announced his purpose and an assembly was gathered to hear him. Simon stated General Hand's query and requested a formal answer.

The council gave him the freedom of the town while they deliberated their response. Having withdrawn from the council house, Simon met up with White Mingo, the war chief who had just returned from Niagara with a horse-load of goods. White Mingo confided that he had made his purchase by trading off some horses that he had stolen a few months earlier near the town of Ligonier, Pennsylvania. He also confided that at the time, he and his war party had taken four white scalps. Girty now had confirmation that some of the Senecas were indeed making war for the English.

Continuing to gather information, Girty later met a returning war party of twenty-five Senecas from the Turtle tribe, led by a chief called Flying Crow. Among the warriors were two whom Girty knew very well: Joneowentashaun, and a man called The Leaf. They told Girty how they had taken two white scalps and a white woman during raids conducted fifteen days earlier, near Ligonier. They even let Girty speak to the captive woman, who related how the warriors had killed and scalped her husband Forbes, and then had beaten the brains out of their only child by slinging it against a tree. From Joneowentashaun, Girty learned of the existence of a British supply depot established at the mouth of the Cuyahoga River, on Lake Erie (present site of Cleveland). From this new base, in the coming spring, the English were planning to supply their Indian allies with food, clothing, guns and ammunition.

Girty also found out about another twenty-seven man war party which was expected back at Connewago at any moment; and, that two American prisoners whom the Senecas had taken in Pennsylvania had already been put to death at one of the Indian towns. That the Senecas had chosen war over neutrality was no longer in question and, with every discovery, Girty's situation was becoming more dangerous. Finally, he was summoned to the council house. When he arrived, Guyasuta was there to address him. Girty and his old friend stood face-to-face before the assembly and the moment was electric. Everyone knew that these two were as close as father and son, and that they were now forced to confront each other as adversaries. Gravely, the fifty-seven-year-old war chief admitted to Simon that the Senecas had indeed decided to make war against the Americans. The Seneca people were certain, Guyasuta explained, that the king's enemies intended to cheat them of all their lands, and because of this, they were joining the king of England's army. Then Guyasuta informed Simon that Colonel Butler at Niagara had promised to supply them and their women and children with every necessity. Led by their principal war chief Kayingwaurto, the Senecas—indeed the majority of the Six Nations—were determined to make war on the Americans in the spring.

Girty responded that he had recently learned that General Burgoyne had just been defeated, and that all of his soldiers had been captured; and, furthermore, everything he was now telling them could be confirmed by their own people. Ignoring Simon's disclosure, Guyasuta advised him that having determined that he had come to Connewago as an American spy, the council had decided that he was to be taken to Niagara and handed over to the British. Simon could either agree to accept the council's decision (i.e. remain relatively free and voluntarily accompany his escorts when the time came to go to Niagara) or he would be bound and guarded.

Simon agreed to accept his fate; a promise he had no intention of keeping. Two days later, he escaped with his horse and rifle. While he fled south, he had plenty of time to mull over his situation. He had been closely united to the Senecas for more than half of his life, but now his ties to Guyasuta and to all of his Seneca friends and relations were severed, perhaps irrevocably. In their eyes, he was now a fugitive, an enemy. Circumstances had forced him to abandon the people he loved and cared for, perhaps more than any others, and return to a world where most of the people did not trust, or even like him. His loyalty to the rebel cause indeed came at a high price.

Abandoning his horse to continue by canoe, Girty reached Fort Pitt on 27 November. General Hand was away at Fort Randolph and in his absence, John Gibson was in command. Simon reported to Gibson and then went to spend time with his family on Squirrel Hill.

Gibson summarized Girty's report in a letter he sent express to General Hand:

Col. John Gibson to Gen. Edward Hand

Fort Pitt Decr 10th, 1777

  ... Simon Girty another Messenger who was also sent by you with Messages to the Seneca towns on the Heads of the Allegheney [sic], Returned and Informed me, that he went to the towns without meeting any Indians, tho by the Marks of the Warrors on the Roads he could Discover they had Been at War, that on his arrival there he acquainted them with the Success of our Army to Northward and Asked them if they had not heard of it. They Replied they had not. He then told them they might depend on it for truth, and desired them to sit still as they would hear it in a few days from their own people. They then told him they looked upon him as a Spy, and that they would take him to Niagara. They informed him that all the Western Nations had taken up the Tomhawk against the Americans Excepting White Eyes and a few Delawares and that they would be Ready to Strike in the Spring. He learned that Seven parties were then actually out against our frontiers, that Guashota [Guyasuta] had been twice at war against our Settlements, that he had killed four people near Ligonier, that the White Mingoe had also Been at War, that the Flying Crow Brought in a White Woman Daughter of Dudley Dougherty who was taken near Ligonier, whilst he was there and some scalps, that All-Face, the head Warrior was out with a party of 25 Men, that the Evening Before they were to set of [sic] for Niagara, he pretended to hunt his horse, and after going out he returned in a Great hurry, saying he saw a flock of Turkeys and snatched up his Gun and Came away. That in the night he came to another town on the River where he got a Canoe and Came by Water, that near the Kittanning Early in the Morning an Indian from the Shore haled him and asked him who he was, that he told him his name was a Chief's name who he left in the towns, that the Indian told him he Lyed [sic], that he knew him to be Girty and desired him to come ashore, that on his Refusal he fired several shots at him.

  He Girty says that he thinks they will wait to hear from the Northward as they are guided by a Chief of the Senecas there, and that the Surrender of Burgoyne's Army will have a Good Effect on them. I am, Dear Sir, with Respect, your most Obedient humble Servt.

Jno. Gibson[29]

___

It is apparent from Gibson's letter that Girty had not revealed to him the existence of the new British supply depot located at the mouth of the Cuyahoga. Simon was saving that information for General Hand.[30]

Hand was at Fort Randolph to investigate the despicable murder of Cornstalk. Apparently, accompanied by a young warrior named Red Hawk, the old Shawnee chief had come to the fort to deliver a warning that except for himself, his wife, and a handful of followers, the rest of the Shawnee nation had decided to go to war for the British. Despite his loyal gesture, he, Red Hawk and another Shawnee were arrested. A few days later, when his father failed to return home as scheduled, Cornstalk's son, Elinipsico, went to Fort Randolph to inquire. Once there, he, too, was quickly arrested and imprisoned. Within hours, a mob of irate soldiers, bent upon avenging the death of a friend who had been killed by Indians, burst into the room where the Shawnee captives were being held and shot all four of them to death.

Returning to Fort Pitt a few days before Christmas, Hand sent for Girty to hear his report in detail. His best spy held nothing back. The general was highly excited to learn about the English supply base at the mouth of the Cuyahoga. The isolated British base represented the kind of opportunity for which Hand had been waiting. Because the British did not expect any American attacks until spring, the Cuyahoga base, located only a hundred miles from Fort Pitt, would be poorly defended, if at all. The warriors of the region would be widely scattered at their winter hunting camps. General Hand reasoned a moderate force of mounted men could slip in and destroy the installation without major losses. Elated by Girty's information, Hand began to plan his attack.

Girty's revelations clearly demonstrate the depth of his loyalty to the American cause. Had he entertained even the slightest thoughts of desertion, he need not have exposed the existence of the Cuyahoga supply depot, nor the other intelligence he had just collected. Notably, during Girty's debriefing Hand made no reference to the promised promotion, nor did Simon.

While General Hand was focusing his attention on attacking the base at Cuyahoga, Captain James Willing of the United States Navy arrived at Pittsburgh seeking to secure supplies, refit a gunboat, and to recruit a 100-man force of marines. Willing's orders were to sail down the Ohio River to the Mississippi, help secure the neutrality of the inhabitants along its banks, and bring back provisions or supplies.

George Girty, who at thirty-two, was "a citizen not without some influence in the community," fell for Willing's recruitment pitch and was commissioned a 2nd Lieutenant. The gunboat that was being refitted was christened *The Rattletrap.*[31]

Of all the Girty brothers, only Thomas escaped combat during the War for Independence. He evidently spent his time farming on Squirrel Hill, where he lived with his wife Ann and two children. Not far away, on the original Girty holdings, John Turner, Jr. still shared a house with his mother. At the time, James Girty was living out at the Shawnee Towns on the Scioto River, where, with George Morgan's blessings, he and his wife maintained a trading post.

By February 1778, the challenge of raising men for the Cuyahoga mission prompted General Hand to seek help from William Crawford at Yohiogania:

Dr. Sir—

As I am credibly informed that the English have lodged a quantity of arms, ammunition, provision and clothing at a small Indian town about 100 miles from Fort Pitt, to support the savages in their excursions against the inhabitants of this and the adjacent counties, I ardently wish to collect as many brave active lads as are willing to turn out, to destroy this magazine. Every man must be provided with a horse, & every article necessary to equip them for the expedition, except ammunition, which, with some arms, I can furnish.

It may not be necessary to assure them, that everything they are able to bring away shall be sold at public venue for the sole benefit of the captors, & the money equally distributed. Tho' I am certain that a sense of the service they will render to their country

will operate more strongly than the expectation of gain. I therefore expect you will use your influence on this occasion, & bring all the volunteers you can raise to Fort Pitt by the 15th of this month. I am, dear Sir, Yr. Obet. Humble Servt.
   Edward Hand

Col. Wm. Crawford
   N. B. The horses shall be appraised & paid for if lost.[32]

Hand was confident of his success. He calculated that his mounted force would traverse from thirty-five to forty miles per day, and that even if light snow fell they would be able to make twenty miles in daylight. At their slowest pace, he figured to reach the mouth of the Cuyahoga, execute the attack, and return to Fort Pitt in no more than ten to twelve days. If his forces were challenged by a few warriors, they would be strong enough to prevail. It would take the enemy a number of days to assemble a force large enough to pose a serious threat.

The forthcoming expedition was Girty's first opportunity to serve under a professional officer—a veteran Continental Army general. He looked forward to receiving his captaincy and, since it was he who had revealed the existence of the secret British base to General Hand, he expected to be awarded the honor of piloting the volunteers. What happened next is best described by an old Inuit expression: *Sometimes you eat the bear, and sometimes, it eats you.*

CHAPTER FIVE
DISILLUSIONMENT

ON 8 FEBRUARY 1778, under a dreary, overcast sky that matched his sullen mood, Girty rode out from Fort Pitt with General Hand and 500 volunteers. Simon had received neither the promised commission nor the honor of piloting Hand's army. That assignment had been awarded by General Hand to a local blacksmith named William Brady (no relation to Samuel Brady). Simon was there because, having divorced himself from George Morgan as well as the Army of Virginia, he had run out of choices. Working for Hand was all that was left to him.[1]

Crossing the Allegheny, the volunteers followed the downstream course of the Ohio River over the ancient Indian trail called the Great Path. Twenty-two miles after leaving Fort Pitt they reached the mouth of the Beaver River. There, Brady led them northward following the Beaver's eastern bank. Anticipating the capture of valuable booty, most of the volunteers had brought two horses; one to ride and an additional packhorse to carry provisions on the outbound leg and to transport plunder on the return. A light snow began to fall, which the men welcomed, because it was covering their tracks.

The disaster began later in the day when the temperature rose and the falling snow turned to rain. Before long the men were soaked through, cold to the bone. Adding to their troubles, the snow on the ground began to melt. That night they were forced to camp under a freezing rain that never ceased. The next day, the streams began to swell, and many of the low-lying areas they had planned to traverse were now flooded. Where they had anticipated crossing over ice-bound streams, they were met by raging torrents. They forded some streams but were forced to ride around the heads of others. The downpour did not let up for days. Even when they were finally blessed with a dry day, the sky remained gloomy and the men stayed damp, cold and miserable. The weather and the blacksmith's piloting were destroying them. Girty knew it but said nothing. The route and the maddeningly slow pace grew increasingly dangerous. Some of the men were coughing and Hand, who was a trained physician, recognized what was happening.

The men were so miserable that at one bivouac, early in the evening, a man walked off and never came back. A search party was sent out to find him the next morning, but they found nothing. It was believed that he had either fallen or thrown himself into one of the rivers and drowned, and that is how his death was recorded.

One morning as the army was breaking camp, Major James Brenton sought out Girty and begged for his help. The major's best horse had wandered off during the night. Not wishing to lose the animal or to be left behind on his own, Brenton asked Girty to accompany him until they found the animal, after which the two of them could ride back together to rejoin the expedition. Simon agreed to help him. There was a frosting of fresh powder on the ground and it was easy to track the wayward stray. Later that morning they found and caught Brenton's horse, and after saddling the animal, the two hurried to rejoin the army. Following the army's tracks, Girty and Brenton were approaching the forks of the Beaver River (where the left branch becomes the Mahoning, and the right fork becomes the Shenango), when they heard the faint sounds of distant gunfire coming from upriver. They spurred their horses on to the sound of fighting.

Seven miles upstream, General Hand's volunteers were engaged in a chaotic assault on a cluster of cabins in the first of the Kuskuskee Towns. Originally built by the Six Nations, the site had been abandoned at the beginning of the French and Indian War. Later, the French had built a number of log houses for their allies; but now only an a few Delawares were in residence.

The shooting stopped long before Girty and Brenton had reached the place, but they arrived in time to watch Hand's men race about in a mad, competitive search for plunder. During the attack an old Delaware chief and a woman had been killed. In front of a nearby cabin, General Hand and a few of his officers interrogated an old woman whose hand was bleeding.

Apparently, earlier that day, while Girty and Brenton were retrieving the major's wayward horse, General Hand and the volunteers had halted at the forks of the Beaver River. The general had already concluded that it was senseless to go on, and he ordered the men to make camp. Although the brigade had been traveling for several days, they had only come some forty miles from Fort Pitt and, at their present rate, it would be weeks before they could reach the mouth of the Cuyahoga. Besides, many of the men were ill. Hand assembled his officers and acknowledged the obvious: the weather had defeated them. They would rest here and prepare to start the return march to Fort Pitt the next morning. Some of Hand's scouts approached and informed him that they had found fresh Indian tracks in the snow alongside the banks of the Shenango, and that the tracks led upstream. Hand sent new scouts out with instructions to appraise the situation. These men returned within the hour, reporting that the tracks led towards the old Kuskuskee Towns seven miles upriver. They guessed as many fifty or sixty Indians might be in residence there.

Thus far, Hand's Cuyahoga campaign had been a disaster, and he grabbed at the opportunity, declaring quickly that any Indians up the river were hostiles and should be attacked forthwith. It was decided to approach and surround the first town with three columns. Hand was to command the center, Colonel Providence Mounts was to lead the left wing, and the right was to be led by Major William Crawford.

Figuring that this would be their only chance to capture anything that they might later be able to sell, the volunteers wasted no time getting ready. During their advance, their discipline evaporated long before they could reach their objectives. The center of the attacking army reached its appointed position on schedule, but was without a commander for, during their approach, General Hand's horse had got mired in deep mud and his men were in such a hurry that they just abandoned him. As soon as the first volunteers got within rifle range of the cabins, they dismounted and began firing. Colonel Mounts' left wing was late and failed to reach its position on time, leaving a gap at the rear of the town. Finally, Major Crawford's right wing arrived and, after dismounting, they too began shooting at the Indian houses.

Girty and Brenton reached the town a few minutes after all the shooting had stopped. Simon was summoned to where the elderly Delaware woman was being interrogated. In anguished tones, she explained that the old warrior who had been killed in the one-sided fight was her husband Bull, brother to Captain Pipe. At the time of the attack, Bull had been digging up stored corn from a hole behind one of the houses when suddenly bullets began to strike all around him. Coming to his senses, the old warrior scrambled for his musket, took careful aim at the nearest of the enemy men, and fired. His ball broke the arm of Captain David Scott. As Bull began to hurriedly reload, a militiaman named Reasin Virgin charged him with a raised tomahawk. Virgin got to Bull before the old man could finish reloading and sank his tomahawk into the Indian's skull. Distracted by the scene, the men nearby did not notice as a woman and several children broke from another cabin and ran for a distant tree line. By the time the volunteers saw them, the woman and children reached the trees and disappeared. More interested in what could be had in the Indian houses, none of the volunteers pursued them.

According to the recollections of Samuel Murphy:

… hearing guns firing, he [meaning General Hand] would ride up to the spot and find they were shooting at nothing & would try to stop them, and then ride off to learn the same result—another volley. Some of the men, in high glee, would say they were 'firing in honor of the day.' A squaw—either Captain Pipe's mother or his brother's squaw—ran out of a cabin and held up her hands imploringly.[2]

Although he was unsure of the identity of this woman at the time, Murphy reported:

… she fell partly against a tree, several ran up, fell upon, shot and killed her.

It was at that moment when Bull's wife ran out from another cabin, and several men began to shoot at her. Shouting for them to cease fire, William Crawford ran after the woman and caught hold of her. Amazingly, her only wound was from having her little finger shot away on one hand.

Girty knew that Bull and Captain Pipe were both strong friends of the Americans, and that there would be a price to pay for what Hand had done that day.

During her questioning, the old woman had mumbled something about ten Muncie warriors making salt at a place further up the Mahoning River. Hand decided to send a strike force "to collect" these men, and he asked Girty to lead it. The general and the brigade would take refuge in the vacant Kuskuskee houses and await Simon's return before commencing their return march to Fort Pitt.

Girty led a dozen or more men to the Salt Lick Town, some twenty-five miles distant (current site of Niles, Ohio). He had a lot to ponder during the ride. The expectations he had about General Hand and the Cuyahoga expedition had been sharply soured. Led by a veteran general of the Continental Army, the first American campaign sent to strike deep into enemy country had managed to kill one old Delaware man and his ancient mother, neither of whom had been at war with the United States.

It was after dark when Simon and his men reached their objective. Originally built by the French for their allies during the French and Indian War, the town's population had peaked in 1764; it was unoccupied now, except when Indians came to make salt. A thin wisp of smoke wafted up from the roof of only one of the scattered cabins, and Girty found it was being shared by five Delaware women. He kept one as a hostage, and turned the others loose. Then, after posting some of his men to keep watch, he and the others ate and slept.

At first light Simon sent men to scout the place and a few minutes later, a shot rang out. An Indian boy who had been hunting birds from the trees with a bow and arrow had been spotted and, according to Samuel Murphy, "several men fired, he was shot and killed, Zach Connell & Squire Forman both claiming the honor."[3]

Girty was summoned to settle the grisly issue. According to Murphy, he decided "in favor of Connell," thereby putting an abrupt end to the bizarre dispute. Within the hour Girty led his boy-killers back to the Kuskuskee Towns.

Soon after his return, Girty was sought out by William Crawford, who told him that General Hand wanted him to pilot the army's return to Fort Pitt. Simon agreed and led the rag-tag collection of volunteers back over a faster and much easier route than the course blacksmith Brady had followed.

On 3 March an exhausted, hungry and unhappy collection of volunteers straggled into Fort Pitt. In addition to a few Indian muskets and some liberated pots and pans, their only trophies were two captive Indian women and a pair of scalps. News of the expedition's failure spread rapidly on the frontier; Hand was jeered for his lack of leadership and the mission to Cuyahoga was dubbed the "Squaw Campaign."

As most of the people on the frontier interpreted it, the failure of Hand's mission was not because a few friendly Delawares had been killed, but because large numbers of Indians had not been slaughtered. Indeed, the only official to express concern over the deaths of the victims was George Morgan, who rushed numerous apologies to the Delawares.

Profoundly disturbed by what had happened, Girty had a lot to mull over. General Hand made his decision to attack the Indians at the Kuskuskee Towns without making any effort to ascertain whether they were friends or foes. Was this just a lapse in Hand's judgment, or did it signify an ominous change to American policy? Girty knew that the majority of the western and northern tribes were already allied to the king. Clearly, if there was no longer any real intention to conduct peaceful trade with the Indians of the Ohio Valley after the war, then there was no reason to maintain peaceful relations with any of them.

As a veteran of the Indian Department at Fort Pitt, Simon knew that Washington, Franklin, Henry Lee and many other leaders of the revolution had all been land speculators. The Indian trade was an irritant to such men, and, as Girty knew, even George Morgan, the fur trade's most vociferous advocate, had clandestinely committed his future to the Indiana Company. If the British lost the war, the Ohio Country wouldn't be dominated by fur traders; it would be seized, sold and settled. Like the Delaware boy who had been hunting birds at the Salt Licks Town, the Indians were disposable.

When Simon was at Connewago, Guyasuta had told him that, in their efforts to enlist the Indians, the British had claimed that if the rebels won their independence, they would come and take all the hunting grounds and destroy the Indians completely. Simon could no longer regard such a statement as rhetoric. So, what course was he to follow? His ties to George Morgan were cut and he could no longer trust General Hand. Too many promises had been made to him and broken. What was left for him to do at Pittsburgh?

Prior to the Squaw Campaign, Simon's commitment to American independence had been steadfast. It was time to look hard at his decisions, and the one he was now pondering would be irrevocable. He made up his mind to talk things over with one of the few men he trusted completely; he went to see his old friend Alexander McKee.

McKee was still at his home, defying repeated orders from Hand for him to go to York Town and face charges of treason. McKee could not hold out much longer and his chances at York Town were nil. There was ample evidence against him, including letters from Lord Dunmore offering him a commission if he would raise a battalion of Tories from around Fort Pitt. He had already sent his wife and his eight-year-old son Thomas to Detroit, where a captain's commission awaited him at the British Indian Department. The only thing that appeared to be keeping McKee at Pittsburgh was his reluctance to abandon his properties and business holdings.

Matthew Elliott was at McKee's when Girty arrived. Driven by motivations that were purely commercial, Elliott had also gone to

McKee to discuss defection. The preceding fall, George Morgan had him out to the Shawnee country to deliver peace messages and to spy. Accompanied by a black servant, Elliott had stopped to rest at a Moravian mission on the Tuscarawas River, where he had been warned that if he continued his journey to the Shawnee towns, he would likely be attacked by "Sandusky Indians." Ignoring the warning, Elliott went on. Then he and his slave were both seized by a mixed war party of Wyandots and Mingoes. Fortunately for Elliott, two Delaware Moravian converts interceded, arguing for his release. Elliott and his servant were let go, but the Wyandot-Mingo war party kept all his packhorses and trade goods. Enraged, Elliott went to the Shawnee towns and spent the winter brooding over his losses. In the spring, he journeyed to Detroit where he confronted Governor Hamilton, and demanded compensation for his losses. Hamilton threw him in irons on suspicion of being an American spy, and Elliott was shipped to Quebec. After several months in custody, he was tried and found innocent. On parole, he was allowed to return to Pittsburgh via New York.

From what he had seen at Quebec, New York and Philadelphia (all of which were now occupied by British forces), Elliott told McKee and Girty that he was convinced that the rebel bid for independence was ultimately doomed. In spite of all that had happened to him, he was still determined to be reimbursed for the losses of his goods and horses, and he reasoned that if he were now welcomed at Detroit, his chances would be greatly improved. He was hoping that McKee would speak on his behalf.

McKee agreed with Elliott's conclusion that the rebels were losing the war. He had made up his mind to defect and he invited Elliott and Girty to join him. Together they would go to Detroit where he would speak for Elliott and do his best to see that Girty was reinstated with the British Indian Department.

Having finally settled on a course of action, Simon returned home to Squirrel Hill, revealed his intentions to his mother and his half-brother, and had a document drawn up to transfer all of his properties to John Turner, Jr.

At the time, James Girty and his Shawnee wife were at Pittsburgh, preparing to carry American gifts and peace messages to the Shawnee Towns on the Scioto River for George Morgan. There can be little doubt but that Simon also told James of his intention to defect.

While working for General Hand, Simon had roomed at Duncan's Tavern and Inn, near Fort Pitt. David Duncan and his wife were friendly, outgoing people, and their place was popular with traders and frontiersmen like John Finley, Matthew Elliott, William Wilson and Simon Kenton. Girty regarded the Duncans as close friends and it appears their affection for him was reciprocal, for even though he was unable to pay his board, they let him stay on. According to the recollections of Major John Finley, Girty was in tears when he bid good-bye to Mrs. Duncan, telling her "he could no longer stay and live with her; that he couldn't work and he wouldn't steal," and added, "I'll do all I can to save your family and kin if they should fall into my hands, but as for the rest, I'll make no promises."[4]

Girty may also have disclosed his pending defection to another close friend, for in her biography of Simon Kenton, Edna Kenton wrote:

There is some evidence that they saw each other again there just before Girty's desertion, and that Girty told Kenton, if not his purpose, at least all his grievances against the Americans.[5]

When Kenton was an old man, he recalled that his two most enduring friendships were those he had had with George Rogers Clark and Simon Girty. The former was America's greatest frontier hero and combat general of the American Revolution, and the latter was the most infamous white renegade of the West. Kenton claimed his relationship to Girty was cemented by a curious pledge:

Girty and I, two lonely men on the banks of the Ohio, pledged ourselves one to the other, hand in hand, for life or death, when there was no body in the wilderness but God and us.[6]

Although the strength of their friendship transcended political loyalties, both men knew that Girty's defection could have deadly ramifications, and that one day they might face each other through rifle sights.

On 25 March 1778, James Girty and his wife left Pittsburgh, leading their packhorse train towards the Shawnee Towns. Three days later, well after sundown on Saturday, the 28th, under a clear but moonless sky, seven mounted men slipped away from Alexander McKee's estate and rode towards the Ohio Country. The riders were Simon Girty, Alexander McKee, Matthew Elliott, a cousin of McKee's named Robert Surphlet, a servant to McKee named John Higgins, and two of McKee's black slaves.

Having received "a hint of McKee's intention," General Hand sent a squad of soldiers to McKee's house to arrest him. They missed McKee by hours.[7]

For General Hand and the rebel leaders, the simultaneous defection of McKee, Girty and Elliott was a civil and a military nightmare. No other trio in America was better suited to incite the western and northern tribes than these three men. News of the event spread explosively from Fort Pitt. General Hand considered the situation so perilous that he wrote to William Crawford on 30 March:

You will no doubt be surprised to hear that Mr. McKee, Matthew
Elliott, Simon Girty, one Surplus and Higgins, with McKee's two
negroes, eloped on Saturday night. This will make it improper
to proceed with the intended expedition to French Creek, which
I beg you may give proper notice of to the gentlemen who are
preparing for it; and as your assistance may be necessary towards
preventing the evils that may arise from the information of these
runaways, I beg you may return here as soon as possible, I am, Dr.
Crawford, sincerely yrs… etc.[8]

Similarly disturbed, George Morgan wrote to Henry Laurens, President of the Continental Congress:

… The elopement of Mr. McKee, late Crown Agent at Pittsburgh
who most dishonourably broke his Parole on the 28th inst.
has somewhat check'd the pleasing expectation I entertain'd

> *respecting the Delawares and Shawnese, tho' I think the former*
> *will not be altogether influenced by him. Four persons accom-*
> *panied him viz: Matthew Elliott, Simon Girty, Robin Surplis*
> *&————Higgins.*
>   *... Girty has served as Interpreter of the Six Nation Tongue*
> *at all the public Treaties here & I apprehend will influence his*
> *Brother who is now on a Message from the Commissioners to the*
> *Shawnese, to join him.*[9]

Hand and Morgan assumed that McKee and his companions would successfully incite the Delawares to take up the hatchet for the British cause. Recently the Wyandots and the British had been pressuring the Delawares to abandon neutrality; however, thanks to the efforts of White Eyes (a Moravian convert and the elected leader of the Delaware nation) the tribe had remained at peace thus far. After Cornstalk's murder, a large number of Delawares had clamored for war; their faction was led by Captain Pipe, whose heart had been irrevocably turned by the killings of his brother and mother at the Kuskuskee Town during the Squaw Campaign.

At the time of Girty's defection, Moravian missionary John Heckewelder and a companion were traveling on church matters from Bethlehem to Pittsburgh. Heckewelder wrote in his journal that:

> *As we drew nearer to Pittsburgh the unfavorable account of the*
> *elopement of McKee, Elliott, Girty, and others, from the latter*
> *place to the Indian country, for the purpose of instigating the*
> *Indians to murder, caused great excitement.... Indeed, the gloomy*
> *countenances of all men, women and children that we passed,*
> *bespoke fear—nay, some families even spoke of leaving their farms*
> *and moving off.*[10]

After leaving McKee's estate, Girty and his companions bypassed the Moravian mission settlements and rode directly to the capital of the Delawares. At Coshocton their unexpected appearance was of major consequence. McKee announced to the Delaware leaders that he, Girty and Elliott wished to address their nation, and runners were sent to summon an assembly.

Coincidentally—or perhaps by plan—James Girty and his wife had arrived at Coshocton one day earlier and, after having conferred in private with his older brother, James announced that he too was joining the British cause. He had confiscated the American goods he had been transporting and was placing them at McKee's disposal.

When the general council finally assembled, both White Eyes' and Captain Pipe's factions were present. The Indians listened intently to what McKee, Girty and Elliott had to say.

Questioned later by Reverend Heckewelder, the Delawares reported that:

The fugitives told the Delawares that it was the determination of the American people to kill and destroy the whole Indian race, be they friends or foes, and to possess themselves of their country; and that at this time, while they were preparing themselves for this purpose, they were also preparing fine-sounding speeches to deceive them, that they might with the more safety fall upon and murder them. That now was the time and the only time, for all nations to rise and turn out to a man against these intruders, and not even suffer them to cross the Ohio, but fall upon them where they should find them, which if not done without delay, their country would be lost to them forever! [11]

Girty, McKee and Elliott all claimed that the English were winning the war. There was no need for them to exaggerate, for at the time, the British occupied Philadelphia and New York, the Continental Congress had been driven to York Town, and Washington and his army were suffering in their camp at Valley Forge.

The speeches provoked immediate debate. Captain Pipe excitedly called for a war vote, and received overwhelming support. Recognizing defeat, White Eyes claimed that if the nation was so inclined, he too would fight the Americans but, he warned, he feared the outcome would bring about the destruction of the Delawares. He asked for a delay of ten days before any hostilities commenced. No one believed that anything would change the final outcome, and the council voted to grant his request.

At Fort Pitt, in a desperate attempt to preserve Delaware neutrality, General Hand, John Gibson and George Morgan hurriedly prepared peace messages and other materials to be sent to the Delawares. Reverend John Heckewelder and his companion, a native convert named John Shebosh, had volunteered to carry these communications to Coshocton, and they departed on 2 April.

Having stirred up a hornet's nest, McKee, Elliott and James Girty were anxious to be on their way to the Shawnee Towns on the Scioto. Simon wanted to go to Detroit to meet with Governor Henry Hamilton and attempt to rejoin the British Indian Department.

There was a young British Indian agent named Edward Hazel then at Coshocton, and he was making ready to return to Detroit after delivering letters from Governor Hamilton to a few of the principal Moravian missionaries. Hazel had an escort of Wyandot warriors, and he agreed to McKee's request to take Girty back to Detroit. McKee quickly penned a report to Hamilton and entrusted it, and a number of documents that he thought the governor might find interesting, to Hazel for delivery.

Somewhere on the Great Path during their journey to Detroit, Hazel, Girty and the Wyandots encountered a war party of Senecas who were en route to the same objective. Recognizing Simon, the Senecas demanded that he be turned over to them. They argued that Girty had been adopted by them and that he had afterward "returned to his countrymen, and joined them in their war against the tribe who now demanded him."[12]

One of Hazel's escorts, a Wyandot chief named Leatherlips, responded that since Girty had been found bearing arms in their country, he was now a Wyandot prisoner. "By your own showing," Leatherlips said, "he only returned to his own country and people. Ever after then you can have no claim upon him as one of your own."[13]

Brought into the conversation, Girty explained that he had been badly treated at Fort Pitt, and that he was on his way now to Detroit to take up arms against the Americans.

It seems the Senecas were not ready to start a war with the Wyandots over Girty. Reluctantly, they withdrew from the conflict and allowed Girty and Hazel to continue on their way.

Girty was facing other problems. Despite McKee's reassurances, he could not know whether Governor Hamilton would welcome him back to the British fold, or have him hanged or shot as a traitor. Unlike McKee or Elliott, Simon had actually spied and conducted military operations against the British and their Indian allies, and the odds were high that Governor Hamilton was aware of this. Simon anticipated that the Senecas would speak against him. However, he had little choice in the matter. If he wanted to serve the British, he had no choice but to face whatever was coming.

By this time, Reverend John Heckewelder and his companion, John Shebosh, had reached the principal Moravian settlement of Gnadenhutten. There, some of the converts told them that due to the rousing speeches made by McKee, Girty and Elliott, many of the Delawares were shaving their heads and making ready to go to war. Seeking security, the Christian Indians at Gnadenhutten were planning to join the congregation at Lichtenau.

The next morning, accompanied by Delaware convert John Martin, Heckewelder hurried to Coshocton. Swimming their horses across the Muskingum River and traveling through woods to avoid war parties, they reached the Delaware capitol at about 10 o'clock in the morning. Their arrival drew a throng of silent, moody Indians who were cold to Heckewelder's greetings.

Met by White Eyes, who swiftly related the content of the speeches of Girty, McKee and Elliott, Heckewelder went to the council house and made his case. He read aloud the peace messages from General Hand and George Morgan, after which White Eyes urged everyone to take notice of the good disposition of the American people towards the Delawares. Then, in closing, Heckewelder held aloft a newspaper containing the story of the capitulation of General Burgoyne's army, which he translated loudly. More than anything else, this startling news made a strong impact on the Delaware leaders, and after lengthy discussion they agreed to back away from their commitment to war.

Girty, Hazel and their Wyandot escorts arrived at Fort Detroit on or about April 20th. Hazel met with Hamilton, delivered the documents given him by McKee, and gave his verbal report, which no doubt included details of the Seneca attempt to seize Girty.

The governor read all of McKee's letters, including one in which McKee vouched for Girty's loyalty and urged that he be taken back into the Indian Department. Girty was hardly an unknown commodity. Many of the officers on Hamilton's staff knew him. Captain William Caldwell had served with Girty during Dunmore's War, and most of the veteran members of the Indian Department knew Girty from his years of service at Fort Pitt. Simon Girty's exceptional talents and frontier skills were common knowledge. Hamilton had to decide whether Girty was sincere about wanting to serve the king, or whether he was a very clever spy.

Only the year before, Hamilton had received orders to assemble as many Indians as he could, and after placing "proper persons at their Head," use them to create an alarm upon the frontiers of Virginia and Pennsylvania. The objective was to cause vast numbers of settlers to abandon their isolated farms and flee to scattered forts and towns. Terror-stricken, the refugees would hopefully clog the roads and rivers, creating chaos. In turn, this would eventually deny the American colonists the ability to feed themselves. Another hoped-for result was that thousands of revolutionaries, who were presently facing British troops in the East under Washington and his generals, would clamor for their release in order to hurry home to defend their homes and loved ones.

Targeting American morale, Hamilton's subsequent campaign had been cunning and perfectly suited to the type of warfare in which the Indians excelled. He had staffed the Indian Department with former fur traders, hunters, intermediaries and interpreters—men who not only knew how to live among Indians, but who also enjoyed it. Quickly accepted by the war parties, Hamilton's agents exerted a strong influence regarding the selection of targets. Thus there was a real need for men like Simon Girty, if his motives were genuine. It was time to see the man.

Hamilton deemed Girty's sincerity to be genuine during their meeting, and a few days later the governor enlisted Simon as an interpreter to McKee with a pay rate of ten shillings a day, the equivalent of a captain's pay. Adroitly, Hamilton put the weight of his decision on to McKee's shoulders. If it turned out that Girty was in fact a spy, McKee would bear some of the consequences.

Simon's acceptance of Hamilton's offer carried with it the certainty that if he were captured, a swift death by hanging or from a firing squad would be the best that he could expect. Expecting nothing less than savagery from their enemies, the Americans responded in kind. Yet, whatever hatred frontier Americans exhibited against Indian captives, it was nothing compared to the rage they reserved for white men who fell into their hands while in the company of Indian raiders. As the Americans saw it, anyone who fought with Indians against whites—for any reason—was someone who had turned his back on civilized conduct in order to delight in savagery.

HESPARIAN, COLUMBUS, OHIO, No. V. v. I, PP 343–349, SEPTEMBER 1838

… one of the boldest and most notorious of these latter (renegades) was Simon Girty–for many years the scourge of the infant settlements in the West, the terror of women, and the bugaboo of children.

HISTORICAL SOCIETY OF NORTHWESTERN OHIO, No. 2, v.10, APRIL 1938

The four Girty brothers, forerunners to the James brothers, the Younger brothers and the other desperadoes of the west, terrorized the entire northwestern country in the period between the revolution and the War of 1812.

Although Simon had not yet lifted a hand or drawn blood against his former countrymen, his defection branded him with a mark of notoriety. As an Indian expert, a frontiersman of note, a scout, a spy, a soldier, and finally as someone who had committed himself to the destruction of their cause, Girty's image provoked fearsome expectations.

Frontier warfare was not set-piece combat with opposing forces of adult males arranged in rigid formations with waving flags, amid the music of drums and fifes. It was a surprise attack by twenty or thirty warriors against an isolated farmhouse in the middle of the night, or a terrifying and deadly ambush on a military wagon transporting wheat to an outpost. It was scalped bodies, burnt out cabins and barns, stolen horses, and dead cattle and pigs. The Indian warriors set loose by Hamilton were cruel and fierce to the utmost of their abilities; it was the only way they knew how to wage war.

From the very beginning, the Americans accused Hamilton of masterminding brutal savagery. The frontier community claimed he incited the "savages" by offering them cash bounties for American scalps—including those taken from women or children. But it was the Indians who had proposed to the governor the idea of payment for scalps upon completion of their raids. As the Indians saw it, scalps and captives were the hard evidence of their actions on behalf of the king. Hamilton agreed with their logic and the bargain was struck. Accordingly, both scalps and captives were carefully inventoried and recorded in British logs and journals (scalps were carefully stored in wooden crates for eventual shipment back to London).

When they returned from raiding, the Indians paraded themselves at Detroit and recounted their exploits. Such events were almost always followed with feasting and celebration, including a disposition of gifts from the British Indian Department, in thanks for the support of the king's Indian allies. There were a number of American prisoners at Detroit to observe such events, and it was natural for them to conclude that Hamilton was buying American scalps (Hamilton's nickname among the Americans was "The Hair Buyer"). What was not apparent to the American captives was that Hamilton was paying additional rewards to Indians who obeyed his requests for them to be humane, and who brought back live prisoners rather than their scalps. At one Detroit Council, Hamilton told a party of warriors who were about to go raiding: "I cannot but praise the behavior of the Indian nations who have taken hold of their father's axe and who have acted as men. I hope you'll act the same part and not redden your axe with the blood of women and children or innocent men. I know that men kill men, and not children. I speak to you who are men."[14]

Despite Hamilton's orders, Indian warriors were murdering men, women and children during their raids on behalf of the king, and Simon Girty would soon become the focal point for rebel hatred.

CHAPTER SIX
SAVING A KENTUCKY HORSE THIEF

GIRTY SPENT HIS FIRST MONTH at Detroit familiarizing himself with the city and its inhabitants. Situated at the head of the Upper Great Lakes, Detroit was where the region's major fur trading routes, military roads and Indian paths all converged. For a man who favored a multi-ethnic lifestyle and an environment in which alcohol was consumed in great volume, Detroit was something of a paradise. During one twelve-month period, 16,000 gallons of rum were delivered to the Detroit garrison, and much of it was handed out at the conclusion of Indian councils.

Primarily comprised of English and French individuals, the white population numbered 1,700 people. Just east of the settlement, in crowded villages located on both sides of the Detroit River, lived over a thousand Indians—mostly Wyandots, Ojibways and Potawatomis.

Soon after his arrival there in 1775, Governor Hamilton surveyed the town, its defenses and people. Then called Fort Ponchartrain, the stronghold had been built four years earlier on a high bank of the river. The installation's palisades encircled four square city blocks and contained more than eighty buildings, most of which were one story log structures. Among these were a church, some twenty stores, an Indian council house and a complex of military buildings, barracks, and parade grounds commonly known as "The Citadel."

Many of the buildings were badly rotted and in great need of repair. Fort Ponchartrain could still withstand an Indian siege (as it had during Pontiac's War), but it was completely vulnerable to an enemy who possessed artillery. Built on a gentle slope, the interior of the fort

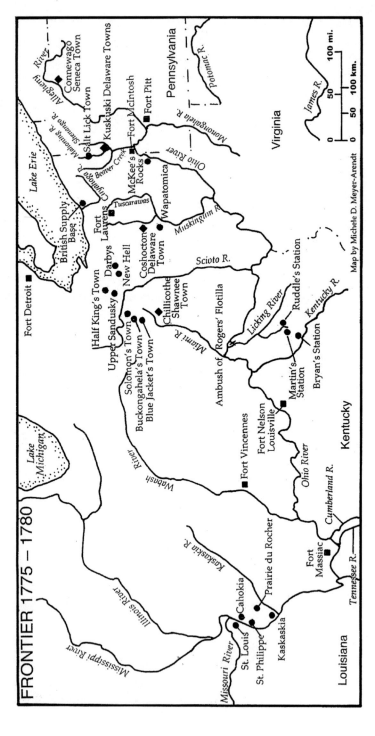

FRONTIER 1775 – 1780

Map by Michele D. Meyer-Arendt

was visible to anyone standing on the opposite shore of the Detroit River. By the time of Girty's arrival, Governor Hamilton was overseeing construction of a new fort, which was being built at the crest of the hill. The new fortress (which would become Fort Lernoult) had thick earthen embankments and could withstand all but the heaviest, most prolonged bombardments.

There were 500 troops at Detroit: four companies of the 8th or King's Regiment, commanded by Major Richard Berringer Lernoult, two companies of Butler's Rangers, commanded by Captain William Caldwell, and a single company of the 4th Regiment, commanded by Captain Thomas Aubrey. In addition, a small but powerful British navy patrolled the Great Lakes.

Detroit was a cosmopolitan city and, echoing it, the agents of the British Indian Department were a mix of Scots, Irish, French and Indian ancestry. Joining their ranks, Girty renewed old friendships and quickly made new ones.

In mid-June, representatives of the Great Lakes tribes assembled at Detroit to take part in councils with Governor Hamilton and other British authorities. Aware of Girty's special problem with the Senecas, Hamilton took care to help him. On the second day of the councils the governor formally presented Girty to the assembly, declared him an interpreter who had recently escaped from the Virginians: "someone who had put himself under the protection of His Majesty, after (having) given satisfactory assurances of his fidelity."[1]

While Girty was being introduced to the Indians at Detroit, in Lancaster, Pennsylvania his former countrymen were declaring him a traitor and were placing an $800 bounty on his head. A proclamation dated 15 June 1778, declared that Alexander McKee, Simon and James Girty, and Matthew Elliott had:

… knowingly and willingly aided and assisted the enemies of the State and of the United States of America, and therefore the Supreme Executive Council did charge and require McKee, Simon and James Girty and Elliott to render themselves to some or one of the justices of the Supreme Court before August 3, to face trial for treason.[2]

As none of the accused men presented themselves to the Pennsylvania Supreme Court, all four were subsequently declared guilty of treason.

At Pittsburgh, General Hand had been replaced by Brigadier General Lachlan McIntosh; and John Turner, Jr. was among the fifty-two volunteers who enlisted to serve in one of two companies raised from Virginia and Pennsylvania to protect the western frontier. Like every recruit, John Turner received a uniform and a bounty of twenty dollars. Strangely, Turner chose to enlist under the name of John Girty, even though by doing so he exposed himself to considerable derision from his barracks-mates.

Simon's enjoyable sojourn at Detroit came to a close when Governor Hamilton ordered him to establish himself among the Wyandots and Mingoes living at a cluster of villages located along the Sandusky River called the Upper Sandusky Towns (about three miles south of present Upper Sandusky, Ohio). The largest of these settlements was Half King's Town, named after the Wyandot chief who made his home there and who was the head of the Sandusky branch of his nation. In 1777, Half King had declared himself against the Americans and since then he had proved his cunning and tenacity in a number of bloody raids and ambushes—including the siege of Fort Henry at Wheeling.

A few miles east of Half King's town were two Mingo villages: Darby's and New Hell. Here, all the inhabitants were Western Senecas who were no longer aligned with the Six Nations. Many of these were people Simon knew and cared for, and amongst whom he felt completely at home.

Girty's first military mission serving under the British flag was described in a secret report sent to George Morgan by Moravian Bishop David Zeisberger. While Zeisberger and his associate Reverend John Heckewelder were professing to British authorities that they and their followers were neutral in the ongoing conflict, in fact, the two missionaries were covertly furnishing military intelligence to the rebels. Zeisberger's report to Morgan of 19 July 1778 stated that:

....A party of 80 Wyandots, mostly from over the Lake, are gone to Weelunk [Wheeling] fort, as much as we know, & many other companies are gone to the settlements.

> *We heard Simon Girty & LaMotte [Captain Guillaume La Mothe] are gone down the river St. Lawrence with as many men as they could spare at Detroit, but have not learnt to what place. The Governor told the Indians that the Passage was stopped & therefore he must open it again. The Trade is also stop'd & no Goods allowed to be brought to Sandusky any more.*
>
> *The newspapers we had from you last [here Zeisberger is referring to the American newspapers that Heckewelder presented to the Delawares at Coshocton, following the anti-American speeches of McKee, Elliott and Girty] are sent to Detroit for which I am much obliged to you & we all long very much to hear from you again. By a Frenchman who came here with the Wyandotts we had intelligence that a company of 40 Indians are gone to watch your boats coming from the Illinois. By all this you will plainly see, there will nor can't be any sort of Treaty with the Chiefs of the Delawares at Pittsburgh for they dare not venture to go there.*
>
> *I am Sir, your Obedt. humble Servt.*
>   *David Zeisberger* [3]

Captain Guillaume La Mothe was a former French-Canadian fur trader who had joined the British service at Detroit in 1777. Simon's foray under La Mothe may have been a result of Hamilton's initial suspicions of Girty's loyalty, and it is likely that La Mothe had been instructed to keep a watchful eye on him. While Girty and La Mothe were "gone down the river St. Lawrence," in one of the most audacious commando attacks in the war on the frontier, twenty-six year old Lieutenant Colonel George Rogers Clark captured the English fort at Kaskaskia, in the heart of the Illinois Country. Clark and his rangers accepted surrender of the stockade and settlement on the fourth of July, without firing a shot. A few days later, they went north and captured Cahokia, Prairie du Rocher, and then St. Philippe. Then Clark defeated the British post at Vincennes, on the Wabash. With this sudden and remarkable string of victories, Clark had boldly wrested control over all the Illinois Country from the English. Simon Kenton was serving as one of Clark's favorite scouts and pilots.

The nature of Girty's mission with La Mothe remains unknown, but Simon was back at Detroit by the middle of August, in time to greet his brother James who had come there from the Shawnee Towns. Governor Hamilton, who was planning a campaign to win back the Illinois Country, took time to meet with James Girty and learn what he had to relate about recent American activities. Impressed by his report, Hamilton granted James' request to join the British Indian Department, and in the same capacity as Simon, he assigned him as an agent to the Shawnees.

Early in September, acting as a military advisor and inter-preter, Simon was part of a large Mingo and Wyandot war party that departed from Upper Sandusky and rapidly moved south. On their way, his group was joined by Shawnee war parties, includ-ing one whose members included his brother James and another Indian Department agent named John Ward. This was Simon and James' first raid against Americans on the frontier. As the war parties moved southeast, small raiding groups comprised of twenty or thirty warriors broke off to deeply infiltrate the American frontier before commencing their attacks. Because of their familiarity with the terrain, the Shawnees were to operate in Kentucky, while the major-ity of the Wyandot and Mingo war parties were to invade western Pennsylvania—surroundings with which Simon was completely familiar. Within days, in raids that were swift and bloody, well-coor-dinated Indian attacks broke out simultaneously over a large region of the American frontier

Reports from survivors claimed that there were white men serving with the raiders, and it was widely assumed that renegades like Simon Girty had motivated, organized, and were in fact commanding the savages.

One evening in the last week of September, Wyandot raiders in Washington County, Pennsylvania surrounded the farmhouse of Robert and Rachel Kennedy. Bursting into the structure without warning, the raiders captured Kennedy, his wife, their children, and two orphans named Stilley, whom the Kennedy family had taken in. Hurrying away, some of the warriors carried off Mr. Kennedy and most of the children. After ransacking the house and setting it on fire, the remaining warriors departed with Rachel Kennedy, one of her daughters, and the two Stilley orphans.

In mid-October, Simon and James Girty and John Ward were with a large war party that was returning to the Shawnee Towns. With them were Mrs. Kennedy, seven children, and a collection of seven enemy scalps. Before embarking on their mission, the three Indian agents had been instructed by Governor Hamilton to do everything possible to "attend to the behaviour of the Indians, protect defenceless persons and prevent any insult or barbarity being exercised on the Prisoners."[4] The Girty brothers and John Ward were following orders. After visiting the first of the Shawnee Towns, the two Girtys, Ward, and an unnamed Indian moved on, bringing with them the captives and scalp trophies that some Wyandot warriors had placed into their care. Their destination was the main Shawnee town of Wapatomica, where James Girty's Shawnee wife anxiously awaited his return.

As they approached Wapatomica in the early afternoon, the town was crowded with visitors from distant villages who had come to be entertained by the burning of a significant white captive—a brave fighting man who had been captured in Kentucky while stealing Shawnee horses. Girty's group was directed to the town's council house, whose split-pole frame and bark-covered exterior stood 16 feet high, 75 feet wide and at least 150 feet long. Invited inside, Girty and the others entered and, as their eyes adjusted to the darkness, they could make out a bare-chested white man sitting on the floor in a corner. The captive's hands were tied and a thong from his wrists led back to an upright post. His upper body and head had been painted black, signifying that he had been condemned to death by fire. Exhausted and dejected, the victim stared at the ground and took no notice of the newcomers.

Girty and his party now had the full attention of the Shawnees, and because it was feared that the condemned man's presence and condition might traumatize the captive woman and children, an escort was ordered to take the condemned man outside. Then Girty and his companions were asked to tell about the raids in which they had participated. Hearing their stories, Shawnee elders determined how Mrs. Kennedy and the seven children were to be distributed and cared for, and after they were led away the condemned Kentuckian was brought back inside. The captive's blackened face was greatly swollen from beatings. He was tall, standing more than six feet. He had a large forehead and blue eyes that were set wide apart.

There was something vaguely familiar about the man to Simon Girty, who asked and received permission to interrogate the prisoner. According to Edna Kenton's biography:

Girty went toward him, threw a blanket on the floor, and told him to sit down. When he did not immediately obey, Girty jerked him by the arm and half threw him on the blanket; then, sitting down beside him, he started to question him about the number of troops in Kentucky. At first, the prisoner's answers were evasive. Girty asked him if he knew one William Stewart?

'Perfectly well,' the prisoner replied.

Girty asked him his name.

'Simon Butler!' Kenton answered, through his blackened lips.

Shocked, Girty suddenly realized that this was his closest friend! Springing up, he pulled Kenton to his feet and threw his arms around him. Kenton's own words describe it best: "... he asked me a good many questions, but I thought it best not to be too forward, and I held back from telling him my name, but when I did tell him, oh, he was mighty glad to see me; he flung his arms round me and cried like a child; I never did see one man so glad to see another yet. He made a speech to the Ingins—he knew the Ingin tongue, and knew how to speak—and told them that if ever they meant to do him a favor they must do it now and save my life. Yes, Girty was good to me."[5]

Since this was perhaps the most harrowing adventure of his life, Edna Kenton can be excused for dramatizing his trial. In truth, since Simon Kenton had never learned to speak an Indian language, he could not have understood anything that Girty said on his behalf. Kenton's later recollections (the source of Edna Kenton's biography) must have come from details that Girty provided him after the incident. However, during the trial, Girty's arguments were voiced by a man who understood very well how to persuade with Indian oratory.

Through all his years of service as an interpreter at Fort Pitt, Girty had been exposed to the most accomplished speakers the Indians could send to the British. His passionate discourse on behalf of his close friend's life must have been impressive. The most powerful members of the council could not ignore that Simon was an agent of the British Indian Department and a man who had the favor of Governor Hamilton. At its root, the contest was a conflict between Girty and two or three angry Shawnee war captains who wanted Kenton to burn. During the debate that ensued, a crowd of onlookers grunted their approval at some statements, and remained silent to signify their disapproval of others. According to Edna Kenton's biography:

> ... *[there] then ensued a long series of speeches for and against the request, until finally the objections filtered down to just one, and that one made by the spokesman for the Indians who had come from a distance to be present at the burning, whose chagrin and disappointment, he said, would be great if they were deprived of the spectacle.*
>
> *Finally silence fell and a war club was raised by the chief at the head of the circle and passed from hand to hand. Those against burning the prisoner handed the club in silence to their neighbors; those for burning him struck it violently on the ground, and as the votes were cast the chief cut notches in a stick he held—on one side the nos, on the other the ayes. The vote went rapidly, for all the old warriors and all the young ones but three 'laid down their clubs easily on the ground, and long before it had rounded the circle, Kenton knew he was free."* [6]

Although the exact details may be suspect, the result as written by Edna Kenton was correct. The Shawnees decided to let Kenton live and they placed him into Girty's care. Following his trial the warriors crowded around their former captive, smiling and offering greetings and words of encouragement. Saved from a hideous death, Kenton was overwhelmed. He later recalled, "They say when a man comes among a parcel of people that are harsh to him and they moderate towards him, he will be more attached to them, and I believe it."[7]

Kenton was adopted by a Shawnee woman whose son had been killed during a raid on Boonesborough. "This form of 'adoption' by some kindly squaw was common among the Indians—the Iroquois called her the 'aunt' or the 'hostess' of such a captive," Kenton recalled years later. His "new" mother led him to her house, where she ceremonially washed away his whiteness and former identity, gave him the name "Great White Wolf" and tended him with great care.[8]

Remaining at the side of his friend while he recuperated, Girty heard Kenton's story of his capture and ordeal. Apparently, after having completed his service with George Rogers Clark, Kenton went to Boonesborough, where Daniel Boone lived after having just escaped from his own captivity among the Indians. Boone was awaiting an attack from the Shawnee chief Black Fish, but, at the end of August, when the expected attack had failed to materialize, Boone suggested to Kenton that they go out on a scout and try to learn what the Indians were planning. If the opportunity came, they might try to retrieve some of their stolen horses. Leaving Boonesborough with eighteen men, Kenton and Boone were promptly ambushed by Shawnees. After a brief skirmish, Boone chose to return to Boonesborough, but Kenton and another frontiersman named Alexander Montgomery decided to continue spying on the Shawnees. Pushing their luck, they stole four of the Indians' best horses and returned to the relative safety of the Kentucky settlements. Not long afterward, Kenton, Montgomery, and another man named George Clark (not George Rogers Clark) went spying on the Shawnees at Chillicothe. Reaching the place on 9 September, they watched for a few days and then stole seven horses. This time, Kenton's luck ran out. Revengeful Shawnees caught up with them the next day, and during the running fight that followed, Montgomery was killed and Simon Kenton was captured. George Clark got away by jumping into a swift-flowing river and hanging on to some floating driftwood.

The Shawnees beat Kenton every day. In addition to being forced to run several gauntlets, his torments included being tied naked to a wild horse which the Indians drove at a run through a thick forest of young trees and tall brush, their branches whipping him senseless. Throughout his ordeal, the Kentuckian exhibited stoic courage, great strength and speed, and even a bawdy sense of humor. Admiring this, his captors brought him to Wapatomica to be burned.

The healing powers of the twenty-three-year-old Kenton were extraordinary, and Girty and Kenton's Shawnee mother had him up and about in less than two weeks. Accompanying him to a store run by an English trader at Wapatomica, Simon bought him a new set of clothes, a rifle, and a horse and saddle, and during the following two weeks, Girty took Kenton on a tour of the nearby Indian towns. They visited Blue Jacket's Town (present Bellefontaine), Buckongahela's Town (three miles north of Blue Jacket's Town), and McKee's Town, where Alexander McKee made the young frontiersman feel at home. After leaving McKee's place, Girty led Kenton to a Wyandot town called "Solomon's Town," (nine miles north of Blue Jacket's Town), on the east fork of the Big Miami River. The former Mingo town was crowded with log and bark cabins, one of which Girty frequently used. About fifty or sixty Indians were in residence. Girty and Kenton remained there a week or more, and were sitting in the shade of a large elm tree one morning, when a delegation of Shawnee ambassadors from Wapatomica approached. The warriors greeted Girty warmly and shook his hand, but when Kenton offered his hand, they shunned him. Their leader—a warrior named Red Pole—spoke at length to Girty.

Translating, Girty explained to Kenton that a war party of Shawnees that had suffered severe losses had returned to Wapatomica after raiding in West Virginia. Hearing of Kenton's release from his death sentence, they demanded that a new council debate his situation and their request had been approved. Red Pole and his companions had been sent to bring Kenton back for his new trial. Girty advised Kenton that he had no choice but to obey.

Once again Kenton's trial was held at the Wapatomica council house, where the war chief of the defeated war party opened debate with a bitter invective against the captive, which terminated with a demand that he be burned.

As before, Girty pleaded eloquently for his friend's life; but this time, his efforts failed. Although Kenton was again condemned, Girty advised him not to give up hope, promising that he would still do everything he could to save him. With the sentence announced, the Indian council turned their attentions to selecting the place of execution. Girty entered the discussion and suggested that since large numbers of people were already assembling then at Upper Sandusky to receive their annual presents from the British, it would be a fine thing to put Kenton to death there, where so many could be entertained. No one objected, and the council arranged for Kenton to be immediately marched to the place of execution, some fifty miles away.

The next morning, five Shawnee warriors drove Kenton on foot before their horses. The captive's hands were tied, he had a rope around his neck, and he had again been painted black from the waist up. He and his escorts had traveled no more than three miles from Wapatomica when Girty overtook them on the trail leading to Solomon's Town. Passing close to Kenton, Girty leaned over and whispered encouragement.

At Solomon's Town, an anxious crowd had awaited Kenton's arrival. As Kenton approached the place, an angry warrior moved up and suddenly swung an axe at his head. Swerving to ward off the blow, Kenton blocked the axe handle with his shoulder, breaking both his arm and his collarbone.

The following day, the injured victim was marched on to a small winter hunting camp where the Mingo chief John Logan was waiting for him. Girty had already seen Logan. The Mingo leader welcomed Kenton, who returned his greeting. Then Logan invited the captive and his escorts into his lodge. Food was served to the Shawnee warriors and to their captive. After Kenton had eaten, Logan saw to it that his arm was splinted and tied down properly to prevent further injury. Speaking in English, he encouraged Kenton, advising him that he had sent two of his own warriors ahead to speak for him. Later, Logan invited the Shawnees to stay the night and join him and his men at daybreak in a hunt for meat. To refuse would have been an insult.

Logan's strategy bought Kenton a welcome day of rest and provided time for the development of other efforts aimed at saving his life. After departing from Logan's camp, Kenton's guards marched him to a plateau about halfway between Logan's and Upper Sandusky, where another crowd had gathered. Kenton was forced to run his ninth gauntlet, which he endured without suffering any serious injuries. He was then informed that he was to be burned to death at daybreak the following morning.

At first light, Shawnee guards escorted their prisoner to the place of execution and were tying Kenton to the stake when the first of several squalls blew into the area, one after the other. The downpours extinguished some of the fires that had been started, and prevented others from being lit. Once again, Kenton's death had to be postponed, and to some of the Indians, the rainstorms were a bad omen. According to Edna Kenton, "on the third date for his burning, there appeared at Upper Sandusky 'a great man,' dressed in scarlet and gold, and known to all the Indians there as one endowed with authority."[9]

The uniformed man was Pierre Drouillard, a long-time Indian trader and one of Girty's fellow agent-interpreters with the British Indian Department. As it was Drouillard who handed out their annual presents and rum, the Indians viewed him as a powerful man. Drouillard had received Logan's messages requesting Kenton's rescue. It was Drouillard's idea to present himself wearing the official dress uniform of an officer of the British Indian Department. In the bright sunshine, he glittered with gold.

In his address to the Indians, Drouillard said that he had received information that "a great American general was coming from Fort Pitt with a large army to invade the Indian country," and that their father, Governor Hamilton at Detroit, was at that very moment preparing to defend them. Then, according to Edna Kenton's biography of her grandfather, Drouillard told the Indians:

... the governor had sent Drouillard to Upper Sandusky to "ask for the loan of the white man; that the information to be got from him was worth more to them than his burning could be; that, after all, they had recovered their horses and had their way up to now with the prisoner; and that for the temporary loan of him to the British governor, he, Drouillard, was ready to pay them the value of one hundred dollars in rum, tobacco, or whatever else they wished; that after the prisoner's examination at Detroit, he would be restored to them, and that they could do with him then

what they wished; that they could if they liked, send some of their men with him and the prisoner to Detroit, to see that the terms of the contract were honorably carried out." [10]

The Shawnees quickly perceived that their refusal would be an insult to Governor Hamilton, and the fact that Drouillard's offer represented only a temporary reprieve for Kenton had considerable bearing on the outcome. Reluctantly, the Shawnees accepted the $100 ransom and assigned a war captain to accompany Drouillard and Kenton to Detroit.

Upon his arrival at Detroit, Kenton was examined and treated by an English physician. The frontiersman's arm had knit poorly and had to be re-broken and properly set—adding another painful round to Kenton's experiences. Following his treatment, Kenton was interrogated by Major Lernoult, who was temporarily in command while Hamilton was away. Later, when he had fully recovered, the likeable Kenton was paroled into the custody of a storekeeper, who put the jovial prisoner to work.

CHAPTER SEVEN
THE SIEGE OF FORT LAURENS

KENTON'S ARRIVAL AT FORT DETROIT followed by a month the departure of Governor Hamilton and his army, who had gone to attempt to retake the towns and outposts that George Rogers Clark had captured the previous July. Among Hamilton's scouts was Matthew Elliott, who, because of his familiarity with the Illinois Country, had finally gained the governor's favor.

In late September British authorities in Canada received reports that a 1,500-man army was assembling at Fort Pitt, most likely for a campaign aimed at Detroit. Simon Girty was sent to Pittsburgh to spy out the truth. Accompanied by his regular escort of loyal Wyandots and Mingoes, he was watching from hiding as General McIntosh led an army of about 1,300 men out from the fort. Girty and his men trailed the American troops as they made their way down the Ohio River to the mouth of the Beaver, where they stopped for a month to build Fort McIntosh.

On 5 November 1778 Girty followed McIntosh and his army north from Fort McIntosh along a trail that led towards the Delaware capital at Coshocton. Piloted by White Eyes, the Americans' most stalwart Delaware ally, the rebel army made good time until the night of the 10th, when White Eyes was fatally attacked by a vengeful Virginia militiaman. The murder of White Eyes was a serious problem for McIntosh; there might be a disastrous reaction if word of the chief's assassination was to reach the Delaware nation. McIntosh had White Eye's body wrapped and taken to Fort Pitt, where it was announced to the public that he had died from small pox.

Girty was still spying on the Americans when they stopped to erect another fort (Fort Laurens), some two and three-quarter miles downstream from the mouth of Sandy Creek. The place was being built to fulfill treaty obligations to the Delawares which required the Americans to erect and maintain a fort within their lands. Situated on a broad plain, the new installation was constructed on high ground some twenty-one feet above the flood plain of the river. Although there were a few scattered knolls, the prairie surrounding the fort was mostly high grass and weeds. Covering about an acre, the fort was outfitted with two gates, one at the rear facing the river, the other on the opposite side facing the prairie. On each side of the river gate, rows of pickets extended down to the low water mark to provide protection for soldiers carrying water. By early December, rough construction was complete. With his army on short rations, McIntosh knew it was too late in the season to launch a campaign against Detroit. He decided to withdraw most of his army to Fort McIntosh for the winter, leaving a garrison of about 150 men under the command of Colonel John Gibson to man Fort Laurens. The defenders had barely enough supplies to last them a month. Soon after McIntosh departed, the weather turned bitter cold. Having watched the progress of the fort and the withdrawal of most of the troops, Girty had seen enough and he and his escorts made their way back to Upper Sandusky.

On 8 December, Governor Hamilton, with an army of close to 500 men (350 were warriors who had joined him during his march to the south), quickly recaptured American-held Fort Sackville, at Vincennes.

At the end of the first week of January, 1779, Simon Girty and his Mingo escorts were sent back again from Upper Sandusky to Fort Laurens where, believing they had been abandoned, Gibson and his hungry garrison were anticipating an attack.

On the morning of 19 January, a Delaware Indian, wearing a deer tail on his head to signify he was a friend of the Americans, approached the fort with a letter for Colonel Gibson from Reverend David Zeisberger. The Moravian missionary warned Gibson that the Delaware chief John Killbuck had heard that Simon Girty was on his way to Fort Laurens. Zeisberger wrote that two Wyandots had told Killbuck:

... that thirteen days ago two companies of warriors, one of seven, the other of eighteen—among the latter is Simon Girty—were gone to Fort Laurens in order to get Colonel Gibson's scalp. Their scheme is to deceive you by carrying deer's tails on their heads and by that means to get into the fort.[1]

On 21 January, escorting a horse train loaded with supplies, Captain John Clark and fifteen men of the 8th Pennsylvania Regiment arrived at Fort Laurens. The supplies they delivered included "46 suits of clothing, 194 shirts, 11 pairs of shoes and five kegs of whiskey." It was decided that Captain Clark and his men should rest within the fort overnight before beginning their return trip to Fort McIntosh the next morning.[2]

Gibson spent the evening writing letters he would entrust to Captain Clark to deliver. One letter was addressed to George Morgan. Hearing from a Delaware that Girty had bragged he "was coming after him," Gibson told Morgan, "Mr. Girty has not yet made his appearance: I hope if he does, to prevent his taking my scalp." In a letter to General McIntosh, Gibson wrote: "I hope, if Mr. Girty comes to pay me a visit, I shall be able to trepan him."[3]

While Gibson was composing letters, Simon Girty and his warriors were huddled in the cold, not far from the fort. They could not have known that Gibson had been forewarned of their coming. The next morning, about three miles below Fort Laurens, Simon and eight of his Mingoes found the tracks left by Captain John Clark's supply train on the road to Fort Laurens. The tracks told the story of their passage the day before. Girty and his companions assumed that the American supply detail would use the same trail for their return to Fort McIntosh within a day or two.

Within hours, Captain Clark, his sergeant, and fourteen men rode through a dense wood. The men's breath smoked in the crisp air. Single file with free hands in pockets, they huddled over their saddles from the cold. The horses' hooves crunched over the frozen snow, and there was the quiet click of metal and the muffled slapping of leather tack. Suddenly Girty and his warriors sprang into view from behind trees on both sides of the roadway and opened fire. The ambushers were no more than twenty or thirty paces from their targets, and the sound from their guns shattered the cold air. Terrified, the startled horses bucked and spun, and two of Clark's men were killed outright. Four more were wounded, and one man was thrown from his horse. Clark and the survivors turned their horses and raced back in the direction of Fort Laurens. The fallen trooper was disarmed and tied. It turned out he was the man who was carrying all of Colonel Gibson's dispatches. There was the smell of gun smoke and steaming blood in the air as Girty inspected the letters. He turned to the captive and threatened to shoot the man unless he read the letters aloud. The frightened trooper blurted that he couldn't read, and his manner was convincing. This may have been one of several times in his life when Simon Girty cursed his own illiteracy. Anxious to get the captured documents back to Upper Sandusky where they could be read to him, Girty and his warriors hurried north with their prisoner, two scalps, five captured muskets, bullets, powder, scavenged clothing, and the letters.

At Fort Laurens, listening to Captain Clark tell how he and his men had been ambushed, some of Gibson's soldiers felt certain that only a handful of warriors had been with Girty, and they asked for permission to chase after him. Thinking that the attack on the supply train might only have been a ruse designed to lure his men outside the fort where they could be overwhelmed, Gibson refused. Bitterly, Captain Clark told Gibson that one of his men who had gone down during the ambush was carrying all the colonel's dispatches. Expecting an attack, Gibson set his men on high alert. If they had had any luck, one of Clark's men would have gotten away and ridden to Fort McIntosh for help. But, if they had had any luck, the ambush wouldn't have happened, and Gibson's letters wouldn't now be in Simon Girty's hands. The only good thing was that the supply train had been hit after it delivered its cargo, and not before. The defenders of Fort Laurens were warmly dressed and enjoyed their first good meal in weeks.

As soon as he reached Half King's village, Girty went to one of the

English traders (most likely Alexander McCormick), to hear what the letters had to say. What Girty heard appears in a summary of Gibson's letters, published in *Frontier Advance on the Upper Ohio*:

Summary: Col. John Gibson, Fort Laurens, Jan. 22, 1779 to General Lachlan McIntosh:

[Gibson] Has received the general's letter of Jan. 8 by Captain Clark, who brought clothing and whiskey. Sends letter from Zeisberger warning him of Girty's proposed strategy, hopes to be ready for him if he comes. If Indians besiege the fort, the defenders will be distressed for supplies. Begs protection for the missionaries and friendly Delawares. Arrangements for under officers.[4]

Alex McCormick, a good friend of the Moravian leaders, paid frequent visits to John Heckewelder at one of the Tuscarawas missions. During their meetings, McCormick provided detailed and timely reports detailing what he had been able to ferret about British-Indian operations. Heckewelder passed McCormick's information on to American officers, including John Gibson, George Morgan and Daniel Brodhead. It was by these means that many British-Indian sorties had been intercepted and defeated.

Believing the information he had captured was important, Girty hurried to Detroit. On 4 February he handed over his prisoner and all the captured documents to Major Lernoult. Simon told Lernoult how he had watched General McIntosh's expedition depart from Fort Pitt the preceding fall, and how he had subsequently witnessed the building of Fort Laurens. After describing his ambush of the American supply detail, Girty said he believed that General McIntosh would make a move for Detroit in the early spring. Next, Girty recited several formal Indian speeches and delivered strings of wampum with which he had been entrusted. The messages and wampum strings that accompanied them had been sent by chiefs of the seven or eight-hundred combined Mingoes, Shawnees, Sandusky Wyandots and pro-English Delawares who were assembling at the Sandusky Towns, before leaving to attack Fort Laurens. Having no cannons, the Indians "had little expectation of making any particular headway against the fortification itself, they would drive off and destroy the cattle; and, if any of the main army from Fort McIntosh attempted to go to the assistance of the garrison, they were resolved to attack them in the night and to distress them as much as possible."[5]

Girty's intelligence put Lernoult into a difficult position. Fearing that Detroit might soon come under attack, he was reluctant to send large numbers of warriors away to harass Fort Laurens. But on the other hand, he could ill afford to ignore the requests of his Indian allies at a time when their loyalty was vital. After giving the situation considerable thought, Lernoult ordered his second-in-command, Captain Henry Bird, to quickly raise volunteers and hurry to the Sandusky Towns to lead the expedition against Fort Laurens.

A few days later, Simon Girty, Captain Bird, some Canadians and ten volunteers from Bird's regiment arrived at Half King's Town just when the inhabitants were intensely occupied torturing an American captive, whom they meant to kill. Enraged by the scene, Captain Bird attempted to intercede on the condemned man's behalf. According to Butterfield, Bird went about:

... begging and praying their head men to save his life, and frequently offering four hundred dollars for him on the spot, and, indeed, was about to offer one thousand dollars, but he found it all to no purpose. He then went to the prisoner, told him he could do nothing; that if he was in his place he would pick up a gun and defend himself as long as he could. But the prisoner seemed pretty easy, and only told the Indians that the time would come that they would pay dear for all their murders. He was then taken away and murdered at a most horrid rate.[6]

Later, the Indians assembled to greet the English captain. With Girty translating, Bird delivered a scathing speech in which he declared that all those who had participated in the torment of the helpless captive were cowards whom he detested, and that he wanted nothing more to do with any of them.

Stung by his words, most of the warriors who had come to fight against Fort Laurens stood up and walked away. Of the

700–800 warriors who had gathered there, now only 180 were still amenable to taking part in the operation. These were a mix of Wyandots, Mingoes, Muncies, and four anti-American Delawares. However, because of what Bird's tirade, not one of these warriors would accept him as their leader.

In a huff, Bird had no choice but to return to Detroit. Girty, the few Canadians and the ten soldier-volunteers from Bird's regiment joined the warriors and started at once for Fort Laurens, where they knew they would be outnumbered.

At Fort Laurens, John Gibson's continued pleas for more food and clothing were finally answered by General McIntosh, who, on 8 February 1779 ordered Major Richard Taylor of the 13th Virginia to deliver 200 kegs of flour, 50 barrels of beef or pork, medicines, clothing and other supplies. Taylor thought it would be best to go by water, and he proposed that with an escort of 100 men, he would travel down the Ohio to the mouth of the Muskingum, then up that stream to Fort Laurens. McIntosh agreed.

Departing for Fort Laurens from Upper Sandusky, Girty and the big war party reached the Mohican River, which they then followed downstream to the Walhonding. After following that river to the Tuscarawas, they turned upstream to reach Fort Laurens. During their journey, Girty and the Indians had traveled almost twice as far as McIntosh's army had gone the preceding fall, and they managed to keep their presence hidden from the enemy. Late in the afternoon of 22 February, they concealed themselves in the tall grass near the fort, taking up positions adjacent to the three sides of the garrison that faced away from the river.

Outside the stockade, American horses, hobbled and wearing bells, had been turned loose to forage all night. Moving slowly and quietly, a few warriors herded these animals to a nearby wood. Once the horses were shielded from view of the fort, the Indians removed the horses' bells and then went back to form an ambush along both sides of the main path that led from the fort through the high grass.

At daybreak, Colonel John Gibson ordered out a 19-man woodcutting detail to locate and gather up the foraging horses. After retrieving the animals, the detail was to hitch up a wagon and move to a nearby wood to load and haul firewood that had been previously cut and stacked there. The men exited from the fort through the main gate.

As the unwitting soldiers approached the warriors who were hidden in the tall grass, the Indians began to ring the stolen horse bells seductively. The lure worked. Following the sound of the bells, Gibson's woodcutting detail was ambushed. In full view of the men of the fort—but well beyond the range of their comrades' rifles—seventeen Americans were gunned down and two were captured.

Perched on the fort's palisades, Gibson's men watched in horror as their dead friends were being scalped, but were helpless to do anything about it. The defenders had no idea how many Indians were opposing them, and they spent the rest of the day watching anxiously.

Out on the prairie, not more than a quarter mile distant from Fort Laurens, was a little rise or knoll. The height of the knoll was such that it shielded the ground behind it from view of the fort. That evening, just after sunset, warriors in war paint emerged from a distant wood and paraded in single file over the top of the knoll. In the gloomy twilight, their numbers were counted by one of Gibson's lookouts. Before it grew too dark for him to see, the soldier had tallied 847 hostiles.

What the Americans could not see was that the Indians, who appeared to walk over the knoll and then drop out of sight behind it, were actually doubling back quickly and re-emerging from the woods again to repeat their charade.

By the time they could no longer see in the darkness, Gibson and his men were certain that they had been surrounded by a vastly superior force. As the night drew on, the Americans watched as the Indians casually lit fires and began to establish a big camp. All of the Indians' actions had been carefully staged to portray the image of a large fighting force, one that was so strong that it had no fear of attack.

On 3 March, a Delaware from Coshocton reached General McIntosh at Fort Pitt to report that Fort Laurens was under siege. Nine days later, a dispirited Major Taylor (the officer whom McIntosh had sent to relieve the garrison at Fort Laurens) returned and reported that he had been ambushed by Indians and forced to turn back. Adding to this bad news, a messenger sent to General McIntosh by John Heckewelder cautioned that American relief columns would be unable to reach Fort Laurens as there were large hostile forces camped in the area.

By this time the besieging warriors were beginning to run out of food and ammunition, and Simon Girty had already left for Detroit to secure supplies from Major Lernoult.

Inside the encircled fort, conditions for Gibson and his men were rapidly deteriorating. By the third week of the siege, meat and flour rations were cut to four ounces per day, per man. To supplement their meager diet, the soldiers began to boil old moccasins and beef hides.

Outside the fort, the Wyandots and Mingoes were frequently visited by Delawares from the Moravian towns who urged them to give up their siege. Finally, hearing that a big American relief column was on its way, the warriors agreed to withdraw. They were delighted with the results of their efforts and in very good spirits. They had never expected to do more than harass the Americans, and this they had done brilliantly. At the end of the siege, only eighty-four warriors remained in action. They were serving in three groups who, hoping to ambush a relief party, spent most of their time guarding the road to Fort McIntosh.

When the fight was a month old, the besiegers sent a proposal to Gibson via a neutral Delaware who was well known to both sides. The Wyandots and Mingoes offered to withdraw, if the Americans would furnish them one barrel of flour, and another of meat.

Gibson desperately tried to fulfill their demand, stuffing one barrel with moldy flour and another with the last of his rancid meat. After nightfall, both barrels were rolled outside the main gate, and on the following morning (20 March), the barrels and all of the warriors were gone.

Three days later, a relief column 700 strong, led by General McIntosh, rode into full view of the fort. Overjoyed, Gibson's men jubilantly fired volleys of shots into the air, and rushed out to greet their comrades. Unfortunately, the shooting and commotion panicked McIntosh's packhorses, and dozens of the animals broke away, racing off in all directions, bucking and scattering their loads. It took two full days before the animals could be rounded up, and considerable quantities of supplies had been lost. The whole episode was a disaster for McIntosh, who, after relieving Fort Laurens, had intended to march north and wipe out the Mingo and Wyandot towns on the Upper Sandusky. Now, with only enough provisions for two weeks, he had no choice but to terminate his planned campaign.

While Girty was helping the Indians lay siege to Fort Laurens, George Rogers Clark had attacked Fort Sackville at Vincennes. The openings between Fort Sackville's picket logs were too wide to provide security for its defenders, and Clark's deadly sharpshooters began to exact a lethal toll. Trapped inside, Governor Henry Hamilton had no choice but to surrender the place early in the morning of 25 February. His capture represented another brilliant victory for the intrepid Clark, and the loss of Fort Sackville was a serious setback for the king's army.

While there were several Americans who interpreted Colonel Gibson's valiant defense of Fort Laurens as a victory, officers like General McIntosh knew better. Instead of providing protection to their Delaware allies at Coshocton, or of serving as a base from which to launch a serious thrust at Detroit (which had been the two primary reasons for building the structure), Fort Laurens had almost been lost, a number of American soldiers had been killed, and the fort's presence had accomplished virtually nothing of military value. Instead of being made to feel secure, the Delawares had become increasingly unsure of American strength and support. Taking Detroit was the objective that Washington had in mind when he put McIntosh in command of the western war; and, thus far, his performance had been dismal. Five days after McIntosh relieved Fort Laurens, Washington replaced him with forty-three-year-old Colonel Daniel Brodhead.

Girty's participation at the siege of Fort Laurens embellished his renegade image. Of the three infamous 1778 defectors from Fort Pitt, the activities of Alexander McKee and Matthew Elliott were, as yet, relatively unknown. But, having been singled out for his audacity in letters authored by Killbuck, Heckewelder, Zeisberger, Gibson and even General McIntosh, Simon Girty's notoriety had grown explosively. Scarcely more than a year had passed since his defection and, in truth, he had only been fighting with the Indians for the last six months. Even so, he had become the most hated renegade on the

American frontier, and his former comrades-in-arms were planning to eliminate him.

In May, approaching the Sandusky Towns from the south, Simon and his escort of Mingoes were scouting a full day in advance of Captain Bird, who was following with a large war party of Wyandots. An Indian warned Bird that up ahead, five Delaware warriors were waiting for a chance to ambush Girty. Apparently, the Americans had posted a new bounty for Girty's scalp, which the five Delaware assassins were hoping to collect.

Bird rushed a runner to warn Girty. Alerted, Simon and his Mingo companions doubled back to pursue the men who were hunting him. There are no records to show whether Girty ever caught up with the Delaware bounty hunters, but the incident illustrates that Simon was bothering the Americans enough for them to take extraordinary measures against him, including posting new bounties and encouraging assassins.

The Americans weren't the only ones impressed with Girty's performance. In a letter dated Friday, 14 May, to Colonel Mason Bolton (who commanded at Niagara), Captain Bird wrote:

[Despite]… the fair promises made by the Chiefs, not a man will turn out to war except a little band of Senecas called Mingalis, consisting of twenty or thirty led absolutely by Girty.

Girty, I assure you Sir, is one of the most useful disinterested friends in this Department (that) Government has.[7]

Another example of Girty's growing notoriety is demonstrated by what happened during an assault of the Shawnee town of Chillicothe by a force of 262 Kentuckians led by Colonel John Bowman. During the fight, a few Shawnee warriors were trapped in the village council house, but before Colonel Bowman's men could burn or overrun the place, returning scouts breathlessly reported that Simon Girty was only fifteen miles away and approaching quickly with one hundred Seneca (Mingo) warriors. Stunned at this news, Bowman ordered an immediate withdrawal, which soon became a costly rout. At the time, Girty was actually nowhere near Chillicothe, and hence knew nothing of the American attack.

By June, 1779, the British-Indians of the Ohio Country were still recoiling from George Rogers Clark's capture of Governor Hamilton, at Vincennes. Because of it, the Indians had begun to believe that the rebel Americans were much stronger than they had anticipated. A few Wyandots and Delawares went to Fort Pitt to talk peace with Colonel Brodhead. Their counterparts went to Detroit, where they attempted to convince the British that they were still their staunch allies. The political situation was fluid, there was a lull in the fighting, and, for the moment, Girty and his Mingoes were the only ones conducting operations from the Sandusky Towns.

In the midst of severe political and military turmoil, Simon Kenton made good his escape from Detroit. By then, Kenton had made many friends and, as he was careful not to violate any of the conditions of his parole, he had full run of the place. Kenton had even earned a little money through hunting and gun repair, and he befriended two local traders: a man named McKenzie and another named John Edgar. Edgar and his wife owned a store near the fort, and an investigation later revealed that Mrs. Edgar had helped Kenton acquire the items necessary for his escape. For this affront, Mr. Edgar was later arrested and punished.

News of Kenton's escape would not have surprised Girty, but it may have saddened him to realize that he would no longer be able to visit his friend at Detroit. It is likely he had some concern for Kenton, for now that the plucky frontiersman had violated his parole, it would go hard for him if he were recaptured—harder still, if he fell into Shawnee hands. However, there was little time for Girty to brood over Kenton's fate, for at the end of June Simon was ordered to slip up close to Fort Pitt to retrieve some important letters deposited by a Loyalist at an established hiding place. Accompanied by eight Mingoes (most likely the same men who had been with him during the January ambush of the American supply detail to Fort Laurens), Girty departed from Upper Sandusky. By now, Simon and his veteran warriors were a cohesive and crafty force, loyal to each other and highly skilled at the art of penetrating hostile country. They would have avoided popular trails or roads, for any travelers whom they encountered had to be viewed with suspicion. In the maelstrom of political upheaval then taking place, a man's tribal affiliations did not necessarily indicate his loyalties. All the western and northern tribes had factions that were neutral, pro-English or pro-American.

Not long after Girty and his escort departed from Upper Sandusky, Alexander McCormick left the same place on a mission of his own. Riding to the Moravian town of Lichtenau (near Coshocton), he met with Reverand John Heckewelder. Late in the evening of June 28, McCormick wrote a letter to Daniel Brodhead revealing Girty's mission to Fort Pitt, and he left it with Heckewelder for delivery.

By 1 July, Colonel Daniel Brodhead at Fort Pitt had McCormick's letter in his hands. Hoping to trap Girty, Brodhead put together a squad of veteran rangers led by Captain Samuel Brady. The famous frontiersman and Indian fighter had recently distinguished himself by pursuing and killing all the members of a Seneca raiding party who had stolen two children. Brady returned with the two liberated captives, neither of whom had been harmed. Brady and his rangers were the most qualified men Brodhead had to try and snare Girty. Helping Brady was a half-breed interpreter named John Montour, who was an outstanding tracker; he also knew Girty and could recognize him. Brodhead also sent word to Chief John Killbuck at Coshocton, asking him to seize Girty if by any chance he was to show himself there.

Notwithstanding all his skills, Brady had been given very little guidance. There were dozens of approaches to Fort Pitt, and the location of the letter drop site was unknown. Hoping for a lucky break, Brady could only send men out in several directions and wait.

The records do not disclose how Alexander McCormick learned of Girty's mission to Fort Pitt. McCormick was not an agent of the British Indian Department, nor was he a military man with access to the chain-of-command. Orders from Detroit for Girty at Upper Sandusky would not have been channeled through him. In order for him to have learned all the details of Girty's mission that were included in his report to Brodhead, he must have learned them from Girty himself, or from one of his Mingoes. By this stage of his life, Simon Girty had been carrying secret messages for the Indian nations and white governments—English and rebel—for more than ten years. He was one of the most experienced military spies on the frontier, and was surely aware of the price he or his men would pay if they were caught. Still, when he was drinking with friends Girty loved to talk, and there should be no question that he was fond of and trusted McCormick. When into the bottle, Girty may have been his own worst enemy.

Unaware that their opponents had been forewarned of their coming, Girty and his escorts nevertheless exercised their utmost skills during their approach to Fort Pitt. Despite Brady's posted lookouts, Girty and his men somehow managed to slip through, retrieve the Loyalist's documents, and then vanish without being discovered. On the 1st or 2nd of July they surfaced again at the settlement called Holiday's Cove, thirty miles west of Fort Pitt (present site of Weirton, West Virginia), where they took an American captive before continuing on to Coshocton, some seventy-five miles away.

During this march, Girty and his men encountered David Zeisberger. The leader of the Moravian missions was on horseback returning to his residence following a visit to John Heckewelder. Zeisberger had taken a wrong turn and was lost. His unexpected confrontation with Girty took place at the foot of a bushy hill, in a wood.

Girty knew it was beyond his authority to arrest, or even to bully any of the Moravian missionaries. However, leveling his rifle at the man, he could not ignore this opportunity to berate his black-coated adversary. During Girty's tirade, two Delawares who had been sent out to find Zeisberger arrived. Finishing his harangue, Girty and his men moved on, leaving the red-faced missionary with his escorts.

The presence of Moravian missionaries in the Ohio Valley had become a cause of enormous frustration for men like McKee, Elliott and Girty. Despite overwhelming proof that the missionaries were providing intelligence to the rebels, the English government continued to protect them. This was no doubt due to the fact that the Moravian headquarters was in London, and the organization's unceasing effort to Christianize the Indians of the American colonies was popular and had been long applauded. Even so, Zeisberger and Heckewelder were well aware that the men of the British Indian Department were calling for their removal, if not their destruction.

Following the run-in with Zeisberger, Girty and his warriors (with their American prisoner) arrived at Coshocton on Sunday, the 4th of July. At the time, the three most powerful chiefs in residence there were John Killbuck, Big Cat and Captain Pipe. Killbuck was decidedly pro-American, Big Cat's allegiance vacillated, and Captain Pipe was resolute in his leadership of the anti-American Delawares.

Attempting to comply with Colonel Brodhead's secret request, Killbuck and some other Moravian Delaware converts discussed a scheme to capture Girty, but Big Cat argued it was the wrong time for the Delawares to alienate the English by seizing one of their best Indian agents and delivering him to the Americans. Big Cat won out.

Unlike Killbuck, Captain Pipe and his people were delighted to see Girty and the Mingoes, and a generous feast was prepared to honor Simon. Present in the Delaware town at this time was a young American hunter named Richard Conner, who had married a former white captive of the Shawnees. Although young Conner and his wife had recently joined the Moravians, Girty did not object to their presence during that night's festivities. According to Heckewelder's account:

Girty told Mr. Conner to tell his brethren the Americans, that he did not desire they should show him any favor, neither [said he] would he show them any.[8]

What Heckewelder claims that Girty told Richard Conner rings true. By this time, Simon was well aware that the rebels were accusing him of the most atrocious and despicable crimes, and that he was becoming a pariah. His statement to Conner indicates his frustration over these developments.

Before departing from Coshocton, Girty let it be known that he and his men had collected the secret documents they had been sent to retrieve, and that he was anxious to have Alexander McCormick read them aloud to him. Delawares quickly brought this news to Heckewelder who, as Girty assumed he would, hurriedly dashed off a letter to Colonel Brodhead at Fort Pitt. Exercising his sense of humor, Simon was using Heckewelder to taunt Brodhead.

Later that month, General Washington wrote to Brodhead, urging him to launch an expedition aimed at the hostiles of the upper Allegheny. The commander-in-chief wanted Brodhead to coordinate his army's movements with that of General John Sullivan who, at about the same time, was set to launch his own campaign from Easton, Pennsylvania, aimed at Iroquois towns in central New York.

Girty went to Detroit and turned over his prisoner and the captured letters. After months of spying and taking part in Indian raids, he must have welcomed Detroit's civility. The place offered him a rare opportunity to take a warm bath, see a barber, get his clothes cleaned, eat hearty meals, and get drunk with friends. He was frequently hosted by McKee and his wife. Alexander McKee's friendship had remained constant and, at Detroit, he was the nearest thing to a blood relation that Girty had. This changed on 8 August when, having recently escaped from the guardhouse of the American fort at Kaskaskia, a bedraggled party of fugitives arrived. The man who had planned their escape, and who then led them safely through a perilous 500-mile journey, was a former lieutenant of the United States Continental Marines who had seen considerable action aboard an American gun boat on the lower Mississippi. Thirty-three year old George Girty had come to join his brothers. The "Injun Girtys" were together again.

CHAPTER EIGHT
RIVER AMBUSH

FEW WOULD HAVE GUESSED that Simon and George Girty were brothers. One was outgoing, brash, with a hearty sense of humor and a quick, witty tongue, while the other was quiet, withdrawn, and frequently somber. Simon blossomed in crowds of whites, Indians, or in mixed company—apparently delighting in the contrasts—while George was uneasy at any gathering of people, particularly if they were white. In spite of their differences, the two brothers shared a full measure of cleverness and aggressiveness, most likely inherited from their father. Both had been raised by Indians to be warriors. At this stage of his life, Simon had mastered the art of slipping unnoticed through hostile terrain, spying, and planning and executing deadly ambushes. The two years George spent as a deck officer aboard a pirate-like gunboat patrolling the lower Mississippi had taught him the savage tactics of riverine warfare.

Under the command of Captain James Willing, the gunboat *Rattletrap* had randomly attacked British plantations along the course of the Mississippi, seizing supplies and provisions wherever they could. Early in 1779 when there was a desperate need for increased American manpower in the Illinois Country, Captain Willing was sent orders to reduce his crew to an absolute minimum and send the excess men north to help reinforce the outposts recently captured by George Rogers Clark. George Girty was among those who were reassigned. Upon his arrival at Kaskaskia he was abruptly informed that his brothers Simon and James were traitors who had gone over to serve the British Indian Department, at Detroit. Instead of being accepted by the men with whom he now had to serve, George became a target for rejection and suspicion. It did not take him long to realize that his loyalty to his brothers outweighed by far his commitment to American independence, and his decision to leave came quickly.

There were a large number of English prisoners of war imprisoned at Kaskaskia. George made friends with some of these men and revealed his intention to defect and go to Detroit. His story of being familiar with the terrain, the Indians and their languages was convincing. If the prisoners were of a mind to join him, he would pilot them over the safest route, all the way to Fort Ponchartrain. Sixteen prisoners volunteered to go with him. Unfortunately for George, one of these men was an informant. A day or two later, George was arrested, charged with treason, and jailed. Kept separate from the British prisoners of war, he was confined in Kaskaskia's guardhouse, awaiting a court-martial. It was a foregone conclusion that following his trial George would stand before a firing squad or be hanged. Motivated by his situation, somehow, just as his brother Simon had done at Fort Pitt, George escaped from the brig on 4 May 1779. But, in George's case, the deed was no prank. Instead of turning himself in the next day, he hiked upriver some fifty miles and then crossed over the Mississippi to St. Louis on the Spanish side, where he presented himself to the Spanish commandant. According to historian Consul Butterfield's *History of the Girtys:*

> *Following a brief interrogation, the Spaniard released him, advising him "that it was not his [the Spanish official's] intention to interfere with or molest any person on either side (of the war), unless for murder or some other capital offense committed against civil society, and that it was his desire to remain in tranquility, and to treat all well who behave as becometh them."* [1]

In his shoes, most men would have thanked God for their narrow escape from death and would have hurried to Detroit. But George spent a month wrestling with his conscience; he knew that because of him, the prisoners he had befriended were suffering punishment and deprivation. On 19 June, four captured soldiers of the King's

Regiment, three American deserters and a Canadian were broken out from confinement at Kaskaskia. Following their rescuer, they spent the next two months traveling the 500 miles to Detroit, where, tired and hungry, they arrived on 8 August, 1779.

Simon and James were quickly reunited with George, and the three brothers celebrated the event at several taverns. The story of George's adventure spread quickly and he received the admiration and respect of a hero. Summoned before Major Lernoult, George retold his story once again, and after hearing it, Detroit's commander congratulated him and at his request, enlisted him into the British Indian Department. George was to be paid at the same rate as Simon and James—sixteen shillings York currency, per day—and he was furnished a new rifle, three horses, a saddle and a bridle. Not long after this, he was assigned to serve the Shawnees at Wapatomica, and the delighted new agent began his duty there disbursing needed supplies and presents.

While George and his two brothers were celebrating their reunion, the Americans launched George Washington's two-pronged campaign against the Lakes Indians. Commanded by Colonel Daniel Brodhead, 600 men were sent 200 miles up the Allegheny Valley, targeting the Mingoes and Senecas in that region. Simultaneously, General John Sullivan, leading 4,000 Continentals, began to propagate destruction among all the Six Nation towns located north of Tioga. Although the two American expeditionary forces failed to link up as had been planned, they were able to wreak considerable damage. As they withdrew from the valley of the Allegheny, Brodhead's men burned all the villages they had missed earlier. By the end of the campaign, the two American armies had destroyed more than 40 Indian towns and some 160,000 bushels of corn.

Although very few Six Nation warriors had actually been killed during the fighting, the Iroquois losses in houses, orchards and field crops were a disaster. What Sullivan's and Brodhead's campaigns ominously proved was that even the five strongest nations of the Iroquois League had been unable to turn back a determined and concerted attack by a large American army. To men like Washington, these astoundingly successful invasions laid the groundwork for future solutions to the Indian problem. To British agents like Simon, James and George Girty, whose futures were now inextricably linked to that of the Indians and to British interests, the Brodhead and Sullivan campaigns led to the uncomfortable and inescapable conclusion that if America won her independence, the outlook for the Indians of the Ohio and Allegheny Valleys, and even for the British in Canada, was grim.

At his headquarters with the Wyandots at Upper Sandusky, Simon received orders to once again spy on Fort Laurens. British military leaders in Canada had received conflicting reports on American activities there, and they wanted the real story. Before departing for Fort Laurens, Girty dispatched the following report to his superior, Major Lernoult:

Sandusky, September 6, 1779
Sir:

I take the liberty to acquaint you that I intend leaving this place tomorrow. There is a party of twenty-five Wyandots that have been turned out to go as volunteers with me on the road I proposed when I left Detroit; likewise a party of ten Mingoes, which party Sandithtas commands. The Wyandots are commanded by Seyatamah.

Sir, I refer you to Captain McKee for the knowledge of the above-mentioned chiefs, if you are not already acquainted with their names. To-morrow, my friend, Nouthsaka, sets off with ten warriors to the falls of the Ohio. Our great friend, Captain Pipe, is gone to Fort Pitt to a council; likewise Naulmatas and Duentate. Six days ago, a party of Wyandots brought here three prisoners from Kentucky. They say there are three hundred men under pay in those parts. They also say there are nine forts in and about Kentucky.

There are no certain accounts of the rebels leaving Tuscarawas [Fort Laurens]. I intend to go there directly, and shall send you the token you gave me at Detroit if they are not there. If the Delawares are in possession of the fort, I intend to turn them out and burn the fort (if my party are able), as you gave me the liberty to act as I thought best, and they and I are not on the best of terms.

Yesterday, Sandithtas arrived here, with the account of ten
parties of Shawanese that are gone to war. This is all I have to
acquaint you with at present.
    I am, etc., Simon Girty [2]

Most likely penned by Alexander McCormick, the construction
and phrasing of Girty's letter are probably his own. The descriptions
are not those one would expect from a rough-hewn frontier illiterate, but are the careful phrases of a man who has a strong feeling for
language. Precise, well organized and highly detailed, Girty reveals
an easy familiarity with the local Indians and their politics, and
demonstrates considerable expertise at collecting and analyzing military intelligence. He reports what he has seen and heard, and then
follows with his interpretation. The letter also indicates that at this
time Girty seldom had command of Indian warriors, for although
both Wyandot and Mingoes have volunteered to go with him to Fort
Laurens, each war party has its own war leader or captain. Shrewdly,
to assure authenticity, Girty uses some code words that only he and
Major Lernoult would know. One of the very few Girty letters on
record, this document reveals many of the true dimensions of Girty's
character.

    In mid-September, Simon was in the Shawnee town of Piqua, on
the Mad River (five miles west of present Springfield, Clark County,
Ohio). At Piqua there were several white captives, one of whom was
a Mrs. Margaret Paulee. Weeks earlier, she and her family had been
attacked while traveling from Virginia to Kentucky. Her husband
and baby girl had been killed, and since then the woman had endured
considerable hardship. Terrified she was going to be forced to marry
an Indian, Girty assured her that she would not be compelled to such
a course.

    Expecting George Rogers Clark to soon lead an army against
Detroit, in hopes of putting the Americans on defense, the British
decided to take the initiative and send a large war party into Kentucky.
The large war party included some fifty Wyandot, Mingoes and
Delawares, as well as Simon and George Girty, and Matthew Elliott.
Traveling south, the raiders halted at the Shawnee town of Chillicothe

(present Old Town, Ohio) to recruit more warriors. Still seething from Colonel Bowman's recent attack on their village (the attack that had terminated abruptly when the Americans heard that Girty was coming with a force of Wyandots), the Shawnees were delighted to greet the white warrior whose name alone had frightened off the Virginia Long Knives. Eighty Shawnee warriors joined the war party. Among these was a youngster named Tecumseh, who was nearing his twelfth birthday. An intense lad, he persuaded his older brother to allow him to come along. Now numbering about 130 men, the British-Indian war party departed for the Great Miami River, which they followed south by canoe all the way to Kentucky.

The afternoon of the 3rd of October found Simon and George Girty, with Matthew Elliott and about half of the war party, camped near the mouth of the Licking River (directly across the Ohio River from present Cincinnati). The remaining warriors were off scouting enemy sign or hunting meat. That evening, some of the scouts returned with an exciting report: several miles downstream, they had seen three big American keelboats slowly making their way against the current, while keeping close to the Kentucky side of the river. The boats were manned by soldiers and appeared to be heavily loaded. The scouts guessed that there were some twenty soldiers aboard each vessel. With their crews poling against the flow, the boats were moving at less than a mile per hour. At this speed, the little flotilla would not reach the mouth of the Licking until the next morning.

Discussions began for devising a trap. Although the war party outnumbered the Americans some two-to-one, the challenge would be to devise a way to lure the enemy boats to shore, where they could be immobilized and overwhelmed. There should be little doubt that the plan that developed was strongly influenced by George Girty, the former marine.

By first light, the trap was set, and everyone was hiding in assigned positions at the river's edge. The Americans had been under continuous observation since the original sighting, with scouts coming in frequently to report the boat's progress. The latest report placed them a few miles away. The estimated time for the ambush was shifted to mid-afternoon. The weather was clear, crisp and bright. Veterans took advantage of the situation and slept. Youngsters like Tecumseh were too excited for sleep, and remained on guard, confronting their fears and trying to imagine what would happen when the battle started.

The American flotilla was commanded by Colonel David Rogers (no relation to George Rogers Clark). Rogers and his forty volunteers had departed from Fort Pitt a year earlier, beginning their long and dangerous voyage south to the Mississippi. Their mission was to obtain vitally needed supplies of gunpowder, lead, money and other goods which American agents had secretly acquired from Spanish sources at New Orleans. Thus far, Rogers had done very well. Now en route back to Fort Pitt, the boats were heavily laden with precious cargo. They had not lost a single man, and they were nearing the final leg of their long and tiresome journey. Their last stop had been at Fort Nelson at the Falls of the Ohio, where they had rested and replenished provisions. There, reinforcing their numbers, Colonel George Rogers Clark had assigned a third boat to accompany them, manned by a crew of twenty-three armed men. Seeking protected transport to Fort Pitt, Colonel John Campbell and a few civilians had also come aboard at Fort Nelson. In addition to his sixty-three soldiers, Rogers had a Negro woman and two Negro boys as galley help. Also aboard the American boats were six English prisoners-in-irons, all of them soldiers captured in the Illinois fighting. At Fort Pitt, the captives were scheduled to be exchanged for American prisoners.

Departing from Fort Nelson, the Americans had traveled seven days without incident. They had seen no one on the river or along the shore after traveling some 130 miles. Crewmen standing on the offshore sides of the boats manned long sweep oars, while other men planted lengthy poles against the river bottom and walked from bow to stern, over and over again. The poling crews worked in shifts; one detail relieving another on a regular schedule. The three boats were in line, moving slowly but steadily. As they approached the mouth of the Licking River, one of the lookouts sang out. Overloaded with seven warriors, a small canoe had been spotted upstream. Caught by surprise, the Indians had been crossing the Ohio from the opposite side of the river, and were only a few hundred yards above the Americans.

Rogers and his men assumed they had come upon a small war party bent upon raiding in Kentucky. Although the Indians were well beyond range of their rifles, a few of the Americans began to shoot. Their efforts appeared to panic the warriors, who were now paddling furiously towards the Kentucky shore. Their overloaded boat was riding so low it was taking water and seemed in risk of capsizing.

Enjoying the moment, and excited by the action, Rogers urged his crews to exert themselves to the utmost. In order to go after the warriors, he beached his flotilla on a sand spit. Posting a few men to guard the boats, Rogers then led the majority of his troops in a mad dash up the brushy riverbank and into the dense forest. After a few moments, the silence was shattered by the sound of heavy firing, and the surprised Americans found themselves surrounded by a superior force. Within moments it was too late for them to fight their way back to the boats, which were now under attack from another party of warriors. During the fighting at the water's edge, soldiers aboard the last of the three keelboats struggled desperately to move their vessel off the sandbar. At last, their boat broke free and as a few men scrambled aboard, other men worked furiously to pole the craft away from the riverbank. Under a barrage of gunfire, the vessel made it out to the current in mid-channel, and safety. By this time, however, the Indians had overrun the remaining two boats.

In the heavy underbrush, where fighting was still going on, Colonel Rogers and what was left of his men desperately attempted to disengage and scatter. Theirs was a running fight through dense shrubbery and trees and during the action Rogers took a rifle ball in his abdomen. He was carried off into a dark, overgrown ravine. Sergeant John Knotts remained with his stricken commander, while the others continued their desperate attempt to escape. Before long Rogers and Sergeant Knotts heard the sound of gunfire become sporadic and finally die out.

Back at the river's edge, Indians were plundering the captured boats, and they discovered their prize was richer than anyone could dream. Against their own losses of two warriors dead and three men slightly wounded, they had killed at least forty Americans and had captured five. One of the prisoners was Colonel John Campbell—an elderly man well known to Girty and to many of the Indians. The captives also included the black woman and two boys who had served as galley help. In addition to these frightened souls, the six delighted British soldiers, former prisoners-of-war, had been liberated.

The spoils were substantial. There was over a ton of gunpowder in forty 50 lb. kegs, two tons of bullet lead in bars, bullet molds, two boxes of new flintlock rifles, forty bales of new clothing, numerous kegs of rum and, finally, a large chest that was brimming with thousands of dollars in Spanish silver. Some of the rum kegs were opened and the men began to celebrate.

Not far away, Colonel David Rogers lay in excruciating pain, tended by Sergeant Knotts. By first light the next morning the colonel was delirious and near death. Aware that Rogers' situation was hopeless, and terrified that Rogers' agonized moaning would likely bring warriors and lead to his own death, Knotts covered his commanding officer with brush and set off through the wilderness in the general direction of some settlements. After suffering great hardship, he reached his home on the Monongahela River. The body of Captain Rogers was never found.

Years later, frontiersman Jacob Drennon (who had worked with Simon Girty as a hunter for George Morgan) claimed it was Girty who killed Rogers, and that Girty had admitted the deed to him:

STATEMENT OF JACOB DRENNON

.... he [Girty] killed Rogers that was in that boat with Benham. When Rogers went to fire, Girty fell down and Rogers' shot passed over him. Girty said he then took as fair aim at Rogers as he ever did in his life at a deer.[3]

There is no other evidence from Simon Girty or anyone else, to corroborate Drennon's claim that Girty shot Rogers.

The warriors swiftly unloaded the captured cargo and disabled the boats. Concerned that an American force might soon be coming to take revenge, it was decided for them to carry all they could to Chillicothe, and to bury the rest. During their return to their home villages everyone carried plunder, including the captives, whose future in the hands of the Shawnees was bleak. Seeking to protect old Colonel John Campbell, Simon took him under his wing. Girty had first met Campbell in 1764, just after his own return from living with the Senecas. At the time, Campbell was a fur trader, surveyor and land dealer (he helped survey and plot the town of Pittsburgh). Later, during the Virginia-Pennsylvania conflicts, when Simon was serving as one of John Connolly's right-hand lieutenants, Campbell had been a fellow conspirator and associate. Now, however, Campbell conducted himself as a strident patriot and he was overtly opposed to men like the Girty brothers, whom he vociferously considered as treacherous turncoats. Even so, Simon retained a fondness for him.

On their approach to Chillicothe, Girty and the Wyandots from Upper Sandusky bid good-bye to the main body of Shawnee warriors, bypassed the Shawnee villages and continued along a trail that led to the Sandusky Towns. Campbell was fortunate that Girty kept him; for once they had arrived at Chillicothe, the Shawnees wasted no time in punishing their American captives. Providing entertainment for the villagers, four prisoners were forced to run savage gauntlets and two others were put to death. In the end, the only survivor of these trials was a young lieutenant named Abraham Chapline, who had been in command of the escort boat that had been assigned to Rogers's flotilla at Fort Nelson. Chapline had withstood his torments so well that the Shawnees had begun to admire his courage, and he was soon adopted.

Upon reaching Detroit, Simon, George Girty and Matthew Elliot reported their victory and turned over Colonel Campbell. While they had been away, Major Arent Schuyler de Peyster had been sent from Michilimackinac to replace Major Lernoult. Delighted by their victory over the American boats, De Peyster wrote to General Haldimand at Niagara:

De Peyster to General Haldiman, 1 November 1779

I… have the pleasure to acquaint you that… Simon Girty, his brother, and Matthew Elliott, have defeated a Colonel Rogers on the Ohio, a stroke which must greatly disconcert the rebels at Pittsburgh.[4]

De Peyster's phrasing was accurate; the rebels at Pittsburgh were indeed "greatly disconcerted," by the debacle on the lower Ohio River. The stories told by the few American survivors of the attack were horrific. Although no mention was made of Matthew Elliott's participation, two of the Girty brothers were held responsible and, within weeks, the only name still being mentioned was Simon's.

Simon returned from Detroit to the Sandusky Towns, and George went back to his Shawnees at Wapatomica. The coldest winter anyone could remember descended. In January 1780, the harbor at New York froze so solidly that the British drove wagons over the ice all the way from that city to Staten Island. In western Pennsylvania, there were heavy snows, and the temperature bottomed out for two months. Among the Indians of the Ohio Valley, the war against hunger now took precedence over the war against the Americans, and the warriors dispersed to winter hunting camps.

By February, the snow in the woods was four feet deep. It was so cold that turkeys froze in their roosts and dropped from icy trees. Unable to find forage beneath the snow and ice, deer, elk and buffalo died by the hundreds. Among the Senecas, whose villages and food stores had been destroyed by the Sullivan and Brodhead expeditions, men, women and children began to die from cold and starvation. Tribes located north of the Ohio River fared better. There, Shawnees, Wyandots, Muncies and Mingoes had put away plentiful stores of corn, and their people passed the winter comfortably.

Simon and fellow agents of the British Indian Department kept busy attempting to supply their allies with sufficient guns, ammunition and clothing to take the warpath against the Americans at the first sign of a thaw.

The rebels spent the winter months building new stations and improving existing forts. Simon Kenton wintered at Lexington, which had been built during his captivity and was the weakest of the new installations in Kentucky. The other new stations in the region were Martin's, McAfee's, Bryan's and Ruddell's. At the latter site, abandoned cabins on the Licking River (first erected by John Hinkson) were being rebuilt and fortified.

In the early spring, De Peyster sent runners on snowshoes to summon McKee, Elliott and the three Girty brothers to Detroit. On 8 March, he listened attentively to their reports of American activities. He was advised that new stations that had been built in Kentucky, and that they were all within two day's journey of each other. In addition, on the east bank of the Mississippi, some five miles below the mouth of the Ohio, George Rogers Clark was erecting Fort Jefferson. At Fort Pitt, Colonel Brodhead was still in command of a small, pitiful garrison that had neither been reinforced nor supplied. Clearly, to De Peyster's great relief, it appeared that the American posture was defensive.

At the time, representatives from the Shawnees, Mingoes, Delawares, Wyandots, Pottawatomie, Chippewa, Ottawa, Miami and other nations were arriving at Detroit to ask for De Peyster's help in curtailing white immigration into Kentucky. The Indians claimed they were ready and willing to assist in opposing rebel advances, but only if British troops would join them in the fighting.

De Peyster knew that the best way he could protect Detroit was to maintain the initiative. What resulted was a plan for a new expedition against Kentucky, timed to coordinate with a secondary British-Indian thrust aimed at the American settlements in the Illinois Country. The Illinois campaign was to originate at Michilimackinac, and was to be led by Emanuel Hesse, a fur trader and former army officer. De Peyster chose Henry Bird to lead the Kentucky expedition. He issued orders for Simon Girty and his fellow agents to help organize the establishment of warrior camps, and to see that supplies were properly allocated. Hoping to keep the Americans off-balance, De Peyster sent smaller war parties out to harass the enemy while Girty and his fellow agents gathered adequate forces for the main campaign. Within weeks, raids were taking place against American outposts and settlements up and down the Ohio River.

CHAPTER NINE
HIGH HOPES, MEAGER RESULTS

THROUGH APRIL AND EARLY MAY OF 1780, Simon Girty was busy distributing food and ammunition, while helping with logistics at the
Upper Sandusky towns where De Peyster's native army was gathering. Warriors were arriving daily from every direction, and many of
them had brought their families. Feasts, dances, games and horse races
gave the camps a festive air. The excitement was fueled by the dimension of the great assembly. In prior marauds, the largest Indian war
parties sent against the Americans had consisted of no more than one
or two hundred men, usually all from the same tribe. The forthcoming campaign would have an army of several hundred warriors from
many tribes, plus British Regulars, Canadian volunteers and militia.
This time, their British allies were also bringing cannons with which to
smash the hated Kentucky stations.

Witnessing the great assembly were a few American captives.
Among these were Lieutenant Abraham Chapline and sixteen-year-
old George Hendricks. Having learned the objectives of the coming
onslaught, the two agreed to risk their lives and warn their comrades.
Slipping away one night late in April, they made their way to the Falls
of the Ohio. Eluding pursuers, they reached Fort Nelson on 19 May.
In one of those strange twists of fate, their disclosures were only partly
accepted because the highest authorities were convinced that their
enemies could not field an army before the end of July. Six days after
Chapline and Hendricks delivered their warning, the largest British-
Indian force ever to go against Kentucky launched from Detroit.

The invaders were aboard a varied collection of sailing vessels, including bateaus and birch bark canoes. The white contingents included Captain Henry Bird, Matthew Elliott, the three Girty brothers, and about 150 assorted militia and volunteers. On one of the bateaus, a squad of artillery men accompanied a six-pounder and two or three smaller cannons. Sailing alongside their British allies were warriors in dozens of big war canoes. As the flotilla passed feeder streams, new canoes, paddled by men in war paint, joined them. Their course took them across Lake Erie to the mouth of the Maumee River, which they followed to the Great Miami. Then they followed that stream all the way to the Ohio River. Ahead, waiting for them at the first portage, was Alexander McKee and six hundred more warriors, with a herd of horses that had been collected to assist in crossing from the Auglaize to the Great Miami.

The second British-Indian expedition (this one directed against the Americans in the Illinois Country) had already launched as planned from Michilimackinac, and was now some four hundred miles to the southwest. When Captain Bird's army departed from Detroit, Emanuel Hesse with 1,000 Great Lakes Indians was only a day's march from Cahokia and St. Louis.

At virtually the last moment, coming quickly from Fort Jefferson with a hundred men, George Rogers Clark made it in time to reinforce the American garrison at Cahokia. Across the river, the Spanish commander at St. Louis had been warned of the British attack and was preparing to repel the invaders.

One day out from Detroit, neither Girty nor any of the men of Captain Bird's expedition were aware that, on the afternoon of 26 May, Emanuel Hesse's army suffered crushing defeats at St. Louis and Cahokia. Badly mauled, Hesse's men were on the run, hotly pursued by three or four hundred American militia reinforced by Spanish and French troops.

The Kentucky expedition now encountered heavy rains, and the rivers turned muddy and began to swell. Boats slowed as men set down oars, paddles and poles in order to bail water. Spirits plummeted. The warriors had never had much confidence in Henry Bird's planning or leadership, and with each passing mile, the fear grew that they were moving towards a confrontation with the seemingly invincible George

Rogers Clark. The sullen mood of the warriors persisted even as their leading contingents reached the Ohio River and halted to make camp. Two days later, McKee arrived, bringing with him reinforcements of veteran Shawnee warriors from Chillicothe. The army now numbered more than seven hundred-fifty men, and the war chiefs went into council with their English counterparts. Accompanied by McKee and Elliott, and with Girty interpreting, Captain Bird pressed for a frontal assault of Fort Nelson at the Falls of the Ohio. The war chiefs were less than enthused. From their point of view, Fort Nelson was a major military installation; not a flimsy stockade that could be easily defeated by a few cannon balls. They knew that at Fort Nelson there were many more cannons than the British had brought from Detroit. The chiefs were in agreement that by now the enemy must certainly have been alerted by their approach; and if so, the garrison at the fort would surely be reinforced and prepared for battle. Some of the chiefs thought that the indomitable Clark and his veterans must already be hurrying from the Illinois to Fort Nelson. The chiefs were concerned that if they were unable to quickly overrun the fort, Clark and his rangers would come at them from the rear and tear them apart.

Against such reasoning, Bird was defeated. Convinced that he had little influence over the war chiefs, he turned to Alexander McKee and asked him to take over and continue to voice the strongest possible arguments in favor of striking Fort Nelson. Then, abruptly, Bird retired from the meeting. Although the Indians had great respect for McKee, they flatly rejected his arguments. Fort Nelson, they responded, was simply too risky. What the Indians wanted to do was to attack the smaller, more vulnerable Kentucky stations situated only a few days' journey up the Licking River. These, the chiefs believed, could be swiftly overwhelmed without much cost, after which their warriors could return to their home villages with considerable prisoners, plunder and horses. Recognizing that continuing to press for an attack on Fort Nelson was hopeless, McKee acceded, and the chiefs began to devise their battle plans.

Ruddle's Station, located on the south fork (Hinkson's Fork) of the Licking River, some twenty-five miles above the Forks of the Licking, stood on a flat piece of ground with a low hill rising behind it. Originally, the settlement had some fifteen cabins, built by pioneer settler John Hinkson (a friend of Simon Kenton's) in 1775. The place had then been abandoned and remained vacant until Captain Issac Ruddle took it over in 1779. Aided by settlers from neighboring stations, Ruddle and his garrison fortified the installation and made it one of the largest and strongest stations in the region.

Like most of the stations in the Kentucky wilderness, Ruddle's was built in the form of a rectangle, with an outside perimeter of log cabins joined together by log picketing that stood from nine to twelve feet high. Two-story blockhouses stood at each of the four corners, extending out over the lower story by about eighteen inches, so that no enemy could reach the outside walls without being exposed to fire. Although the solid walls of the cabins and picketing were impervious to rifle or musket fire, they were vulnerable to cannon shells. The cabins had clapboard roofs, slab doors hung with deer thongs, and windows covered with oiled paper. All the windows and cabin doors faced the center of the enclosure; the only openings facing outward were firing ports carved in the mortar between each cabin's logs.

The surrounding countryside was dotted with farms. Fearing Indian attacks, the settlers had come into the station for safety. In addition to Captain Ruddle and his forty-nine-man garrison, the place was crowded with 300 men, women and children. Among the latter was frontiersman John Hinkson, who had just arrived from Limestone with a pack train of settler's goods. Hinkson's family remained back at the Falls. Although Ruddle's Station was crammed with refugees, the families that were there were unaware of any imminent danger.

By the time the Girty brothers and the rest of Bird's army arrived at the Forks of the Licking, they found the water was too shallow to accommodate the heavier boats. A camp was built, and shelters were erected to keep the stores dry. Scouts were sent ahead. These men learned that the path leading to Ruddle's Station was soft and muddy, and much of the trail would have to be widened to allow for the transport of the cannons. On 20th of June, Bird sent McKee with an advance party of two-hundred warriors to isolate the station, and to capture any Americans attempting to enter or leave the place. If prisoners could be taken, they were to be interrogated in order to learn the true conditions within the fort. Aware that the station was crowded with non-combatants, Captain Bird was seriously concerned about their welfare once the place was surrendered, and he mentioned this in a letter to De Peyster, written just after the attack on Ruddle's Station:

BIRD TO DEPEYSTER, 1 JULY 1780

I had before that day entreated every Indian officer that appeared to have influence among the Savages, to persuade them not to engage with the fort, until the guns were up—fearing if any were killed it might exasperate the Indians & make them commit cruelties when the rebels surrendered.[1]

Prior to the attack on Ruddle's Station, Bird asked the Girtys and all the other white agents to obtain promises from the Indians to refrain from killing any cattle, as Bird planned to use the captured animals to provide meat for his men and for the prisoners during the army's return to Detroit. In exchange for sparing the cattle, the Indians were to receive all the horses that were captured.

Before daybreak on 22 June, hoping to snare a prisoner or two, McKee's men encircled the station and lay quiet. At sunrise, a small party of men exited the main gate to cut grass for fodder. Prematurely, some of the younger warriors began to shoot, and the work party hustled back inside the fort. Intermittent firing soon broke out from both sides. During the opening scrap, one Canadian inside the station was killed, and a warrior suffered a shot through his arm. Sporadic firing continued all morning, without causing additional casualties to either side. At noon, Bird and the main force arrived with the artillery. A violent downpour began, limiting visibility. Despite the rain, one of Bird's smaller guns was put into action and two shots were fired in rapid succession. Shortly thereafter, firing ceased from within the fort, but there was, as yet, no sign of surrender. The sounds of gunfire from the station were replaced by the braying of frightened cattle. The rain let up, visibility improved, and Bird ordered his big six-pounder gun wheeled into plain view.

From a high position within the station, Captain Ruddle saw the gun and knew that within minutes such a cannon would reduce his installation to matchsticks.

Simon Girty was standing beside Captain Henry Bird when the defenders showed their white flag. Bird sent Girty forward. Carrying their own white flag, Simon could see dozens of rifles pointed at him as he approached the station's main gate. After identifying himself, he was admitted and ushered to Captain Ruddle. Girty advised Ruddle that unless his station was surrendered right away, the occupants might all be slaughtered at the hands of the Indians, for if they suffered further casualties, they might get so angry they could not be controlled.

Measuring Girty, Ruddle mulled the situation and then agreed that he had no choice but to surrender, but that he would do so only conditionally. He wanted reassurance from the British officer in command that the people in his care would be placed into custody of the whites, not the Indians. He also wanted assurance that all the captives would be taken to Detroit.

Girty brought Ruddle's terms back to Bird, and a few minutes later, both Bird and McKee entered the station to iron out details. In general, Bird agreed to Ruddle's demands, but he confided that he and his men were greatly outnumbered by the Indians, and that he was in no position to force anything upon them. As Bird and Ruddle were discussing the situation, the gates burst open suddenly, and a horde of screaming warriors rushed inside. Chaos ensued. The warriors raced about grabbing captives, each one seizing the first person he could lay his hands on. Amidst screams, shouts and crying, families were separated from one another, husbands from wives, children from their parents. There were but half as many prisoners as there were captors, and the warriors who had been unable to take prisoners, raced through the station buildings competing with each other for plunder. Frustrated, an angry Shawnee shot a cow. In a moment, his action was echoed by two more warriors, and then a dozen more joined the game. Soon all the cattle within the station were dead or dying. The attempts by Girty, Bird and McKee to stop the mayhem were futile, and during the melee that ensued, a wounded American was tomahawked. Adding to the chaos, a young pregnant woman named Mary Kratz began to deliver her baby. Demonstrating compassion for the welfare of the mother and the child, her Indian captor took her inside a cabin. Kratz's husband, Leonard, had already been led off by another Indian, and when next seen he was carrying a big, heavy copper kettle tied to his back. Soon all the captives were loaded with plunder.

Eventually, order was restored, but Bird was seething over the killing of the cattle, which he knew was a real disaster. Nevertheless, he stifled his anger, and eventually the chiefs came to him. Excited by the easy victory, they invited him to join with them for a similar assault against Martin's Station, which was located only a few miles away. Quietly, Bird admonished them for not controlling their men and for the loss of all the cattle. Then he offered his ultimatum: unless the chiefs gave their promise that the prisoners taken here and during the remainder of the expedition would be turned over to him, and that no more cattle or horses would be slaughtered, he was ready to terminate British participation at that very moment, including the use of his cannons.

The next morning, the majority of the captives were turned over to him, and the chiefs swore their word to his requirements with a string of wampum. On the 27th, McKee dispatched spies to Martin's Station. They returned with a prisoner who was caught after the man had exited the little fort, having been sent to alarm nearby stations of the British attack. The next morning, Bird's army surrounded Martin's Station and, after showing the captured American his artillery, he sent the man back to the station to inform the defenders that the King's forces had the means to completely destroy the place, and that their situation was hopeless.

With no way to defend against English cannons, Martin's Station surrendered. Once again, delirious with their victory, the warriors went wild and shot all the cattle. However, none of the new prisoners were harmed and all of them were turned over to Bird's men. After looting the station and setting it afire, the warriors followed the British contingent and the prisoners back to Ruddle's Station. Bird now had more than 380 captives to manage and care for, and he knew that within two or three days, there would be nothing to feed his own men, the Indians, or the prisoners.

Energized by their success, the chiefs seemed oblivious to the situation. They pressed Bird to continue the campaign and attack Bryan's Station and then Lexington.

Bird declined and began the march back to the Forks of the Licking, where his stores and boats were waiting. While the majority of the prisoners from the two captured forts ended up in Bird's care, the remainder was in the hands of Indians whose intent was to ransom them at Detroit. Following the surrender of Martin's, it rained for days and the captives were wet, hungry and miserable as they were marched to the waiting boats. Bird reached the Forks of the Licking on 29 June.

One of the captives was John Hinkson, the noted pioneer, and one of Simon Girty's former friends. During Dunmore's War, Hinkson had served as a captain of rangers, and he and Girty had known each other for years. Delighted to see him again, Simon Girty marched beside him, and the two swapped stories. Hinkson had spent a good part of the preceding winter in the company of Simon Kenton (the two had helped build a crude blockhouse at the mouth of Limestone Creek), and Girty was glad to hear news of his friend. But he knew that once the news of what had happened to Ruddle's and Martin's stations reached George Rogers Clark, he would send his best spies to locate the captives. However, any contemplation of a confrontation with Kenton was put aside, for it was Hinkson who was in great need of his attention. In 1774, Hinkson had killed an Indian called "Wipey," who was quite popular among the whites of western Pennsylvania. At the time, the incident had attracted considerable attention. What Girty feared was that one of the Indians on the expedition would recognize Hinkson, and once that happened, nothing would save him. During one of the rest stops, acting as though it were a prank, Girty exchanged clothes with his friend. Later, Simon went to Bird and told him that Hinkson was "very supple and active," and that, in his opinion, unless the American were removed from the custody of the Indians and placed under close guard of English soldiers, he would surely get away. Bird had no reason to reject Girty's advice. Even so, that night, during a downpour, Hinkson somehow escaped. Rumors quickly circulated that Simon had aided his escape, but no one was prepared to accuse Girty to his face, nor were any charges ever filed against him in the matter.[2]

A few black slaves had also been captured in Kentucky, and these had been divided among the members of the Indian Department and some of the Indians. Simon Girty and Alexander McKee received one man each, and Matthew Elliott was presented with two others. The name of Girty's alleged slave was Scipio. According to Mrs. Margaret Paulee, "McKee and Elliott's slaves remained slaves. Girty and the Indians adopted their slaves or set them free."[3]

When Bird's returning army reached the west bank of the Ohio River (at present Cincinnati), the Indians detached themselves and started their journeys back to their home villages, taking their prisoners and booty with them. Simon and James Girty remained with their Indian contingents, the former headed back to Upper Sandusky and the latter to Wapatomica.

Bird retained George Girty to serve as one of several hunters employed to harvest meat for the expedition. Assuming he was pursued, Bird pushed his men and the prisoners relentlessly. According to one of the captives, George Girty was angry at Bird because none of the meat that he brought in went to the captives, not even to the women or children. On 24 July, when Bird's tired and hungry entourage finally arrived at Louis Loramier's trading house at the headwaters of Loramier's Creek (present Piqua, Miami County, Ohio), George Girty quit to return to Wapatomica.

As Simon Girty most likely suspected, Simon Kenton was indeed one of the first spies sent by George Rogers Clark to ascertain details of what had happened in Kentucky. Kenton's narrative on the subject states: "Charles Gatliffe and myself went on to Riddle's and Martin's Stations, and found them both taken, and a number of people lying about killed and scalped. We then took Captain Bird's trail from there on to the South Fork of Licking, where Falmouth now stands; and when we got there, we found where Captain Bird had built a blockhouse, and made a stockade fort—and that Bird and the Indians had left there. We returned back to Harrodsburg."[4]

HISTORY OF WETZEL COUNTY, W. VIRGINIA, JOHN C. McELDOWNEY, JR., 1901

> In Kentucky and Ohio he sustained the character of an unrelenting barbarian... his name was associated with everything that was cruel and fiendlike: to the women and children particularly, nothing was more terrifying than the name of Simon Girty.

Itching to strike back, Clark began to raise men and provisions. His immediate targets were the Shawnee towns of Chillicothe and Old Piqua. By the end of July, he had assembled a force of one thousand men, with adequate provisions and ammunition to sustain them.

On August 4, Bird reached Detroit with about 150 captives. Two days later, Indians brought in another 200 captives, whom they ransomed.

When Simon Girty returned to Upper Sandusky, the Wyandots and Mingoes celebrated their recent victories. Having suffered only a few men killed and wounded, the combined British-Indian expedition had destroyed two Kentucky stations, captured over four hundred white prisoners, nearly as many horses, and had liberated an enormous amount of plunder. By their standards, the campaign had had been a resounding success.

De Peyster and the British authorities saw it differently. The military objectives of the twin campaigns of Hesse and Bird were to capture St. Louis, destroy the American installations on the Illinois, and finally, to overthrow and capture Fort Nelson—Clark's American fortress at the Falls of the Ohio. Hesse's campaign was a disaster, and Bird's attacks on Kentucky had accomplished nothing of value except to pinprick an enemy who, having been provoked, was more dangerous now than before.

As Girty had suspected, news of pending American retaliation came fast. On 5 August John Clairy, an American deserter from Benjamin Logan's unit of Clark's army, brought word that Clark, with a thousand men and artillery, was about to attack the Shawnee towns along the Little Miami River.

Seeking help from Detroit, Shawnee leaders hurried to De Peyster, who was non-committal. The men who had just returned with Bird from Kentucky were exhausted, and the fort at Michilimackinac was also begging for reinforcements. Still, De Peyster refrained from abandoning his Shawnee allies. He rushed Matthew Elliott, James and George Girty and several other whites to Piqua and Chillicothe. Alexander McKee and Simon Girty were also sent there, but did not arrive until after the fighting was over.

Before dawn on 6 August, Captain Simon Kenton (who had been promoted and now commanded a company) led Clark's leading elements into Chillicothe. The Shawnees had abandoned the place. All the Indian houses, as well as the British stockade, had been set afire the day before. Clark halted his army there overnight and then moved on to Piqua, where he ran into heavy resistance.

According to Kenton:

We pursued on to a place called Pickaway Town and there the Indians embodied and fought us all day, and we whipped them, and for two days afterwards we were busily employed in cutting down their corn. On our return we stopped and cut down all their corn at Chillicothe, and then returned back to Kentucky, which finished our campaign.[5]

After the fight, the Shawnees lauded James and George Girty's efforts. Indeed, the two Girtys had fought so well that McKee made mention of it in a written report to De Peyster.[6]

Once again, the unbeatable George Rogers Clark had caused the Indians great distress, but he failed to follow-up with a lunge at Detroit. When it was over, both sides claimed they had inflicted significant losses upon their opponents; but, in reality, only twenty Americans had been killed and some forty wounded. The Indians suffered only six men killed and three wounded, but with winter coming on fast, the loss of Shawnee corn reserves was a disaster.

The three Girtys spent the winter of 1780-81 in Indian villages, and lent their hunting skills to the common need. For a few months, the war was forgotten and the "Injun Girtys" were left to recharge themselves in a primitive environment among close-knit families who appreciated their company and their friendship.

CHAPTER TEN

STRUCK DOWN BY ONE OF HIS OWN

WHILE THE GIRTYS HUNTED WINTER MEAT, De Peyster worked at securing supplies that would enable his Indian allies to resume their marauding
early in the spring. Anticipating the arrival of those supplies, McKee
spent the winter erecting a large storehouse near Roche de Bout, on
the Maumee River (near present Waterville, Ohio).

In Kentucky and Virginia, the rebels strengthened their defenses
by building several fortified stations.

In Pennsylvania, Fort Pitt's ragtag garrison suffered from a lack
of warm clothing and adequate food. Aware that his inability to
wage war might cause increasing numbers of Delawares to pick up
the British hatchet, Brodhead prayed for reinforcements and supplies,
and sent numerous messages to the Delawares pleading for their continued loyalty:

BRODHEAD TO THE DELAWARE INDIAN KNOWN AS "WILLIAM
PENN," 2 DECEMBER 1780

*... Brother: There is Alexdr' McKee & some others who do great
harm to your Grand Children by the Lies they tell them, & now I
desire you will send four or five of your strong men to take McKee
& more if they can & bring them to me so that I may have a piece
of meat.*

*Brother: I will pay sixty Bucks to your men that bring McKee
& twenty Bucks for any of the Girtys.*[1]

Simon must have welcomed the winter, for with the snows came sweet relief from the threats and stresses of war. If he was not coursing the hunting grounds on snowshoes, he was inside a winter hunting camp hut, enjoying the fare, the fire, gambling games, and conversations that were spiced with teasing, storytelling and laughter. He spent the hunting moons as an Indian, living among small, intimate groups of men and women, people who cared for and enjoyed one another.

While Simon was savoring the company of his favored Mingoes, his commander at Detroit concluded that his talents were being wasted. As De Peyster saw it, the Mingoes were too few in number to make a significant contribution in the upcoming battles. Late in January 1781, Girty received orders to move to Half King's Town at Upper Sandusky and establish himself with the Wyandots. As soon as weather permitted, he was to make his way to the Falls of the Ohio and spy on George Rogers Clark.

Although he did not welcome leaving his Mingo friends and relations, Girty had no choice in the matter. Fortunately, he already had a good relationship with Half King (also known as Pomoacan), and upon his arrival at Half King's Town, he was warmly welcomed and given a good house. Within days, he and his hand-picked escorts departed on snowshoes for Fort Nelson. As Girty's war party moved south along the Scioto River they were joined by a few Shawnees. It was 20 February when they reached the Falls of the Ohio. With fresh snow on the ground, they were able to track down and snare three hapless rebel soldiers who had been sent out to find meat. Girty interrogated each man out of earshot of the others. Expecting the worse for having fallen into the hands of savages and for facing the notorious Simon Girty, the captives were overly cooperative. They corroborated several points: George Rogers Clark had been acquiring supplies to support a spring offensive, and he had recently gone to Wheeling and Fort Pitt to raise two thousand men who were destined to join another thousand-man army that was being raised in Kentucky. In the early spring Clark would move down from Fort Pitt with men and supplies, and then clear out the Indian country as far north as Detroit. In addition to this information, Girty's captives claimed that another expedition, which was aimed at Michilimackinac, was to launch at about the same time from Fort Jefferson on the Mississippi.

Girty had what amounted to an intelligence bonanza, and he knew it. Leaving a few of his warriors to spy on Fort Nelson, he and the others hurried the captives to McKee at Roche de Bout, arriving there before 1 March. After hearing Simon's report, McKee sent a hurried express to De Peyster at Detroit, in which he urged his superior to rally warriors from the north and south to stand against Clark's invasion. McKee believed the coming fight was a turning point; for if Clark's campaign against Detroit failed, it was likely that all the American settlements on the south side of the Ohio River would fall. Thanks to Simon Girty, as the most critical phase of the frontier war approached, George Rogers Clark had lost the crucial element of surprise, and De Peyster could anticipate the moves of his enemy.

After Girty returned to Upper Sandusky, Half King asked him to carry a speech to De Peyster. The Wyandot chief wanted the British commander to know that his people and the Delawares understood that they had been deceived by the Virginians, that they would never again listen to them, and that they were now fully committed to waging war against the Americans. This was news that Girty was delighted to carry to Detroit.

Pleased with the Wyandot and Delaware promises of support, De Peyster wrote an answering speech which he then read to Girty, who easily repeated it in its entirety word for word. Simon was to deliver the speech first to the Wyandots at Upper Sandusky, and then to the Delawares at Coshocton.

Always conscious of his image, as Girty rode in to Upper Sandusky he was appropriately costumed in the full dress uniform of an officer of the British Indian Department. As he approached the council house, a young captive broke free from his guards and raced towards Simon. Pursued by three warriors, eighteen-year-old Henry Baker reached Girty's position and breathlessly begged for his life. Simon motioned for the approaching warriors to stand off so he could hear the youngster's story.

Baker explained that he had been captured by Wyandot raiders near Catfish Camp (present Washington, Pa.), after which he had been taken to Chillicothe and then on to Upper Sandusky. Here, he explained, the Indians had grouped him with nine other American prisoners. Then, day after day, one by one, each of his fellow captives had been put to death by fire. Now he was the only one left, and the Wyandots were making ready to burn him too. Simon took Baker into his protection. Trailed by the three warriors, he and the captive made their way to the council house where Girty's pleas for the boy's life were successful (Baker was later taken to Detroit and ransomed). Girty then called for an assembly, to hear De Peyster's speech. After delivering De Peyster's address to a large audience of Wyandots, Girty departed to voice the same speech to the Delawares at Coshocton. Speaking for De Peyster to both audiences, Girty explained:

Indians of Coshocton! I have received your speech sent to me by the Half King of Sandusky. It contains three strings, one of them white, and the other two checkered. You say that you want traders to be sent to your village and that you are resolved no more to listen to the Virginians, who have deceived you. It would give me pleasure to receive you again as brothers, both for your own good and for the friendship I bear to the Indians in general.[2]

A few days after Girty left Coshocton the town was attacked by three hundred mounted troops under the command of Colonel Daniel Brodhead. Secret letters from Heckewelder and Zeisberger had alerted Brodhead to the Delaware's recent decision to fight for the British; having finally received reinforcements and supplies, the frustrated colonel struck at his former allies. After slashing at Coshocton, Brodhead camped his army on the banks of the Tuscarawas River and sent for Heckewelder. Brodhead was concerned that due to his attack on the Delawares, the Moravians might suffer reprisals. When the missionary arrived, Brodhead invited him and his converts to vacate their Ohio Valley settlements and move to Pittsburgh, where they would benefit from his protection. Heckewelder declined the offer, arguing that such a move was unnecessary.

Hearing of Brodhead's attack on Coshocton, Girty dictated the following letter to De Peyster:

May 4, 1781 Upper Sandusky

We sent to Coshocton twenty of our men [Wyandots] some time ago and they have returned with the following news:

20 April. Colonel Brodhead, with five hundred men, burned the town and killed fifteen men. He left six houses on this side of the creek that he did not see. He likewise took the women and children prisoners, and afterward let them go. He let four men go that were prisoners who showed him a paper that they had from Congress. Brodhead told them that it was none of his fault that their people were killed, but the fault of the militia that would not be under his command. He likewise told them that in seven months he would beat all the Indians out of this country. In six days from this date, he is to set off for this place [Upper Sandusky] with one thousand men; and Colonel Clark is gone down the Ohio River with one thousand men.

There were one hundred and twenty Wyandots ready to start off with me, until this news came. Your children [the Wyandots] will be very glad if you will send those people you promised to their assistance; likewise send the Indians that are about you, to assist us. The Christians [Moravian converts] have applied to us to move them off before the rebels come to their town.

I have one hundred and sixty Indians at this place. Their provisions are all gone; and they beg that you will send them some.

Mr. Leveyer [Francois Le Villiers], when he heard that the rebels were in the Indian country, went off to the lower town where there was not a man but himself, and told the women and children that the rebels was close by. He ran off in the night without giving notice to the chiefs or me. He minds trading more than the King's business.

I will be much obliged to you, Sir, if you send me a little provisions for myself, as I was obliged to give mine to the Indians.

I am Sir, your most obedient and humble servant,

[Signed] Simon Girty

To Major DePeyster, Commanding Detroit [3]

Girty's reference to the Moravian Indians' request to be removed from their mission settlements "before the rebels come," reveals a fear shared by their Delaware converts that was not embraced by their white leaders. Zeisberger and Heckewelder had repeatedly assured their followers they were safe from American attack. To men like Girty, McKee and Elliott, the missionaries' claims were absurd.

The Delaware survivors of Brodhead's attack on Coshocton fled to the Scioto and Mad rivers, and to Upper Sandusky, which was now the rallying point where Girty, McKee and other British agents were helping to raise a native army. In early May, accompanied by forty warriors, thirty-nine-year-old Mohawk Chief (and British Captain) Joseph Brant arrived from Detroit. Brant's presence signaled forthcoming Iroquois support. To honor him, the western Indians slaughtered two oxen and hosted a feast. The Mohawk leader delivered stirring speeches from Colonel Guy Johnson and five of the Six Iroquois Nations, after which his hosts presented him an ornate coat bearing 700 silver brooches. Despite all the pomp and ceremony, inwardly the western tribes regarded Brant with suspicion. Many considered him an imperious braggart who was to be tolerated only because his warriors were needed.

Among the American borderers responding to General Clark's call, Colonel Archibald Lochry, County Lieutenant of Westmoreland, was able to muster 107 volunteers. Intending to join with Clark's army at Wheeling on 24 July, Lochry and his men departed from near Hanna's Town for Fort Pitt.

Aware that the Moravian missionaries were disloyal, and fearing for the safety of their Delaware converts, De Peyster ordered all the Moravians to be removed from their missions on the Tuscarawas River. For political reasons, he arranged for the removal to be carried out by a combined force of Wyandots, Delawares and Shawnees led by Half King, with Matthew Elliott present as his official voice.

At Upper Sandusky, Girty, McKee and their fellow agents were learning once again that it was much easier to recruit warriors than to retain them while a suitable army was being assembled. Bored, the Indians spent their days playing games and gambling. Before long, many had lost the clothing and ammunition provided to them from

British stocks. As food diminished, some of the warriors left to hunt meat, and others went to steal horses. By early August, acknowledging that they would only continue to lose more men by further delay, Joseph Brant and George Girty started for the Ohio River with ninety warriors and a few of Butler's Rangers. By this time Brant's welcome at Upper Sandusky had worn thin. Except for the forty Mohawks who had come west with him from New York, none of the Iroquois warriors he had promised had arrived. George Girty's complement of fifty warriors was comprised of Muncie Delawares, Wyandots, and a few Shawnees. When Simon Girty and McKee gathered enough men, they intended to reinforce George Girty and Joseph Brant, who would be waiting at the Ohio River. The reinforcements were to include a hundred more of Butler's Rangers, led by Captain Andrew Thompson.

George Rogers Clark's efforts to raise two thousand men at Pittsburgh were a dismal failure. The majority of the local militia had already marched east to fight against Cornwallis in Virginia, and, anticipating Indian raids, others refused to leave their homes undefended. Clark got no help from Brodhead, who disliked him, opposed the proposed expedition, and flatly refused to provide him with even a single company. Exasperated, Clark lost his temper and began to impress men, and as a result his desertion rate soared. Determined to curtail further losses, the red-headed Virginian departed for Wheeling on 8 August, leaving orders behind for Archibald Lochry to hurry and join him as soon as he could. Ironically, Lochry and his men reached Wheeling only a few hours after Clark's departure. Seeking further instructions, Lochry rushed an officer and escort down the Ohio by fast canoe to catch up with Clark.

Clark wanted Lochry to come down the river at once. At a site called Camp Three Island, Lochry would find a large boat with provisions for fifteen days that Clark would cache for him. Then, as Clark and his soldiers continued down the Ohio, Lochry and his men would have to catch up as quickly as they could.

Early in the morning of 18 August, Joseph Brant, George Girty and their warriors lay hidden in brush along the banks of the Ohio River, near the mouth of the Great Miami. No one moved, no one spoke, and no one coughed or sneezed. Heartbeats were as loud as drums. Only a few yards off the bank, George Rogers Clark and his army paddled by. Greatly outnumbered, the British-Indian force had no choice but to remain hidden. Brant was astonished to see that the great American war chief was traveling with only four hundred men. Seething with anger because promised reinforcements had not yet joined him, the Mohawk rushed a message back to the Scioto urging McKee and Girty to come on if they wanted a fight. If they were quick enough, Brant reasoned, the combined force could still overtake and destroy Clark before he reached Fort Nelson and safety.

Six days earlier, Clark had sent Major Charles Cracroft with an escort of eight men back upriver to deliver the boatload of provisions for Lochry. Cracroft had orders to guard the boat until Lochry arrived; but, during the first or second night at Camp Three Island two of his men deserted, and after a full week passed and Lochry still had not arrived, Cracroft abandoned the supplies. He hurried downstream with his remaining six men to rejoin Clark, paddling right into the hands of George Girty and Joseph Brant, who were still awaiting reinforcements at the mouth of the Great Miami. Brant's interrogation was swift and brutal. One of the captives said that Lochry was coming down river with a hundred men. The impatient Mohawk sent off another message to hurry McKee, advising him that whether or not he was reinforced in time, he meant to strike and annihilate the approaching Americans.

When Lochry reached Camp Three Island he found the provisions Clark had left for him but, to his consternation, no ammunition had been packed. He sent off men by canoe to find Clark and bring back powder and shot. After the provisions were distributed and he and his men had eaten, Lochry launched his boats once more down river.

Like Cracroft and his escorts, the men that Lochry sent for ammunition were also snared by Brant. Then, just as Brant, George Girty and their men were taking positions to ambush Lochry, they were reinforced by sixty more warriors, bringing their total strength to 160 men. On 25 August, some eleven miles south of the Great Miami River (and just inside the present Indiana border), Lochry's boats were lured to shore and trapped by warriors in canoes, who swiftly cut off any chance of escape. The Americans were overwhelmed, and Lochry and thirty-seven of his men were killed during the sharp firefight that ensued. Afterward, severely wounded Americans were put to death by tomahawk. The remaining captives were to be marched to Detroit. The warriors had been lucky. Not one of Brant's or George Girty's men had been killed.

Two days later, McKee, Simon Girty, and Captain Andrew Thompson joined Brant and George Girty, bringing with them 300 warriors and 100 more rangers. In the war council that followed, Brant speculated that due to the loss of Lochry's men, Clark would forego his planned campaign against the Sandusky Indians and Detroit. McKee argued that the best way to be sure of Clark's intentions was to pursue and destroy him. Brant acquiesced. Leaving a few men behind to escort the captives north, the rest of the army set off down the Ohio River in high spirits.

After five day's travel, it became obvious that they would not be able to catch Clark, and the British-Indian force made evening camp on the banks of the river. It was time to rest and to celebrate their defeat of Lochry. Captured rum and whiskey were handed out, and before long Brant began to boast of *his* great victory. The more he drank, the more he bragged about "how many prisoners he had taken and of his great prowess." The Mohawk's interminable arrogance grated against Simon Girty's nerves, and finally he snapped. He stepped up to Brant and called him a liar, claiming that if any credit was due, it was to his brother George, who had masterminded the ambush. The tent went dead quiet. Everyone waited for Brant's response. Although stung, the Mohawk refused Girty's challenge and walked out of the place with a sneer.[4]

Later that night, inside the tent where the men were drinking, or just outside it, Brant came up from behind Girty with a drawn sword and struck him viciously over the top of the head. Simon dropped like a sack of flour. Brant's blade had cut deeply into his skull. One account of the event claimed that Girty's "brain could be seen beating." A prominent Wyandot medicine man was summoned, and during the commotion, Brant slunk off. Believing that he had killed Girty, the Mohawk was hurriedly preparing to flee when McKee confronted

204 Simon Girty TURNCOAT HERO

him, warning him to remain, and adding that "if Girty dies, I'll have you hung."[5]

When he sobered, Brant expressed sorrow for what had happened and blamed his actions on his drunkenness. Supposedly, "Brant shed tears and begged Girty's forgiveness." If so, the Mohawk's words were not heard by Simon, who was deep in a coma, hovering between this world and the next.[6]

Girty was carried to Mingo Town (Logan County, Ohio) and later transported to Upper Sandusky. Some accounts claim that a Wyandot medicine man removed bone shards from Girty's brain, that he was trepanned, and that a silver plate was embedded in his skull.

Two days after Girty was struck down, George Rogers Clark and his little army reached safety at Fort Nelson, but not before three more of Clark's men had been captured. Interrogated, these hostages confirmed that due to the loss of Lochry and his company, Clark had terminated the scheduled campaign.

Frustrated by Clark's failure to attack Detroit, General Washington ordered Colonel Brodhead to relinquish his command to John Gibson and, at the end of September the Commander-in-Chief sent Brigadier General William Irvine to Fort Pitt to take command of the western war.

There were many at Upper Sandusky who believed that Simon Girty would never see the spring. Some speculated that even if he lived, he would never be more than an unresponsive, crazed cripple. McKee continued a constant vigil, monitoring Simon's condition, hoping for the best. It is difficult to know what outcome Joseph Brant wished for Girty, for back in New York among his own people, he never mentioned the incident.

Chapter Eleven

MASSACRE AND CONSEQUENCE

A MONTH AFTER HIS WOUNDING, Simon continued to slip back and forth between consciousness and oblivion. While he struggled, the removal of the Moravians from their missions on the Tuscarawas River got under way. Following De Peyster's orders, Matthew Elliott, Half King and a few hundred warriors collected the missionaries and their Indian converts and marched them to a site about three miles southeast of Upper Sandusky that would soon become known as "Captive's Town." The converts had been forced to abandon most of their cattle and to desert their fields before their corn could be harvested. The place where they were taken was bleak and empty. They built tiny brush shelters and scavenged for food. Heckewelder describes their plight:

> ... the cold during the nights became almost insupportable; the more so, on account of the smallness of our huts, not permitting the convenience of our having large fires made within them, and even wood being scarce where we were. Our houses having no flooring, whenever a thaw came on, the water, forcing passages through the earth, entered in such quantities that we scarcely could keep our feet dry. The cattle finding no pasture in these dreary regions, and we not being able to procure any for them, now began to perish by hunger, and, as provision for so many people could not be had even for money, famine took place, and the calamity became general; many had now no other alternative but to live on the carcasses of the starved cattle, and in a few

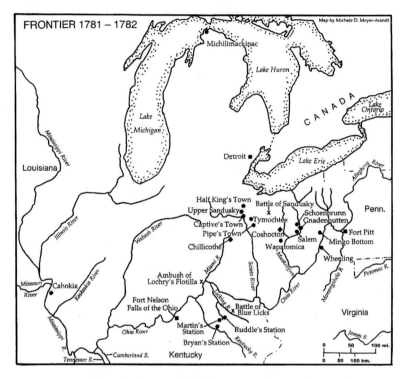

FRONTIER 1781 – 1782

Map by Michele D. Meyer-Arendt

instances suckling babes perished for want of nourishment from the mothers' impoverished breasts.[1]

Much to the surprise and delight of those who were caring for him, Girty's condition began to improve in October, and by late November he could manage short walks. To cover the deep, ugly scar that furrowed from his forehead to his left ear, he wore a red silk bandana—a practice he would continue for the rest of his life. Plagued by chronic spells of dizziness, blurred vision, and agonizing headaches from which there was no escape, Simon dulled his senses with rum or whiskey when it was available.

By January 1781 he felt strong enough to attempt a trip to Detroit, where, soon after his arrival, he was informed that a wounded American named Samuel Murphy had asked to see him. Girty went to the hospital to find Murphy, and shuffled about looking at each of the patients. Disoriented, he finally stood in the middle of the open ward and called out, "does anyone here know me?"[2]

Murphy was recovering from a gunshot wound to his hip suffered when he had been captured the preceding fall. He and Girty had been good friends at Pittsburgh and had served together in the Squaw Campaign. Realizing that Simon was in distress, Murphy identified himself and reminded him of their former exploits. Even so, Simon was still unable to place him. A few days later, an attendant handed Murphy a pound of tea and five or six pounds of sugar wrapped in a new, red handkerchief.

Returning to Upper Sandusky, Simon and Half King paid a visit to the suffering Moravians at Captive's Town. Heckewelder did not welcome their presence:

NARRATIVE OF JOHN HECKEWELDER

The missionaries had at this time reduced their daily allowance of provision for bread to a pint of Indian corn per man, a day. Now and then Mr. McCormick sent them a leg of venison purchased of the hunters. Yet, in this wretched situation, the hungry Wyandots would often come in our huts to see if there was any victuals cooking, or ready cooked. At one time, just as my wife had set down to what was intended for our dinner, the Half King, Simon Girty and another, a Wyandot, entered my cabin, and seeing the victuals ready, without ceremony began eating.[3]

According to Heckewelder, before Girty and his companions could finish their meal, two or three Delaware converts entered the hut and reminded them that the Moravians had been falsely promised food and provisions. Girty and Half King were told that they should "go out in the snow and find a cow carcass upon which to feed." After which, Heckewelder asserted, "Girty and his two companions quietly departed."[4]

The plight of the converts worsened, and in February a delegation went to Half King to beg permission for some of their people to return to the deserted missions to try and harvest what corn they could find from the frozen fields. Feeling sorry for them, Half King acquiesced. About 120 men, women and children departed for the Tuscarawas Valley. It was a bad time for them to be traveling, as

Wyandot and Shawnee warriors had been raiding American frontier farms and outposts in that region. On Raccoon Creek, in Hanover Township, Washington County, Pennsylvania, Robert Wallace's house was struck while the owner was away. Mrs. Wallace and three children were carried off. When Wallace returned and saw what had happened, he spread the alarm. By their tracks and other sign, a mob of American militiamen estimated that the Indian raiders numbered less than thirty men, and that they were heading in the direction of the Ohio River. The pursuers soon discovered the bodies of Mrs. Wallace and her youngest child hidden in underbrush. They had been killed and scalped. Another local named John Carpenter had also been carried off, but he escaped and made his way back to Fort Pitt. There he claimed that four of his captors had been Wyandots, and that two others had "told him they were Moravian Indians."[5]

In response, one hundred volunteers rushed from western Washington County to rendezvous at Mingo Bottom (on the west bank of the Ohio River, some seventy-five miles below Pittsburgh). Under the command of Colonel David Williamson, they set out to strike the vacated Moravian missions they believed were being used as bases by the raiders.

Although Half King was sorry for the plight of the Delaware converts wintering at Captive's Town, he had no sympathy for their missionary leaders. Two of his sons had been killed in raids against American outposts that had been forewarned of their coming. With good reason, Half King and Simon Girty both believed that the warnings had been sent by Zeisberger or Heckewelder. Without success, the two had repeatedly asked De Peyster to remove the missionaries from Captive's Town, and in February, Half King decided to try again. He went to Alexander McCormick to have him pen a letter to De Peyster. The Wyandot chief informed De Peyster that he would be "uneasy in his mind as long as the teachers remained at Sandusky," and that he "feared some misfortune and requested the commandant to take them away as soon as possible; but that, if he refused, he himself would know what to do!"[6]

Recognizing the threat, De Peyster responded. His letter arrived at Upper Sandusky about 1 March, and Simon Girty and Half King hurried to McCormick's place to hear De Peyster's response. As soon as it was read to them, Half King sent a messenger to summon Heckewelder and Zeisberger. After walking eight miles through the snow, the missionaries learned that De Peyster had ordered them to be removed from their followers, and, if he was not otherwise engaged, Simon Girty was to escort them to Detroit. Additionally, De Peyster ordered Girty to see that the missionaries were not plundered, molested or otherwise physically abused.

Toward the middle of the month the French trader Francois Le Villier arrived at Captive's Town from Lower Sandusky, telling Heckewelder and Zeisberger that Simon Girty had gone off with a war party to "make war on the Americans," and that Girty had appointed him to conduct them to Detroit. As Heckewelder explains:

He told us that Girty had ordered him to drive us before him to Detroit, the same as if we were cattle, and never make a halt for the purpose of the women giving suck to their children. That he should take us round the head of the lake [Lake Erie] and make us foot every step of the way.[7]

If Girty had indeed instructed LeVillier to drive the missionaries like cattle, the French trader ignored the order and conducted the missionaries and their families to Lower Sandusky with considerable care. There, waiting in relative comfort, they awaited further instructions and a boat to carry them to Detroit.

It was a full seven months since his wounding before De Peyster judged that Girty was mended enough for active duty. He sent Simon off to meet with some Loyalist informants at a predetermined location somewhere on the border, in an area frequently patrolled by American militia. On snowshoes, with their canoes over their shoulders, Girty and nine Wyandot warriors left Upper Sandusky on 17 March. One of Girty's companions was Half King's eldest son, Scotash. Portaging to the Scioto River, they canoed downstream, and just before reaching the Ohio River they were joined by twenty Wyandots led by a war captain named Abraham Kuhn. Returning scouts reported that enemy patrols ahead were unusually active, and Girty concluded that the original mission was too dangerous. He and Abraham Kuhn decided to divide their men and strike targets of opportunity. Girty took sixteen warriors south to cross the Ohio River, and Abraham Kuhn led his men northeast towards Fort McIntosh.

After crossing the river, Girty's party split up. Scotash took ten warriors upstream, and with the remaining six, Simon entered modern-day West Virginia, where he and his companions slipped up close to the home of a man named Zachariah Spriggs. While they were watching the place a pair of men approached. During the ambush that ensued, one of the two Americans was captured, and the other killed. A little later, Girty's men caught one of Sprigg's black slaves. That night, while Girty and the others were crossing back over the Ohio River in canoes, Sprigg's slave suddenly leapt from the boat, dove beneath the water, and escaped.

Reaching the north bank, Girty interrogated his remaining captive, a soldier named John Stevenson. It was Stevenson's brother who had been killed in the ambush. Terrified that he was about to be put to death, Stevenson blurted out everything he knew. He claimed that Fort Pitt had come under the command of General William Irvine, who had replaced John Gibson, and that General Irvine was preparing to lead a campaign out from Fort McIntosh against the Sandusky Indians. Stevenson thought Irvine's army would consist of five hundred men on foot, with another three hundred mounted. Stevenson figured the expedition would start early in the spring. Probing the man further, Girty was startled to hear that about three weeks earlier, a unit of Virginia militia had arrived at the Moravian mission of Gnadenhutten and had rounded up and put to death about one hundred Indian converts. Led by Colonel Williamson, the Virginians had been in pursuit of warriors who had murdered a white woman and her child. According to Stevenson, approaching the Gnadenhutten mission early in the morning, Williamson and his men came upon a hundred Moravian converts collecting frozen corn from the fields. The friendly Indians were gathered up and put to death the next day, after which the militia ransacked the mission buildings. During their return to Fort Pitt, Stevenson claimed that Williamson and his men attacked a few Indian camps located near the fort—all of them occupied by Delawares who supposedly were friendly to the United States. Many of these Indians were slaughtered, but some managed to flee inside the fort, where John Gibson had opened the gates to provide them refuge (Gibson was in temporary command while General Irvine was away at Carlisle). According to Stevenson, Williamson and his men were outraged by Gibson's action and they threatened to kill and scalp him too.

Girty soon received confirmation of Stevenson's bizarre account of the Gnadenhutten massacre, as well as other details, from a Delaware, a former prisoner at Fort Pitt who had recently escaped. On 8 April, Scotash, whose war party had captured a young man named Thomas Edgerton, rejoined Girty's war party. During their return to Upper Sandusky, Scotash confided to Simon that he had come to like young Edgerton and had made up his mind to present the captive to his mother as a gift, in hopes that she would accept him in replacement for one of her two younger sons who had been killed the previous fall.

By the time that Girty and the others reached Upper Sandusky, Abraham Kuhn and his warriors had already returned from their raiding, bringing with them fourteen scalps and four American prisoners. After hearing their story, Girty took captive John Stevenson and hurried to Lower Sandusky. Upon his arrival on 12 April, Simon dictated the following letter to De Peyster:

.... We killed one soldier and took one man prisoner, and arrived [back] at Upper Sandusky the 8th of April. The said prisoner informed me that General Irvine had returned from the Congress to Fort Pitt; that he had been down for two battalions of troops; but whether he had obtained them or not, he could not tell. He further says on his [Irvine's] arrival at Fort Pitt, he had called all the militia officers together and likewise the regular captains to a council of war, and that it was determined to start in a few days on a small campaign, their number to consist of about 500 foot and 300 horse; that they intended to go to Sandusky—and are to march from Fort McIntosh.

The Moravians that went from Upper Sandusky this spring to fetch their corn from their towns where they lived last summer,

are all killed by the Virginia militia; the number of dead amounts
to ninety-six men, women and children.

.... The small parties that I served out ammunition to, the 1st of
March last, are all returned, except one party. They have brought
in fourteen men's scalps, and four men prisoners; so that there
have neither woman nor child suffered this time. There is one
Indian killed and three wounded. I shall leave this place tomor-
row morning, and proceed to Upper Sandusky. I take with me one
hundred pounds of powder and two hundred pounds of ball, and
eight dozen of knives for the use of the Wyandots, Monseys and
Delawares. I was obliged to purchase some little necessaries from
Mr. Arundell, that were not in the King's store, which I hope you
will be good enough to excuse, as I did it for the good of the service.
I should be very much obliged to you, if you would be kind enough
to order me out some few stores, that I may have it in my power to
give a little to some Indians that I know to be deserving.

I remain, with much respect, sir, your most obedient humble
servant,

    Simon Girty[8]

Considering the dimension of the Gnadenhutten massacre, Girty's report is amazingly brief for, more than any other event, this atrocity would become the catalyst to unite the western and northern tribes against the United States. The Indians concluded that if the Americans were capable of slaughtering Christian converts (the only natives still friendly to their cause), there could be little doubt of what was in store for everyone else if the rebels won their independence from the English king.

Perhaps Girty's report was low-keyed because, as horrific as it was, the slaughter of the Delaware Moravian converts would hardly have come as a surprise to someone like him. By this stage of the frontier wars, the pattern of American militia killing Indian men, women and children had been well established. The irony of the Gnadenhutten massacre was that the Moravian converts were the only Indians in the entire region who, advised by their missionary leaders to expect friendship and justice from Americans, would have actually welcomed Williamson and his volunteers.

Girty knew that the missionaries had been warned several times but had rejected every offer to move their followers to safety. He blamed them for what had happened and he went to pay them a visit at Lower Sandusky, where they were still awaiting transport to Detroit. Heckewelder's journal tells what happened:

… he [Girty] did return, and behaved like a madman on hearing that we were here, and that our conductor had disobeyed his orders, and had sent a letter to the commandant at Detroit respecting us. He flew at the Frenchman, who was in the room adjoining ours, most furiously, striking at him, and threatening to split his head in two for disobeying the orders he had given him. He swore the most horrid oaths respecting us, and continued in that way until after midnight. His oaths were all to the purport that he never would leave the house until he had split our heads in two with his tomahawk, and made our brains stick to the walls of the room in which we were. I omit the names he called us by, and the words he made use of while swearing, as also the place he would go to if he did not fulfill all which he had sworn that he would do to us. He had somewhere procured liquor, and would, as we were told by those who were near him, at every drink renew his oaths, which he repeated until he fell asleep.

Never before did any of us hear the like oaths, or know anybody to rave like him. He appeared like an host of evil spirits. He would sometimes come up to the bolted door between us and him, threatening to chop it in pieces to get at us. No Indian we had ever seen drunk would have been a match for him. How we should escape the clutches of this white beast in human form no one could foresee. Yet at the proper time relief was at hand; for, on the morning, at break of day, and while he was still sleeping, two large flat-bottomed boats arrived from Detroit, for the purpose of taking us to that place.[9]

Despite Heckewelder's claim that the only thing that prevented Girty from committing mayhem was a barred door, Girty must have been satisfied to remain outside the cabin. Otherwise, he could have simply picked up an axe and chopped the door to pieces.

Simon was sober enough the next morning to ride his gray mare back to Upper Sandusky where, at the end of April, he visited fourteen-year-old Thomas Edgerton, the young captive whom Scotash had captured and wanted his mother to adopt. The boy was disconsolate and apprehensive. Girty told Edgerton about his captor, pointing out that Scotash was the only remaining son of Half King, and that he was fast becoming a great warrior. Then he described the details of a bloody, hand-to-hand fight Scotash had survived during a recent skirmish with some Virginians, and from which he was the only Indian to emerge alive. Finally, Girty informed Edgerton that Scotash liked him well enough that he was going to present him to his mother the next day, for adoption into their family. Edgerton never forgot his meeting with the notorious Simon Girty.

Another American captive to benefit from Girty's attention was seventeen-year-old Christian Fast, who had been wounded during the attack on Lochry's flotilla. First taken to Half King's Town, he had subsequently been adopted by a Delaware woman, and was now living at Captain Pipe's Town. Longing for his Pennsylvania family and home, Fast later recalled that he had been sitting on a log in the woods meditating when Girty came upon him. Speaking the Delaware tongue, Girty asked him what was he thinking about. Fast answered that he was feeling lonesome. "That's not it," Girty corrected. "You are thinking of home. Be a good boy, and you shall see your home again." Years later, Fast remembered that Girty visited him several times after that, and that he did him many favors. Eventually, Fast was allowed to accompany a war party to the settlements, where he escaped and made his way home.[10]

When they reached Detroit, the Moravian missionaries suffered lengthy examinations, but were ultimately set free without any punishment. Determined to rebuild their ministry, Zeisberger and Heckewelder obtained permission from the Ojibwas to erect new missions along the Huron River, thirty miles north of Detroit. Then the two missionaries sent messages to their convert refugees, summoning them to a new settlement, which once again was to be named Gnadenhutten.

Following the Moravian massacre, Indian spies had been sent out in large numbers, and in mid-May reports of American military activity began to reach Detroit. At the time, Girty was at Detroit interpreting for the Indian Department. Responding to Wyandot pleas for help, De Peyster arranged for the ship *Faith* to carry Irish-born Loyalist Captain William Caldwell, along with some Canadian volunteers and one-hundred of Butler's Rangers, across Lake Erie to the Sandusky River. Simon Girty and other officers of the Indian Department were ordered to rally the Indians. The warrior army was to be assembled at Half King's village.

With General Irvine's approval, American mounted volunteers (most of them from Washington and Westmoreland counties, Pennsylvania) were once again to rendezvous at Mingo Bottom. Once assembled, they were to form companies and elect leaders. Colonel David Williamson would be present, as would Colonel William Crawford of the Continental Army. To promote their recruitment, volunteers were promised they would be excused from two regular tours of duty, and if any of their horses were lost during the operation, they would be replaced with horses taken from the Indians. The following are General Irvine's orders to whoever was elected to lead the expedition:

The object of your command is, to destroy with fire and sword (if practicable) the Indian town and settlement at Sandusky, by which we hope to give ease and safety to the inhabitants of this country: but if impractical, then you will doubtless perform such other services in your power as will, in their consequences, have a tendency to answer this great end.

… Should any person, British, or in the service or pay of Britain or their allies, fall into your hands—if it should prove inconvenient for you to bring them off, you will, nevertheless, take special care to liberate them on parole, in such manner as to insure liberty for an equal number of our people in their hands.

There are individuals, however, who, I think should be brought off at all events, should the fortune of war throw them into your hands. I mean such as have deserted to the enemy since the Declaration of Independence.[11]

Those signaled out "as have deserted to the enemy" were, of course, the Girty brothers, Alexander McKee and Matthew Elliott.

By 24 May 1782, the volunteers for what was already being called the "2nd Moravian Campaign" had all arrived at Mingo Bottom. Many of the 480 men present had taken part in the massacre at Gnadenhutten. Forming eighteen companies, the volunteers went about electing company captains and brigade leaders. The two candidates for commander were David Williamson and sixty-year-old Colonel William Crawford (the latter was Irvine's choice). When the votes were tallied, 230 had been cast for Williamson and 235 for his opponent.[12]

Among the volunteers were many men with whom Girty was familiar, including Major James Brenton (the officer whom Girty had helped to find his lost horse during the Squaw Campaign), as well as frontiersmen Jonathan Zane, John Slover and Thomas Nicholson—all of whom were selected to serve as guides or pilots for Crawford's expedition.

News of the gathering of an American army at Mingo Bottom reached Sandusky within a day after the first American volunteers had arrived on the north shore of the Ohio River. By the time Captain William Caldwell and his two companies of British rangers arrived at Upper Sandusky, two hundred warriors were there waiting for the Americans to invade the Sandusky region. There were Ojibwas, Lakes Indians, Wyandots, Delawares, Mingoes, Shawnees, and Miamis. All three of the Girty brothers, as well as Alex McKee and Matthew Elliott, were either at Half King's Town or en route to it. As the army gathered, one of two survivors of the massacre at Gnadenhutten told his story. The gruesome details quickly made the rounds of the various camps. Every warrior learned how at Gnadenhutten the Americans had disarmed their captives, separated the Delaware men from their women and children, and then herded everyone inside two cabins. Then, led by Williamson, the militia voted whether to convey the Indians to Fort Pitt or execute them. The vote was for death. Informed that due to their participation in recent attacks on settlers they were to be put to death the next morning, the Delawares vehemently protested their innocence—to no avail. Resigned to their fate, they spent their last night praying and singing hymns.

At dawn, groups of male converts were tied and conveyed to a small shed where, forced to stand facing the walls, their skulls were smashed by their executioner, who moved behind them wielding a big cooper's mallet. After the men had all been killed, the white soldiers marched the women and children into the bloody shed. Later, after the wooden mallet had fallen for the last time, the militia scalped the crushed skulls, piled the bodies into heaps inside the cabins, and set everything afire. At Upper Sandusky, the telling and retelling of the grim story primed the massing warriors who sought revenge.

The rebel militia at Mingo Bottom assembled at the same place where Williamson's earlier expedition had rendezvoused; and, when they departed on Saturday the 25th, they rode out over the same trail that Williamson's force had taken on its way to Gnadenhutten. Like the First Moravian Campaign, the Second was determined to destroy any and all Indians it encountered: Christian or heathen, man or woman, child or infant. According to writing carved on trees after the bark had been peeled, there was to be no quarter given. After the Americans departed from Mingo Bottom, Indian spies made careful tracings of the inscriptions, transferring them to deerskins with pieces of charcoal. Brought to Upper Sandusky, the skins were translated and their messages read for everyone to understand. War chiefs huddled together, formulating battle plans. Half King's Town and Captive's Town had already been abandoned to draw the Americans deeper into Indian lands. The women, children and the aged were evacuated to Half King's New Town, seven miles downstream on the Sandusky River.[13]

On Tuesday, 28 May, Crawford's army reached the west bank of the Tuscarawas River, just below the upper Moravian settlement of New Schonbrunn (slightly south of present New Philadelphia, Ohio). There they camped amid the ruins of the mission that was previously sacked and burned by Williamson. Having left Mingo Bottom four days earlier, they had come only sixty-plus miles. After feeding their horses on Indian corn, the men poked about the abandoned mission buildings, looking for plunder. That night, Major John Brenton and Captain Joseph Bane reconnoitered and spotted two Indians, whom they fired on from a great distance. The Indians ran off, and Brenton and Bane returned to camp and reported the incident. Everyone understood that their presence had now been discovered, but even so, they started out the next morning for the Sandusky River, still one hundred miles distant.

After marching a full week the Americans reached Hell Town, a Delaware settlement that had recently been abandoned. Crawford called his staff together. Wanting action, Williamson asked Crawford to let him take fifty men to go and set ablaze the nearest village (Half King's New Town). Crawford, who was against dividing their forces, refused. Thus far they had not fought anyone, and everything they had seen led to the conclusion that the Indians were hastily retreating before them. Even so, Crawford may have had a premonition of danger, for he expressed apprehension about going on. After some discussion, the junior officers won out and the decision was made to continue to advance at least a few more miles.

With thoughts of women and children being clubbed to death, the avengers waited at Half King's New Town. The combined British-Indian force was commanded by Captain William Caldwell, with Matthew Elliott his second-in-command. It was Elliott's responsibility to coordinate the movements of the Indians who were to fight under the command of their own war chiefs. Half King would command the Wyandots, and the Delawares were to be led by Captain Pipe and Wingenund. Simon Girty was to fight with the Wyandots, and George Girty was with the Delawares. Runners were sent to James Girty and Alexander McKee, asking them to come on fast with reinforcements from the Shawnee towns.

On the morning of 4 June, the Americans were crossing plains where the grass stood nearly as tall as a man. Slowly, they worked their way through the deserted ruins of Captive's Town, and then through Half King's Old Town. Finally, Crawford halted the army by some springs (now downtown Upper Sandusky), and sent twenty-four scouts ahead to search for the enemy while he and the main force took their noon meal. The trail that the scouts followed skirted a nearby wood that would later become known as "Battle Island." The fighting started when dismounted Wyandots and Delawares appeared suddenly and opened fire at the scouts. The point of conflict was about three miles in advance of the main army and within sight of McCormick's Town. Pursued by warriors racing through the tall prairie grass, Crawford's scouts retreated into the nearby woods. After sending a few riders back for help, the remaining men dismounted to take cover and defend themselves. Pushed back through the trees, the scouts had almost been overrun before Crawford and reinforcements arrived and, with an aggressive bayonet charge, drove the Wyandots out of the woods. Crawford then ordered the army to take up defensive positions within the grove. By four o'clock in the afternoon the fighting had stalemated, with both sides satisfied to take long range shots at each other.

Arriving reinforcements enabled the Wyandots to completely surround Battle Island and Crawford's forces. Soon after, Caldwell arrived with a few of his rangers and strengthened the encirclement. As he was dismounting, an American marksman put a rifle ball through both of Caldwell's legs. At the same moment, across the meadow and along the edge of Battle Island, another bullet smashed William Crawford's powder horn. The impact knocked the American commander down, but he was not seriously injured. During the opening action, Simon Girty reportedly fired from afar and wounded Captain Joseph Bane, who was carried for treatment to surgeon Dr. John Knight. Sporadic firing continued with expert riflemen from both sides doing the most damage.

That morning, before the fighting had began, the trader Francois Le Villiers bragged to the Wyandots that he "had a special magic" to protect him from enemy bullets. He even had his Indian wife sew a circular, crimson patch over his heart, on the white ruffled shirt he was going to wear into battle. Just before sunset on that first day of battle, an American sniper, hiding in the shadows of Battle Island, sighted on the conspicuous red patch and shot him dead.

After sundown, the shooting died off, and the opponents lit big bonfires along their fronts to disclose enemy movement. Thus far, the Americans had five dead and nineteen wounded, while the British-Indian forces had suffered five dead and eleven wounded.

Like a scene from a Shakespearean tragedy, as the night advanced a low, foreboding mist spread over the ground. Posted in pairs, a few Americans stood guard in the eerie light while their comrades tried to sleep. Harassing them, Indians periodically screamed war cries and fired their muskets. Occasional groans issued from deeper in the woods, where the wounded men were being tended. At the time, Crawford's army was equal if not superior in number to its enemy, but to the volunteers who were lying in the damp, dark woods, listening to the moans of the wounded, it was easy to convince themselves that they were already greatly outnumbered. Adding to their woes, ammunition and water were running low. In spite of the fires that burned all night, fifteen Washington County deserters managed to slip away. Reaching Pennsylvania, they reported that "all in the army was cut to pieces."[14]

At first light, both sides resumed firing at each other again from the trees and in the high grass. As the morning wore on Indian reinforcements kept arriving. Williamson went to Crawford and asked permission to counterattack from the eastern end of the woods with fifty men on horseback, and another fifty on foot. The two men argued and Crawford "talked of taking the sense of his Field Officers." Williamson's request was put aside. Early in the afternoon, a torrid sun bore down and the stench of the dead began to grow intolerable.[15]

Taunting their opponents, some of the warriors exposed themselves recklessly, drawing fire in order to expend the enemy's ammunition. Infrequently, Americans responded with oaths and jeers. Matthew Elliott (who had taken overall command after Caldwell had been wounded) was content for the situation to remain static, for he knew that another detachment of rangers was coming with two small cannons and a mortar. McKee and James Girty were also expected soon, with Shawnees from Wapatomica and the Mequashake Towns. Elliot summoned Simon Girty and, following a brief discussion, Girty mounted his horse. Wearing his red bandana, riding his big gray mare and vigorously waving a white flag, he emerged from the tall grass, approximately 150 yards from the Americans. The shooting died off, and when it stopped, Girty slowly advanced towards the enemy lines. When he figured he was close enough, he halted his horse and called out loudly for the Americans to discuss surrender. The line of defenders facing him from the woods was almost a quarter mile long, and he had no idea where to aim his voice. He repeated himself, facing in different directions. Accounts vary regarding Girty's attempt to parley, some claiming that he addressed himself to Crawford, with others equally certain that he directed his demands to Williamson.

When his repeated requests went unanswered, Girty wheeled his horse, lowered his flag and quickly rode out of sight. Years later, an American sharpshooter named Myers admitted that, at the time, he had been up a tree taking careful aim at Girty with his rifle, and had started to squeeze the trigger when his target disappeared.

Just after sundown on the second day of fighting, McKee and James Girty arrived with 140 Shawnee warriors who quickly reinforced the encirclement. Shortly thereafter the Indians fired their muskets into the air in a rolling volley that traveled the full length of the siege line, all around the trapped Americans. By this time Crawford had had enough and he ordered his officers to prepare to withdraw. They were to retreat along the same route by which they had arrived. Orders were issued for the dead to be hurriedly buried and for fires to be set over the graves to disguise them. Horse litters were to be contrived to carry away all the wounded.

At nine o'clock that night, Indian sentries fired their muskets in alarm as the first units of Crawford's army suddenly broke from the woods. At the sound of their shooting, panic swept the American ranks. A large number of men led by Williamson broke out to the west, in the opposite direction from the first detachment. The action left Indians milling about and confused in the darkness. Fleeing south, groups of militiamen reached the ruins of Half King's Old Town, where they re-assembled. By morning, Williamson commanded about 250 men, whom he led on a hurried march homeward. Crawford was missing and Williamson presumed him to be dead or captured.

Instead of pursuing and destroying the retreating Americans, the majority of the Indians, including women, raced into the woods of Battle Island to collect abandoned horses, saddles, knapsacks, weapons, clothing and cooking utensils. Joyful celebrations began as word of the great victory spread.

Simon was at the Wyandot village of Half King's New Town when he was informed that some Delawares had captured the "Big Captain" of the invading army. The captive had repeatedly asked to meet with Girty, and he was being brought to McCormick's Town for that purpose. The Delawares intended to burn the prisoner, and, as they were apprehensive about losing him to the more powerful and numerous Wyandots, they would not bring the American commander directly to Girty at Half King's Town. Their fear was well founded. Under the influence of Girty and other agents of the British Indian Department, the Wyandots were now ransoming virtually all their American captives at Detroit—where a ranking American officer brought substantial reward. In addition, Girty's stance regarding white captives was well known, for he had consistently acted on behalf of prisoners who were threatened by torture or death. While the Delawares were willing to allow their captive to meet and talk with Girty, they were reluctant for the event to take place at a site where they were greatly outnumbered by Wyandots who were under the British agent's influence.

Accompanied by two warriors, the captured American officer was brought to McCormick's Town on Sunday night, 9 June. For his meeting with Girty, the prisoner was taken either to McCormick's house or another near-by cabin. There were several people to witness the meeting, including a Moravian Indian named Tom Jelloway, and a young captive American woman named Elizabeth Turner.

The Delawares believed that they had caught the American commander responsible for the massacre at Gnadenhutten, the infamous David Williamson; but the moment he saw the prisoner's gaunt face, Girty knew it was William Crawford. He also knew that unless there was a miracle, the colonel was going to suffer a horrifying death.

CHAPTER TWELVE
A FATEFUL PENALTY

WILLIAM CRAWFORD HAD BEEN A CAPTIVE for two days when he met with Girty. Following the chaotic retreat of the Virginia militia from Battle Island on the night of 5 June 1782, Colonel Crawford had lingered in the woods, searching unsuccessfully for his son John. Giving up the search, he encountered the militia's surgeon, Dr. John Knight. On foot, the two men then attempted to rejoin the retreating army. The next morning they were joined by five stragglers, and the following day all of them were captured by seventeen Delawares. Since then, Crawford had been beaten and force-marched almost sixty miles. He was bruised, exhausted, forlorn and desperate.

Seeking to calm him, Girty said that Shawnees had captured both William Harrison (Crawford's son-in-law) and William Crawford (his nephew), that they were unharmed, and their lives were to be spared. In fact the Shawnees had already put both men to death at Wapatomica and it is likely that Simon knew it. Next, Girty explained to Crawford that his particular situation was grave because the Delawares blamed him for the Gnadenhutten massacre.

Crawford reacted as though he had been slapped. He adamantly denied participating in any way in that tragedy, and he pointed out that during his campaign not a single Moravian convert had suffered. Not one. His conduct had been honorable and he begged for Girty to convince the Indians of that truth. Then he allegedly told Simon that if his life were spared, he would divulge some important military intelligence, but that nothing else could make him do it. Some accounts allude that he also promised Girty a large sum of money if he would save him.[1]

Elizabeth Turner (who later married Alexander McCormick) told historian Lyman Draper that she was present at the initial meeting of Crawford and Girty, at which time Girty suggested an escape plan that, if successful, would have left Crawford safe in British hands at Detroit. But, according to Elizabeth, the American officer "seemed disheartened, with no pluck to make the effort." Nevertheless, Girty had promised Crawford that he would do all he could to save him. When their meeting concluded, Delaware guards led Crawford away to where he was to spend the night.[2]

The next morning Crawford was marched south six miles to Half King's Old Town, where several other American prisoners (including Dr. John Knight) were being held. Upon his arrival, Knight asked Crawford if he had met with Girty and what had happened. According to Knight's published narrative, the colonel told him:

Girty had promised to do every thing in his power for him, but that the Indians were very much enraged against the prisoners; particularly Captain Pipe one of the chiefs....[3]

Crawford's fate was to be decided later that evening by a council of chiefs at Pipe's Town, and Simon Girty was to translate for the prisoner. By then, others were scrambling to save Crawford, including Matthew Elliott, who sent urgent requests for help to McKee and to two traders at Lower Sandusky whom Elliott hoped would assist him in an attempt to ransom Crawford.

As the day drew on, a sullen crowd of Delaware men, women and children gathered at Pipe's Town to see the White Chief burn. As the captives were marched north from Half King's Old town, nine of the eleven American prisoners were tomahawked and mutilated. Crawford and Knight were forced to run a gauntlet that left both men bruised and in pain. As the two captives approached Pipe's Town, the Indians held Knight back to prevent him from attending Crawford's trial.

Jeers erupted from onlookers as Crawford was brought before an assembly of Pipe and other chiefs. Men and women shouted obscenities and accusations. One of the loudest of the protestors was Pipe's sister-in-law. Crawford and Girty exchanged greetings and it was apparent that the colonel still hoped to talk his way out of the situation. The "trial" began with Delaware chiefs angrily blaming Crawford for the massacre at Gnadenhutten.

Recalling Crawford's trial, Delaware chief Wingenund later told Heckewelder:

These Indians [the victims of the massacre at Gnadenhutten]
believed all their teachers had told them, of what was written
in the Book, and strove to act accordingly! It was on account of
the Great Book you have, that these Indians trusted so much to
what you told them! We knew you better than they did! We often
warned them to beware of you and your pretended friendship: but
they would not believe us! They believed nothing but good of you,
and for this they paid with their lives! [4]

With Girty translating, Crawford answered his accusers by again denying any involvement with the massacre at Gnadenhutten, and by voicing sincere regret for what had happened there. The Indians listened intently. Taking a new tack, Crawford then asked Girty to explain that he had also "very much favored the Indians at the Salt Licks of Mahoning," (referring to his conduct during the "Squaw Campaign").[5]

A moment later, Pipe's ancient sister-in-law, Micheykapeeci, moved to the chief's side, and was granted permission to speak. During the American attack on the Kuskuskee Towns, in February of 1778, it was Crawford who had saved her from being gunned down. But, much to Crawford's misfortune, this was not what she was about to recall. Instead, in loud, anguished tones, she accused Crawford of being one of the war chiefs who led the white soldiers when her husband Bull—Pipe's brother—and his mother were both murdered, the very same morning when her fingertip had been shot off.

Acknowledging her story, Pipe condemned Crawford to death by fire. When the approving shouts of the crowd died down, Girty attempted to bargain for Crawford's life. According to Joseph Jackson, who was living with the Shawnees, and who later professed that he had discussed these events with Girty shortly after their occurrence:

Girty said he had interceded for Crawford to be spared, even got on his knees and begged their favor, as Crawford was an old friend. The reply of the Indians was, that as Crawford was the commander of the whites, he must suffer; that they must have revenge for Williamson's cruel tragedy at the Moravian towns on the Muskingum; if Crawford had been but a private soldier, Girty's request would have been granted—as it was, they could not spare him, unless Girty would take his place at the stake.[6]

Elizabeth Turner McCormick agreed that Girty tried to save Crawford. As she tells it:

He offered a beautiful horse which he had with him, the stock of goods he then had on hand, if he would release him, but the chief said 'No! If you were to stand in his place it would not save him.'[7]

During an 1864 interview, Girty's daughter Sarah told historian Lyman Draper that her father often said that he did everything he could possibly do to save Crawford from the stake. According to Sarah Girty Munger, Girty pleaded with Pipe:

... offering for his ransom all the property he was possessed of in the world... The Indians said Crawford could be saved only on the condition that Girty would take his place.[8]

Threatened with death if he did not cease his appeals for Crawford, Girty said nothing more. The issue was closed, and Crawford was led to where Dr. Knight was being held.

Girty now concentrated on seeking help from others. There can be little doubt that he conferred with Matthew Elliott, whose efforts on behalf of Crawford had also been unsuccessful. Although Elliott had considerable influence with the Shawnees, nothing that he had been able to say or offer to the Delawares had deterred Pipe or Wingenund, who were determined to see Crawford die.

The location of the place of execution was a ceremonial grove of oaks on Tymochtee Creek, three quarters of a mile west of Pipe's Town. On the afternoon of the 11th, Knight and his guards followed along behind Crawford's party, with the two groups separated by about 150 yards. Ahead of them, awaiting them on the trail was Girty and a few mounted Wyandots. When Crawford reached Girty's position, the two men spoke briefly. Knight remembered seeing them talking together, but he was too far away to hear what was said. Shortly thereafter, Crawford's party continued on their way, and Girty waited for Dr. Knight. As the captive drew near, Simon inquired "if he was the doctor?"[9]

According to Knight's account, he answered "yes," and went toward him, reaching out his hand. Girty allegedly refused his hand, called him "a rascal" and threatened that he would soon be taken to the Shawnee Towns "to see his friends."[10]

At the ceremonial site, crowds of Delawares and other Indians were gathered. Crawford and Knight were led to a fifteen-foot post, erected in the center of a clearing. Six or seven yards away, a fire blazed. The fire was fed by long hickory poles, burning through at the middle, each end of the poles remaining about six feet in length.

The two captives were made to sit on the ground and then the Indians beat them with fists and sticks. Finally, Crawford was hauled closer to the fire and stripped naked. His hands were bound behind his back with rope, and another rope was attached that connected his tied wrists to the foot of the post. The longer rope was rigged to allow the condemned man to walk around the post once or twice in either direction.

Enduring the humiliation, Crawford called out to Girty, imploring "if they intended to burn him?" Girty answered affirmatively, and Crawford nodded, stating softly that "he would take it all patiently."[11] Then Crawford began to pray. According to the Wyandot Scotash, Crawford "talked much God and all the time looking up."[12]

Girty once again tried to intercede for Crawford but Pipe threatened him with death if he spoke another word for the condemned prisoner. Girty yielded, and Pipe delivered a rousing speech that evoked cheers from the onlookers. As soon as Pipe's tirade concluded, warriors with muskets screamed and surged around Crawford, firing powder charges into his body at close range, striking him from his feet to his neck. The gunpowder burned deep into Crawford's flesh, creating black and bloody wounds that smoked. Knight estimated that more than seventy such charges were fired.

Wearing his full dress officer's uniform, Matthew Elliott stood by helplessly. After the shooting of powder charges ended, an old man stepped close to Crawford and cut off his ears. Next, the warriors picked up hickory poles from the fire and began to press and jab the blazing ends against the doomed man. Scrambling around the pole in agony, Crawford tried to evade the fiery prods, but no matter which way he went they stabbed into him. Eventually hot coals were tossed beneath his feet and toward the end of the ordeal, he sank to his knees. An Indian with a knife moved up behind him and cut off his scalp. Finally, what was now William Crawford slumped over on his stomach. Using a thin board to scoop up hot coals, a woman poured them over the victim's wounded back and bloody head. Crawford groaned, rose to his feet and began to shuffle once more, although he no longer reacted to the burning poles. Shortly afterward, he fell forward on his stomach again and expired. His body was thrown on the fire. From start to finish his ordeal had taken a little more than three hours.

Years later, Elizabeth Turner's son recalled her saying: "Girty shed tears while witnessing Crawford's agonies at the stake, and ever after always spoke of Crawford in the tenderest terms..."[13]

SIMON GIRTY, THE OUTLAW. U.J. JONES, HARRISBURG, PA. 1843

In the midst of these extreme tortures he called upon Girty for God's sake to shoot him.

'Why my friend, that would put an end to the sport,' said the Outlaw derisively.

Eighty-two years after the event, Girty's daughter told Lyman Draper: "While Crawford was being burned... he requested Girty to shoot him, and Girty replied that it was Indian custom that no one could interfere with a prisoner condemned to death, without himself being shot down on the spot..."[14]

En route to the Shawnee Towns where he was scheduled to be

burned, Dr. John Knight was able to overpower his single guard and escape into the wilderness. On the 4th of July, he arrived at Fort Pitt, exhausted and half-starved. Knight was incoherent when he related his story to General Irvine. A week later, Irvine wrote the following to George Washington:

GENERAL IRVINE TO GEORGE WASHINGTON, FORT PITT, JULY 11, 1782

Sir—Dr. Knight, a surgeon I sent with Colonel Crawford, returned the 4th instant to this place. He brings an account of the melancholy fate of poor Crawford. The day after the main body retreated, the colonel, doctor and nine others, were overtaken, about thirty miles from the field of action by a body of Indians, to whom they surrendered. They were taken back to Sandusky, where they all, except the doctor, were put to death. The unfortunate colonel, in particular, was burned and tortured in every manner they could invent.

The doctor, after being a spectator of this distressing scene was sent, under guard of one Indian, to the Shawanese town, where he was told he would share the same fate the next day; but fortunately found an opportunity of demolishing the fellow, and making his escape. The doctor adds, that a certain Simon Girty, who was formerly in our service, and deserted with McKee, and is now said to have a commission in the British service, was present at the torturing of Colonel Crawford, and that he, the doctor, was informed by an Indian, that a British captain commands at Sandusky; that he believes he was present, also, but is not certain; but says he saw a person there who was dressed and who appeared like a British officer. He also says the colonel begged Girty to shoot him, but he paid no regard to the request.[15]

The day after Crawford's burning, Girty went to Lower Sandusky to report to Captain William Caldwell what had happened. Caldwell rushed the following message to De Peyster at Detroit:

CALDWELL TO DE PEYSTER, JUNE 13, 1782

Simon Girty arrived last night from the upper village (Half King's town) who informed me, that the Delawares had burnt Colonel Crawford and two captains, at Pipes-Town, after torturing them a long time. Crawford died like a hero; never changed his countenance tho' they scalped him alive, and then laid hot ashes upon his head; after which, they roasted him by a slow fire. He told Girty if his life could be spared, he would communicate something of consequence, but nothing else would induce him to do it. He said some great blows would be struck against the country. Crawford and four captains belonged to the Continental forces. He [Girty] said fourteen captains were killed. The rebel doctor and General Irvine's aid-de-camp [Rose] are taken by the Shawanese; they came out on a party of pleasure.[16]

The story of Crawford's death swept the frontier and was sensationalized in American newspapers. Girty's supposed participation in the victim's execution served as a dark indictment from which his reputation would never recover. Strangely, although Knight's narrative made it clear that Matthew Elliott was also present at Crawford's burning, his role is rarely mentioned in American accounts and he escaped the despicable notoriety that was to descend upon Girty. A good illustration of how Girty was regarded is demonstrated in the lyrics of a folk song entitled "Crawford's Defeat," which was popular along the frontier following the American Revolution:

Our officers all so bravely did fight,
And likewise our men, two days and a night,
Until a reinforcement of Indians there came,
Which caused us to leave the Sandusky plain.

Then said our commander, "Since we have lost ground—
By superior numbers they do us surround—
We'll gather the wounded men, and let us save
All that's able to go, and the rest we must leave."

There was brave Colonel Crawford upon the retreat,

Likewise Major Harrison and brave Doctor Knight,
With Slover, the pilot, and several men,
Were unfortunately taken on the Sandusky plain.

Well, now they have taken these men of renown,
And dragged them away to the Sandusky town,
And there in their council condemned for to be
Burnt at the stake by cruel Girty.

Like young Diabolians, they this act did pursue,
And Girty, the head of this infernal crew—
This renegade white man was a stander-by,
While there in the fire their bodies did fry.[17]

Heckewelder wrote that shortly after Crawford's death Wingenund went to Detroit and was censored by British authorities for not acting to save the life of his old acquaintance. Reportedly, the Delaware chief listened calmly to his accusers and then confided to Heckewelder: "These men talk like fools. If King George himself had been on the spot with all his ships laden with treasures, he could not have ransomed my friend."[18]

On 18 July 1782, De Peyster bemoaned Crawford's death in a letter to Thomas Brown, the Superintendent of Indian Affairs at Detroit:

Sir—I am happy to inform you that the Indians from this quarter have gained a complete victory over six hundred of the enemy who had penetrated as far as Sandusky, with a view of destroying the Wyandots, men, women, and children, as they had done with ninety-six of the Christian Indians at Muskingum a few weeks before.

… Colonel Crawford, who commanded, was taken in the pursuit and put to death by the Delawares, notwithstanding every means had been tried by an Indian officer present, to save his life. This Delawares declare they did in retaliation for the affair of Muskingum [the massacre at Gnadenhutten].

I am sorry that the imprudence of the enemy has been the means of reviving the old savage custom of putting their prisoners to death, which, with much pains and expense we had weaned the Indians from, in this neighborhood....[19]

As soon as the survivors of the defeated Sandusky expedition returned, Americans aching to avenge Crawford pressed for a campaign to annihilate all the Indians of the Sandusky area. Such a thrust was a subject of correspondence between General Washington and General Irvine.

Following their victory in the Battle of Sandusky, the Delawares and Shawnees announced that from then on, they would torture and put to death any American who fell into their hands. When this information reached De Peyster, he ordered McKee to advise the Indians that if they continued such a policy, he would be forced to deny them any further aid.

After reporting Crawford's death to Captain William Caldwell, Simon Girty departed from Lower Sandusky with a party of Wyandots to participate in war councils at Wapatomica. Flushed with victory, the Ohio tribes were anxious for more action.

On his way to the war councils, Girty paused near Chillicothe to visit nine-year-old Jonathan Alder, who had been captured by Shawnee raiders the previous year. Although a kindly couple had adopted the boy, he was underweight and weak. Alder was concerned that his Indian father "had no intention of permitting him to return" (to his real parents), even though this had been promised to him. As Howe explains in his *Historical Collections of Ohio*:

He (Girty) took him to one side where they had a long talk. He inquired all about the parents and relations, where they lived, and how he liked to live among the Indians, and if they treated him kindly and he thought to be satisfied to live with them. Having responded in a satisfactory manner, to all these questions, the strange white man said his name was 'SIMON GIRTY.'—that he was formerly from Pennsylvania and that if he (Alder) was not satisfied he would buy him and send him across the lake into Canada, among the British, and they would learn him a trade, but continued saying, 'If you stay with these people,

someday you will be exchanged for another prisoner and have a
chance to get back to your mother.' And further, 'You will be more
likely to get back to your people, if you stay with the Indians than
if with the British. Besides, you will soon get to like the Indians
and will not care to leave them, even to go home. And further, the
war will not last always, for the whites will conquer the Indians,
and then there will be peace, and then you can go where you
please. Reflect on what I have told you and I will be back in about
two weeks and if you are not satisfied by that time, I will do as I
have said, buy you and send you to the British across the lake.'

…. Girty returned as agreed and inquired of young Alder if
he had made up his mind. He says, 'I told him I had and that I
would stay with the Indians.'

Girty seemed pleased at this decision and talked for sometime
giving him much good advice—telling him to be a good boy and
someday he would be sure to get back to his folks.[20]

Simon, with his brothers George and James, was at Wapatomica
in July when Captain William Caldwell arrived with eighty British
rangers. Caldwell asked for Shawnees to join him for an attack against
Fort Henry and Wheeling, and three hundred warriors responded.
The Girty brothers, McKee and Elliott joined Caldwell's forces.
Departing from Wapatomica, they were two days out when runners
caught up to them with alarming news: George Rogers Clark was on
the move "with a train of artillery and a large body of troops," and
was heading for the Shawnee Towns.[21]

Startled, Caldwell sent two Frenchmen and forty warriors east
to spy on the Americans, and then rushed his army back to defend
Chillicothe. At the same time, De Peyster received reports that
General Irvine at Fort Pitt was organizing another expedition aimed
at the Sandusky Indians, and perhaps at Detroit itself. Wishing to
reinforce Caldwell, the governor rushed a company of rangers under
the command of Captain Andrew Bradt to Chillicothe.

Reaching Chillicothe, the Girty brothers, McKee, Elliott, and
other British agents began to raise an army of warriors. A great council
was held, attended by anxious Shawnees, Delawares, Wyandots,

Mingoes, Ojibwas, Ottawas, Pottawatamis, and Miamis. The Indians had confirmed the news that Cornwallis had surrendered, and that the war between England and the United States was drawing to a close. They feared that once the British put down their tomahawk, the Americans would come full force at them—particularly the Long Knives (Virginians) and their indomitable leader, George Rogers Clark.

For Girty, his brothers, McKee and Elliott, there was no way to avoid the ironic truth that although they and the Indians had won every important battle of the western frontier wars, to the east the English had lost enough money and blood to conclude that the war was no longer sustainable. At Chillicothe, the main issue was not the war between the American rebels and King George, but whether the Indians would be able to keep their homelands north of the Ohio once the British surrendered. As the Indians saw it, their only choice was to keep fighting to prevent new white settlements from being established on their side of the river. Properly armed, supplied and led, they might just be able to accomplish this.

In an address to the warriors, Girty delivered a powerful speech in which he outlined the situation at such a pivotal moment. As one nineteenth century historian wrote:

---

*Girty recited to them [the Indians] their wrongs, the encroach-
ments of the whites, the value of Kentucky as a hunting ground,
the necessity of combining their strength to regain possession of
their lands and prevent the final loss of their homes and means
of living, and extinction as a people. The warriors roared their
approval and the tribes were determined to continue the war.*[22]

The massacre at Gnadenhutten had brought about the American defeat at Sandusky, which, in turn, fueled morale, unity and purpose among the northern and western tribes. When the Chillicothe war talks concluded, eleven hundred warriors were ready to fight. Captain Caldwell and the war chiefs decided to strike the expected American invaders at Piqua (some forty miles south), where, two years earlier,

Clark had driven out the Shawnees. Enthused over the size of the British-Indian army, McKee wrote De Peyster:

We had on this occasion, the greatest body of Indians collected, on an advantageous piece of ground near the Picawee village that has been assembled in this quarter since the commencement of the war.[23]

Demoralized by the American defeat at Sandusky, George Rogers Clark was unable to raise the men he needed and the anticipated expedition failed to materialize. Caldwell and the Indian agents tried to keep their warrior army together, but it was impossible. The first to return to their villages were the Shawnees. Soon afterward, other warriors began to go home.

Before their warrior army completely disintegrated William Caldwell, Simon and George Girty, Alex McKee, and Matthew Elliott marched to Kentucky with fifty rangers and three hundred warriors (mostly Wyandots). Their objective was Bryan's Station, some five miles northeast of present Lexington.

Chapter Thirteen
AMBUSH AT BLUE LICKS

THE OUTSIDE WALLS of Bryan's Station were two hundred yards long and fifty wide, enclosing more than twenty cabins. In each of the corner blockhouses there were gun ports positioned from which riflemen could protect the front, rear and sides of the fortress with devastating crossfire.

On the night of 14 August 1782 Caldwell's forces surrounded the stronghold, taking positions beyond the effective range of the defender's rifles. Following their battle plan, at dawn a hundred warriors started to shoot at the fort from the southeast. Caldwell kept the main body of his force in hiding, hoping that some of the American garrison could be lured out into a trap. If so, when the moment was right, the main body of warriors would emerge from hiding, storm the undefended side of the fort and set the palisades ablaze with torches. Simon Girty had been assigned to the latter group.

Sounds coming from within the fort made it clear that the Americans were active. In fact, having only that day received a request for help from a nearby station, the garrison had spent the night casting bullets and making ready to depart at first light.

At dawn, the Wyandots southeast of the station emerged from the shadows of the woods and began to fire their muskets. Suspecting a trap, the Americans ignored the provocation and instead sent two men out on fast horses to request help. Rather than reveal their positions, Caldwell's force remained in hiding and let the two riders go off unmolested. By this time, the station's defenders had taken positions on the palisades and the shooting died down.

The defenders were short of drinking water and the summer day turned blazing hot. The station's water came from a spring situated outside the palisades, near the front gate. The Kentuckians assumed that some Indians had already hidden themselves near the spring in order to ambush any men who went there for water. Some brave women suggested that they get water, and they were instructed to act as calm and ordinary as possible. Once again the Indians declined to reveal their positions. They let the women pass freely, draw and fetch water.

What happened next is explained by Alexander Scott Withers in his *Chronicles of Border Warfare*:

When a sufficiency of water had been provided, and the station placed in a condition of defense, thirteen men were sent out in the direction from which the assault was made. They were fired upon by the assailing party of one hundred, but without receiving any injury; and retired again within the palisades [sic]. Instantly the savages rushed to the assault of, what they deemed, was the unprotected side of the station, little doubting their success. A steady, well directed fire, put them quickly to flight. Some of the more desperate and daring however, approached near enough to fire the houses, some of which were consumed; but a favorable wind drove the flames from the mass of the buildings and the station escaped conflagration.[1]

Without artillery Caldwell knew it would be impossible to overrun the fort, but nevertheless he continued the siege. He assumed that the two riders who had left would return with reinforcements, and he deployed men to ambush the rescuers. His guess was correct. Some thirty Americans later arrived, half of them mounted and the rest on foot. They were immediately engaged. The horsemen charged through a cornfield and made it to the safety of the fort. According to Butterfield's account:

.... Those on foot were driven back with the loss of one killed and three wounded. It is said that one of the settlers—a stout, active

young fellow—who had come to the assistance of his besieged friends, was so hard pressed by a white man and several savages that he turned and fired, and the white man fell. The latter, it is claimed, was Simon Girty. 'It happened, however, that a piece of thick sole-leather was in his shot pouch at the time, which received the ball and preserved his life, although he was felled to the ground. The savages halted upon his fall and the young man escaped.[2]

There are no other accounts to corroborate Girty being hit that day by a rifle ball. Because he was wearing his trademark red bandana, the defenders recognized Girty and assumed that he was in command of their enemies. After the siege, the Girty legend was enhanced by a story that claimed that when Simon attempted to persuade the defenders to surrender, he was sharply rebuked by a young, audacious trooper named Aaron Reynolds. According to this tale:

In the twilight of evening, Simon Girty covertly drew near, and mounting on a stump from which he could be distinctly heard, demanded the surrender of the place. He told the garrison, that a reinforcement, with cannon, would arrive that night, and that this demand was suggested by his humanity, as the station must ultimately fall, and he could assure them of protection if they surrendered, but could not if the Indians succeeded by storm; and then demanded if 'they knew who was addressing them?'

Aaron Reynolds allegedly bellowed back:

We all know you! I have a good-for-nothing dog named Simon Girty because he looks so much like you. Bring on your artillery if you've got any, and be damned to you! We, too, are expecting reinforcements; the whole country is marching to us, and if you and your gang of murderers stay here another day we will have your scalps drying in the sun.[3]

To which Girty supposedly replied: "that it was no time for joking." Then Reynolds allegedly responded with another insult. It is unlikely the dialogue between Girty and Reynolds ever took place; detailed official reports of the attack make no mention of the defenders being addressed by Girty or anyone else.

While Caldwell retained some of his warriors to keep the station under siege, he turned the majority loose to raid nearby farms. These raiders stole horses, slaughtered livestock, and set cabins and crops ablaze. More than 300 hogs and 150 cattle were killed and that night the Indians gorged themselves on domestic meat.

At daybreak on the morning of 17 August Caldwell withdrew his forces, leading them first to the ruins of Ruddle's Station and then on to the Lower Blue Licks. An easy-to-follow trail was left behind.

Later that day, 170 avenging volunteers led by Colonel John Todd arrived at Bryan's Station and after a short visit departed to pursue the enemy. Among Todd's men were Daniel Boone and his twenty-one-year-old son, Israel. In his written report of that day's events, Lieutenant Colonel Levi Todd, brother of the colonel, recollected:

On the morning of the 18th we pursued on their Trail. On the morning of the 19th we came within sight of the enemy about 3/4 of a mile north of the Lower Blue Licks—we dismounted & began the attack with vigor, from our left the enemy retreated & we gained ground. Our right, within a minute or two gave way & found themselves to be flanked by the enemy. Our Line then gradually gave way from our Right to our Left till the whole broke in Confusion. The action lasted about five minutes. Our Loss, as near as we can ascertain is sixty six, among whom were our commanding officer Colonel John Todd, Col. Trigg, Capts: Gordon, McBride, Kinkaid & Overton, Major Harlan, Major Bulger (who since died of his wounds) Mr. Jos: Lindsay & several gentlemen of note—the enemy we supposed consisted of three or four hundred—they took some prisoners, we suppose tho' very few, upwards of 40 were found, but we think a number more lay near the battle ground. The enemy must have suffered considerably, a great part of our men fought with much Resolution & Activity. The Conduct of the Officers is by some censured & charged with want of prudence in attacking at any Rate, but as he had no chance to know their number, we thought ours was not much Inferior & supposed we should by a fierce attack throw them in confusion and Break their lines...[4]

Levi Todd's report omits mentioning that when the Americans halted at the Licking River a bitter argument broke out between Daniel Boone (who suspected an ambush and wanted to go no further without reinforcements) and Major Hugh McGary, of Harrodsburg. After listening to Boone, McGary mounted his horse and spurred it into the river, yelling, "Them that ain't cowards follow me!" Caught in the spirit of the moment, Colonel John Todd and his men followed after hothead McGary. To avoid being left behind, Boone joined the others. In the chaotic and bloody five-minute firefight that ensued, Boone's twenty-one-year-old son Israel was among the first to be slain.

Racing from Bryan's Station to reinforce Todd with 154 more Kentucky volunteers, Colonel Benjamin Logan's scouts were commanded by twenty-seven-year-old Captain Simon Kenton. Helping to build a station near Danville, Kenton had answered the call for volunteers as soon as news of the siege at Bryan's Station reached him. Six miles from Blue Licks, he and his men began meeting up with frightened and exhausted stragglers returning from the fight. The survivors reported that they had been overwhelmingly outnumbered by Girty and the Indians. There was a good chance now that Kenton's best friend was just ahead, waiting for him. However, the scope of the disaster shocked Colonel Logan, and he was apprehensive that the enemy might come after the retreating Kentuckians. Prudently, he halted where he was, ordered his men to prepare defensive positions and sent messengers to summon reinforcements. For the moment, Kenton's possible clash with Girty was postponed.

Five days later, having been reinforced, Colonel Logan led 470 volunteers down to where the fighting at Blue Licks had taken place. The only living thing they found was an engorged buzzard that flew off at the intrusion, its wings flapping loudly as it labored to gain altitude. The stench of rotting flesh was everywhere. Logan sent Kenton and Boone to scout the place, and they soon confirmed that Girty and the Indians had indeed left the area. In his postmortem of the battle, Colonel Logan reported to a Governor Harrison that:

BENJAMIN LOGAN TO VIRGINIA GOVERNOR BENJAMIN HARRISON:

... from the situation of the ground, on which our men were drawn upon, I hardly know how it was possible for any to escape...

... Our men marched over upon the Hill. The Indians had a very strong line in front which extended from one point of the river to the other. They had flankers and also a party in the rear in order to prevent a retreat. As the river was very deep only at the Licks and the cliffs so steep that a passage was impracticable only where they first marched in—thus circumstanced the Savages, sure of victory rushed immediately up and threw our men into confusion. What escaped returned mostly by way of the Lick.[5]

Boone's biographer, John Filson wrote:

Being reinforced, we returned to bury the dead, and found their bodies strewed every where, cut and mangled in a dreadful manner. This mournful scene exhibited a horror almost unparalleled: Some torn and eaten by wild beasts; those in the river eaten by fishes; all in such a putrefied condition that none could be distinguished from another.[6]

During the frightful moments of the ambush at Blue Licks, seventy-seven Kentuckians had been killed and a half-dozen more were captured. The relief column found only forty-three bodies, which were collected and buried in a common grave.

The devastating defeat had immediate consequences. Enough of Kentucky's militia had been wiped out to cause settlers to vacate their homes and farms and move east to safety. Boone begged the governor for an additional 500 militiamen.

British and Indian losses at Blue Licks had been negligible. The rangers suffered one man killed; and the Indians had only ten men killed and fourteen wounded. But, due to rumors that the English were actively seeking peace, the warriors considered the victory bittersweet. For Girty, Blue Licks was his last fight of the Revolutionary War. Erroneously credited by the Americans for leading the enemy forces at the Battle of Sandusky, for being responsible for Crawford's death, and now for the disastrous defeat of the Kentuckians at Blue Licks, Simon Girty had become a monster in their eyes. Referring to a proposed expedition against Sandusky by General Irvine, Colonel Arthur Campbell wrote that he was:

... disappointed in Clark's co-operation, which he [General Irvine] was promised; and, it is said he will set out with only 1,200 men. Simon Girty can outnumber him; and, flushed with so many victories, to his natural boldness, he will be confident.[7]

In Pennsylvania a new, 1,500-pound reward (half the value of Crawford's estate,) was posted for Simon Girty's capture or killing.

SIMON GIRTY: THE WHITE SAVAGE, CHARLES MCKNIGHT, PHILADELPHIA, 1880

The outlawed white man by Ohio's flood,
Whose vengeance shamed the Indians's
    thirst for blood;
Whose hellish arts surpassed the redman's far;
Whose hate enkindled many a border war,
Of which each aged granddame hath a tale
At which man's bosom burns and
    childhood's cheek grows pale.

The war was winding to a close. English diplomats were meeting with their American counterparts to open the way to peace talks. For men on both sides, there was a burning hope that they would soon be able to put down their rifles, reunite with their wives and families, go back to their shops or farms and live in peace. This dream was not shared by any of the Indians living north of the Ohio River, nor by their white brother who had become "Dirty, Dirty Simon Girty." The Indians were locked in a battle for survival in which the Revolutionary War was but a passing phase.

CHAPTER FOURTEEN
A FRAGILE PEACE

INSTEAD OF CELEBRATING their victory over the Kentuckians at Blue Licks, the warriors who accompanied Girty back to Half King's Town were grim and tense. Word had come that General Cornwallis had surrendered his army at Yorktown. If so, England might quit the war and the Indian nations would no longer have redcoats to fight by their side. But it wasn't English blood that was necessary for victory against the Americans; it was their muskets, gunpowder and food supplies that were vital. If their English father abandoned the war, would he continue to supply his children north of the Ohio River? Men like Simon Girty, Alexander McKee and Matthew Elliott had no answers.

At Wapatomica, the Shawnee chiefs wanted to strike the Americans once again while British soldiers, supplies, ammunition and weapons were still available. Succumbing to their urging, in September 1782 Captain Andrew Bradt departed with James Girty, 238 warriors and forty British rangers to attack Fort Henry at Wheeling. Just as they were leaving, instructions from General Sir Frederick Haldimand, Governor General of British North America, reached De Peyster (at Detroit), advising him that peace negotiations with the rebels were underway and ordering him to immediately cease all offensive operations. De Peyster rushed stand-down orders to Captain Bradt, but they arrived too late. Bradt, James Girty and the Shawnees were already besieging Fort Henry and facing stiff resistance. Unable to overrun the place, they harassed the Americans for two days and then withdrew. Before crossing back over the Ohio River, Bradt paused to attack an isolated outpost known as Rice's Fort, but once again

246 Simon Girty TURNCOAT HERO

a small but determined garrison repulsed his warriors and troopers. The American's initial paralysis, brought on by their disaster at Blue Licks, had dissipated. Bradt's failures against Fort Henry and Rice's Fort reflected a growing determination on the part of the enemy.

Seeking to avenge the disaster at Blue Licks, the Americans evolved a two-prong strategy which called for George Rogers Clark to lead a Kentucky army north against the Shawnee Towns on the Great Miami while General Irvine was to simultaneously march a second army from Fort McIntosh against the Sandusky Indians. On 4 November 1782, Clark's army of 1,050 men assembled at the mouth of the Licking, crossed the Ohio, and started for Old Chillicothe. Kenton, along with Boone and Clark's pilot Phil Waters, marched in the vanguard. None of them were aware that General Irvine had fallen behind schedule and was not yet ready to march from Fort McIntosh, nor could they have known that several weeks later, on 30 November, the United States and Great Britain would sign preliminary articles of peace. Four days later General Irvine received orders to abort his operation. Stand-down orders had also been sent to General Clark, but they failed to reach him in time to prevent his initial attack. On the evening of the 10th he and his Kentuckians crept within two miles of Chillicothe before their presence was uncovered. In Clark's written post-mortem, he wrote:

> ... they [his command] discovered a solitary straggler, who instantly fled to the village, yelling like a demon at every jump. The troops pressed on with all possible speed, but upon entering the town found it deserted. So precipitate had been their retreat, however, that the enemy left the fires burning, pots boiling, and meat roasting on sticks. This was a treat to the almost famished Kentuckians, who, after full indulgence, proceeded to destroy the town, corn and everything tending to support the savage foe. It is said that on the approach of the army, men, women and children fled to the forest, leaving everything behind them.[1]

Clark reported that there had been very little fighting. Having received the belated stand-down orders, he reluctantly withdrew. His

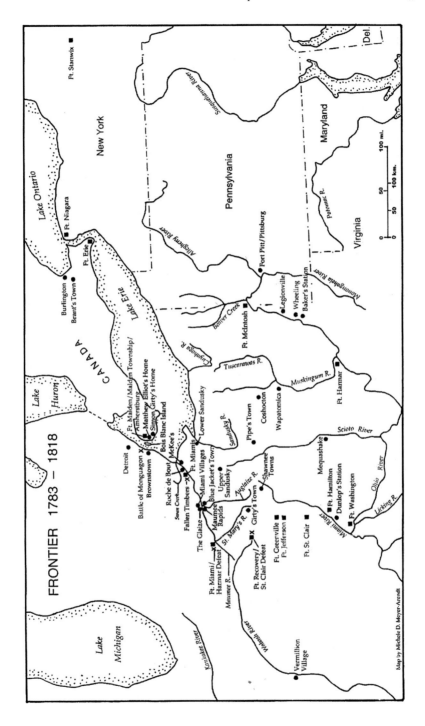

FRONTIER 1783 – 1818

Lake Michigan

Lake Huron

CANADA

Lake Ontario

New York

Pennsylvania

Maryland

Virginia

Del.

Ft. Stanwix

Ft. Niagara

Burlington
Brant's Town
Ft. Erie

Lake Erie

Susquehanna River
Allegheny River

Fort Pitt/Pittsburg

Legionville
Wheeling
Baker's Station

Monongahela River

Potomac R.

100 mi.
100 km.
50
50
0
0

Detroit

Ft. Malden/Malden Township/
Amherstburg
Matthew Elliot's Home
Simon Girty's Home
Bois Blanc Island
McKee's

Battle of Monguagon X
Brownstown
Roche de Bout X
Ft. Miamis
Miami Villages
Blue Jacket's Town
Upper
Sandusky
Lower Sandusky

Cuyahoga R.

Beaver Creek
Ft. McIntosh

Tuscarawas R.
Muskingum R.
Ft. Harmar

Coshocton
Pipe's Town
Wapatomica

Scioto River

Sandusky R.

Swan Creek
Fallen Timbers X
The Glaize
Maumee
Rapids
Auglaize R.
Girty's Town
Shawnee
Towns

Mequashake

Ft. Hamilton
Dunlop's Station
Ft. Washington

Ohio River
Licking R.
Miami River

Ft. Miami/
Harmar Defeat
St. Mary's R.
Ft. Recovery/ X
St. Clair Defeat
Ft. Greenville
Ft. Jefferson
Ft. St. Clair

Maumee River

Wabash River

Kankakee River

Vermillion
Village

Kentuckians had destroyed ten thousand bushels of corn and had burned out six villages.

However, only twenty warriors had been killed, and Shawnee fighting strength and morale remained intact. Impatient to retaliate, their chiefs hurried to the British for help. To their consternation, their allies urged them to refrain from striking back, instead of joining them.

At the time, Simon Girty was at Detroit interpreting at councils attended by anxious deputies from the Senecas, Shawnees and Delawares. On 24 January he and McKee received orders from De Peyster to do all they could to restrain the warriors and get them into a defensive posture. De Peyster's letter to McKee accented the finality of the English decision to quit the war:

…. Having received orders from the Comm' in Chief to lesson the Indian Department I have struck off several of the interpreters. Simon Girty continues his pay—till further orders, but McSurphlet, George Girty, James Girty and others who had two dollars are reduced to one, with which please to acquaint them. You will please to dismiss such of your four shilling men as you have not an absolute occasion for.

P.S. All prisoners shall have provisions till they go down the country.[2]

By the end of February 1783, the rolls of the British Indian Department show that only thirty men were still employed. By mid-May a total of forty-seven men had been discharged, and Captain Simon Girty was one of the few field agents to remain in service at full pay.[3]

Divorced from Indian Department service, James Girty and his Shawnee wife Betsey established themselves at a fortified trading post south of the Auglaize River. Independent Indians soon took up residence adjacent to James Girty's store; and in time, the village became "Girty's Town." Today the place is known as the city of St. Marys, Ohio.

Certain now that the English were quitting the war, the chiefs were acutely aware that none of them had had been invited to take part in any of the peace negotiations. Sensing disaster, they feared that their most powerful ally would soon abandon and betray them. The dynamics of these apprehensions must have fallen like hammers upon Girty and the other field agents of the British Indian Department. Living among the Indians, Girty and his compatriots served the Indian interests as translators, traders and emissaries. They were the only avenue of communication to the crown. With no knowledge of treaty details, Girty and his fellow agents were unable to field questions about what British Indian policy might be after the war. All they could do was attempt to allay Indian apprehensions, offer ambiguous promises, and repeatedly urge the chiefs to refrain from further raiding on American outposts and settlements. The challenge was all the more difficult because, at De Peyster's urging, McKee and Elliott had for weeks been denying to the Indians that Cornwallis had surrendered at Yorktown. When that deception was no longer possible, the two men had claimed that Cornwallis's defeat was but a minor setback—not one that would lead to total capitulation.

What the Indians understood for certain was that they remained unconquered and in possession of their homelands and hunting grounds, and that they had not lost the war that they had been waging against the Americans for six years. Indeed, their collective victories were stunning. Iroquois, Wyandots, Shawnees and Delawares had defeated the Americans at Oriskany, Wyoming Valley, Schoharie Valley, Cherry Valley, Minisink, the Battle of Sandusky, the destruction of Hanna's Town, and finally at Blue Licks. There was a growing consensus among the tribes that no matter what peace terms were agreed to by the Americans and the English, the Indians would not suffer the surrender of any of their hunting grounds north of the Ohio River. Consequently, before one war had truly ended, the foundations for another were being erected.

Confronted daily by the Indians, and unaware of what was occurring at the highest levels of authority, Girty and his fellow agents had no option but to continue stalling and to maintain their ambiguity. Considering their frustration, the chiefs were remarkably patient and cooperative, and for the most part they were able to restrain their warriors.

Touring from one village to another, Girty met and encouraged nine-year-old James Lyon who, along with his brother, had been captured during an Indian raid on their parent's farm near Turtle Creek, Pennsylvania. Years later Lyon remembered how Simon had put him on his knee and "caressed him and treated him so kindly that when Girty was about to leave, he wanted to go with him."[4]

General Haldimand was unsure of enemy intentions, and in the early spring he wrote to De Peyster and urged him to send "an intelligent" spy to Fort Pitt. Girty received the assignment in late April. His orders included a request for him to capture a prisoner, if possible.[5] Accompanied by seventeen trusted Wyandot veterans, Simon surreptitiously made his way to Pittsburgh where, on 5 May, he and his men captured fourteen-year-old John Burkhart. The kidnapping was witnessed and it provoked a strong reaction from the locals. Thirty to forty angry men soon gathered near Fort Pitt, voicing their suspicions that Simon Girty was involved and that John Turner, Jr. must have aided and abetted his outlaw half-brother. They talked about marching on Turner's farm, burning out his buildings and driving him off, or worse. They were checked somewhat by a local man of influence named Pat Murphy who argued convincingly on John Turner's behalf.

Word of the ongoing meeting soon reached Turner and within hours he presented himself before his accusers. Highly annoyed, he told the ringleaders that unless his neighbors let him alone and had confidence in him he would "of necessity, not choice" be forced to join the British. Impressed by his courage, and by more of Pat Murphy's assurances, Turner's accusers relented and he was allowed to return home without further incident.[6]

Whether Simon actually visited his half-brother at the time of John Burkhart's capture cannot be verified, but—given Simon's nature—it is more than likely. For most of the combatants of the frontier war (rebel or Loyalist), the prospect of peace brought with it the tantalizing possibility that at last there might be an opportunity to safely travel back to their former homes to visit friends and relatives. Such fantasies were out of the question for the Girty renegades, whose break with America was irreparable. Branded as war criminals and social demons, and with prices on their heads, they could never return home. Interviewed in 1846 by Lyman C. Draper, ninety-year-old James Blashford, reflecting back more than six decades, remembered that, "about 1783, a party of 17 Indians captured John Brinkhart [sic] on Squirrel Hill, 5 miles from Pittsburgh...." By mentioning the location as "Squirrel Hill," Blashford's statement indicates Girty's presence in the same area where John Turner, Jr. resided. It is difficult to believe that Simon did not take advantage of such an opportunity. In addition to John Turner, Jr., Simon's aged mother still resided on Squirrel Hill.[7]

As Simon and his Wyandots retreated with their young captive they heard Fort Pitt's heavy cannons being fired. Pausing to listen, Girty asked Burkhart why he thought the big guns were being discharged. The boy replied that it was to celebrate the end of the war. Girty hurried back to Detroit where Burkhart's answer was confirmed.

Officially, peace terms had been signed on 17 April, but it was not until 6 May that De Peyster received notification. He immediately rushed orders to McKee to see that all war parties were recalled and to arrange for early meetings with principal Indian leaders. As instructed by General Haldimand, De Peyster omitted any details of the peace terms in his written orders, for fear of angering the Indians.

In mid-June, Simon Girty and agent William Tucker were serving as interpreters at a council between the Indian Department and Wyandot leaders at Detroit. Representing the king were Lt. Colonel De Peyster, Captain Henry Bird, and four lieutenants. According to the recorded minutes of this meeting, Half King (principal speaker for the Wyandots), addressed De Peyster as follows:

MINUTES OF COUNCIL MEETING, DETROIT, 14 JUNE 1783

Father!

Listen to me since this is the day that the Great Spirit has allowed us to meet you in this Council House where you have seen us often assembled.

Father!

These strings were delivered us by Simon Girty whom you sent to acquaint us that it was your desire we should sit still and not go to war until we had heard from You. There are the strings and we have listened to them. You also desired that we should send a few young men by Simon Girty in order to take a prisoner to give you intelligence. You were so particular as to Desire that none might go on this errand that had lost friends in the war. That Father, would have been a difficult matter as most of our nation have suffered. We however went to take a prisoner and here he is, we present him....

Further notes in the minutes describe what happened next:

[Half King] Delivers the prisoner John Buircart, 10 years of age, taken on the Nine Mile Run....

.... He was asked by the Colonel how he was treated since taken? The boy answered they had treated him quite well.[8]

Following orders, De Peyster and his subordinates refrained from disclosing any prohibited information, and made no promises to their guests. While the councils were taking place, arrangements were already underway to transport American prisoners to Montreal for repatriation, and young Thomas Edgerton (whom Girty had earlier befriended) was among the first group of 492 Americans whom De Peyster sent home. This was but the beginning of the gargantuan task of delivering prisoners taken along the Ohio frontier to the American officials in the East. Although most of the returnees had been quartered at Detroit, there were still hundreds of captive American men, women and children held by Indians at remote villages. Finding these people, redeeming them from the Indians, and bringing them to Detroit for eventual transport to the United States soon became an important preoccupation for all the Indian Department's field agents—including Simon Girty.

Sent under a white flag by General George Rogers Clark, Major

George Walls met with Alexander McKee at the Shawnee Towns to discuss repatriation. Accompanied by a Shawnee captive whom the Americans were returning as a sign of good faith, Walls explained that he had been sent to arrange for prisoner transfers. Then he inquired specifically as to the situation of a Mrs. Charles Polke and her children—all recently captured. Walls explained that her husband, a captain serving on General Clark's staff, was greatly concerned.

McKee sent an express letter to De Peyster, who responded quickly, instructing McKee to ask Major Walls to please inform the people of Kentucky that the British were doing everything possible to restrain the Indians. Walls was also to be told that until the conditions of the peace terms were known, it would be unsafe for Americans to travel in Indian country. As for Mrs. Polke and her children, De Peyster was happy to report that they were all safe and well, and were in fact quartered within his own house.

Only months after the preliminary articles of peace had been signed in Paris, the Americans made their first attempt to take lands across the Ohio River without spending blood or money (both of which they had very little to spare). On 16 June, American envoy Major Ephraim Douglas arrived at Captain Pipe's village at Upper Sandusky, accompanied by Captain George McCully and a guide. Before the war Douglas had traded out of Fort Pitt, and he was once a good friend to Matthew Elliott. Douglas had left from Pennsylvania a week earlier with orders to inform the western and northern tribes that Great Britain "had been compelled to make peace with the United States, to cede all the lands to the Mississippi, and to vacate the forts at Detroit and Niagara." Douglas was also to advise the western and northern tribes that the United States now claimed possession of all their lands by right of conquest. It was all a bluff. Men were leaving the militias and going home in droves. Hundreds of soldiers were being discharged from the Continental Army, which was out of supplies and quickly running out of money. Still, the scheme that Douglas had been sent to effect was worth a good try. If it failed, they would make other attempts. Thousands of acres were needed to fulfill the enlistment promises of free land that had been made to officers and men. If there was no other way, America would clear the Indians off by force.

Douglas asked Captain Pipe to arrange for him to deliver his message to a large assembly of Indians.[9]

Pipe was cordial to Douglas, but the wily old Delaware told him he could not participate in any peace talks until the Americans had first treated with his more powerful neighbors, the Shawnees and Wyandots. Having already ascertained that Half King was the most significant Wyandot leader in the region, Douglas hurried to Upper Sandusky to see him, but the chief was away attending talks at Detroit. Pomoacan's wife told Douglas she expected him to return within a few days. At her urging, Douglas agreed to wait. While he waited he wrote to Matthew Elliott, asking his support in persuading Shawnee leaders to come to Upper Sandusky to meet with him. Instead of answering his old friend's request, Elliott rushed a copy of Douglas's note to De Peyster. De Peyster immediately invited Douglas to come to Detroit, and to be accompanied by Matthew Elliott.

By the end of the month Sir John Johnson, British Superintendent General of Indian Affairs, had arrived at Detroit where Lt. Colonel De Peyster had already gathered chiefs from eleven tribes. Although he was ill, Girty worked the meetings as principal translator. Representing the king, Johnson and De Peyster announced to the Indians that peace was at hand, that they should bury the hatchet; but that they should remain ready to defend themselves vigorously if they were invaded.

On 4 July 1783, when the councils were well underway, Ephraim Douglas arrived with Matthew Elliott. Meeting Douglas in private, De Peyster was courteous and hospitable, but he flatly rejected the American's request to address the Indians. De Peyster was justifiably concerned. If the tribes learned that England had been forced to give away their lands all the way to the Mississippi and the Great Lakes without considering, involving, or even mentioning their native allies in the peace terms, the consequences would be catastrophic. Nevertheless, after he returned to the councils De Peyster told the Indians essential elements of Douglas's message: that England and the United States had made peace, and that the Americans now wanted to make peace with all the Indians. Supporting him, Sir John Johnson tactfully communicated that the king would no longer be able to assist the Indians in making war against the Americans. Although they were denied direct access to Ephraim Douglas, the chiefs expressed their willingness for peace by surrounding his quarters and saluting him whenever he was visible through a window.

Pressed by Douglas, De Peyster finally told the persistent American that he, as the commander of Detroit, lacked authority to deal with such matters. He urged Douglas to travel on to Niagara where he could discuss the issue with General Allan MacLean. Douglas agreed. Provided an escort, the American ambassador left Detroit for Niagara on 7 July.

On the same day, De Peyster wrote to General MacLean that "Simon Girty, a Principal Evidence, is too ill to proceed to Niagara."[10]

There are no further details about Girty's illness, which may have stemmed from a local virus (both Joseph Brant and Alexander McKee were also ill) or from recurring problems of his head injury. Despite his condition, he took time to seek out John Burkhart to let him know that arrangements had been made for him to return home. The boy was to be sent back to Fort Pitt in the company of one of the guides who had come to Detroit with Major Douglas. Simon wished Burkhart well, and the former captive always remembered him in a kindly way.

Despite British efforts to keep the surrender terms from the tribes, the truth erupted simultaneously at Oswego, Niagara, Quebec and Detroit. Rumors ran rampant about the desertion of their British allies on all counts—including abandonment. Refusing to consider themselves a conquered people, the Indians were outraged to learn that their lands had been surrendered to the Americans without their consent. Still, despite their feeling of having been betrayed, the chiefs could not afford to sever cordial relations with English authorities.

Next, most likely provoked by Douglas, rumors reached the chiefs that the United States would soon declare that every Indian nation who had fought as allies to the British during the war had abrogated all their land rights; and as a result, these nations should move off at once to Canada or west of the Mississippi. On paper the Americans could claim anything they liked, but the eviction of the tribes from their homelands was something that could only be accomplished by considerably larger and more effective armies than any the United States had fielded during the frontier war of the Revolution. The unintended result of the great American deception was the rapid growth of a deep sense of need for confederation among the western and northern tribes.

Ephraim Douglas arrived at Niagara on 11 July, by which time Joseph Brant and some 1,600 other Six Nation warriors and sachems had gathered to meet with General MacLean and Sir John Johnson (who had not yet arrived). MacLean received Douglas cordially but, as De Peyster had done, he withheld permission for the American to formally address the Indians. When Douglas protested, MacLean suggested he travel to Quebec to meet with General Frederick Haldimand. Frustrated, Douglass said he had done enough in an effort to complete his mission and expressed a desire to return home. MacLean gladly arranged immediate passage for him to depart aboard a vessel bound for Oswego, New York.

On 18 July, after Sir John Johnson finally arrived at Niagara, the meetings with Joseph Brant and the Six Nations commenced. Girty was either at Detroit or Upper Sandusky where, in early August, news of what had transpired at Niagara reached him. He, McKee and Elliott learned most of the details from official reports and from what they were able to glean from returning interpreters. Seeking to appease their Indian allies, the British offered land in Canada for the use of any Mohawks or Senecas who wished to leave New York. Joseph Brant was already evaluating tracts located along the north shore of Lake Ontario for that purpose. Sir John Johnson had assured the Indians that the placement of boundaries, as stated in the peace treaty with the Americans, had nothing to do with the Indians' right to their own lands. Those rights, Johnson emphasized, had been indelibly established by the treaty of Fort Stanwix in 1768 which, in spite of the current peace accord with the United States, was still in force. Once again Johnson urged the Indians to avoid launching any offensive attacks against the United States, but advised them to be prepared to strongly defend their lands if they were invaded.

Responding to Johnson, Kayingwaurto, principal war chief of the

Senecas, declared that if the Americans attempted to take any part of their country the Six Nations would instantly go on the warpath and ask assistance from the king. Johnson had no response.

At the close of the Niagara councils Brant, along with some fifty other Six Nation chiefs and warriors, received Johnson's blessings to go to Lower Sandusky to organize a confederation with thirty-five western nations. From the British perspective a strong anti-American alliance among the western and northern tribes was good for the defense of Canada. To demonstrate British support for the proposed alliance and to help assure a significant and enthusiastic audience for Brant at Lower Sandusky, the schooner *Faith* was secured, heavily loaded with presents at Niagara, and sent on its way. Word of the vessel's cargo, sailing and purpose was sent ahead to the western tribes.

For Girty, the news that Joseph Brant was coming must have overshadowed everything else. He had not seen Brant since the fateful night two years earlier when the arrogant Mohawk had nearly killed him. Although Simon had been told that Brant had apologized profusely for what he had done to him, Girty had been waiting a long time to confront his assailant.

On 18 August when Brant and his Six Nation deputies arrived at Detroit to conduct some preliminary business before going on to Lower Sandusky, Girty was there waiting for him. According to notes taken from an 1864 interview of Girty's daughter, Mrs. Sarah Munger, Lyman C. Draper wrote that:

Girty brought two pistols and two swords and laid them on the table, and told Brant to take his choice and they would fight it out—not go sneaking behind his back, but come boldly and bravely before his face. Brant shed tears ... and begged Girty's forgiveness, and Girty forgave him. They subsequently served together, but Girty always represented that Brant never placed himself where there was danger.[11]

Whether or not Simon Girty's daughter exaggerated the account of her father's confrontation with Brant is unknown. Other records support her claim, indicating that after his injury, Girty's first meeting with

Brant did take place at Detroit, about mid-August of 1783. It is also well established that Girty generally wore two pistols tucked in a sash about his waist, and swords were readily available. Rather than slap Brant in the face with a glove and issue a gentlemanly challenge, it was Girty's style to barge into Brant's room, dump two pistols and a pair of cutlasses on a table, and then dare his opponent to pick one or the other and fight him face-to-face. On the other hand, Girty was a consummate schemer, and he had several months to plan his confrontation. Believing his opponent a coward, he may have gambled that if he took Brant on in private, the Mohawk would back down. However their confrontation unfolded, Brant's response most likely was (as Mrs. Munger disclosed) a sincere apology—which the frontiersman evidently accepted. Both participants had good reason to avoid a physical clash. Brant knew that Girty was important and highly respected among the western nations, and that if he slew or seriously wounded him just before the Sandusky meetings the odds for achieving a successful Indian confederation would be dramatically reduced. He needed Girty's support, not his blood. As for Simon, he knew that the English government earnestly wanted the proposed Indian alliance behind which Brant was the driving force; and, while he craved personal revenge, he too was strongly in favor of the proposed confederation. Without a committed alliance with which to oppose the land-hungry Americans, the Six Nations, the Ohio Indians—and perhaps Canada too—all faced bleak and uncertain futures.

In a letter dated 11 August, De Peyster advised General MacLean that "I have delivered up the management of the Indian Department to Mr. McKee, so [I] have got rid of a deal of trouble."[12] McKee's promotion reinforced Girty's job security. Shortly afterward, Girty was pleasantly surprised at the sudden and unexpected appearance of his brothers Thomas Girty and John Turner, Jr.

Simon's brothers had traveled with another Pennsylvanian named McCarty. Thomas was forty-four years old now, and John was twenty-eight. The two "American Girtys" had come to Canada to see their brothers and to explore the possibility of moving there. Both men had suffered because of their ties to their notorious siblings, and they had no reason to believe their situations would improve in the future.

They explained that they were also representing other Pennsylvanians who faced persecution for not supporting the American cause. They wanted to see what encouragement there might be for them all to move to Canada and settle under British rule. In order to facilitate a complete reunion, George and James Girty were summoned to Detroit and Simon remained there with his brothers until late in the month, when he departed for Lower Sandusky in order to participate in the confederation councils.

Simon had never seen Lower Sandusky so crowded. Concerned for the future, and attracted by the promise of English presents that were being unloaded from the schooner *Faith,* more than 1,500 Indians (including women and children) had gathered. In addition to Joseph Brant and his entourage, there were Hurons from Upper Canada; Wyandots, Delawares, Shawnees, Mingoes, Miamis from the Ohio Country; Ottawas and Chippewas from the Great Lakes; and Creeks and Cherokees from as far south as Florida. Strangely, Girty's old friend and patron Guyasuta was notably absent.

On Monday, 1 September, Half King arrived with 300 of his people. Two days later the Shawnees turned up. An initial meeting between the Indians took place on Friday the 5th, and Girty served as one of its three interpreters. The Cherokees and Shawnees told Brant and the Six Nations representatives "of their willingness to join in defence of their country, which appeared to them at this time more necessary than ever, as the Americans were encroaching upon different parts of it...."[13]

General meetings commenced on the 6th of September. Representing English interests were Alexander McKee, Deputy Agent for Indian Affairs; Captain Isidore Chesne, Ottawa and Chippewa Interpreter; Captain Matthew Elliott, head of all Indian agents; Lieutenant W. Johnson, officer of the Royal British Marines; and Simon Girty, interpreter for the council. Speaking through Chesne and Girty, McKee saluted the nations which had assembled, and then began the conference by restating what Sir John Johnson had said at Niagara—that the Indians' right to occupy their homelands had not been given away by the recent treaty with the Americans and that the Fort Stanwix boundaries were still in effect. McKee then elaborated

on the relationship between the Indian nations and the British Crown
and how the Indians should behave in the future:

---

*… the King still considers you his faithful allies as his children
and will continue to promote your happiness by his protection
and encouragement of your usual intercourse with Trade, & all
other benefits in his power to afford you. Therefore I do in the
most earnest manner recommend to you for your own advantage,
to bear your Losses with manly fortitude, forgiving & forgetting
what is past, looking forward in full hopes and expectation that
on the return of the Blessings of Peace, and cool and just reflection, all animosity and enmity will cease, conciliation succeed,
and Friendship be renewed, and as a proof of your Inclination to
promote that desirable end, let me once more recommend to you
to collect and give up without exception all Prisoners that may
be yet among you, and as an inducement to comply with what I
recommend, and as a proof of His Majesty's bounty and attention:
I have brought up a large assortment of everything necessary to
supply your wants.*[14]

On the 7th, Brant's moment came. Speaking through Girty and
Chesne, the Mohawk consoled the Indian nations for all the warriors
they had lost during the war and explained why the Mohawks had
joined the British cause. Then Brant summarized what the British at
Niagara had told the Six Nations, after which he asked the assembled
Indians to refrain from taking any independent actions against the
Americans and to set all their prisoners at liberty. Finally, he asked for
their commitment to confederation:

---

*Brothers and Nephews. You the Hurons, Delawares, Shawanese,
Mingoes, Ottawas, Chippeweys, Pouttewatamies (sic), Creeks and
Cherokees. We the Six Nations with this belt bind your Hearts
and minds with ours, that there may be never hereafter a separation between us, let there be Peace or War, it shall never disunite
us, for our Interests are alike, nor should anything ever be done
but by the voice of the whole as we make but one with you.*[15]

Brant's appeal for confederacy was well-received, as the Ohio Indians were already having problems with the Americans. Before any confederacy would work for the benefit of all, the Indians, with the Six Nations as their collective voice, had to deal directly with American encroachment occurring along the Ohio River boundary. Addressing McKee as a trusted friend, Half King, responded on behalf of the Indians in general.

> *Father! Listen! As also our Brethren the Six Nations, you have told us there is peace. You know the Rights of our Indians in this Country, and you also know that the Tomahawk is now laid down. Brethren the Six nations, you know where the Boundary Line was fixed, since you were the people who fixed it. We now inform you that the Virginians are already encroaching upon our Lands, and we desire you and our Father to be strong, and desire them to desist from encroaching upon us, otherwise, they will destroy the good work of Peace which we are endeavoring to promote. This is all that we have to say.*[16]

Taking advantage of the high note of hope, McKee thanked the assembly for complying with the King's requests and for being unanimous in "doing right. I am well pleased." McKee closed the assembly by complimenting the various representatives working together as one body with like needs and interests.[17]

Brant closed the conference by symbolically binding the nations together and by promising that on its behalf the Six Nations would now confront the Americans over the encroachment of the Virginians. The bulk of the English presents were distributed on the 9th, and within a few days the delegates started to leave Lower Sandusky for their home villages. From both the English and Six Nation perspectives the conference had been a resounding success. Some thirty-five Indian nations, most of which occupied the Ohio Country and the approaches to Canada, were now united against the Americans. Although Girty's only role had been that of interpreter, his presence and attitude had demonstrated his support for the alliance. Apparently Girty was able to work cooperatively with Joseph Brant even though he had no respect for the man. In Girty's heart, a deep, cold chasm would always remain between them.

The Indian leaders understood that the current peace between their people and the Americans was temporary. They also recognized that the new confederation gave them a strength they had never had before in dealing with the Americans who wanted to emigrate west into the Ohio Valley. More importantly they had heard enough from McKee and the other English representatives to gamble on the premise that when they needed them, the British would be there to supply food, muskets, gunpowder and lead. After all, McKee had just told them that trade would continue. What the chiefs accurately perceived was that their father, the English king, was afraid of losing Canada.

Girty's communication skills had served a vital role building a verbal bridge between the Indians and the British, and he had successfully reconfirmed his commitment to protecting the Indians' homelands. Like everyone who attended the confederation councils, Simon knew that the current peace was smoldering and would eventually be destroyed by a raging conflagration.

CHAPTER FIFTEEN
THE RESCUE OF CATHERINE MALOTT

AS SOON AS THE CONFEDERATION councils concluded, Girty started back to Detroit where John Turner and his elder brother were still contemplating a move to Canada. During his journey, Simon had time to digest what had taken place during the Sandusky meetings. Despite their dislike for each other, he and Joseph Brant had worked very well together. Brant had been brilliant at keeping the meetings on course, and in the end the confederation they had worked for was a reality. McKee expected Simon to help the tribes maintain the unity they had just achieved. This was no easy task. In the past, even a few stolen horses or a drunken brawl had been enough to tear apart confederations which at the onset had seemed all-powerful. Nevertheless, with skill, rips in the fabric of intertribal unity could be mended. It was when the enemy succeeded in making a deal on the side, and a trusted member of the longhouse betrayed all his brothers, that serious, possibly irreparable damages could occur. There was no doubt in anyone's mind that the Americans would attempt to break the confederation.

John Turner was eagerly awaiting Simon's return to Detroit. When Simon arrived, Thomas was across the Detroit River inspecting lands that might be suitable for farming. Before he had left for the confederation councils at Sandusky, Simon had encouraged both of the "American Girtys" to move to Canada. Thomas was still undecided, but John had made up his mind. He informed Simon that he was going to stay at Pittsburgh, and then he revealed his affection for a beautiful young woman named Susannah York, who awaited him there. John confessed that his trip to Canada had only made him realize how much he longed for her, and he had decided to marry her as soon as he returned. He had been ready to go home for some time, he explained, but had waited to see Simon once again, to tell him his decision and to say good-bye.

Both men realized they might not see each other again for a long time, if ever. There should be little doubt that Simon was saddened by that reality, yet, at the same time, it must have pleased him that his twenty-eight year old half-brother had found a woman who brought him such joy and longing. There was little else for him to do but swallow hard, wish John the best, and then try and arrange a suitable escort for his half-brother's long and dangerous journey home.

Sometime after John had departed, the thought of his younger brother's happiness may have prompted Simon to reflect upon his own situation. He was now forty-two and still without a family or land of his own. For the first time in years there was time for him to look for a companion, but where? If she were Indian, she would have to be comfortable in the white world, and if she were white, it was the other way around. Girty also knew there was more to it than just needing a woman who easily moved between two opposing cultures. He had learned that lesson from his affair with Elizabeth Lowrey, the beautiful half-breed woman he had lived with at Pittsburgh. She had enjoyed the company of whites, or Indians, or both, and she had shined in any crowd where people were drinking, talking, laughing, and having fun. But his work and life required him to be away for long periods of time, and for this and other reasons, their relationship had soured.

Simon was at Upper Sandusky during the first week of October 1783 when two Americans en route to Detroit paused there. One was Jonathan Zane, the veteran frontiersman whom Simon had served with during Dunmore's War, and the other was a young officer named Captain Charles Polke. Zane was happy to see Simon again, now that the hostilities were over. He introduced Polke and explained that he was guiding him to Detroit, where he would collect his captive wife and children, whom he had recently learned were quartered in De Peyster's house. Girty knew of them and reassured Polke that his family was healthy and doing well. Zane and Polke's horses needed a breather, and Girty invited the two men to remain at Sandusky as his guests. There was a lot to share, and the two men quickly agreed.

Polke had last seen his wife, their seven-year-old son and three younger daughters late in August a year earlier, just after the big American defeats at Sandusky and Blue Licks. At that time Polke had been serving in the defense of several small forts or stations located near Louisville, and he and his family had quarters at a place called Kincheloe's Station. Hearing that a large war party was headed their way, Polke's superior, Colonel Isaac Cox, rushed a messenger to him asking him to bring as many of his men as he felt could be spared from the defense of Kincheloe's Station and rendezvous with another officer and a number of soldiers. The proposed meeting would have enabled the American defenders to move quickly to the defense of any of the local settlements that might be attacked. Unfortunately for Polke, Kincheloe's Station was under enemy observation at the time, and it was attacked an hour before daybreak the day after he and his men left. During the initial assault, Indians scaled the walls and quickly broke through the roofs of many of the perimeter cabins. One man, a woman and a child were killed, while two men, four women and a boy escaped and made their way to the next station, where they revealed what had happened. All in all, some thirty of the inhabitants, men, women and children, had been captured, including Mrs. Polke and all her children. Adding to the stress of her dire situation, the young mother was seven months pregnant. A full year had passed before Polke finally learned that his family was alive and together at Detroit, and that two months after her capture, his wife had given birth to their second son.

Girty knew that it was Zane who had piloted Crawford's army to Sandusky, and he was concerned that if Zane tried to take Polke on to Detroit, he might be recognized by some warrior and made to suffer. He voiced his apprehensions and advised Zane that it might be best for him to start back for home as soon as his horse was ready to travel. Girty promised Zane that he would see to it that Polke was safely taken to Detroit, and that the captain and his family would be escorted home with reliable guides. Zane was grateful for Simon's warning and, after obtaining Polke's permission, he took Girty's advice.

Because of congenial meetings like the one he had just had with Polke and Zane, it may have been difficult for Girty to comprehend the depth of hatred and fear that most Americans on the frontier had for him. There were thousands who had heard nothing but the worst about him, and who knew him only as the frontier's most treacherous, blood-thirsty renegade. Most of these folks would have paid to watch him hang. At the same time frontiersmen and soldiers who knew him from before the war, and even some who had later served against him, had few if any reservations about dealing with the infamous "white savage," or trusting his word. Captain Polke was not the least disturbed at the prospect of placing his life and that of his loved ones into Simon Girty's hands.

After Jonathan Zane departed for his home at Wheeling, Girty provided Polke with an Indian escort and sent him on to Detroit. On 15 October, Polke returned to Upper Sandusky accompanied by his relieved and happy family, plus four other American children whom De Peyster had placed into his care. De Peyster had also provided Polke with a passport to return through the Indian country, and had sent an officer as far as Sandusky with a speech for the Wyandot chiefs, warning them not to molest the Polkes while they were passing through their country. Polke told Girty that many of the prisoners at Detroit wanted to leave for home with him, but that De Peyster had refused to let any of them go, except for three young sisters (the daughters of a widow who had escaped during the attack on Linn's Station), and the son of the only man who had been killed there. Polke had promised to see these youngsters back safely to their families. De Peyster furnished them all with adequate clothing, and had even made a present of a horse and saddle to the eldest of the three sisters, an eleven-year-old who had lived with De Peyster's family, and who had been treated as one of their own.

Simon explained to Polke that he had arranged for his older brother Thomas to accompany him and his family on the trip south from Sandusky. However, it would be two days before Thomas Girty was due to arrive and, eager to renew their relationships, the Polkes made good use of this free time.

Wishing to increase their security, Captain Polke hired an aged Delaware as another guide and intermediary, and he hired one of that man's younger relations to serve as a hunter. Anxious to be on their way, the Polkes departed almost immediately after Thomas Girty's arrival.

Like John Turner, Thomas Girty had also decided to remain in Pennsylvania. In good spirits, Simon rode along with his brother and the others for a few miles. When Polke showed interest, Simon toured him over the battleground at Sandusky where Crawford had been defeated, detailing the moves of both sides for the captain's benefit. He concluded his tour by confiding to Polke that, in his opinion, had Colonel Crawford continued the initial pursuit some ten minutes longer at the start of the fighting, the Americans would most certainly have defeated them, for at that moment, "the Indians were about commencing a general retreat." Fearing an ambush, Colonel Crawford had instead halted his advance to take up defensive positions in the timber, and that was his fatal decision. Sorry to lose their company, Girty finally bade goodbye to his brother and the Polkes, wishing them all a safe journey.[1]

At the end of the month General Haldimand gave permission to General MacLean to go home to England, replacing him with De Peyster, who immediately departed for Niagara to take command of the troops in the Upper Country, as well as the King's Regiment. Haldimand appointed a former fur trader named Jehu Hay to serve as Lieutenant Governor and to take over command at Detroit.

As the winter drew on, American leaders backed away from their designs of expelling all the Iroquois from New York, and of forcing the western tribes to move off their lands and pay war reparations. It was apparent that the Indians were angry, that they were determined to resist, and that they had formed alliances. In truth, neither the American Confederation government nor any of the individual states were prepared to take on the united tribes. In July 1783, General Philip Schuyler of New York wrote to the president of Congress, assuring him that continued wars against the Indians were unnecessary.

Schuyler contended that if the Indians were allowed to remain within the United States, their presence would not prevent American settlers from inhabiting some of the lands the Indians now held. There would surely be cessions, as a result of America having defeated England. Then, according to Schuyler, whatever lands the Indians still retained would steadily erode, because:

> ... *for as our settlements approach their country, they must, from the scarcity of game, which that approach will induce to, retire farther back, and dispose of their lands, unless they dwindle comparatively to nothing, as all savages have done, who gain their sustenance by the chase, when compelled to live in the vicinity of civilized people, and thus leave us the country without the expense of a purchase, trifling as that will probably be.*[2]

As John B. Ingram pointed out in his thesis *Simon Girty: Degeneration Through Violence:*

> *In short, the presence of whites on ceded territory near Indians would drive away the game on which the savages were dependent. As a result the Indians would willfully abandon to the whites lands which had been granted the red men in perpetuity.*[3]

What Schuyler proposed was ecological warfare. Quick to endorse the new strategy, George Washington joined Schuyler in advocating that new land treaties be made with the Indians, not in order to preserve their lands, but "to preserve American peace while taking Indian land."[4]

In Canada, General Frederick Haldimand was devising countering strategies. As Robert S. Allen mentioned in his book *His Majesty's Indian Allies,* the general was concerned that the situation between the northern and western tribes and the United States might explode, and in a November 1783 letter to Lord North, Halidmand proposed that British posts in the country northwest of the Ohio River be maintained indefinitely.

Soon, the conflicting strategies of Haldimand and Washington would have a direct and dangerous bearing on Simon Girty's life, but for the moment he was happily occupied. In the interests of promoting the fragile peace, the British Indian Department had been assigned the responsibility of locating and securing the release of all the American captives being held by Indians. In November, among the list of captives whom Girty was ordered to try and find was an eighteen-year-old woman named Catherine Malott. The girl's mother, Sarah Malott, had visited the Indian Department office at Detroit to beg for help in locating and securing the release of her missing children.

Helping to repatriate captives suited Girty's nature. For someone who was multi-lingual and who enjoyed traveling from one Indian town to another, finding and liberating American captives was an ideal assignment. The detective work was both interesting and difficult as there were no photographs and, due to the lengths of time in captivity, even physical descriptions of missing people, particularly young people, were unreliable. This was especially true in the case of children who had matured during their captivity. For the searcher, even a captive's English name was of little use; once they had been adopted, the individual would have been given an Indian name early in the resocialization process. The most dependable information the rescuer had to work from were the descriptions of where and when the captive had been taken, their age at the time of capture, their coloring and general description, and any information that might reveal the tribal affiliations of the captors.

The most that Girty could have learned about Catherine Malott was that she had been taken the last week of March 1780, some three years and four months earlier, at which time she had been fifteen-years old. She would be close to nineteen now, tall, brown-eyed and dark-haired. According to Sarah Malott, she and her husband Peter, along with their two daughters Catherine and Keziah, and son, Peter Jr., were among a large party of settlers traveling to Kentucky via the Ohio River. They were aboard three flat boats floating downstream on the river when they were attacked. Mr. Malott was aboard a stock boat that was carrying the party's cattle while his wife and children were on another boat. Somewhere near the mouth of Captina Creek (which empties into the Ohio some twenty-one miles below Wheeling), a mixed war party of Muncie Delawares, Mingoes and Wyandots attacked the three boats, capturing two of them. Several men and a child were killed during the attack, and some twenty-one people were captured. The stock boat, with Peter Malott aboard, escaped and continued downriver, and Mrs. Malott did not know whether her husband had survived. Along with some other of the captives, she was eventually taken to Detroit and ransomed, but her children remained with the Indians. By the time Simon Girty received the details, Peter Malott, Jr. had been retrieved, but both Malott daughters were still missing. For Simon, familiarity with the tribes of the warriors involved in the capture was only a starting point, for captives were often traded or given away to members of other tribes.

There is some uncertainty about exactly where and how he found her, but in the spring of 1784, following a long, bleak winter, Girty reluctantly handed Catherine Malott back to her mother at Detroit. There can be no doubt that he regarded this gesture as a loan. During their journey north, Catherine had stolen the heart of her rescuer. By all accounts the nineteen-year-old was an extraordinary beauty. In his 1870 book *Our Western Border,* Charles McKnight wrote:

> One of the captives said she was 'a right pretty girl,' reported to be the prettiest in Detroit.[5]

According to a booklet published by the former Henry Hotel, Pittsburgh:

> Picture No. 32 forms one of the decorative features of the bar. Its subject is a dusky but beautiful maiden, garbed in savage drapery, crossing a stream upon the stepping-stones of a rocky ford. Its title is 'O-ta-wa-ta,' which, translated from the Indian tongue, means 'White Pigeon.'
>
> O-ta-wa-ta was the heroine of a life drama as full of adventure and romance as was ever coined in the imagery of fiction. She was a white girl of French descent, born in Maryland in 1764, and named Catherine Malott ... [etc.][6]

Although the Henry Hotel painting of Catherine Malott (which was painted in the late 1800s) was unquestionably a product of the artist's vivid imagination, its existence nevertheless serves well to illustrate Catherine's legendary beauty.

According to Girty descendants, the 43-year-old Simon "fell hard for Catherine Malott the moment he first saw her, and by the time the two of them reached Detroit, they were deeply in love." The family story further claims that in order to secure her release, Simon either bought her freedom or tricked the Shawnees who held her, telling them that he only wished to take her to Detroit to visit her mother, after which he promised that he would return her. When he interviewed Catherine Girty, the widow of Simon's son Prideaux, early American historian Lyman Copeland Draper was told the same story.[7]

While Girty had been chasing down Catherine Malott, negotiations had been ongoing between the Wyandots, Ottawas and British authorities at Detroit concerning a valuable, seven-square mile tract of land situated some eighteen miles below the fort on the east side of the Detroit river. One of the most favorable spots in Upper Canada, it was ideally situated on the line of communication between Detroit and the Maumee Valley, and allowed access to the whole country stretching down to the Ohio and along the Wabash. The Indians wanted to award this land to the Indian Department officers and interpreters who had fought with them during the war. Although several years would pass before final legal transfers were to be approved, General Haldimand gave his approval for the Indian Department men to take possession. Among the nine to receive lots in this tract were Simon Girty, Alexander McKee, Matthew Elliott, Henry Bird, and William Caldwell. Taking up residence in late 1783, Elliott and Caldwell were among the first to build improvements on lots located opposite the lower end of Bois Blanc Island. This was the beginning of the Township of Malden, County of Essex, and in early spring of 1784, Girty was happy to provisionally receive his own 164-acre parcel. The place was a fine, flat piece of land which looked out on Lake Erie at the very mouth of the Detroit River. In August, with Sarah Malott's approval, Simon and his beautiful young bride were married by an "itinerant" preacher of the Church of England—most likely a man named Robert Pollard. Simon, at last, had roots.

Girty wasted no time erecting a two-story frame house and having some of his farmland cleared. By then, Catherine was carrying their first child. A sociable character, Simon was an energetic host. Catherine was sure of herself and it appears she enjoyed entertaining frequent guests, red and white alike. Early in 1785, their son John Girty was born. A few months later the infant took ill and despite every effort by Simon and Catherine, he died about mid-year. Grief-stricken, Simon buried his little boy not far from the house.

Although Simon could not have learned about it until a much later date, his mother Mary Girty-Turner also died in 1785, and was buried on 31 July by John Turner, Jr. on Squirrel Hill. Many years later, Turner donated the land where his mother was buried to be used as a community cemetery, and for the building of a church to be erected adjacent to the graveyard.

While Girty and his young bride were recovering from the loss of their first-born, the United States attempted to break the Indian confederation by signing treaties with individual tribes. The first of these treaties took advantage of the Six Nations, whose homelands were isolated from the other western and northern tribes. The negotiations began at Fort Stanwix on 12 October 1784. By 20 October discussions had ended, with the American commissioners dictating terms and demanding specific land cessions.

Because of their alliances to the United States during the war, the Oneida and the Tuscaroras were granted possession of their lands, but the remaining Iroquois nations were forced to give-up all of their holdings west of Pennsylvania—in essence Ohio. Following the Fort Stanwix meetings, U.S. Commissioners Arthur Lee and Richard Butler (Girty's old rival from Pittsburgh) met with Indians from beyond the Ohio at Fort Pitt in early December, and again at Fort McIntosh in January 1785. As at the Fort Stanwix meetings, Indian claims were stated to no avail. The treaties the Wyandots, Delawares, Chippewa and Ottawas were forced to sign gave away what is now all of eastern and southern Ohio. The Shawnees, who had resumed raiding along the American frontier for almost a year, were conspicuously absent from both treaties; and, except for the Oneidas and Tuscaroras, the Indians who met with the American commissioners were disgruntled and angry. Faced by aggressive American commissioners, the Indian leaders were cowed into ceding lands that they loved for terms they despised. Initially, the Indians were swayed by the power of the United States' victory over the English. That perception began to erode when the chiefs began to realize that although bands of Shawnees were actively raiding against the Americans, no white army had come forth to punish them. The leaders of the western and northern tribes began to question Yankee strength. Simultaneously, they knew that the English continued to retain possession of their western posts—including Fort Detroit—without rebuke.

Although the British government was treading lightly, in order to avoid outright resumption of war with the Americans, it was nevertheless determined to retain its hold over the Ohio Country and its people, and to dominate the fur trade of the region. This policy was one that coincided ideally with objectives of the commanding officers of the Indian Department; for, in addition to their status as civil servants, McKee, Elliott and Caldwell were all active traders. Indeed, Elliott and Caldwell had just formed a trading company based at Detroit, and the partners had received Haldimand's enthusiastic consent to quickly establish operations in the Ohio Country. Although he did not share his contemporaries' zeal for commerce, Girty was a willing and enthusiastic instrument of current British Indian policy, which centered on the tribes retaining their homelands on the north or westerly side of the Ohio River.

In late 1784 or early 1785, Simon was awarded a pay raise, approved by Superintendent General of the British Indian Department, Sir John Johnson. His new salary was £85.3s annually (85 pounds sterling, 3 shillings). He was asked to continue touring the villages of the Ohio Country for several months, during which time Catherine, still glum over the loss of her infant, was left alone to manage their home at Malden.

Traveling from one village to another, Simon encouraged and cajoled Indian leaders to remain united and stand firm, and his efforts were noticed by the United States. On 18 May 1785, Girty was at Wapatomica interpreting, when chiefs from the Shawnees, Mingoes, Delawares and Cherokees met with United States commissioner James Sherlock and four other Americans—one of whom was William Wilson, an old friend of Simon's. Wilson was in partnership with Girty's former friend David Duncan (owner of Duncan's Tavern and Inn at Fort Pitt). As a gesture, the Indians had brought a young captive with them, eighteen-year-old John Crawford (no relation to William Crawford). A Mingo named Black Wolf had recently captured the young man on the Indian side of the Ohio. Years later, Crawford told his story in a letter to historian Lyman C. Draper:

We were nine days going from where I was taken, to the new Chillicothe town, on waters that ran into the Scioto. And four days waiting there, till they gathered in the council, and sent to Sandusky, for Girty, about 60 miles. I was in eight different towns on my route. When they made me run, instead of running the gauntlet, about twenty-five or thirty men came along by me, and each one gave me a slap on the head or face. When Girty arrived, he came and talked with me. Said he didn't think the Indians would kill me. I was but a boy. He inquired if I was a relation of Colonel Crawford. When the council assembled, they let me right in the midst of them. The council sat two hours in perfect silence. At length, Blue Jacket rose, and made a big speech. Girty interpreted and Wilson, the trader, wrote it down . . .

. . . . They were determined to make the Ohio the line; and after this, to burn every prisoner they caught on this side of the river. That they had been driven further and further back, etc. That they would all die before they would give up an inch more of their land. They killed two traders while I was there, and brought in their fresh scalps on a Spontoon [a long stick, with a spear point on the end]. These were Silas Zane [brother of Girty's friend Jonathan] and George Green. They lived at Wheeling.[8]

Unfamiliar with the geography of the area, John Crawford was mistaken about where he was when he was freed. The event he wrote about actually took place at Wapatomica, not Chillicothe, as he stated;

the Shawnee chief who made the speech that he remembered was not Blue Jacket, but a tall and generally bright-natured Shawnee called Captain Johnny. In a detailed report created later at the headquarters of the British Indian Department at Detroit, Simon dictated Captain Johnny's speech word for word:

You know Brethren Virginians you kindled a council fire at Fort Stanwix, the Six Nations led us by the hand to it, but we heard nothing there that was good from you. Afterwards you kindled another council at Beaver Creek. There two men spoke and we could hear nothing good from you. You told us that all the country was yours. You have kindled two council fires at the first you know how you have treated our Brethren the Six Nations, seized and detained them as prisoners. You have now behaved in the same manner at Fort McIntosh, presently you will kindle another council fire, but if you do it any place near us we will not go to it or listen to you, but if you kindle it at Detroit where our forefathers did, then we will think you are there for some good. Where our Brethren who stand at our backs will hear you. But we see your Intentions, you are drawing close to us. You are so near our bedsides that we can almost hear the noise of your axes felling our trees and settling our country. According to the lines settled by our forefathers, the Boundary is the Ohio River, but you are coming from the ground given us by the Great Spirit. We wish you to be strong and keep your people on that side of the river. We have no objections to carry on trade with your traders, provided they do not attempt to settle in our country, but it is now clear to us your Design is to take our country from us. We remind you that you will find all the people of our color in this Island strong, unanimous and determined to act as one man in defence of it. Therefore be strong and keep your people within bounds or we will take up a Rod and whip them back to your side of the Ohio. It is now incumbent on you to … listen to us, otherwise the consequences of what may happen hereafter will be your fault.

You are always calling to us for your flesh and blood. No doubt you are fond of them. We have them by the hand to deliver to you, if you listen to us, and the contrary if you do not, you will never see them at any other time. What we three nations say to you, are the sentiments of the Six Nations and that of those to the Setting of the Sun.

What we have said we are determined to do without the council or advice of our Father, who formally assisted us when requested.

We have called in Simon Girty that our words should be fully explained to you before him.

The foolish young man [John Crawford]) who was taken in our country encroaching upon us, we deliver to you, that he may serve to prevent others doing what he has done. His companions were sent back when taken.[9]

Two weeks later, Lt. Colonel Josiah Harmar, commanding the new First American Regiment at Fort Pitt, complained to the Secretary of War about Girty's influence.

… Speeches have been continually sent by the British from Detroit to the Indians since the treaty, and I have good intelligence that several traders have been among them, using all means to make them entertain a bad opinion of the Americans. One Simon Girty, I am informed, has been to Sandusky for that purpose. I have taken every means in my power to counteract their proceedings, and have directed the Indians not to listen to their lies, but to tie and bring in here any of those villains who spread reports among them injurious to the United States, in order that they may be punished.[10]

There were now 45,000 settlers in Kentucky and several thousand more had located north of the Ohio River. By August of 1785, small bands of Wyandots and Delawares began to raid those who had settled on "their side" of the river. In September, Girty was called away from home when the British Indian Department learned that American commissioner Richard Butler was on his way to Coshocton to forge a new treaty with the Wyandots, Shawnees, Mingoes, Cherokees, Pottawattamies, Kickapoos and Miamis (all of whom had formed an alliance). In an attempt to prevent these nations from meeting with Butler, Girty and William Caldwell were rushed to Sandusky. Although their efforts to prevent or impede the treaty meeting were unsuccessful, their activities were carefully noted in a report authored by U.S. Commissioner Samuel Montgomery.

In early October, according to journal entries by American emissaries Daniel Elliott and James Rinken, Girty was at the Shawnee town called Mequashake (on Macochee Creek, just east of present West Liberty, Ohio) when the two Americans arrived there for a council. Serving both sides as an interpreter, Simon participated in the return of a captive white woman, Mrs. Thomas Cunningham:

JOURNAL OF DANIEL ELLIOTT

October 8. Was informed by Simon Girty of a prisoner woman that was lately taken by some Mingoes and Cherokees from Monongahela, and was now at the Mingo Chief's house. We spoke to the Wyandotte chief about her, & gave him a string of wampum to speak to the Mingo, which he did cheerfully.

The 9th, Simon Girty and the Mingo chief, with the woman above mentioned, came to our camp, which was along with the Wyandottes, which we looked on to be much the safest. The Mingo made a very long speech, directing his discourse first to the Wyandotte, then to us. When he had finished, he jumped up, caught the woman by her arm, and putting her hand in one of mine, and giving me a string of wampum in the other hand, said, "I deliver you your flesh and blood." We thanked him. We asked Girty to interpret what he said to us; he answered it was not his business, but said it was chiefly forbidding the Half King to go to the treaty, and that he would advise his young men to quit stealing horses and going to war, for he had lost his son at the taking of that woman he was about to deliver up.

The woman's name is Cunningham, [Mrs. Thomas Cunningham] and says that four of her children were [killed or

> *taken] on the eighth day of August last, by five Mingoes and one Cherokee.*[11]

The Yankee strategy of attempting to influence individual tribes was failing, and Girty had become an annoying thorn in America's hide.

At the end of December, by which time all their efforts to bring a majority of the Shawnees to the treaty table at Fort Finney had failed, the Americans sent a new ambassador to the Shawnee towns to speak the American voice—Chief Wingenund of the Delawares. But Wingenund had little favor among the majority of the Shawnee leaders, who stayed away. Still, some Shawnees from the Mequashake region who were in dire need of provisions took their people to Fort Finney. Approximately three hundred Shawnees (men, women and children) were present there on 18 January 1786, including the aged chief Moluntha, who was one of the few Shawnees inclined to make peace with the Americans. Seemingly unaffected by low attendance and the absence of key Shawnee leaders, the Americans nevertheless proceeded with their well-orchestrated program. As at Fort Stanwix and Fort McIntosh, the commissioners dictated all the treaty terms. Shocked by such blatant aggressiveness, the Shawnee chiefs protested they would be left no land upon which to live or raise corn, "God gave us this country," Chief Kekewepellethy (Tame Hawk) argued, "we do not understand measuring out the lands, it is all ours."[12]

No doubt enjoying the moment, Richard Butler admonished the Shawnee leaders: "We plainly tell you that this country belongs to the United States—their blood hath defended it, and will forever protect it." Continuing, Butler summarized the attitude of the Washington administration towards the western Indians, claiming that the government's "proposals are liberal and just; and you instead of acting as you have done, and instead of persisting in your folly, should be thankful for the forgiveness and offers of kindness of the United States."[13]

Chief Kekewepellethy again spoke against the treaty and delivered a string of black wampum to Butler. Butler decided he had had enough. Facing Kekewepellethy, he warned: "the Shawnees could choose peace or war; and if war, it might begin at once." Then he turned and stalked out of the meeting, dashing the string of black wampum against the council table as he left. After a moment, George Rogers Clark stood up and used his cane to push the wampum string off the table, and he trampled it as he walked out.[14]

Left to discuss their situation in isolation, Shawnee resistance rapidly collapsed. The Americans were summoned back to council, and meekly, Chief Kekewepellethy told the commissioners that they had misunderstood him. "Brethren," he said, "our people are sensible of the truths you have told them. You have everything in your power—you are great, and we see you own the whole country."[15]

Butler quickly produced the treaty documents that had been previously prepared, and the Indians were compelled to sign. With their marks, the Shawnees ceded everything east of the Great Miami to the United States.[16]

By the end of January, the Americans had successfully dictated three treaties and, on paper, the signatory tribes had given up all of what is now eastern and southern Ohio. Behind the scenes, Clark was seeking support for a military strike that he wanted to conduct against some of the western tribes, to establish that the United States held the power to destroy the Indians whenever it wished to do so. Clark's proposition was gaining favor.

While the Americans redrew their maps, the anger of the western tribes escalated. Encouraged by British agents like Simon Girty, Alexander McKee and Matthew Elliott, the Indians were determined to overthrow all their hated treaties. As the spring of 1786 drew on, the Shawnees increased their raids against the Americans. With little faith that the Federal government would come to their aid, alarmed settlers in Kentucky began to organize an expedition on their own. As the fever for blood heated up along the Ohio, the British Indian Department took advantage of Simon's influence and kept him busy traveling from one Indian town to another. While he was away, Catherine was isolated at their home, facing another pregnancy and longing for her husband.

In June, Girty, McKee and Elliott were summoned to Niagara by Sir John Johnson, British Superintendent General of Indian Affairs, to take part in councils with representatives from the Shawnees, Wyandots, Ottawas, Chippewas and the Six Nations. Although he had not seen his wife or his home for months, Girty had no choice but to attend. The three Indian agents sailed from Lower Sandusky on June 7th. At Niagara they each played a supportive role to Johnson, who told the Indians they should all be one people, and then, whether they chose to declare war or peace, their pronouncements would be understood much more keenly by their enemies. While they had access to Johnson, the three agents pressed for legal titles to the lands across the river from Detroit, upon which they had already settled.

Girty's activities against American interests were brought to the attention of Congress, when, on 19 June 1786, the deposition of William Doleman was heard. Doleman was a frequent resident of the Shawnee village called McKee's Town (Kispokotha Town, present Logan County, Ohio). According to congressional records:

The deponent saith that Simon Girty, Thomas Smith, Robert Surpluss [Surphlet], McGillis and a Captain William Caldwell are emissaries, paid by Alexander McKee the British Agent at Detroit, to carry messages to, and transact other business with, the Indian Nations....

... That Simon Girty, another of the said emissaries, had said in public where he, the deponent was, that he was sent from Detroit to prevent the Indians from attending the treaty with the United States, which was to be held at the Miami.[17]

As the Americans saw it, Girty and his comrades were the driving force behind Indian resistance northwest of the Ohio River.

Indian raids against the Americans continued, and in response to an urgent request from Governor Patrick Henry of Virginia, on 30 June 1786 Congress ordered Colonel Josiah Harmar and two companies of infantry to march to Louisville. Entirely inadequate, it was the largest force the federal government was able to provide. Governor Henry quickly notified Kentucky officials to organize the militia and actively defend their lives and property by joining the federal forces recently come to their aid. By August, men were assembling; George

Rogers Clark was appointed commander-in-chief, with Colonel Benjamin Logan as his second-in-command. Now a major, Simon Kenton was still serving under Logan.

The Americans struck in early October, during the height of a prolonged drought. Executing a two-pronged attack, Clark and Logan led separate columns deep into Indian country. Due to low water, the supply boats carrying vital provisions were unable to reach their scheduled rendezvous and Clark's campaign against the Wabash tribes fizzled. As the Kentuckians ran out of food, morale plummeted. After a few mutinies and desertions, Clark had no choice but to withdraw before making contact with the enemy. Although Clark's expedition was a disaster, Benjamin Logan's 500-man army was more fortunate. With Major Simon Kenton and Colonel Daniel Boone as pilots, Logan's force surprised the Shawnee towns on the Mad River just when a major council between leaders of the western tribes and the Six Nations was about to commence. In quick succession eight Shawnee towns and hundreds of cornfields were burned. Joseph Brant, who was there representing the Six Nations at the councils, was nearly captured. After inflicting their damage, the invaders quickly withdrew. When it was over, the Indians had suffered twenty warriors killed and eighty captured, along with a winter's supply of food lost, and the homes of hundreds destroyed.

News of the attack reached Simon Girty just after he had returned to Upper Sandusky from the Wabash, where he had been sent to spy on Clark's army, and to bolster Indian resistance. Girty immediately dictated the following report which he rushed to McKee:

Sir,

I inform you that on the 8th Inst. there arrived an Express from the Shawanese Towns to Upper Sandusky, that the American Army had arrived at the Shawanese Towns, and I [receiving] the news made no delay but immediately sent two Runners to said Towns to know the certainty thereof and this day the Runners arrived to me again, and gave me an account that the American Army came into the Town at 12 o'clock in the day; and some time before the Army had arrived in Town, there came in a Deserter who told the Indians that the Yankey [sic] army was coming but the Indians would not believe the Deserter, that they were [a coming] when the Army appeared in sight—Shortly after the Indians of the Maycockey Town (Mackashack), on seeing them [run] their Yanky [sic] Colours to receive them, but [hauling] their colours was to no purpose, the Army immediately destroyed the Town, then proceeded to [Wapatomica] Town and destroyed that likewise, then proceeded from thence to Your House and destroyed that, immediately from thence proceeded to Blue Jacket's and brought that immediately to the ground; and then returned instantly back to [Waketumekin] & there encamped and remained on the Ground that night, the next day made a retreat back again. Whether they have made a total Retreat or not I cannot tell as yet, but this is the word at present. In short, I will be able to acquaint you farther—The number of Indians that were killd I do not know, but in the Town where Capt.n Elias lived, there were 10 Indians found lying in the town dead, and among them was the Chief of the Town slain, and an Indian named [Shade] and another [Missquangheanacke]. The Indians there do say the Yankeys [seized] him up and Burned him, and Mr. Coon's Brother is likewise killd: the number which is killed I do not know yet, but they have taken the women and Children prisoners along with them.

Capt.n Brant if he is alive, I dare say that he has wrote the particulars to you before now; Tomorrow I am determined to proceed to the Shawanese Towns myself to know the certainty thereof, and likewise I am informed that there is an Army to set off from the mouth of Muskingam for the Wayandot Towns, but I am not certain thereof, and the Runners that arrived this day say that an Army is on the way to the White River, that a party went out to spy on them and two of them got killd. And then an Indian arrived from Fort Pitt and gave me an Account that there is no more Indians at that place and they have all left it and come off. The bearer of this letter, I hope you will satisfy,

I remain "etc.,"

Simon Girty

> *Capt.n Alex.r McKee*
>
> *NB—I have farther to inform you that there is one of the Ottawa Chiefs killed among those of the Indians. The reason of the Express being conveyed by a woman is that none of the Indians dare leave [here], the Chiefs of each village orders them to remain in their Towns till further Orders.*[18]

While Simon was preparing and sending his report to McKee, Catherine Girty was at home, delivering their daughter Nancy Ann. Physically, mother and daughter were doing fine, although it had now been months since Catherine had last seen her husband.

Logan's attack on the Shawnee towns failed to achieve any positive results. If anything, it embittered the Shawnees and reinforced the western tribes' desire to unite and stand fast. Intertribal meetings that had been set to take place at Mequashake were rescheduled to be held at Detroit at the end of November. Unless some dire emergency intervened, Simon would then be able to visit his wife and see his new daughter.

Commenting on Clark's failure at the Wabash, McKee wrote Sir John Johnson on November 12, 1786, explaining:

> *… Simon Girty who was sent towards the Wabash, is this moment returned and brings an account that the Americans are actually gone back from St. Vincents. Letters from the Traders there confirm this also, and that Body of men are left there by General Clark to erect a Fort which was already begun, to which place He is to return in the spring with sufficient force as He has proclaimed to reduce all the Indian Nations to his own terms on his way to Detroit. It is said that the force collected by the Indians to oppose the Americans on the Wabash was equal to them, which occasioned their return without attempting anything against them. We have sent people who have continued their way to the Wabash to know for certain whither any accommodations had taken place between the Indians and the Americans before their retreat.*[19]

It was mid-November before Simon was finally able to go home. At Malden, he found that a bitter winter cold had descended—both outside and inside his house.

CHAPTER SIXTEEN
SIMON AND THE DEATH OF ABNER HUNT

SIMON HAD BEEN HOME only a week when McKee summoned him back across the river to Detroit, where delegates from the Six Nations, Wyandots, Delawares, Shawnees, Ottawa, Chippewa, Potawatomi, Miamis, Cherokees and the Wabash were meeting to decide their future relations with the Americans. According to Butterfield, "At this council Simon Girty was extremely active, along with McKee and Elliott, in stirring up the minds of the savages against the Americans."[1]

Once again, Joseph Brant opened and chaired the meetings, which this time plunged into conflict. While most of the Wyandots and Delawares favored conciliation with the United States, the Shawnees, Miamis and Wabash tribes were against any form of appeasement. The arguing continued until the middle of December, when a compromise was finally reached, and a carefully-worded speech to the American Congress was drafted and dispatched. The confederation declared that all the treaties recently authored by the Americans were invalid, and they demanded recognition of an Ohio River boundary. In the interests of peace they asked to meet with American officials at a halfway place yet to be agreed upon. Until such meetings were concluded, they warned, no further American encroachments were to take place. Unless the United States wanted war, they must not send surveyors or any other people across the Ohio River.

A month later, on 25 January 1787, Governor Randolph of Virginia issued a proclamation opening lands north of the Ohio River to settlement.

At home during the opening months of the new year, Simon was frequently interrupted by McKee summoning him to Detroit. During one of Girty's trips across the river, an American captive—seventeen-year-old James Moore—sought him out. Moore told Girty how he had been captured by Shawnees three years earlier, and that he was now living with a kindly French trader named Baptiste Ariome, who had purchased him from his captors. Moore liked Ariome and was quite content living with him. He made it clear to Girty that he wanted nothing for himself; his concern was for his sister. Moore explained that a few weeks earlier he had learned that the Shawnees had captured his younger sister, and that she was now living not far from Detroit with a white trader, a Loyalist named Stockwell. Having obtained permission from Ariome to go and find his sister, Moore had traveled to Frenchtown where he found the girl (Mary Moore) half-starved, clad in rags, and living in wretched conditions. His sister told him that Stockwell had purchased her from a Shawnee for half a bottle of rum, and that he had made a slave of her. Her situation was intolerable, and Moore was desperate for Simon's help. Girty took him at once to see McKee, who promptly filed charges of ill-treatment against Stockwell. In a subsequent investigation, Stockwell prevailed, but a civil decision was reached which led to the return of both James and Mary Moore to Virginia in the fall of 1789. Moore's memories of Simon Girty as a helpful and considerate man contrasted sharply with the hateful character that dominated prevailing perceptions.

During the period of October 1786 thru May 1787, while the western tribes awaited a formal answer to their letter of demands to the American Congress, a total of 177 boats, containing some 2,689 invading settlers, passed Fort Harmar on their way down the Ohio River. Considering the 1785 Treaty of Fort McIntosh to be a valid agreement, on 13 July 1787 the American Congress enacted the Northwest Ordinance, which asserted United States authority over the eastern part of the Northwest Territory. George Washington appointed Arthur St. Clair as its first governor. St. Clair immediately organized his government while, simultaneously, a number of land companies began the colonization of their Revolutionary War-era land grants. With his aggressive nature and disregard for Indians, St.

Clair's antagonistic tactics conflicted with the policies of Secretary of War Henry Knox, who knew that there were neither sufficient funds nor troops available to effectively engage in a war with the western tribes. Nevertheless, St. Clair and Indian Commissioner Richard Butler kept pressuring the Indians, and Knox wrote to them both, sternly advising caution.

Early in the autumn of 1787, Girty, Brant and McKee were at the foot of the rapids of the Maumee, where representatives from several of the confederated tribes gathered to receive the official response of the American government to their earlier demands. Notably absent were any Wyandots and Delawares, which signified major problems with the confederation. Distressed, McKee dispatched Girty to Sandusky to try to mend the tear. Simon was successful, and the entire confederation met at the Maumee where they waited day after day, without any word from the Americans. After a few frustrating weeks, McKee and Joseph Brant helped the Indians draft and expedite another message to Congress, this one stating that they awaited an answer at the Maumee. Once again the Indians were rewarded with silence. Frustrated and in disarray, the assembly broke apart after agreeing to meet again the following year at the same time and place.

In his efforts to destroy the Indian confederation, Richard Butler, U.S. Commissioner of Indian Affairs, began to recruit agents who, disguised as traders, were to interact with the Indians, spy, carry messages, and otherwise help Butler affect his schemes. Oddly, one of the men he was able to buy was Thomas Girty.

Simon hurried home after the pointless assembly at the Maumee. His relationship with Catherine was on the mend and by mid-November she was carrying another child. In the summer of Simon's forty-sixth year, Catherine delivered a healthy young boy whom they named Thomas, after Simon's elder brother.

Forced by Secretary Knox and a Congress that was determined to avoid the disastrous expenses of a new war, St. Clair and Richard Butler sent invitations in December 1787 to five of the confederated nations to meet and discuss peace with representatives of the United States at the Falls of the Muskingum (present Taylorsville, Muskingum County, Ohio). In due course, a few American troops were sent there to build a council house and a warehouse to store the presents that would be distributed.

The five confederated nations accepted the American invitation and agreed to meet with each other beforehand to formulate a policy. The Wyandots and Delawares wanted these organizational meetings to take place at Upper Sandusky, where they could exert maximum influence, but Joseph Brant stymied their effort, and the meeting was scheduled to take place at the foot of the Maumee rapids. In the summer of 1788, as the first Indian delegates arrived, Thomas Girty was present in the guise of an American trader. His sojourn as an American spy working for Richard Butler is curious. For years, Thomas had assiduously avoided political or military service. Perhaps he needed cash, or maybe he was simply taking advantage of a good opportunity to meet with his brothers. At any rate, having collected whatever information he had been sent for, he returned to Pennsylvania before Simon, James or George arrived.

Once the organizational meetings began, Simon immersed himself in the politics of the matters at hand. Butterfield wrote that his role was impressive:

> *No white man so readily entered into fellowship with many of the chiefs there assembled as he. His acquaintance with individual members of the various tribes was much extended. He spoke with many of them in their own tongue. He was recognized now more than ever as the true friend of the Indian. Still, the peace party gave him the cold shoulder. He was the mouth-piece for McKee and powerfully aided Brant. Whatever were their counsels were his. In the meetings he was a most prominent figure, but a silent one; his work was prosecuted outside the council-house.*[2]

After the meetings, Girty went home to celebrate his son's first birthday. While he was home, a rogue ten or twelve-man Chippewa war party attacked the American troops who were preparing the proposed council site at the Falls of the Muskingum. During a brief fight, two privates and a Negro slave were killed and three men were wounded. After coming under determined fire, the Chippewas withdrew, leaving behind one of their dead. The Americans believed that two more raiders had been wounded. News of the attack reached Fort Harmar a day later and outraged St. Clair, who rushed the following message to the western tribes:

The flag of the United States has been fired upon and when a small party of soldiers were sent to watch the council fire, kindled at your request; to build a council house for you to meet in, and to take care of the provisions sent there to feed you, you have fallen upon them, and killed them.... In the name of the United States I require an immediate explanation of these transactions, and demand satisfaction and the restitution of the prisoners [several soldiers were reported as missing]. Until these are made, as there can be no confidence, it will be improper we should meet one another in council.[3]

To emphasize his anger, St. Clair proclaimed that the council fire at the Falls of the Muskingum was permanently extinguished—any treaty involving the western tribes would now have to be held at an American site. There was no formal answer from the confederation to St. Clair's ultimatum, but responses from individual leaders of the Indians confirmed that the hostile Chippewa raiders responsible for the attack had acted completely on their own. Towards the end of October, intelligence collected by agents for Butler and St. Clair indicated that the Indians were firmly resolved to insist on an Ohio River boundary, and that under no circumstances would they go further east than the Falls of the Muskingum to meet and talk peace with the United States.

By now, Joseph Brant was working feverishly to preserve the confederation. Siding with the Senecas, Wyandots and Delawares who wanted peace, he dealt with their opposition. As there already were a large number of Americans settled on the north side of the Ohio River at Marietta, Brant somehow persuaded the Shawnees and Miamis to agree to vacate all their lands east of the Muskingum if, in return, the Americans would show that they truly meant to come and treat fairly. Once more the Indians asked the United States for restoration of the Falls of the Muskingum as the prospective meeting site, and once again St. Clair stubbornly rejected their request. By 8 December the issue was dead. The Mohawks, Shawnees, Miamis and a few Delawares returned to their home villages.

Misreading the situation, St. Clair believed he had struck a mortal blow against the western confederacy. Pressing what he perceived was an advantage, he sent agents to arrange for meetings at Fort Harmar with the pro-American Senecas, Wyandots and Delawares. His efforts brought a poor response; only 200 Indians met with St. Clair at Fort Harmar in mid-December. Nevertheless, St. Clair proceeded with his agenda, and on 9 January 1789 a pair of new treaties was signed: one by a Six Nation representative, and the other by some Ohio Wyandots and Delawares. At St. Clair's direction, with their signatures (or marks), these Indians legalized all the cessions of the former treaties. Delighted, St. Clair bragged about his accomplishments. A dramatic escalation in raids conducted against American settlers located on the Indian side of the Ohio River was a much truer indication of the efficacy of St. Clair's Fort Harmar treaties.

Among the signatories of these treaties were the totem marks of Simon's old patron, Guyasuta, as well as those of his close friends Half King and Captain Pipe. On paper, they and their people were finally "at peace" with the Americans. Once again, events beyond his control had put Simon Girty at odds with Indians he cared for and with whom he had long been affiliated. Perhaps because he was disheartened and tired of the confederation's continual turmoil, or maybe because he was now forty-eight years old and becoming ever more enamored of domestic life with his wife and children, Simon abandoned the turmoil to go home to Malden, where he remained until the end of 1789. His absence from the Ohio Country did not preclude him from being blamed for playing a bloody role in murderous Indian raids that were taking place on the frontier. One such alleged attack on Van Meter's Fort, Ohio County, Virginia, is described in Doddridge's *Notes on the Settlement and Indian Wars,* first published in 1824. In his book, Doddridge claimed that:

> *Mr. John Van Meter at one time lived in this fort … It was during his occupancy of this farm, in 1789, that a party of Indians visited his peaceful domicile, murdered his wife, daughter, and two small sons, taking the three elder sons prisoners, and burning the house.*
>
> *Hanna, the daughter who was killed, was washing at a spring a short distance from the house; she had on a sun-bonnet and was stooping over the tub, unconscious of danger, when one of the savages stealthily advanced and, supposing her to be an old woman, buried his tomahawk in her head. When the Indians saw her face and perceived that she was young and beautiful they deeply lamented their precipitancy, saying, "She would have made a pretty squaw." This information was subsequently communicated by the notorious Simon Girty, who was one of the party which committed the murders.*[4]

Once again, while the real Simon Girty was at home tending to his family and farm, his notorious legend grew without any basis in fact.

In the spring of 1789, the constitutional government of the United States of America was established and, on 30 April, George Washington took the oath as its first President. To protect American citizens from the Shawnees and western tribes (and from any other enemies—North American or European) the Commander-in-Chief had at his disposal a Federal army consisting of just 672 men. Their pay was so low (a private received $6.67 per month without subsistence or forage) that recruiters were enlisting drunks, drifters and other undesirables from city slums in order to meet their quotas.

In the autumn of 1789, John Turner, Jr. traveled to Canada to visit Simon, and he was warmly received. Simon introduced him to Catherine and to Nancy Ann and little Thomas. The situation required tact, as John's marriage to Susanna had been unproductive. In that regard, John revealed that he and his wife were seriously contemplating taking orphans into their home. John was also able to report that he had at last received title to Simon's old property on Squirrel Hill. Taking great pleasure in his presence, Simon charmed

John into staying on as his houseguest through the New Year. There can be little doubt that while he was staying at Simon's home both James and George Girty came to visit him.

In the spring of 1790, vexed from having their peace offers rejected by the Wabash tribes, the Americans mounted a minor campaign to punish hostiles located near the mouth of the Scioto River. These Indians were routinely attacking the boats of settlers as they descended the Ohio River. On 15 April, General Josiah Harmar, with 120 troops, sailed out on barges from Fort Washington and made their way to Limestone (present Maysville, Kentucky). There, General Charles Scott and 200 Kentucky militiamen joined Harmar's forces. Under Harmar's overall command, the army then moved overland to the Scioto. Warned that their enemies were coming, the Indians simply melted away. After fifteen days without making any contact, the Kentuckians began to grumble that they wanted to go home. Disgusted, Harmar terminated his sorry expedition. On 12 May, the Indians he had sought retaliated by attacking a Federal convoy of six boats on the Ohio River, once again near the mouth of the Scioto River. During that attack, five Americans were killed and eight more were captured.

British Indian Department records show that on 19 May, Simon Girty and Isadore Chesne were interpreters at a council held at Detroit between delegates from the Ottawas, Chippewas, Potawatamis and Hurons, and about twenty English officers, including Alexander McKee and Major Patrick Murray, commanding the King's 60th Regiment. The subject matter that was being discussed was inconsequential. The Indians were there to assess the British mood.

As the summer season drew on, McKee regularly sent Girty to the Ohio Valley. One of these sorties is highlighted in the notes of historian Lyman C. Draper, taken when he interviewed Alexander McCormick's son Alex. Mr. McCormick told Draper that, in 1790, Girty and his father were instrumental in finding and retrieving the children of John and Elizabeth Quick from their Indian captors. Draper wrote the following in his notes:

John Quick was a native of Jersey. Was living in the Wheeling region in 1782 and saw Dr. Knight when he came in from captivity. Quick settled in Kentucky (above Maysville on the Ohio, early in 1790: LCD) where he and his wife Elizabeth, and ten children were all taken. Girty and McCormick [Alexander McCormick] managed to buy them from Indians, and when Girty could not get them to consent to sell, he would steal them off—all the children were obtained except one girl, who was never recovered. The whole family at once settled in Canada.[5]

In the fall of 1790, the Americans launched a major punitive expedition aimed at seven villages clustered around the confluence of the St. Joseph and St. Mary's Rivers (present Fort Wayne, Indiana). The villages were inhabited by Shawnees, Delawares and Miamis, and the largest was the Miami town of Kekionga. Governor St. Clair and General Harmar planned a two-pronged attack, one army launching from Vincennes to assault the Wabash villages, while a larger army starting from Fort Washington was to hit Kekionga. The Wabash thrust, comprising about 400 Kentucky militiamen and 100 federal troops, was to be led by Major John Hamtramck. General Harmar was to lead the main force with about 1,200 militiamen from Kentucky and Pennsylvania, reinforced by some 300 federal regulars.

Seeking to avoid direct conflict with British troops, Secretary of War Knox ordered St. Clair to send a messenger to Detroit to advise Commandant Major Patrick Murray that the forthcoming expeditions were not aimed at any British post, but were being pursued with the sole design of humbling and chastising some of the rampaging tribes. St. Clair also requested that the British refrain from alerting or aiding the hostiles in any way. As soon as he received St. Clair's letter, Major Murray notified McKee, who, in turn, ordered his field agents to warn the Indians.

On 30 September, Major John Hamtramck's force started for the Vermillion village, a Kickapoo town located at the mouth of the Vermillion River and the Wabash, arriving there on 10 October. The place had just been abandoned. During the march out from

Vincennes there had been considerable dissention and disarray among the militiamen, some of whom had already deserted. Rumors began to circulate that there were some 750 warriors waiting for them just ahead. Having no confidence in his command, Hamtramck withdrew and returned to Vincennes without making contact with any hostiles. His diversionary thrust was meaningless.

Approximately 150 miles to the east, General Harmar's army reached the Miami villages on 15 October only to find that they had just been abandoned. Some of the towns, recently set on fire by their former inhabitants, were still burning. Harmar's troops looted any of the Indian houses that still stood, and then set about burning their planted fields. On the 18th, still hoping to make contact with the enemy, Harmar sent Lieutenant Colonel James Trotter with 300 men to the northwest, in the direction of some Kickapoo villages. Trotter also failed to make contact and soon returned. Next, Colonel John Hardin asked for and was given permission to try, and he departed on the 19th with 150 militiamen and about 30 regulars. Seven miles above Kekionga, Hardin's company was brilliantly decoyed and ambushed by 150 warriors led by the veteran Miami war chief Little Turtle. At the start of the attack the majority of the militiamen broke in panic and ran for their lives, while the regulars (with nine militiamen who stayed to fight) took cover and attempted to hold their ground. These brave soldiers were quickly overwhelmed. Fleeing back to the main force, Hardin reported the debacle to Harmar. The cowardice of the militiamen had been matched by the bravery of the regulars, whose losses were high. More than 30 regulars were missing, along with another 100 militiamen. A few days later another ambush by Little Turtle and Blue Jacket decimated a 400 man military unit. American losses were severe, with over 330 killed. According to British estimates, Indian losses for all this fighting were between ten and forty warriors killed. The Americans estimated Indian losses to be at least 100 and later, according to St. Clair's reports, this total climbed to 200.

Despite having suffered serious losses in houses, crops and stored provisions, the Miamis and Shawnees considered the battles they had just fought to be significant victories. Instead of demoralizing and forcing the Indians to the treaty table, the American punitive expeditions convinced the warriors that they could whip their white enemies in the field. The Americans learned that undisciplined militiamen were no match for their native opponents.

In the fall Girty joined other British Indian agents in getting food, clothing and ammunition to the Kekionga Shawnees, who were facing a winter of hardship. By mid-November, Girty joined the chiefs of the confederated tribes gathered at the foot of the rapids of the Maumee to plan their next moves. When deliberations commenced, Simon advocated the sending of speeches to all the confederated tribes asking them to assemble at the foot of the Maumee in the early spring to form an army to repel American attacks. By the time the talks concluded in December the confederated tribes had agreed to go to war. War belts were sent to every nation and a delegation was selected to go to Quebec to secure Lord Dorchester's help. Before the delegates returned to their villages, Girty proposed a raid-in-force be conducted at once against some American stations situated north of the Ohio River. Not only was Girty's proposal accepted, but the chiefs honored him by asking him to lead the foray. Simon's relationship with the tribes had reached a new and very rare plateau.

Plans were contrived to simultaneously attack Baker's and Dunlap's stations. The first of these was located not far below Graves Creek on the Virginia side of the Ohio River, and the second was about seventeen miles up from Cincinnati on the east side of the Great Miami River. When it departed, Girty's large war party consisted of some 300 Shawnee and Miami warriors.

On the night of 7 January, having no reason for alarm, surveyor Abner Hunt and three companions were camped just above Dunlap's Station. Early the next morning they were attacked, and during the assault one man was killed, Abner Hunt was captured, and the two remaining Americans escaped (one of whom was badly wounded).

The two who escaped made their way to Dunlap's Station and raised the alarm. At the time, the station was sheltering a number of women and children and was defended by a force of some thirty-five men and boys commanded by a regular officer, Lieutenant Jacob

Kingsbury. It was assumed that the attack on the surveyor's party had been the work of a small party of warriors out looking to steal horses.

Four days later, the siege of Dunlap's Station began. Immediately following the fighting, Lieutenant Kingsbury wrote his official report of the action, which he addressed to General Harmar. Kingsbury's report is by far the most credible and accurate account of the conflict:

LIEUT. KINGSBURY TO GENL. HARMAR, DUNLAP'S STATION, 12TH JANUARY, 1791

Dear General—

Monday morning, about sunrise at half past seven, the Indians surrounded this garrison—the Indians consisting of nearly two hundred. After they had completely surrounded us, Mr. Hunt, a prisoner (taken last Saturday within one mile of this place) demanded the surrender of this garrison by order of the Indians. I informed them that we were happy to see them, that we had plenty of men, arms, ammunition and provisions, and we had been waiting impatiently for them for several days. They then began a very heavy fire, but have wounded but one man, which is McVickar of Capt. Freeman's company, shot through the arm. They demanded the garrison several times, but to no purpose. We have killed and wounded not less than twelve or fifteen. The savages have killed most part of the cattle belonging to the station, and burnt all the buildings outside of the garrison, and have destroyed most part of the corn belonging to the inhabitants.

The Indians appeared to come prepared for a siege, as they had a number of pack-horses with heavy loads on them, and were loaded themselves with large packs on their backs. The savages raised their siege yesterday morning about eight o'clock, after keep-ing up a heavy fire for nearly twenty-five hours. They threatened to starve us out, or storm our works, and to set fire to our garrison. They attempted to set fire to our garrison with arrows, but could not bring any of their plans to bear. They informed me that Girty was there, and called me by name, and told me they would wish to see me outside of the garrison.

Hunt, the prisoner, they murdered within two hundred yards of the garrison. I have the pleasure of sending you two scalps; hope before long to send you several more, but have them to take first.

The inhabitants will some of them leave this place, others will remain here. I had of my men and the inhabitants in the attack thirty five men, old and young, sick and well. I shall now be a little weakened by the loss of some of the inhabitants who are about to leave this place. Captain Sloan, the bearer, received a wound in his side but was of great service to me in the attack. I yesterday morning sent off an express to you, but they met the militia and returned.

I am, dear General, with the utmost respect, your most obedt. Humble servant, Jacob Kingsbury, Lieut. Commdg Dunlap's Station.[6]

From Kingsbury's report it's clear that neither he nor anyone inside the besieged station saw or heard Girty during the conflict. Kingsbury simply states: "they [the Indians] informed me he was there." In fact, there is considerable evidence that the leader of the warriors who besieged Dunlap's Station was the Shawnee chief Blue Jacket, who may have figured there would be an advantage to making the Americans believe that Girty was present. There is stronger evidence that at the time Girty was miles away leading the attack on Baker's Station. The earliest and most credible version of this event appears in *American Pioneer*, 1843, in the article "First Settlement of Grave Creek," written by A.B. Tomlinson, based upon the experiences of his father. The following account is excerpted from this article:

Baker's Station was next attacked by about three hundred Indians, with Simon Girty at their head. The whites had sufficient warning of their approach to enter the fort, and were prepared for its defence. When the Indians advanced along the hill-side, (near the base of which the fort stood,) Simon Girty called out to those in the fort to turn out and surrender. The voice of Girty was recognized by some of the men, who answered him by curses, telling him, if they did not leave before morning (this being between sundown and dark) they would come out and drive them from

*the country. The Indians, however, fired upon the fort; and
perceiving that their shots would not take effect from their present
position, they proceeded further up the hill, in order the more
easily to discover those in the fort. From this position they engaged
the fort all the next day and part of the next night. But the whites
concealed themselves under cover of the walls so securely that no
one sustained any injury. The Indians finding their efforts to be in
vain, abandoned the attack and went off without effecting their
purpose. During the attack on the second night, a Mr. Downing
left the fort to give the alarm to those at Grave creek, and, if
possible, to get assistance. Some seven or eight men returned with
Mr. Downing early next morning, but the Indians had left, and
all was peaceable.*[7]

As he had been blamed for Crawford's death, Girty was now held
responsible for Abner Hunt's murder. In the story that rapidly spread
throughout the frontier, Abner Hunt had been forced to tell the
people inside Dunlap's Station that if they didn't surrender, he would
be put to death, and when the defenders refused to comply, Girty and
the Indians spent hours burning the hapless screaming man to death.

In his *History of the Girtys,* Butterfield argued that Girty must
have been present when Hunt was killed, because Baker's Station was
east of the Ohio River, on the side where Girty never set foot after the
end of the Revolutionary War. But Simon Girty was His Majesty's
foremost frontier spy, and there is solid evidence he crossed over into
Pennsylvania several times after the end of the revolution. Indeed, the
following letter written by Lord Dorchester, claims Girty's presence
at Pittsburgh just three months prior to the attacks on Baker's and
Dunlap's stations:

LORD DORCHESTER'S TO MR. GRENVILLE No.79,
OF 23 JANY 1791

*The Information of Simon Girty Detroit 5th November 1790
    The information of Simon Girty states: that on the 18th
October last, he arrived in the neighborhood of Pittsburg
[sic], where he was informed that the American Army, gone to*

take possession of the Indian Country consisted of Two thousand five hundred men, whereof four hundred were Prisoners, Packhorsemen & Bullock Drivers that they made not the least doubt of succeeding, that they were to establish Forts this fall at the Miamies, Lower Sandusky and Guyahoga, and next Spring were to send troops to take possession of Detroit, and settle that part of the country, wherein if they failed, they were to raise another Army to take it; that officers were sent to reconnoitre Beaver Creek to know how far up that River, towards the head of Guyahoga, Craft could proceed—He further adds, that a few days before his arrival at Pittsburg [sic], he learned that the Corn Planter, a Chief of the Five Nations set out for Philadelphia to counsel with congress about keeping The Five Nations quiet, while the Americans were taking possession of the Western Country.[8]

In addition, the records indicate several instances of Simon Girty visiting his younger half-brother John Turner, Jr. at Pittsburgh, and there is even a statement from Girty collected by historian Lyman C. Draper, in which Simon claimed that in 1792 or 1793, he was present in disguise at Duncan's Tavern at Pittsburgh when General Anthony Wayne was at the same establishment, drinking with his friends. One can choose to disregard the story of Girty being in the same tavern with General Wayne as being far-fetched, but it is impossible to ignore British Governor General Sir Guy Carleton's (Lord Dorchester) letter to Mr. Grenville containing military and political intelligence Simon Girty gleaned at Pittsburgh in October 1790.

Considering the degree of his notoriety, the price on his head, and the hatred directed toward him, Girty's audacity was astounding. His confidence came from years of successful role playing, combined with a hearty appetite for living on the edge.

CHAPTER SEVENTEEN
NATIVE WARRIORS HAND ARMY WORST DEFEAT

FOLLOWING THE SIEGE of Baker's Station, Simon hurried home to be with Catherine when she delivered. On April 18, 1791 she gave birth to their second daughter, Sarah, who was named after her maternal grandmother.

Like most of the frontiersmen of his era, Simon disdained the manual labor of farming, and often hired people to do his plowing, planting and harvesting. His access to inexpensive farm labor improved dramatically in the spring of 1791, when large numbers of Moravian converts took up residence next door. The Christian Indians, whom Elliott had helped remove from their Tuscarawas missions back in 1781, had been living at New Salem on the east bank of the Pequotting River since 1787 (Huron River in present Milan, Erie County, Ohio). At the beginning of 1791, fearing the outbreak of a new Indian war, Reverend Zeisberger recognized that his flock was again rooted in a no man's land between the British and the Americans. This time, he acknowledged the need to quickly move the community to safety. The missionary went to Matthew Elliott for help, and Elliott, agreeing with his concern, took the issue to McKee. The British agent arranged for the Moravian converts to settle along the Detroit River, but until a permanent location could be found, the converts would stay at the Detroit River plantations of McKee and Elliott. The Moravians arrived in May, naming their new community Warte or Watch-Tower. Amused by their presence, Squire Girty took immediate advantage of the situation. According to Butterfield:

> *Planting soon followed the arrival of the "Moravians" and the*
> *harvest came on in due time; but there was trouble among the*
> *"Christian" Indians; "for," as Zeisberger declares [in his diary],*
> *"there was drinking in the neighborhood, so that our people were*
> *led astray." Girty was, in particular, a thorn in the side of the*
> *missionary; as he not only employed some of the "Moravians," but*
> *paid them in rum, making them drunk.*[1]

While Girty devoted himself to domestic tasks, American militia conducted three small raids against some of the Wabash towns. These actions were followed by reports that a major Yankee army was assembling at Fort Washington. This time, the news was accurate. Determined to offset General Harmar's defeats, Secretary of War Knox called for the procurement of a 3,000 man army that St. Clair was mandated to lead against the Miami Towns. Since there were only 600 regulars on the frontier, Congress approved the six-month recruitment of 2,000 more men. In addition, St. Clair was granted permission to raise another 1,000 militia from Kentucky and Pennsylvania. Girty's old nemesis Richard Butler (now General Richard Butler) was second-in-command.

The magnitude of the latest American build-up at Fort Washington made it clear to the British and their Indian allies that the forthcoming fight would be crucial. Gathering to oppose the invaders were warriors from the Delawares, Shawnees, Wyandots, Miamis, Ottawas, Kickapoos, Chippewas, and Potawatamies, plus some Mohawks from Canada, and even a few Creek Indians. By the end of the summer, Girty, McKee and Elliott were in the Miami Towns distributing war materials and provisions shipped down from Detroit. While Girty was so preoccupied, back at Malden a tanner named George Setchelstiel filed the following complaint against him, alleging:

> *That on Sunday the 21st of August 1791, being on horseback ...*
> *he [Setchelstiel] was assaulted by said Simon Girty who seized*
> *his horse by the bridal, making use of abusive words, and after*
> *[Setchelstiel] had found means to turn his horse away and get at*

some distance, said Girty threw too [sic] stones at him, the latter of which struck him in the head & gave him a wound from which much blood gushed out, all of which bad treatment he received without having given any provocation prior to having received the wound.[2]

There is neither any further explanation of this incident nor any hint of how it was finally resolved. Simon was too busy to pay it much attention. As the Indian army was assembling at the Miami towns, spies were sent to observe enemy activities and intelligence streamed back daily. By mid-August, advance contingents of American soldiers were observed moving from Fort Washington to a location some six miles north, a place called "Ludlow's Station." Early in September, troops from Ludlow's Station were moved forward twenty miles to the banks of the Great Miami where they began to construct Fort Hamilton (present day Hamilton, Ohio). By this time, several thousand warriors had arrived at the Miami Rapids and the men of the Indian Department struggled to supply and keep them at hand.

At the beginning of October, Governor St. Clair joined his advance troops at Fort Hamilton. Heavy rains greeted his arrival, and morale plummeted with the downpours. St. Clair was stricken by a painful episode of gout and hurriedly returned to Fort Washington where, from his bed, he penned a letter to the Secretary of War stating that he now had a total force of some 2,300 men combined of regulars, levies (six-month federal troops), Kentucky and Pennsylvania militia.

On 4 October, Shawnee and Miami spies reported that the Americans were beginning to move north from Fort Hamilton. St. Clair and his staff hurried from Fort Washington in order to overtake Butler the following day. By their course of travel it seemed certain that Butler was marching for the Miami Towns. His was a strange and arrogant army, reminiscent of that of General Burgoyne's campaign of 1777. Consisting of some 200 camp followers and a long train of baggage wagons, a menagerie of some 2,700 people, including officers, soldiers, scouts, surgeons, cooks, washerwomen, seamstresses, wives, lovers and even children, trudged along at a ponderously slow pace. In five days, the Americans progressed only some twenty-five miles. Ominously, the weather turned colder and early frosts began to kill the forage upon which the Yankees depended for the sustenance of their horses and draft animals. Simultaneously, the American troops discovered that their uniforms were poorly made, their new shoes were falling apart, and that their rations were inadequate. They began to fall ill from the cold, and desertion rates soared. Neither St. Clair nor Butler was aware that their army's presence and disposition was well-known to waiting hordes of warriors. After eight days of travel the Americans averaged nine miles per day and had come only seventy miles from Fort Washington. Days of intermittent rains were followed by barrages of hail and sleet, and desertions accelerated. Some of these defectors made their way to Detroit—providing the English with more accurate and detailed intelligence. On 14 October St. Clair paused to build a station on a low, rounded knoll located five miles south of modern Greenville, Ohio. Hoping to stem the tide of desertions, St. Clair assembled his men on the morning of 21 October and forced them to witness the hanging of three deserters who had been caught in the act. By the 24th, the new installation had been roughed in and the extra baggage was deposited, to be guarded by a small garrison comprised mostly of sick men. Resuming their march, St. Clair and Butler managed to go only about five miles before they were forced to halt for lack of rations. They were now about eighty miles away from Fort Washington, and the supply convoy upon which they depended would not reach them until the 28th.

On that same date war parties started moving south from the Miami Towns. Before he departed, Simon Girty dictated the following report to McKee:

Miami Delaware Town October 28th, 1791
Sir:

This is to let you know that 1,040 Indians are this day going from here, to meet General Butler and his army, with an Intention to attack him on his march to this place; I am informed that he is likewise to leave his last Post on his way here this same day, and that he has 2,200 men which account is confirmed by the report of Deserters and Prisoners that are daily brought in

*who also say that he is to bring with him five pieces of cannon and
two Cohorns [small bronze mortars mounted on wooden blocks]
for the Post he intends there. He has 320 Kentucky militia with
him and 100 Light Horse. The militia demanded of Governor St.
Clair five shillings per day, which he refused to allow them, this
is the reason so few of them have turned out, having also insisted
upon being commanded by their own officers only. The deserters
say that bad usage & scarcity of provisions obliged them daily to
quit the army. The Indians were never in greater heart to meet
their Enemy, nor more sure of success, they are determined to
drive them to the Ohio, and starve their little posts by taking all
their horses and cattle.*

*Their principal officers are St. Clair, Butler, Gibson and
Duncan, all of whom you know as well as I. This is all I have to
let you know till they return.*

And am your humble servant "etc." Simon Girty [3]

Wyandot leaders had just awarded Simon one of his greatest honors—bestowing upon him full battlefield command of their warriors in the coming fight. Everyone's future depended on the outcome of the forthcoming battle, and Girty openly disregarded standing orders from his British superiors prohibiting him from engaging in direct combat with the Americans. More than 400 Wyandot warriors volunteered to follow Girty into battle. At the time, the enemy was only seventy-five miles away. Unlike their foes, the warriors were unencumbered by excess baggage, artillery or camp followers. They knew what they were fighting for, and had intelligence of everything they needed to know about their enemy. A great victory was anticipated.

On 29 October, to accommodate his artillery and the many wagons, Butler sent a 120 man detail forward to carve a road in advance of the army. One day later he prodded his main force forward once again. Two days later he had to halt once more to wait for provisions, during which time sixty more discontented Kentucky militiamen deserted. Convinced that the Indians were afraid and would not fight, and concerned that the deserters who had just departed might stop and steal food from the supply convoy that was en route to him, St. Clair sent Major John Hamtramck and the 1st Regulars—300 men—back to locate and protect the supply train. St. Clair issued this order even though numerous reports had come in from outlying sentries that Indians had been sighted. It was presumed by the American commanders that these were lone hunters and their presence was disregarded. On 1 November St. Clair's gout flared, and the army remained immobile. The next day the Americans marched about eight miles through low, swampy terrain under a faltering rain that finally turned into snow. On the 3rd, the snowfall became intermittent, and a number of men and officers became sick. By mid-afternoon the Americans had marched roughly six miles before St. Clair halted to establish a camp on six acres of high ground bordered by low, swampy terrain.

Starting from the Miami Towns, Girty and the warrior army easily traversed fifty miles in four days, setting up their own camp only some two and one-half miles from the most forward American positions.

The morning of 4 November dawned clear and cold. St. Clair and the main force were bivouacked on the east bank of the Wabash River, with an advanced camp of Kentucky militia just across the water-way. The Americans had already called their early morning assembly and been dismissed at daybreak, so that the men could build up their cooking fires and prepare breakfast.

The Indian battle plan called for Girty and his Wyandots (rein-forced by a handful of Six Nation warriors) to attack on the right. Shawnees, Miamis and Delawares were to hit the American center and Lakes Indians—Ottawas, Chippewas and Potawatomis—were to strike from the left. To facilitate an ultimate encirclement, the pattern of the attacking Indians was to be a semi-circle.

The fighting commenced when Girty and his Wyandots attacked the Kentucky militia. After returning a single volley, the Kentuckians panicked. Pursued by hundreds of warriors, they ran back towards the main American positions. Those who made it across the shallow Wabash ran through St. Clair's main camp in terror, just as the regulars and levies were atempting to form battle lines. During the result-ing chaos the center of the American positions was soon inundated.

Fronting the Wabash, four 6-pounder and three 3-pounder guns were quickly wheeled into action, detonating round shot and canister which added ear shattering blasts to the cacophonous confusion. Girty and his warriors were too close for the gunners to lower their barrels enough to bear, and their salvos harmlessly raked the treetops above the attacking hordes. The warriors replied with withering musket fire and within minutes the big guns fell silent. Then, in a desperate but brave attempt, 300 American regulars and twenty-five cavalry-men charged across the Wabash River towards the former Kentucky militia camp. At first, Girty and his Wyandots were forced to give way, but the American charge ran out of steam, and the Wyandots were able to beat them back across the river. At this point terrified camp followers and cooks, who had been occupying the very center of the American positions, started screaming and scattering while being hacked to pieces by merciless Shawnee and Miami warriors. By 9:30 a.m. the outcome was apparent and, in desperation, St. Clair ordered a full retreat. Survivors raced back along the road over which they had come. Behind them small pockets of resistance continued to fight, but the gunfire was already beginning to die off. Exultant with their stupendous victory, warriors now rushed to kill and scalp the wounded and loot the camp. The desire for booty was so strong that only a few warriors pursued the fleeing American troops who had broken through the encirclement and were now scrambling eastward. According to historian Wiley Sword:

Richard Butler—who had once imposed a humiliating treaty on the Shawnees, asserting that the English king had given away the Indian lands, and that he (Butler) would decree the terms on which peace might be restored—had been greatly weakened by the loss of blood [he had received a musket ball in his side]. With a cocked pistol in his hand, he now lay propped up against a large sprawling oak tree, cold and alone, awaiting the inevitable.

Two warriors, said to be Shawnees, approached through the lingering haze of gun smoke. Butler raised his pistol and fired. He was reportedly attempting to grasp a second gun when the blade of a tomahawk ripped through his skull, abruptly ending his life.[4]

Moments later, Girty recognized Butler's body and pointed him out to some of the Indians. Girty's lifelong enemy was scalped and his heart torn out, "to be divided into as many pieces as there were tribes in the battle, and eaten."[5]

Several years after the event, Girty himself described Butler's death during a 1799 conversation with Thomas Silk (who had befriended Girty at Pittsburgh before Simon's defection during the Revolutionary War). Relating this conversation, Silk told the following to historian Lyman C. Draper:

Girty inquired if the people around Pittsburgh did not blame him for General Richard Butler's death? Yes, said Silk. Girty said he had no part in it, but did see Butler, wounded and sitting up by a tree, snapped his pistol at a white man with the Indians & the latter shot Butler dead.[6]

In another strange story related by Butterfield, just after the fighting ended, Girty allegedly took possession of a frightened white woman. Seeing this, a Wyandot squaw became incensed and demanded the prisoner on the ground that it was customary for all female captives to be given to the women who accompanied the braves. Girty refused, but a number of warriors came up and forced him to comply with this rule. "To the great relief of the prisoner," Butterfield commented, as though the poor woman was more frightened of what might happen to her in Girty's hands than if she were left to the Indians. In due course the woman was sold to a respectable French family at Detroit.[7] In addition to picking up booty, Indian women were busy lifting American scalps, and in some cases dispatching wounded men, cutting off their privates and stuffing their mouths with dirt, since it was land for which they had come and died.

The defeat of St. Clair's army was an astounding victory for the Indians. Among the captured booty were two traveling forges, two baggage wagons, 384 common and 9 horseman's tents, 1,200 muskets, 163 felling axes and 8 cannon. For his bravery during the fight, the Wyandots paid homage to Girty by presenting him with three of the big American cannons that were captured. Later, the guns had to be buried, as there was no road over which they could be transported northward. Following the battle, Girty was seen with a new pair of silver-mounted pistols in his belt, obviously pilfered from some high ranking officer—perhaps even Butler himself.

With 630 dead or missing, and the wounded numbering 31 officers and 252 enlisted men, St. Clair's defeat remains the greatest loss ever suffered by American soldiers in battle with native warriors (in 1876, 7th Cavalry losses at Custer's last stand totalled 260). In proportional terms, it remains as the greatest defeat that United States forces have ever endured in battle. Reported Indian losses in the fight against St. Clair were 21 killed and 40 wounded.

Panicked American survivors began arriving at Cincinnati on 9 November, traversing in just four days the same mileage it had taken them five weeks to cover when the invaders had marched north to encounter the Indians. One of the survivors was George Gibson, brother to Girty's old enemy John Gibson. Badly wounded, George died on 12 November at Camp Hamilton.

As word of the terrible slaughter spread, Simon Girty was accused of being in command of all the Indians engaged in the defeat of St. Clair. According to an interview of W. Curry Jr. by Rev. Shane, immediately after the defeat of St. Clair:

"Congress offered $10 a head for every Indian prisoner brought in alive and 500 guineas for Simon Girty and $40 a month as long as he lived, and drew it in any state in the Union."[8]

Written three weeks after the defeat of St. Clair, the following extracts from an anonymous letter provide the British perspective:

The American Army of which no doubt you have this summer heard, had advanc'd on the third of this month to within Forty Miles of the Miamis Towns, they were there encountered by near Two thousand Indians, who on that day took from them the greatest part of their horses and cattle …

… besides the Commanding Officer, the Adjt. Genl. & Surgeon Genl., Twelve hundred are said to have Fallen in

the Assaults & Pursuits—you however know the Indians, most
probably this Number is exaggerated we do not hear of one
prisoner—about 50 of the Indians are said to be killed & wounded,
the Numbers at first were American Regulars 1500, Militia 800,
in all 2300—of Indians nearly 2,000. Two Forts they had erected
on their Rout nam'd Hamilton & Jefferson, are said to be surrounded by the Indians, they contain 100 Men each with but
little provisions; the truth of this information may be depended
on, Simon Girty, if not in the action, was within view of it. He
had join'd Coll. McKee at the foot of the Rapids, brought the
American Orderly Books & all their papers—Butler's Scalp was
brought in, & is sent they say to Joseph Brant with a severe
Sarcasm for his not being there—he is at the Grand River with
the Six Nations ... Humanity shudders at the number of poor
wretches who have fallen in this Business, but as they were clearly
the aggressors, they merit less pity, the horrible Cruelties that
may probably now fall on the defenceless Frontiers of the Western
American Settlements, is infinitely more dreadful & claims from
every person who can feel as a man, every preventative that can
be devis'd; I have this morning wrote to our Friend Mr. Askin
strongly pressing him to join the Trade in inspiring the Indians
with moderation. The Americans must be severely hurt at this
Blow, however willing to resent it, they will find great difficulty
in raising another Army for this service. They would probably
listen to any Reasonable Terms of accomodation, if they saw a
prospect of its being establish'd on solid Grounds, perhaps this
can only be affected by the influence of the British Government
& Trade with the Indians—The terms the Indians ask'd were, that
the Ohio shou'd be esablished as the Boundary to the American
Settlements, & that they shou'd enjoy unmolested their hunting
Grounds, to the West & North of that River, some of the Branches
of the Ohio to the Southward of this come within a few Miles of
the Genesea River, which runs into Lake Ontario Sixty Miles
east from the Fort of Niagara—If these two Rivers by the interposi-
tion of Government cou'd be fix'd as the Boundaries between
the Americans and Indians, & between them & us, we shou'd

*secure our Posts, the Trade, & the Tranquility of the Country; you
will know that the present lines must furnish a source of constant
Contention & dispute–The others now propos'd being on Streams
not navigable, will be free from this, the Indians not having as
yet sold their Country between this & the Genesea nor does any
of the American Settlements extend to the West of that River, but
they very soon will–I wish our Peacemakers of 83 had but known
a little more of this country. I wish our present Ministry were
informed of the actual situation–perhaps this is the important
moment in which the unfortunate terms of the Peace may be
alter'd–Perhaps this moment may never return.*[9]

As soon as the fighting stopped, Girty collected papers, ledgers, and other intelligence from the battlefield, which he presented to McKee. After pausing to observe two small American forts that the Indians were harassing, Girty went home to Catherine and his three children, joining them near the end of December.

Even as the young nation reeled from news of the bloody disaster, Secretary of War Henry Knox proposed the formation of a new, larger, federal army. Knox was convinced that with the strong taste of victory in their mouths, the Indians would be disinclined to entertain any peace offers on reasonable terms. Once enacted, Knox's proposal would establish an army of 5,168 men, all of whom would serve for three years. Pay rates were to be liberally increased, the cavalry service was to be expanded, and an entire regiment of riflemen was to be recruited. Projected costs were to be $1,026,477 "a staggering sum for the time and nearly double the original estimate for 1792."[10]

Endorsed by Washington, the administration's bill came before the House of Representatives. Despite a tough floor fight, it was enacted on 5 March 1792. The President understood that the country could ill afford another disastrous defeat at the hands of the Indians. He also knew that without gaining the warriors' respect for American might, there was little hope of securing peace treaties accompanied by land cessions from across the Ohio River. In order to gain the appropriation that would fund his new army, Washington was compelled to undertake serious efforts to obtain peace from the Indians—even if he believed such efforts would prove futile. Even so, his peace attempts might serve to deflect the Indians' attention from raiding. They would also buy valuable time for his new army to become operational by causing both sides to spend weeks, if not months, debating the issues.

Washington's immediate challenge was to select the man who could assemble, train and lead the new American Legions, as they were soon to be called. This was no easy task. Having failed with previous choices of Harmar and St. Clair, the president could ill afford to err again. What had become abundantly clear was that untrained militia led by officers who had little if any combat experience fighting Indians always led to disaster. Washington drew up a list of twenty men for his cabinet to consider, but all were rejected for being either too old, too infirm, too much a drunk, and an assortment of other reasons. The job finally went to forty-seven year old Brigadier General (retired) Anthony Wayne, although the president had considerable misgivings about his choice. A poor businessman, Wayne was out of work and in financial difficulties. Like Harmar and St. Clair, he was overweight, a heavy drinker, a womanizer, and also had a reputation for vanity. Officers who had served with him at Brandywine, the Paoli Massacre, Monmouth, Valley Forge, Stony Point and Yorktown found him offensive and difficult. His nicknames were "Dandy Tony" and "Mad Anthony." Militarily, he was regarded as conservative yet aggressive; a tenacious yet adaptable disciplinarian. Even so, after weighing the man's complexities, Washington finally gave him the nod on 3 April 1792.

As Wayne began to organize his staff at Pittsburgh, Secretary of War Knox sent six peace messengers off to the Maumee Villages, all bearing invitations for the chiefs to meet in council with the Americans. By mid-April it was known that three of the messengers had been killed and that the other three were missing. The missing party, comprised of Major Alexander Trueman, his body servant William Lynch, and his interpreter, William Smalley, had had been sent to the Miami villages via Fort Washington. On 13 April, Private William May was sent to locate Trueman's party, having been instructed that if he was taken by Indians he was to pretend that he was a deserter.

Months later, May reappeared at Pittsburgh and was debriefed personally by General Wayne, who repeated May's story for Congress (the following is taken from the Congressional Record):

Personally appeared before me, a certain William May, a private soldier belonging to Captain Armstrong's company, of the late first regiment; was born at Dover, in the State of Delaware, aged about thirty-one years, who upon oath, saith: That, on or about the 13th of April, he was sent from fort Hamilton, with orders to follow on the trail of Trueman, who, with a French baker, and another man, were sent as a flag to the Indians. That, after passing Four-mile creek, he steered a north course, by a pocket compass, to General Harmar's route, which he reached the seventh day, and followed it about eleven miles, where he discovered Trueman, and the two other men, lying dead, scalped and stripped. He then steered west for General St. Clair's route. After traveling twelve or fourteen miles on that course, he fell in with three Mingoes, and soon after with eleven Chippewas, who took him prisoner about eleven o'clock the same day; and the next, at three o'clock reached General St. Clair's field of battle, where they remained two or three hours, and took a straight course, frequently falling in with the same Indian path which Gen. St. Clair followed. He knows it to be the same; and that, from the field of battle to a little village, burned by General Harmar, situate on the St. Josephs, is fifty-seven miles; from thence, they struck across the country for about fifty miles, when they fell in with a Delaware town, on the Tawa river, where he was much beat; from thence he was carried down the side of the said river, passing through several little villages, about ten miles, to a trading town, where many of the principal traders live, among whom are Messrs. McKenzie and McDonald, Robert Wilson, and two by the name of Abbet, to whose father, and to Simon Girty, it is said, Major Trueman had letters which mentioned his name, as Captain Armstrong had requested the major to make inquiries after him in particular, which had nearly occasioned his being put to death. At this place the river Glaze forms a junction with the Tawa, and is the principal town, or Indian head-quarters, where there were 3,600 warriors....

That Alexander McKee is the principal Indian agent, and keeps his stores at the rapids, sixteen miles above the mouth of the river. From the mouth of the river to Detroit is one hundred and eight miles, or ninety miles along the lake, and eighteen miles up the river to Detroit. That he was condemned to die, but saved by Simon Girty, and sent to war with twenty-two Indians, on or about the beginning of May, and reached fort St. Clair in eight days, where they killed one man, and returned through the field of battle, where he discovered the cannon, two of them in Hiskee Creek, one of them a six-pounder; that he put his hand into it; the other three are under a fallen hollow tree, on the opposite side of the creek from the field of Battle. Just at the rising of the hill there is a hollow tree standing close by the fallen tree; these three were given to Simon Girty by the Wyandots, whom he commanded on the day of battle. The Shawanese did not behave well on the day of action, and were called cowards by the Wyandots and Mingoes; but that the Wyandots made them a present of two cannon in the creek...[11]

On 21 July 1792, Girty was at Blue Jacket's Town, at the confluence of the Auglaize and the Maumee rivers, where he interviewed eleven-year-old Oliver Spencer, who had been captured two weeks earlier by Shawnees near Columbia—a settlement just above Cincinnati, on the north side of the Ohio. According to Spencer's recollections, not long after his capture he was placed in the custody of an old Indian widow who was also taking care of an Indian girl of thirteen, and a boy of ten, allegedly a son of Simon Girty. According to Spencer's account, the widow and a friend took him along when they went to pay their respects to Blue Jacket, arriving at his house about dinner time. Spencer recalled that Blue Jacket was six feet tall, finely proportioned, stout, and muscular; his eyes large, bright and piercing, his forehead high and broad; his nose aquiline, his mouth rather wide, his countenance open and intelligent.

As Butterfield tells it:

On the day of their visit to Blue Jacket, this chief was expecting
what, to him, was distinguished company; it was none other than
Simon Girty, accompanied by a chief of a neighboring village—the
Snake, a Shawanese warrior.... In honor of the occasion, Blue
Jacket was dressed in splendor; had on a scarlet frock, richly laced
with gold, and confined around his waist with a parti-colored
sash; also, red leggins and moccasins, ornamented in the highest
style of Indian fashion. On his shoulders, he wore a pair of gold
epaulets, and on his arms broad silver bracelets; while from his
neck hung a massive silver gorget, and a large medallion of his
majesty George III. Around his lodge were hung rifles, war-clubs,
bows and arrows, and other implements of war, while the skins
of deer, bear, panther, and otter, the spoils of the chase, furnished
pouches for tobacco, or mats for seats and beds. His wife was a
remarkably fine-looking woman; his daughters, much fairer than
the generality of Indian women, were quite handsome; and his
two sons, about eighteen and twenty years old, educated by the
British, were very intelligent.

The expected visitors soon came; and, to young Spencer, who
had often heard of him, Simon Girty was a person of more than
usual curiosity; and he subsequently wrote of his personal appear-
ance in an exaggerated manner.

Girty wore an Indian outfit, but without ornament, upon
this occasion; and his silk handkerchief, while it supplied the
place of a hat, hid the unsightly scar in his forehead, caused by the
wound which, the reader has already been told, was given him
by Captain Joseph Brant. On each side, in his belt, was stuck a
silver-mounted pistol, and at his left hung a short, broad dirk,
serving occasionally the uses of a knife. He made many inquiries of
Spencer; some about his family and the particulars of his captivity,
but more of the strength of the different garrisons, the number of
American troops at Fort Washington, and whether the President
of the United States intended soon to send another army against
the Indians. He spoke of the wrongs he had received at the hands

*of his countrymen, and, with fiendish exultation, of the revenge
he had taken.... He ended his talk by telling young Spencer that
he would never see home again; but, if he should turn out to be
a good hunter and a brave warrior, he might one day be a chief.
The captive boy then returned, with the old squaw, up the river.*[12]

There were four important councils that took place at "The Glaize"
over the summer of 1792, and according to many accounts, once again
Simon Girty was the only white man permitted to attend. It was now
well known by everyone that while the Americans were sending peace
messengers to the confederated western tribes, they were also building a new army some twenty-one miles south of Pittsburgh. Between
21 July 1792, at which time Girty interviewed young Oliver Spencer
at The Glaize, and the end of September, when Girty was present
for the most important of the four great councils, Simon's activities
remain a mystery. There is nothing to place him either at Malden or
at The Glaize through most of August and September, and this might
well be because the British had sent him on a dangerous mission to
Pittsburgh.

During an interview with historian Lyman C. Draper in 1850,
Girty's old friend Thomas Silk recalled a meeting he had had with
Simon in 1799. Draper took careful notes. According to Silk:

*Girty said he was disguised at Duncan's Tavern in Pittsburgh
when Gen. Wayne was there—mixed with the American officers
at the Tavern, who did not suspect him, was taken for an old
Frenchman.*[13]

Although Silk's recollection of his 1799 meeting with Girty did
not specify the date of Girty's alleged spy mission to Pittsburgh, the
evidence suggests that it took place early in September 1792, when
Wayne's army was there in training. There are a number of factors that
support Girty's dramatic revelations to Thomas Silk. For one thing,
Duncan's Tavern would have been a relatively safe house for Girty, as
Simon and the Duncans were good friends. Indeed, just before Girty
defected, he was rooming at their establishment. Duncan was also

friendly with Matthew Elliott, and not long after the end of the war, Duncan and William Wilson's trading company did business with one owned by Matthew Elliott and William Caldwell based in Detroit. It is also interesting to note that Duncan and Thomas Girty were friends, and that both were licensed estate appraisers at Pittsburgh. Lastly, Duncan's Tavern was among the most popular watering holes at Pittsburgh, and there can be little doubt that General Wayne—an enthusiastic drinker—frequented the place.

Less than a decade after the incident, Girty told Thomas Silk that he was disguised as an old Frenchman the night he saw General Wayne at Duncan's Tavern. A gifted linguist, Simon had been living among French-speaking people at Detroit for years, and speaking a broken English dialect with a French accent would have been easy for him. It has been assumed that Girty's spying consisted of watching forts from hidden positions in the wilderness, but if he also used disguises, as he revealed to Silk, it is not unreasonable to credit him with mingling with Americans to glean intelligence. It should also be realized that during combat he always wore the same costume: a red silk bandanna covering his head, a sash around his waist in which he tucked two pistols, and a long knife or sword at his side. This garish outfit has all the earmarks of a signature—something Girty thoughtfully contrived—and which he evidently wore whenever he wanted his identity to be recognized by Americans. An amazing aspect of such a signature is that simply by changing into drab, common clothing and swapping the red head scarf for an old hat, he could go about unmolested. By 1792, fifty-one-year-old Girty had spent almost twenty-five years spying—on the Indians, on the British, or on the Americans. Whether or not Girty actually spied on General Wayne at Duncan's Tavern cannot be verified. But, if he did, the people most likely to recognize him (the Duncans, Thomas Girty, William Wilson, and others) would never have given him away.

Considering the many real adventures of Simon's life, there is no conceivable reason for him to have fabricated such a tale. The way that Silk recalled Girty's conversation with him indicates that the Wayne incident at Duncan's Tavern was immediately preceded by Simon having asked Silk if he was being blamed for Richard Butler's death—which occurred in November 1791. It is logical that while discussing important events of his life in a chronological manner, Girty's mention of Butler's death triggered his recall of what to him was the next most significant event—his presence, in disguise, at Duncan's Tavern while General Wayne was there. Among the subjects Girty revealed to Silk was how Girty and McKee had both tried to save Colonel Crawford. Notably, all the other incidents Girty revealed to Silk are apparently true.

Finally, there is no doubt that General Wayne was at Pittsburgh on 14 September 1792, at which time he penned the following letter to Henry Knox, in which Girty's old Seneca patron Guyasuta is mentioned. Apparently, the ancient warrior was by this time firmly in the American camp, and had fallen on hard times:

ANTHONY WAYNE TO SECRETARY OF WAR HENRY KNOX,
14 DECEMBER 1792

… on Sunday last I was honored by the Company of Genl. St. Clair to dinner—who was on a flying visit to this place upon private business the same day Old Geyesutha arrived from Fort Franklin and deliver'd the enclosed talk—not Officially from the Nation, but his own Voluntary Act & private Opinion—the principal Object of his Visit, was evidently a supply of Clothing for himself—which the Governor, gratified him.…[14]

If Simon was spying at Pittsburgh in September 1792, he may well have clandestinely visited with his half-brother, John Turner, Jr. If so, he would have learned that back in February Thomas Girty had transferred half of their mother's land on Squirrel Hill to John "for the sum of £40 in Gold and Silver lawful money of State," and that Thomas then sold the other half of their mother's land to Jacob Caselman.

Late in September, McKee planned to send Girty with a mixed war party of some 247 Wyandots and Mingoes to harass the Americans at Fort St. Clair or Fort Hamilton, but at the last moment McKee aborted this mission. The opening date of the most important of the four Grand Councils at The Glaize was approaching, and McKee wanted Girty in attendance. Although he and Matthew Elliott were not allowed to actually take part in the councils, they were both at The Glaize, doing their best to influence the outcome. McKee had orders to pursue the concept of establishing an Indian buffer state, and to secure Indian approval for the English to serve as mediators in all their future negotiations with the United States.

Representatives were present from twenty-eight eastern and western tribes, including Sauks and Foxes from the north, the Seven Nations of Canada (Iroquois dissidents who sided with the British), neutral and pro-American Six Nation's tribesman like the Senecas of Cornplanter's sect (which included old Guyasuta, who did not attend), as well as Creeks and Cherokees from the south. The most hostile members were the Shawnees and Miamis, followed by the Potawatomis, Ottawas and Wyandots. Although there was harsh dissention among the opposing factions, everyone understood that in order to project real power the results of the Grand Council had to be inclusive. Girty's voice was added to those who insisted upon an Ohio River border.

Butterfield's description of The Glaize is an accurate one:

The place where the council was held was high ground, on the point between the Auglaize and the Maumee. Here, extending from the latter river up the first-mentioned stream, was an open space, on the west and south of which were oak woods, with hazel undergrowth. Within this opening, a few hundred yards above the point, on the steep, high bank of the Auglaize, were five or six cabins and log-houses, inhabited principally by Indian traders. The most northerly, a large hewed log-house, divided below into three apartments, was occupied as a warehouse, store, and dwelling, by George Ironside, the most wealthy and influential of the traders "on the point." Next to this was the house of Pirault, a French baker, and McKenzie, a Scotchman, who, in addition to merchandising, followed the occupation of a silversmith, exchanging with the Indians his brooches, ear-drops, and other silver ornaments, at an enormous profit, for skins and furs. Still farther up, were several families of French and English; and two American prisoners, Henry Ball and wife, were allowed to live

there. They were captured in St. Clair's defeat, and were permit-
ted by their masters to work and earn the price of their ransom; he
by boating to the Rapids of the Maumee, and she by washing and
sewing.

Fronting the house of Ironside, and about fifty yards from
the bank, was a small stockade, inclosing two log-houses. In one
of these, McKee and Elliott stored their supplies of arms, and
other articles which were now being handed out to the savages in
lavish quantities; in the other, lived a trader, mention of whom
will hereafter be made, and with whom Simon Girty had his
home while the council continued. From this station, a fine view
could be had of a large Indian village—more than a mile south,
on the east side of the Auglaize—and of Blue Jacket's town; on the
Maumee river and down that for several miles below. An exten-
sive prairie, covered with corn, directly opposite, could also be
seen—the whole forming a very handsome landscape.[15]

The deliberations of the council were dominated by Messquakenoe of the Shawnees and Red Jacket of the Iroquois, who were strongly opposed. On 7 October the Shawnees asserted that the Six Nations were nothing more than agents of the United States, who were avoiding participation in the defense of the country against American aggression. Restating the position of the western nations, Messquakenoe reasserted that the Ohio River must be the boundary between the red and white people. He said that if America was serious about wanting peace, the forts on the west or north side of the Ohio should be removed. Only then, he claimed, could peace be achieved. After meeting in private, the Six Nation representatives returned and agreed to the demand for the Ohio line. Finally, the full council resolved to meet with the Americans at Sandusky the following year to negotiate a settlement. Although the Grand Council concluded on 9 October with apparent consensus, there were still problems between the Shawnees and the Iroquois League. It was decided that the reso-lution of the council would be delivered by the Six Nations to the American agent to the Iroquois, General Israel Chapin.

On 6 November, leading some 200 warriors, Little Turtle and

Blue Jacket attacked a large Kentucky brigade encamped some two hundred yards from Fort St. Clair. The Kentuckians had about 100 men and the same number of packhorses. Catching the Americans completely unaware, the Indians attacked on three sides, and immediately the battle turned to hand-to-hand combat. The majority of the Kentuckians broke and ran to the fort for safety. American casualties were six killed, five wounded and four missing. Twenty-six horses were killed, ten wounded, and the remainder were taken by the Indians. The loss of so many packhorses was a devastating blow. In camp at Legionville, on the Ohio River, General Wayne ached to respond, but was ordered not to launch any offensive operations.

On 6 December, Secretary of War Knox mentioned Girty in a letter to President Washington:

SECRETARY OF WAR HENRY KNOX TO PRESIDENT GEORGE WASHINGTON, 6 DECEMBER 1792

Sir:

… Besides the papers transmitted by Mr. Chapin, the interpreter says, that a list of the tribes which composed the council at the Au Glaize, on the Miami river of Lake Erie, was taken by Mr. Chapin, but he omitted to transmit it.

He was informed by the chiefs of the Six Nations, that, at the council of the hostile Indians, which was numerous, but the numbers not specified, no other white person was admitted but Simon Girty, whom they considered as one of themselves….[16]

Between October 1792 and February of 1793, Girty's activities are unknown. Butterfield speculated that he remained at The Glaize over the winter, but it is far more likely that he went home to his family at Malden. Meanwhile, Mad Anthony Wayne continued to hone his new army.

CHAPTER EIGHTEEN
THE FINAL CLASH

IN FEBRUARY 1793, Secretary of War Knox's answering letter to the confederacy's fall proposals finally reached the Indians. Simon hurried to The Glaize to join Shawnee and Miami leaders who had gathered to study the document. Encouragingly, Knox wrote that President Washington had welcomed their peace messages and that early in the spring the United States would send commissioners to discuss peace with them at the Miami Rapids. In the meantime Knox promised that the Americans would prevent any of their parties from going into Indian country and, in return, he asked the Indians to suspend their offensive operations.

Knox's letter omitted any mention of an Ohio River boundary or the removal of American forts or settlements already situated north of that river. These demands were two of the principal points of contention that the Six Nations had reluctantly agreed to the preceding fall, and they were supposed to have been included in Joseph Brant's presentation to the Americans. Knox had also declared that the peace meetings were to take place at the Miami Rapids and not at Lower Sandusky as the confederation had originally requested. As a result, there was growing uncertainty about exactly what Brant had communicated to the Americans. Because of this ambiguity, a message was rushed to the Six Nations inviting Brant and their delegates to attend preliminary councils at The Glaize before the spring meetings with the Americans. After lengthy discussions, a terse response was sent to Knox in which the Indians complained that it appeared to them that the Americans were preparing for war rather than peace.

They also informed the Secretary of War that the forthcoming negotiations would have to take place at Lower Sandusky and nowhere
else. Closing on a positive note, the Indians agreed to call back their
war parties until the treaty convened.

At the end of February, signaling compromise, Knox responded
that the United States commissioners would be pleased to meet with
the Indians at Lower Sandusky on the first day of June. But once again
his letter failed to mention anything about the removal of American
forts or settlements across the Ohio River.

Flushed with recent memories of their overwhelming victories,
the fragile confederacy disregarded any sense of urgency and debated
interminably.

While the chiefs argued, twenty-one miles south of Pittsburgh, at
Legionville, "Mad Anthony" Wayne conducted advanced marksmanship training and put his troops through rigorous tactical maneuvers
and war games. His riflemen had been armed with Lancaster County
Rifles, with which he had them practice at ever-longer ranges. Paper
targets were affixed to trees so that lead bullets could be retrieved,
melted and recast. Wayne's regular infantry were equipped with
standard smoothbore muskets that fired modified paper cartridges—
preloaded not with just one lead ball and powder, but with a single
large ball plus three heavy buckshot placed in front of a stout black
powder charge. The infantry were being trained to move rapidly in
lines, firing waist-high as they advanced. Their buck-and-ball paper
cartridges would enable them to reload faster, and to deliver far more
devastating firepower than their opponents.

Wayne's tactics were designed to disorient the enemy and to dis-
lodge them by waves of rapid movement. Once he had the warriors on
the run, he meant to keep them moving and deny them any opportunity to rally. When eighteenth century infantry charged, their
principal weapon was the bayonet. Wayne knew that in the heat of
close combat there was nothing more frightening than a rapid, coordi-
nated bayonet charge. The general's officers drilled and re-drilled their
men on this murderous method, using the latest techniques to maintain formations while charging at a run. Wayne's discipline was as
severe as his training. Deserters first had the word "coward" branded

across their foreheads, and then they were shot or hung. Unlike his predecessors, General Wayne was not relying upon unruly militia who were more interested in looting than soldiering. Mad Anthony was creating a legion of deadly, professional soldiers.

In March 1793, Brant wrote to McKee saying that in his view, the Americans were sincere in their desire for peace. He urged that the western nations be restrained. The Six Nations had just concluded that the Muskingum Line of 1788 now presented the only realistic chance they had to settle with the Americans, and whether it meant war or peace, the Iroquois tribes were insisting on that compromise. This was the same proposal Brant had first pitched to the Shawnees and Miamis two years earlier, which allowed the Americans to retain their existing settlements east of the Muskingum River.

What had now become glaringly apparent to Simon Girty, Alex McKee and Matthew Elliott, was that the western tribes of the Ohio Country and the Six Nations of New York were inexorably opposed on the central issue. Once again, evolving politics had made Girty and Guyasuta, his mentor and friend, opponents in a matter of vital concern. While McKee may have inwardly agreed with Brant that the Muskingum Line proposal was the confederacy's best chance to achieve lasting peace, he and his agents were given no leeway in the matter. Provincial Lieutenant Governor John Graves Simcoe ordered them to discreetly and cleverly encourage the Shawnees and Miamis to maintain their demands for an Ohio River boundary.

Late in April, Benjamin Lincoln, Beverley Randolph and Timothy Pickering were appointed to represent America at the forthcoming June treaty meetings. Lincoln was a retired general who had compiled a distinguished record during the War for Independence, Randolph was a recent governor of Virginia, and Pickering was a brilliant Harvard graduate who had served as a captain during the revolution and who had recently been appointed postmaster general. The commissioners were to be accompanied by a pious entourage of Pennsylvania Quakers and Girty's old Moravian nemesis, Reverend John Heckewelder. They had instructions to initiate confirmation of all the treaties and boundaries that the Americans had established in the 1780s. However, if during the course of negotiations, they deemed that it was the only way to preserve peace, they could retreat from the terms of the 1789 treaty of Fort Harmar—but not too far. Under no circumstances were they to agree to any boundary demands that would result in the removal of settlements or forts that had already been established across the Ohio River. Finally, for military reasons, the commissioners had been instructed to conclude negotiations by the beginning of August and immediately inform General Wayne of their results. President Washington had already ordered Wayne to have his army ready for action no later than 20 July.

At the end of April, 1793, General Wayne and his army sailed aboard keelboats and barges to Fort Washington, located just outside of the fledgling settlement of Cincinnati. There, he established a camp for his men on swampy terrain about a mile south, at a place he named "Hobson's Choice."

As the opening date for negotiations approached, the players included the English, who wanted to maintain as large a buffer state as possible between the United States and their holdings in Canada; the alliance of western nations, led by the Shawnees and Miamis, who wanted American recognition of an Ohio River boundary or war; the Six Nations, who were willing to give away everything east of the Muskingum River in pursuit of peace; and lastly, the Americans, who were determined to hold on to what they had stolen in postwar treaties. Simon Girty must have realized that what was at stake was the future of red and white America.

Accompanied by six Quakers and John Heckewelder, the American delegation arrived at Niagara on 16 May, and Lieutenant Governor Simcoe hosted them at his home. Simcoe made every effort to see that his guests were treated hospitably and politely. Having enjoyed a feast and attended a ball, Simcoe's evident sincerity and trustworthiness beguiled the American delegation, and they began to reveal their innermost concerns and intentions—exposing far too much to their formerly overt and presently covert foe. The commissioners were so taken in by Simcoe's cooperative facade that they even requested him to provide British military officers to attend the forthcoming negotiations, ostensibly to assist the Indians in understanding American proposals, maps and intentions. Simcoe rushed a stream of secret communications to McKee at The Glaize, including startling news that he had just received which indicated that since February, France and England had been in a state of war. Simcoe warned McKee that the Americans might soon join their French allies, information that McKee no doubt shared with Simon Girty.

Recognizing the need for urgency, Girty and McKee pressed the confederated nations to resolve their differences. The number of Indians coming to attend the councils was growing daily, and more than a thousand had already gathered. At Detroit, Matthew Elliott was working to keep the delegates provided with a steady stream of provisions, arms and ammunition.

On 22 May, accompanied by seventy members of the Six Nations, as well as a few representatives from the Delawares at the Grand River, Joseph Brant finally reached the Maumee Rapids. Another three weeks were to pass before all the principals from the western tribes had arrived and meetings could commence.

Waiting for the Indian delegation, the Americans at Niagara grew uneasy. Their apprehensions were fed by a rumor that claimed that if the Indians were unable to successfully achieve peace, they "would commence hostilities by sacrificing the commissioners on the spot."[1] Late in June, the American delegation decided to move to Detroit in order to be closer to where the Indians were meeting. On the 26th they went to Fort Erie, intending to sail to Detroit aboard a British schooner, but the winds were unfavorable. The Americans were still waiting to sail to Detroit when, on the 5th of July, the English vessel *Chippewa* arrived, carrying Simon Girty, Indian agent John Butler, Joseph Brant, and an Indian delegation comprised of some fifty chiefs and sachems. Girty was wearing his signature outfit. Although the arrival of the Indian delegation was a surprise, an agreement was reached for the initial treaty meetings to take place back at Niagara two days later.

The meetings finally began on 7 July under Lieutenant Governor Simcoe's clandestine supervision. By mid-morning the temperature was 102° F in the shade. Brant served as spokesman for the Indians, and began by informing the commissioners that the confederacy was alarmed at General Wayne's movement towards Fort Jefferson, and

that the chiefs were determined not to meet with the commissioners at Sandusky under such circumstances. Then, after reminding the
commissioners that he and his friends had been deputized to represent all the Indians who owned land north of the Ohio, he bluntly
asked the Americans if they had been "properly authorized to run and
establish a new boundary line between the lands of the United States
and the lands of the Indian nations?"[2]

Brant's question went unanswered for the moment. Several
members of the Indian delegation alertly noted that the Mohawk chief
had omitted mentioning anything about the dismantling of existing
forts or settlements. The following day the commissioners replied to
Brant's question, and assured the Indians that no hostile actions were
being taken against them, as President Washington, General Wayne,
and the governors of Pennsylvania and Virginia had all taken measures to preserve the peace. As proof, copies of proclamations to this
effect were exhibited to Brant and the Indian delegation. Next, the
commissioners revealed that they did, in fact, have the authority to
run a new boundary line, but that the location of that line was one of
the issues to be discussed at the coming meetings at Sandusky, where
they thought concessions might be necessary from both sides. At
this point, the meeting was postponed in order to give Brant and the
Indian delegation time to discuss and formulate their response.

The next day Brant addressed the Americans in conciliatory tones.
He said that he believed the prospects for peace were good and that
the western nations had agreed to meet with them at Sandusky. He
added that when he had left the Maumee twelve nations had already
arrived and more were coming every day. Having concluded their
business, Girty and the Indian delegation withdrew and started back
for The Glaize. Once again Simon and Brant had worked in harmony
together.

Thus far the American delegates believed that things had gone very
well, and they again made ready to sail to the mouth of the Detroit
River (a short distance from Girty's home).

By the time that Girty, Brant and the others reached the Maumee
Rapids on 21 July, the assembly there had grown to some 1,500 men,
women and children. Included were about 166 people from the

American Six Nations, a larger delegation from the Seven Nations of Canada, and Creeks and Cherokees from the South, who reported that recent fighting with the Americans had broken out on the Georgia frontier. Brant's account of the negotiations thus far outraged the Shawnees, Wyandots, Delawares and Miamis, all of whom accused him of deviating from the ultimatum that he had been charged to deliver. Brant angrily responded that he and the other delegates had not been empowered to fix a new boundary, but only to determine if the Americans had been authorized to make one. Brant threatened that if the western nations remained rigid on this issue, he and the Six Nations might withdraw. The Ottawas, Chippewas and Potawatamis signified that they sided with Brant. Faced with the prospect of their confederacy coming apart precisely when unity was vital, the western tribal leaders hurriedly withdrew to confer among themselves.

Meanwhile, the American delegation was housed at the estate of Matthew Elliott, located at the mouth of the Detroit River, next door to Girty's homestead. They had been directed there because (for military reasons) Simcoe did not want the American commissioners to see Detroit. Elliott's family played the role of good host, with his slaves providing for the visitors' every need. Lincoln, Pickering and Randolph had been quartered inside Elliott's home, and the Quakers and Moravian missionaries occupied tents that had been erected on a pleasant green before the house.

On 26 July, things came to a head at The Glaize. Led by the Shawnees and Miamis, the hostile faction came to council with flintlock pistols tucked in their belts. Captain Johnny spoke for the Shawnees, declaring that they and their allies were committed to sending a message to the Americans that the Ohio River boundary, as described in the Fort Stanwix Treaty of 1768, had to be preserved. A written draft of this message had been prepared for all the tribes of the confederation to sign, to be delivered to the Americans by a new delegation.

Infuriated, Brant refused to sign. He guessed that McKee had prompted the Shawnee actions, and he was probably right. Regardless of Brant's displeasure, Simon Girty, Matthew Elliott, Thomas McKee (son of Alexander) and another interpreter named Thomas Smith departed with a thirty-plus delegation to meet the Americans. Led by the Wyandot chief Sa-wagh-da-wunk, the Indians included principal chiefs of the Shawnees, Miamis and Delawares. The delegation arrived at Bois Blanc Island, opposite Elliott's farm, late on 29 July and crossed over to Elliott's place on the morning of the 30th. Girty again wore his signature costume and, according to Heckewelder, "supported his insolence by wearing a quill or long feather run through the under part of his nose cross ways."[3]

Speaking through Simon, Sa-wagh-da-wunk opened the meeting by greeting the Americans, and then he delivered the written ultimatum which demanded an explicit answer to the question: Are you fully authorized by the United States to firmly to fix the Ohio River as the boundary between your people and ours?

Taken aback, the startled commissioners said they would reply the next day. On the morning of the 31st Timothy Pickering responded for the United States. Regarding the American settlements situated across the Ohio River, Pickering informed the Indians that these had been acquired through treaties, and that the lands had already been resold. There had been improvements built and there would be too much expense involved for practical removal. The Americans wanted confirmation of the Treaty of Fort Harmar. In addition, General George Rogers Clark wanted a small tract of land at the Rapids of the Ohio. In return, Pickering promised that the Indians would be paid very well for these concessions. On their part, the commissioners were willing to negotiate a boundary somewhere between the new settlements and the line established by the Fort Harmar treaty. More importantly, the commissioner explained, the United States was ready to acknowledge the Indians' right to all the remaining lands north of the Ohio River.

This was the pivotal moment of post-Revolutionary War white and red relations—and there can be little doubt that America's eventual boundaries, and thus her power, hung in the balance. Had the consummate Brant still been conducting negotiations for the confederacy, an agreement might have been achieved in which westward expansion by the whites would have been retarded, if not prevented, for decades. But Brant wasn't there, and it was So-wagh-da-wunk who answered. According to Butterfield:

> *The rejoinder was made on the 1st of August by the same*
> *Wyandot (Girty again interpreting), the purport of which was*
> *that they would lay the written document of the Commissioners*
> *before the warriors upon the Maumee; but he added, so Girty*
> *interpreted, that they (the Commissioners) might "now go home!"* [4]

According to historian Wiley Sword, So-wagh-da-wunk's actual response was:

> *… this side [of the Ohio] is ours," and "you have your houses and*
> *people on our land," the Wyandot speaker asserted, "We cannot*
> *give up our land." "You may return whence you came and tell*
> *[President] Washington," he admonished.* [5]

At this point Matthew Elliott interrupted, claiming that Girty had not properly interpreted the Wyandot's closing statement. Turning to the Shawnee chief Kakiapalathy, Elliott sought agreement. After a quick, terse conversation between Elliott, Girty, and the Indians, Simon issued a new interpretation of the Wyandot speaker's closing line: "Instead of going home," Simon corrected, "we wish you to remain here for an answer from us … We have your speech in our breasts and shall consult our head warriors." [6]

The American delegation agreed to wait for a reasonable period for the Indian response. Four days later, Quaker William Savery wrote in his journal:

> *3d. The vessel called Detroit, bound to Fort Erie, appearing in*
> *sight, I wrote a hasty letter. Appointed a meeting to be held at*
> *Simon Girty's tomorrow at ten o'clock.*
>
> *4th. First-day morning. Very rainy, and much wet in my tent;*
> *rose about three o'clock, bundled up my mattress and tied it in*
> *a painted cloth, and sat upon it till sunrise. The rain continuing,*
> *three of us went to Simon Girty's, but finding none met, except*
> *the family, returned. Captain Hamilton, an amiable man, and*
> *an officer in the Fifth Regiment dined with us. The Chippeway, a*

vessel bound from Fort Erie to Detroit, brought one hundred and eighty Indians and landed them at the Miami [Maumee] river. The afternoon being pleasant, had a meeting at Simon Girty's, about one and a half miles from our camp, at which a number of Indians were present and behaved soberly. General [Benjamin] Lincoln, General Chapin, Captain Hamilton, Lieutenant Givans, and several seamen, also attended; I believe it was to satisfaction. The few scattered white people in this Indian country, many of whom have been prisoners of war, have no opportunity of public worship; yet some of them are glad of our meetings; among whom was the wife of Simon Girty, who also had been a prisoner among the Indians.[7]

In addition to confirming that Catherine Girty apparently enjoyed taking part in Christian activities and prayer meetings during her husband's prolonged absences, Quaker Savery also noted that Indians who visited the Girty farm felt at home there.

While the commissioners languished at Elliott's estate, awaiting the final message from the western tribes, harsh infighting was taking place back at The Glaize. Having learned from the Shawnee leaders that no compromise was possible, Brant told his tribesmen to make preparations to go home. On 9 August, he addressed the general council of nations, once again reminding everyone that what he had proposed—a Muskingum boundary line—was the same boundary the confederacy had proposed two years earlier during meetings with Lord Dorchester. Brant argued that a compromise now, by everyone, was preferable in every way to a tentative war.

Brant was unable to budge the Shawnees and their allies, whose leaders met with McKee later that night. Speaking before a general council on 12 August, Captain Johnny once again insisted that the Ohio River must remain the final boundary.

Brant had had enough. Refusing to sign the final declaration, he and the rest of the Six Nation delegates departed for a camp eight miles away to make ready to go home.

With Alexander McKee's assistance, the Shawnees framed the formal written response that was to be delivered to the Americans. The final declaration was signed by sixteen nations, with signatures from the Six Nations noticeably absent. On 15 August, two Wyandot runners delivered the document to the American commissioners. Dooming the creation of an Indian-governed country whose borders would be recognized by its most powerful enemy, the declaration included the following phrases:

You agreed to do us justice, after having long, and injuriously, withheld it. We mean in the acknowledgement you now have made, that the King of England never did, nor ever had a right to give you our Country, by the Treaty of peace, and you want to make this act of Common Justice a great part of your concessions, and seem to expect that, because you have at last acknowledged our independence, we should for such a favor surrender to you our country.

… money to us is of no value … and as no consideration whatever can induce us to sell the lands on which we get sustenance for our women and children; we hope we may be allowed to point out a mode by which your settlers may be easily removed, and peace thereby obtained.… We know these settlers are poor, or they would never have ventured to live in a country which has been in continued trouble ever since they crossed the Ohio; divide, therefore, this large sum of money, which you have offered to us, among these people … and we are persuaded, they would most readily accept of it, in lieu of the lands you sold them.… If you add also, the great sums you must expend in raising and paying Armies, with a view to force us to yield you our Country, you will certainly have more than sufficient for the purposes of repaying these settlers for all their labor and improvements.[8]

Amounting to a declaration of war, the document was signed by the Wyandots, Seven Nations of Canada, Delawares, Shawnees, Miamis, Ottawas, Chippewas, Senecas of the Glaize, Potawatomis, Conoys, Muncies, Nanticokes, Mahicans, Mississaugas, Creeks and Cherokees.

The Americans responded that there was no point in continuing negotiations, and within hours they began to load their belongings aboard the *Dunmore*. The next morning they sailed for Fort Erie. A message had already been sent to General Wayne advising him "we did not effect a peace."[9]

In November, Thomas Jefferson wrote:

THOMAS JEFFERSON TO CHARLES PINCKNEY,
27 NOVEMBER 1793

Our negotiations with the northwestern Indians have completely failed, so that war must settle our difference. We expected nothing else, and had gone into negotiations only to prove to all our citizens that peace was unattainable on terms, which any one of them would admit.[10]

As the confederacy reeled from the loss of Brant and the Six Nations, it appeared that the Americans were going to undertake offensive operations. However, due to a wave of smallpox and influenza, and a lack of sufficient supplies at his forward bases, General Wayne was unable to proceed farther than seven miles in advance of Fort Jefferson, where he erected a fortified camp (site of the future Fort Greenville), as winter came on.

When word reached the foot of the Maumee Rapids that the Americans were advancing, McKee removed his heavy baggage and personal papers to Swan Creek, near the mouth of the Maumee. The following entry appears in his journal on 15 November:

Sent off Simon Girty to the Glaize for intelligence with directions to return the moment he shall have learn't any certain accounts of the American army.[11]

Girty performed the assignment with his usual attention to detail. Upon his return to Swan Creek, he reported to McKee that General Wayne and the bulk of his army were encamped some six miles north of Fort Jefferson, where it appeared they would remain until spring. Grateful for his help, McKee let Simon go home, where he enjoyed a respite until early the next year. The Americans were now offering $1,000 for his scalp.

On Christmas Eve, 1793, the surveyor general's office at Detroit awarded Simon Girty: "one thousand acres on the North Side of River La Tranche (present Thames River)."[12]

On the same day, General Wayne, accompanied by eight companies of infantry and some artillerymen, undertook a rapid march from recently built Fort Greenville (site of present Greenville, Ohio) to the grounds of St. Clair's defeat, arriving there on Christmas Day. Scattered all about them was debris from the disaster, including some skeletons of the defeated. Under a large oak tree, where his brother had died, Captain Edward Butler found Richard's remains—identified only by a former thigh injury. Altogether, Wayne and some of his men interred some four to six hundred skulls. The rest of the soldiers began to construct Fort Recovery. Thanks to the debriefing of former captive William May (who had only recently returned from Canada), Wayne was able to locate some of St. Clair's cannons, which had been hidden by the Indians. Three of the eight big guns were recovered, remounted, and made ready for action. Ironically, these were the same three guns the Wyandots had awarded to Simon Girty. On 28 December Wayne returned to Fort Greenville with most of his men, leaving behind a company of riflemen and a company of artillerymen to garrison the new installation.

On 3 February 1794, Girty was met by an American named Jacob Lewis, who had come from New Jersey to secure freedom for his sister, who was a captive of the Indians. The story Lewis later related of his meeting with Girty appears to have been dramatized. As Butterfield tells it:

JACOB LEWIS

One day while sitting talking with a gentleman—Dr. Freman—at his house in the outskirts of the town, the latter suddenly exclaimed: "Here comes Simon Girty." As Lewis had heard of the renegade, and knew what his reputation was among Americans, he was not only surprised but alarmed. Girty entered the house without knocking; and without saying a word, stood looking at the American stranger. He had evidently been drinking, which fact made his presence any thing but agreeable. After a few

*minutes, in which he stood still as a statue, Lewis asked him if he
had ever seen him before. "No," was his emphatic answer; "but if
ever I see you again, I shall know you," at the same time drawing
out from its sheath a large butcher-knife and throwing it down
between the American and the gentleman with whom the latter
was conversing. It was not long, however, before he picked up the
dangerous weapon and left the house. Lewis saw Girty several
times afterward, and he was always well treated by him.*[13]

Eventually Jacob Lewis succeeded in rescuing his sister. About the same time that he met with Girty at Detroit, Governor General Sir Guy Carlton (Lord Dorchester) was at Quebec, advising a delegation from the Seven Nations of Canada that, "I shall not be surprised if we are at war with them [the United States] in the course of the present year ... I believe our patience is almost exhausted."[14]

In an effort to bolster Indian confidence, Dorchester sent Simcoe to establish a military post on the Maumee, and to garrison it with regulars from Detroit. This, of course, was an overt act of aggression and in complete defiance of the peace agreement England had signed with the United States.

Lieutenant Governor Simcoe arrived at Detroit on the 2nd of April, and four days later he traveled to the Maumee Rapids with Elliott and McKee to arrange for construction of Fort Miamis, which was to be erected across the river from McKee's place, about a mile downstream. British troops were also stationed at other strategic points. On 14 April, the governor stood before a large assembly of western Indians and repeated Lord Dorchester's inflammatory Quebec speech. The Indians were intoxicated by vociferous encouragement from Girty, McKee and Elliott; by the building of a British fort and the establishment of other posts manned by English soldiers; by the promise of a flood of arms and supplies; and by the likelihood that British troops would once again be fighting by their side in a new war against the United States. The decision was made for The Glaize to be the warriors' point of assembly.

Throughout May, Girty, McKee, and Elliott were busy at the Maumee. As the month ended there was news that the Indians had attacked an American supply train somewhere between Fort Washington and Fort Hamilton, resulting in the taking of forty scalps, with the loss of only one warrior. The Lakes Indians (Ottawa, Chippewa and Potawatomi) were gathering, and by 3 June McKee was able to report that that he expected the entire Indian army would be together at The Glaize within two weeks. On the 10th of the month, 500 more Indians came to the rapids and were ready to join the warriors at The Glaize. On the 15th, the Wyandots arrived, and were greeted by 600 warriors who honored them by firing a fusillade. Including Miamis, Shawnees, Delawares, Wyandots, Ottawas, Chippewas, and Potawatomis, the Indian army now numbered about 1,200 men, and was one of the largest assemblies of warriors ever drawn together to fight the United States. British traders and other Canadians were also coming in daily, and an Indian council of war determined that all the whites in the vicinity would have to join the Indian army. To ensure that there would be no mistakes during the heat of battle, the whites were to wear Indian dress. The only sour note was disquieting news that some twenty-seven Lakes Indians from Mackinaw and Saginaw had committed depredations, and had raped women in the Indian villages through which they had passed. The problems caused by these particular Indians were just beginning.

Outwardly, the Indian army that Chief Little Turtle led from The Glaize on 17 June appeared powerful and unified. But the truth was the warriors had few provisions, almost no logistical support, and ten percent of them were without firearms. A combination of several tribes who did not trust one another, the alliance was fragile and volatile, and whatever unanimity there was at the start of the campaign rapidly dissipated. As the collective voice of the British government, McKee, Elliott and Girty had been the glue that had held the Indians together, but now that the warrior army was underway and native leaders were in control, things began to unravel. The chiefs were unable to agree upon even basic objectives.

McKee advocated for continued attacks on Wayne's supply lines, a strategy by which the Miamis and Shawnees had been achieving good results with only minor losses. The Lakes Indians, however, were in favor of an assault on Fort Recovery. The conflict simmered for days, and the dissension was nurtured by the dismally slow pace of the marching army. Due to the lack of provisions, the warriors were forced to make camp early each afternoon in order to send hunters out to scour game from the surrounding countryside. In three days of travel Little Turtle's army had come only sixty miles. On 26 June, advance scouts encountered a small party of Chickasaws, who were spying for General Wayne. One of the enemy spies was killed and scalped, but the remainder of the Chickasaws escaped. Little Turtle, Blue Jacket and the other war chiefs were concerned that their presence was now known. There could be no more time for arguing. Although the ranking British officer present adamantly opposed the plan, in order to keep their forces together, Little Turtle and Blue Jacket bowed to the Lakes Indians and the decision was made to attack the nearest American installation—Fort Recovery.

The 200 man garrison at the fort was commanded by a Virginian, Captain Alexander Gibson (no relation to John Gibson). An energetic and disciplined veteran, Gibson had cleared the surrounding ground for two hundred yards in order to provide a clear field of fire. He had also raised the four blockhouses of the fort to two stories, and had continually drilled his men and compelled them to practice their shooting. In addition to the three St. Clair cannons which had been recovered, Gibson's men had discovered a brass three-pounder and an iron four-pounder that had been buried by the victors of St. Clair. All of these guns had been reconditioned, remounted and positioned, creating a formidable defense. In addition, a large shipment of gunpowder had arrived in March. Gibson's only shortall was his lack of provisions. Fort Recovery operated hand-to-mouth and depended entirely upon what Wayne could supply it from Fort Greenville. On 29 June Major William McMahon led a heavily escorted supply mission to Fort Recovery. Fifty dragoons and ninety riflemen accompanied 360 packhorses laden with some 1,200 kegs of flour. McMahon's supply train reached the fort on the evening of the 29th. It was too small to comfortably accommodate McMahon's men overnight, so a camp was set up for them about a hundred yards from the main gate. The most accurate account of what took place the next morning is revealed in

General Wayne's report of the event to Secretary of War Knox, dated 7 July 1794. In his letter, the American commander reports:

Head Quarters
Greenville

Sir

At 7 O'clock in the morning of the 30th. Ultimo one of our escorts consisting of Ninety Riflemen & Fifty Dragoons Commanded by Major McMahan was attacked by a very numerous body of Indians under the walls of Fort Recovery, followed by a General Assault upon that post & Garrison in every direction. The enemy were soon repulsed with great slaughter, But immediately rallied & reiterated the attack keeping up a very heavy & constant fire, at a more respectable distance all the remainder of that day, which was answer'd with spirit & Effect by the Garrison & that part of Major McMahans Command, that had regained the post.

The Savages were employed during the Night which was dark & foggy, in carrying off their dead by torch light, which Occasionally drew a fire from the Garrison—They nevertheless succeeded so well, that there were but Eight dead bodies left upon the field & those close under the influence of the fire from the Fort.

The Enemy again renewed the attack on the morning of the 1st Instant but were ultimately compeled to retreat about One O'clock of that day with loss & disgrace from that very field where they had upon a former Occasion been proudly Victorious.

Enclosed is a particular & General return of the Killed, Wounded & missing, Among the Killed we have to lament the loss of Four good and Gallant Officers VIZ Major McMahan, Capt Hartshorne, & Lieut Craig of the Rifle Corps & Cornet Torry of the Cavalry, who all fell in the first Charge, among the Wounded are the intrepid Capt Taylor of the Dragoons & Lieut Drake of the Infantry.

At the end of his letter to Knox, Wayne dissects the conflict, noting everything of military value that had been revealed by the Indians.

Although the conflict appeared to be a solid victory for the Indians, Wayne seemed unperturbed, taking note of the weaknesses the enemy had revealed:

It would appear that the real Object of the Enemy was to have carried that post by a coup de main for they cou'd not possibly have received intelligence of the Escort under Major McMahan which only marched from this place on the morning of the 29th Ultimo, & deposited the supplies the same evening at Fort Recovery, from whence the escort was to have return'd at Reveille the next Morning. Therefore their being found at that post was an accidental, perhaps a fortunate event, By every information as well as from the extent of their encampments which were perfectly square and regular, their line of March in seventeen Columns, forming a wide & Extended front, their Numbers cou'd not have been less than from 1500 to 2000 warriors, it wou'd also appear that they were rather short of provision as they killed & ate a number of Pack Horses in their encampment the evening after they assault, as also at noon next encampment [during] their retreat, which was but seven miles from fort Recovery, where they remained two Nights, probably from being much encumbered with their dead & wounded a considerable Number of the pack Horses were actually loaded with the dead....

... The horses that were killed, wounded & missing in the Assault against Fort Recovery will not in the least retard the Advance of the Legion after the arrival of the Mounted volunteers Because I had made provision for these kind of losses & contingencies which from the nature of the service must be expected & will unavoidably happen.

I have the honor to be with every sentiment of Respect & Esteem Your most Obet & very Huml Sert.

Anty Wayne[15]

During the initial attack against McMahon's supply train some forty Americans had been killed and more than 300 packhorses had fallen into Indian hands. Little Turtle, Blue Jacket and Captain

Johnny were satisfied with what had been achieved, and were all for splitting up and waylaying other American supply trains. However, flushed with excitement, the chiefs of the Lakes Indians (whose warriors numbered almost half of the combined Indian forces) argued for a renewed full frontal assault on Fort Recovery. Egos were involved, and finally, for the sake of preserving unity, the Shawnee and Miami war chiefs reluctantly agreed.

The ensuing attack was a disaster. In a foolhardy effort to storm the fort the Lakes Indians exposed themselves, charging wildly over the open grounds surrounding the installation. Gibson's men responded with deliberate, well-aimed rifle fire. A moment later several of the American cannons roared and one warrior was reportedly decapitated by a cannon ball. The impetuous assault was decimated, and the surviving warriors were driven to cover. Although the siege was to continue for another full day, it was apparent from that moment on that without any cannons of their own, the Indians were incapable of overwhelming the American post. Lacking any cannons of their own, they would never be able to do so.

What Wayne's report failed to mention, and what evidently must have gone unnoticed by Gibson and his garrison, was that during the latter part of the siege Shawnee warriors at the rear began to fire directly at the backs of Lakes Indians who were engaged closer to the enemy fort. This no doubt was in payment for the rapes and other depredations they had committed earlier. What had begun as a glorious show of Indian spirit and unity changed to betrayal, disappointment and disarray. As the Indian army retreated, their mood turned disconsolate. Simon Girty and a few other whites who had taken part in the fight had nothing but bitter disgust for what they had witnessed. Thomas McKee was apprehensive about the useless loss of lives wasted against the fort, which would bring lasting damage to the confederacy.

By 2 July morale was so low that the Indian army began to disintegrate. First the Lakes Indians turned away and started for home, followed at once by 800 disaffected Ottawas and Chippewas who had suffered the greatest casualties during the belated siege. The Shawnees blamed the failure at Fort Recovery on the Lakes Indians and the northern tribes; while the Ottawas and Chippewas countercharged that the Shawnees had fired on their rear while they were attacking the fort. Adding to the gloomy chaos was news of a fresh outbreak of smallpox in the Illinois Country. The result was the rapid dispersal of what shortly before had been a great Indian army. It was more a loss of spirit than substance. With the benefit of hindsight, there is no question that had the Indian army concentrated on destroying Wayne's supply columns, thereby isolating his forts, the outcome would have been different.

Tactically, General Wayne considered his losses at Fort Recovery to be a minor setback. What was important to him was what the delayed attack and its aftermath taught him about his enemy. Some of Wayne's Indian spies, whom he had sent out a few days prior to the siege at Fort Recovery, had fallen in with the enemy, and were present during the action. In his report to Knox, Wayne relates what they learned:

WAYNE TO KNOX, 7 JULY, 1794

... these Indians all insist, that there were a considerable Number of armed white men in the rear, who they frequently heard talking in our language & encouraging the Savages to persevere in the assault, that their faces were Generally blacked except three British Officers who were dressed in scarlet & appeared to be men of great distinction, from being surrounded by a large party of White men & Indians who were very attentive to them, these kept a distance in the rear of those that were engaged.[16]

From this intelligence, Wayne understood that the Canadian militia—who took part in the fighting—had been disguised as Indians, while the uniformed British officers had taken great care to avoid being caught in an overt act of war. Their actions coincided with his knowledge that diplomatically, British officials were in the midst of negotiating peace terms with the United States which would result in their relinquishing all of their Northwest Territory posts—including Detroit. Under such circumstances, he reasoned it was likely that once he made his move, he would not face anything more than Indians supported by a few Canadian militia.

Focusing on the intelligence which indicated that his opponents were poorly provisioned and not nearly as well prepared to wage war as he had assumed, Wayne was like a shark scenting blood. Here was the opportunity that he had been waiting for. The outcome of the impending conflict between the army of the United States and that of the western tribes was in a large sense the result of what Wayne learned from the Indian attack on Fort Recovery.

The challenge for Girty, McKee, Elliott and the other members of the Indian Department was to heal the great wounding of the confederacy before the clash with Wayne. Holding councils, receiving tribal delegations, and pointing out the increased shipments of provisions and gunpowder that were being sent to the garrison at Fort Miamis, they endeavored to arrest Indian discontent and allay apprehensions. Late in July, as Fort Miamis was being stockpiled, the Shawnees and Lakes Tribes regained their confidence and agreed to table their differences, at least for the present.

Wanting assurances and a clear demonstration of British fidelity, Little Turtle went to Detroit to meet with Colonel Richard England, whom he asked point blank to provide two cannons and at least twenty men for another assault on Fort Recovery. Unable to grant his request, the colonel met with the Miami chief for two or three days, after which he mistakenly believed he had placated him. Far from being placated, Little Turtle was now firmly convinced that the British were neither capable, nor inclined, to furnish the Indians with direct military aid.

The question of British fidelity was forcing Girty, McKee and Elliott into an uncomfortable corner. By now, all three were aware that once the shooting started, direct British military assistance to the Indians would be withheld. There was little else the trio could do except obey orders and continue to allude to the chiefs that, if needed, British troops would come to their aid. The Indian agents were trusted so completely that their precarious charade was remarkably successful in rebuilding unity after the debacle at Fort Recovery. It appeared that when Wayne began his final advance there would be a strong and sufficient force to oppose him.

The war chiefs knew they could not overwhelm well-defended American forts. They reasoned that once the enemy offensive began, their white opponents would not be protected by palisades and cannon, but would have to maneuver out in the open, where in every major confrontation over the last twenty years the Indians had handed them devastating defeats. Girty, McKee and Elliott had good reason to believe that if they were to reverse their course and warn the Indians that under no circumstances would British troops come to their aid, their will to resist "The Black Snake," (as Wayne was now called) would be broken and their chiefs would seek reconciliation with the United States. The Indians would lose everything in any subsequent treaties. The three men realized that if Wayne was defeated in the coming conflict the Indian agents would retain their credibility. If the Indians lost—their credibility wouldn't matter.

In mid-July, Wayne was informed that 760 mounted Kentucky volunteers were en route to him, and that the balance of the 1,500 militia he had been promised were only a day behind the first contingents. Wayne ordered his men to prepare to move out at a moment's notice. On the 25th the reinforcements arrived. Early the next morning, with 2,200 regular infantry and 1,500 Kentucky militia, Wayne started for The Glaize. The Americans followed the same trails the Indians had used when they had attacked Fort Recovery. Ahead of the American army, a large vanguard of veteran scouts—both white and Indian—fanned out in front of the formidable force. The woodsy spies had only one responsibility: to make certain that Wayne's army was not surprised.

In council at The Glaize, as reports came in Little Turtle pointed out that the open villages along the Maumee were indefensible, and these towns were quickly evacuated.

On 1 August, Wayne's forces reached the headwaters of the St. Mary's River, where they paused two days to build Fort Adams. During the work, a large tree fell on Wayne's tent while he was inside. When the debris was cleared, panicked rescuers discovered Wayne alive but with a badly bruised leg and ankle. He had survived a close brush with death.

On 8 August, destroying crops and burning abandoned homes along the way, the Legionnaires, as the force was called, pushed through recently vacated towns of the confluence of the Auglaize and Maumee rivers. Here Wayne paused to build Fort Defiance. On the 13th, he dispatched a peace message to the enemy. Stating that he was now in control of their major villages and farms, Wayne said that only immediate action on their part could save their women and children from starvation during the coming winter. He warned the Indians to ignore the British who had been giving them very bad advice.

Downstream, the allied warriors, some 1,500 strong, met in council. Little Turtle cautioned:

We have beaten the enemy twice under different commanders. We cannot expect the same good fortune to attend us always. The Americans are now led by a chief who never sleeps. The night and the days are alike to him, and during all the time that he has been marching on our villages, notwithstanding the watchfulness of our young men, we have never been able to surprise him. Think well of it. There is something whispers to me it would be prudent to listen to his offers of peace.[17]

Blue Jacket and other warriors were quick to oppose the Miami leader, insisting that if they remained resolute, the tribes of the confederacy were strong enough to defeat Wayne's forces. Little Turtle agreed to help during the fight, but only as the leader of the Miamis and not as war leader of the confederacy. Without dissent, Blue Jacket (whose leadership was supported by McKee) replaced Little Turtle. Large numbers of warriors had still not arrived, including those from the Six Nations. The immediate problem was how to stall the opening of hostilities until the entire Indian army was assembled to fight. To gain time, it was decided to deceitfully answer General Wayne's peace feeler with a conciliatory message.

From this point forward, Blue Jacket and the other war chiefs were in charge. McKee had already received explicit orders that in the coming fight, neither he nor any of his agents were to enter combat—there were to be no exceptions. With this in mind and with little to contribute to the war-planning, McKee withdrew and took Girty with him to attend to another crisis. Hundreds of refugees from abandoned villages were streaming into the area near Fort Miami, and he and Simon commenced a new preoccupation—keeping the refugees from starving. Begging for supplies, McKee sent desperate messages to Detroit.

Girty and McKee may have welcomed their new preoccupation as a respite from having to continually support the promise of active British military aid once the fighting began. That bluff was growing old.

English leadership, however, grasped every opportunity to embolden the warriors. Fort Miamis was reinforced by Major William Campbell and a few companies of the 24th Regiment, followed quickly by the arrival of Colonel William Caldwell with about one hundred Canadian militia. Caldwell let it be known that he was prepared to lead his men in a combat role, if necessary. Convinced by these actions that they would indeed have British military support, Indian morale began to soar.

In a great stroke of luck, an American deserter informed Blue Jacket of Wayne's intended line of march. The war chiefs decided to place their warriors at a spot along the Maumee River about five miles south of Fort Miamis. The position took advantage of a dense, twisted thicket of timber that had been ravaged by a tornado two or three years before. Expecting to go into combat the next day, on the 18th, the warriors followed their tradition of fasting the day before a fight as they took up defensive positions. They comprised a formidable army, including Wyandots, Delawares, Shawnees, Miamis and Ottawas. There were over 1,200 warriors ready for battle, and their spirits were high.

On the evening of the 18th, Wayne's Legionnaires reached Roche de Bout, a large limestone outcrop and landmark on the Maumee River. Earlier some of Wayne's scouts had been ambushed and this, combined with other intelligence, indicated that the Indians were preparing to fight. To assure his army easy mobility when it engaged in battle, Wayne ordered the immediate construction of a "place of deposit" where all their heavy baggage would be stored.

During the ambush against some of Wayne's scouts, Blue Jacket's warriors captured William May. He was the same American spy whom Girty had saved from being put to death at the hands of his Indian captors some two years before. Recognized by the Indians, May was thoroughly interrogated, and he provided detailed information about Wayne's line of advance. He also told the warriors that the Americans intended to attack on the 19th unless it was decided to build a fort for the deposit of baggage, in which case the fighting wouldn't start until the 20th. At the conclusion of his questioning, the Indians informed May that he was to be shot to death the following morning. Later, his shattered body was found tied to a tree, riddled by more than fifty bullets.

On the morning of the 20th of August, 1794, having manned their positions for three days with little or no food, the Indians were weak from hunger. One end of the Indian front line abutted the west bank of the Maumee River, with the opposite end terminating to the northwest almost three quarters of a mile away. The weather was grim, damp and rainy. Several hundred warriors slipped away from their positions to hurry to Fort Miamis to locate food and bring it back to their comrades. Girty, McKee and Elliott were on horseback heading towards the Indian line when the fighting began.

Wayne began the conflict by moving forward with a spearhead of mounted Kentucky militia, followed closely by regulars whose front lines were longer than those of the Indians. When the shooting commenced the warriors drove back the Kentucky militia and, sensing victory, several hundred Indians charged the Legionnaires. They were abruptly stopped by volleys of deadly fire from Wayne's regulars, who then executed a series of quick bayonet charges. Wayne's troops kept on, moving with such rapidity that the Indians were denied any opportunity to reload. The warriors buckled under the onslaught, and their retreat soon became a rout. At the same time, at the northwest end of the Indian positions, other American elements outflanked and savaged the Canadian militia, who were crudely dressed as Indians.

Kept in check by McKee, Girty and Matthew Elliott could only observe from a distance as the panicked Indians retreated and erupted from the forest maze. Recognizing what was happening, Blue Jacket and Little Turtle attempted to rally the warriors, but their efforts were to no avail. Remaining on horseback, Girty and his associates took no part in the actual fighting.

Along with the Wyandots, the rear guard of the Canadian militia fought valiantly, providing cover fire for their fleeing comrades. From his position Girty watched the retreating Indians hurry towards Fort Miamis and the protection they believed its big guns would provide. When they approached, however, the British cannons remained silent and the gates were shut against them. It was a nightmare come true as the English betrayed the warriors in an astonishing and final outrage. Aware that the American army was fast approaching, confused clusters of disillusioned warriors milled about, and then hastened away. They did not stop until they reached Swan Creek (near the mouth of the Maumee, present site of Toledo, Ohio), where hundreds of their families were waiting. Girty, McKee and Elliott hurried there too. Considering that they had played key roles in the great British deceit that had seduced the Indians, their journey to where the defeated warriors were now gathering took considerable courage. It can be argued that all three of these men related more closely to the Indians than to the English, and there should be no doubt they clearly grasped the dimensions of the disaster. In addition, McKee and Elliott had family members among the refugees.

The fighting at the Battle of Fallen Timbers, as it was later called, had lasted less than an hour and fifteen minutes. Yet, in this short span of time, the last big fight of the Great Indian Wars destroyed any hope the British had to maintain an Indian buffer state in the Ohio Country. The door was now opened for massive American westward expansion. After Fallen Timbers, the ultimate defeat of all the natives residing from Ohio west to the Pacific Ocean was a foregone conclusion to American leaders. While there might be occasional defeats for American military power, these would only amount to temporary setbacks. The main issue would never again be in doubt. Wayne's victory would serve as the blueprint for continental conquest. The Indian Wars were to end with a whimper, not a bang.

Losses for both sides were relatively minimal. The Americans suffered 33 dead and about 100 wounded. Indian casualties were estimated to be no more than 40 warriors. Disdaining the conflict,

Wayne's officers did not consider the action to be a battle, but only a skirmish.

Deserted by their British allies, confused and thoroughly defeated, the warriors melted away. As the afternoon wore on, Wayne's troops formed up on a clearing just outside British Fort Miamis and boisterously began to celebrate. The English and American commanders who now confronted each other were brave, aggressive men who were equally determined to avoid being blamed for starting another war. They were satisfied to send harsh messages back and forth and to trade insults.

On the 22nd, Wayne's soldiers took delight in burning McKee's house and stores, while other Legionnaires torched Indian fields, homes and orchards throughout the countryside. Then, astounding everyone, Wayne assembled his army on the 23rd and began to withdraw. He reached Fort Deposit that evening, and was back at Fort Defiance by the 27th. Having destroyed vast quantities of the Indian food reserves and hundreds of Indian homes, Wayne was sure of his control of the entire region.

At first, Girty, Alexander, Thomas McKee and Matthew Elliott attempted to rally the warriors at Swan Creek, but their efforts were rejected. If not for the fact that the people there were facing starvation, and were in desperate need of supplies, the three Indian agents may well have been murdered. Despite their betrayal, the British military remained as the Indians' only source of provisions, clothing, blankets, arms and ammunition. By mid-September approximately 2,500 men, women and children were residing in makeshift huts at Swan Creek, and Girty and his associates had only ninety-four barrels of pork and twenty barrels of flour with which to keep them from starvation. Ominous night frosts signaled an early winter. There can be little doubt that Girty understood the ramifications for the Indians and himself. Soon the Ohio Country would be irrevocably lost, and he would begin a new life of exile in Canada. Although Catherine and his three children were waiting for him in their snug home at Malden, Simon chose to remain with McKee at Swan Creek.

Chapter Nineteen
DARK DAYS

BRITISH MILITARY LEADERS in Canada were dumbfounded when Wayne retreated following his astounding victory at Fallen Timbers. They knew that Indian morale had bottomed and that there was nothing to stop Wayne from taking Detroit or, for that matter, all of Upper Canada.

McKee traveled to Detroit to plead for more supplies for the refugees at Swan Creek. Soon after his arrival, British authorities made him aware of a pressing need for credible information about General Wayne's whereabouts and movements. After receiving his orders from McKee, Britain's most capable frontier spy left Swan Creek to conduct one of his last covert actions against the United States. Simon Girty's reports confirmed that General Wayne had settled in to winter quarters at Fort Greenville, and for the moment Canada was safe.

In the fall of 1794 Joseph Brant arrived at Detroit with a retinue of one hundred Six Nations representatives. He immediately requested that a council of the western nations be convened at the Wyandot village at Brownstown, located on the west bank of the mouth of the Detroit River—just across from Girty's home. Happy for an opportunity to bolster Indian morale, Lieutenant Governor Simcoe made preparations to attend. Girty was summoned to serve as one of the council's principal interpreters, and he left Swan Creek for home. The site for the council was near enough to Malden for Simon to ride a small ferry across the river and attend the meetings by day, while spending his nights at home with his family. He was at Brownstown on 9 October when the meetings began.

From the start, the Brownstown council was strained. Simcoe and his entourage faced Brant and his Iroquois delegation, as well as large numbers of cynical Wyandots, Delawares, Shawnees, Miamis, Lakes Indians and Cherokees. The governor attempted to persuade the western nations to stall the Americans until spring, at which time he wanted them to resume their fight against Wayne. He urged the chiefs to reject any American peace terms that failed to secure an Ohio River boundary, and he invited them to convey all of their lands situated on the west side of the Ohio River to the king, where they would be held in trust for them. Simcoe sought a pretext for the British to deal directly with the Americans on behalf of the Indians. He closed his address by announcing that he had just issued orders to Colonel Campbell at Fort Miamis to fire on any American forces that approached that installation.

Joseph Brant and Simon Girty both supported Simcoe, agreeing with the governor that the western nations' struggle should resume in the spring. Their words fell on deaf ears. The chiefs no longer had faith in British intentions or loyalty. Brant clearly perceived the situation, and boldly challenged Simcoe to provide a specific commitment of British military assistance for launching a joint attack against an American position in the spring. Simcoe remained evasive. Pressing him, Brant requested that he ask Lord Dorchester to name a date when direct military assistance would be provided. Simcoe had no response. After a few electric moments, Brant turned and addressed the assembly in both English and Algonquin, calling for the present council to conclude, and reconvene at the same location in the spring. Until then, the Mohawk cautioned, the western nations should avoid making separate treaties with the Americans. On this dark and sour note, the councils adjourned.

Turning back to their home villages, most of the chiefs were convinced that there was nothing they could do but submit to the Americans and evacuate their people to land west of the Mississippi. Their homelands, they reasoned, were soon to be lost forever.

Returning to Niagara, Simcoe received more bad news. He was

advised that as a result of peace negotiations just concluded with American Chief Justice John Jay, he was required to evacuate and abandon all of the British posts ceded in 1783 by no later than June 1796. The list included the great prize of Fort Lernoult at Detroit. Simcoe's dream of retaining an Indian buffer state between Canada and the United States was shattered.

Girty spent the remainder of the winter of 1794 at Swan Creek with McKee and Elliott, attempting to alleviate the hardships of nearly 5,000 refugees. The unceasing efforts of the three Indian agents did much to offset doubts of their loyalty, but nothing they could say or do rallied Indian confidence in British support. The chain of trust had been broken at Fallen Timbers, and so many chiefs had been killed there that the Indians suffered from a lack of leadership. The Wyandots had lost all of their principal chiefs, including Half King. In mid-November, Wyandot chief Tarhe (The Crane) was among the first chiefs to make peace with General Wayne at Fort Greenville. By January 1795, chiefs from the Wyandots, Chippewa, Pottawatomie, Sauk and Miamis had all signed American preliminary articles of peace at Greenville and they had agreed to meet there with Wayne again in mid-June to establish a permanent peace. Finally, on 24 January, heading a Shawnee delegation accompanied by one from the Delawares, Blue Jacket left Swan Creek to go and meet with Wayne at Fort Greenville.

In a last-ditch effort to discourage the most obstreperous member of the confederacy from settling with the Americans, Simon Girty was ordered to intercept and dissuade Blue Jacket. Simon reached his old friend in time, but his efforts at persuasion were to no avail. Girty returned to Detroit to report that the chiefs were united in their determination to bury the hatchet. With nothing more to do, he departed for home in a sullen mood.

In August 1795, nearly one hundred chiefs, representing twelve nations of the Ohio Valley and Great Lakes regions, traveled to Greenville and signed the treaties General Wayne had prepared for them. What they relinquished was nearly all of southern and eastern Ohio, most of present Indiana, the entire region comprising Illinois, Michigan, and Wisconsin, and all of Minnesota east of the

Mississippi River. The Indian Wars were over. Governor Simcoe was planning the evacuation of Detroit, which, according to the terms of Jay's Treaty, was to be completed no later than June the following year. Construction of Fort Malden, a new administrative center and headquarters for Indian Affairs located on the Canadian side of the Detroit River, had already begun.

Since his defection in 1778, Simon Girty had spent sixteen years of his life in support of the Indians' struggle to retain their home-lands in the Ohio Country. Between July and December of 1794, his old friends Half King and Captain Pipe had died. After taking up residence on the streets of Greenville, the once great Seneca Chief Guyasuta spent his last months as a lonely, old alcoholic beggar whom General Wayne favored with a little drinking money and used clothing. In 1795 Guyasuta fell ill, died and was buried in northern Pennsylvania. Simon's memory would no doubt have rejected the image of Guyasuta as a tragic old drunk. To him, Guyasuta would always remain the intelligent, vital, giving man who, acting more like a substitute father than a patron, had watched over him during his first years among the Senecas. It was Guyasuta who had guided his training as an interpreter, and it was Guyasuta who had brought him to Alexander McKee. In the 1770s, the times Simon spent by Guyasuta's side as his traveling companion, interpreter and body-guard were among his fondest memories. Guyasuta (who, after the French and Indian War had joined with Pontiac to lead the Indian rebellion against the British) was Girty's role model—a dedicated, loyal leader who had the strength to sacrifice his personal needs in an instant if the outcome was of benefit to his people. Girty could remember back to when General Hand had sent him to Connewago to inquire whether the Iroquois tribes were at war with the Americans. He recalled how Guyasuta had appeared and sounded when he looked into Girty's eyes and told him that the council had agreed that he was there not as a peace emissary but as a spy, and that he was to be turned over to the British. Even at that terrible moment, Simon had nothing but respect and admiration for Guyasuta, and he never thought of him in any way but as his true friend. The thought of how Guyasuta spent his final months evoked great sorrow and bitterness.

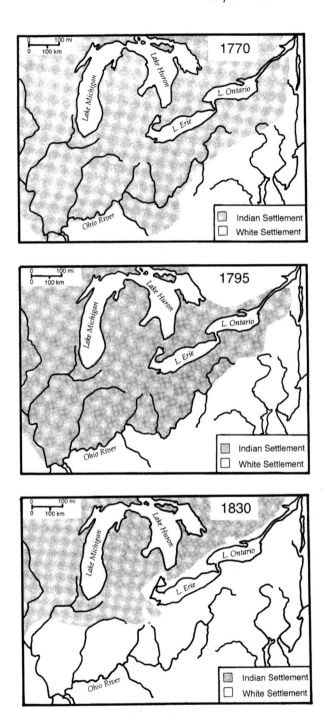

It was time for Simon Girty to stop fighting and go home. At fifty-four years of age, both his marriage and his finances were in shambles. The state of his mind is revealed in his resignation letter to McKee:

GIRTY TO MCKEE, 10 NOVEMBER 1795

Sir:

I take the liberty of advising you hoping to meet with your condisansion [sic], that is to say, that it has been a number of years since you & I have had any settlement together, and as Messrs Luth & Sheperd seems to be doubtful of their payments are not willing to advance me the Necessaries for my family nor any other thing I might want from them, I am at present in town, and hope to have the pleasure of seeing you before my departure, at which time should I remain Indebted to you (I) shall take the first opportunity of Disposing of a part of my property to satisfy you and all others to whom I may be indebted as I intend taking a New Course of Life for the preservation of myself and Family.

I remain Sir, your very Humble Servant

Simon Girty [his mark][1]

Girty went home. Retired, he received a pension of half his active duty regular pay, supplemented by income working part-time for the Indian Department as an "additional interpreter." For that service Girty was paid a dollar a day, except when employed at major councils or treaties, when his pay was increased to three dollars per day. As an additional interpreter, Girty's home was always open to Indians who came to Malden to deal with British authorities. It would be Simon's job to prescreen native visitors, ascertain their needs or complaints, and then either resolve their issues outright or escort them to the Indian Department headquarters at Fort Malden. Providing a valuable service to the Indian Department, Girty and his peers were reimbursed for their expenses. Although barely moderate, Girty's monthly income from the government left him and his family comfortable.[2]

Comparable fates were shared by the other two "Injun Girtys" following the Battle of Fallen Timbers. James Girty and his Shawnee wife Betsy (along with their two children James and Ann) opened a store on Middle Sister Island and then settled on a farm in Gosfield, Essex County, Canada. George Girty resided among a small community of Delawares situated not far from James's place where, sober or not, he too served as an "additional interpreter" to the Indian Department.

Simon was like a war-horse put out to pasture. From Catherine's perspective, the husband and father who had enjoyed only infrequent visits with his family, but who had seemed genuinely happy to be with them when he did so, seemed a different man. If Catherine expected to finally receive regular attentions and care from a cheerful, doting farmer-husband, Simon let her down. He began to drink heavily and spent considerable time away from home. Unable to reach or to please him, it was natural for Catherine to resent both his moods and his binges, and the long-festering problems of their marriage began to surface. Shortly after his retirement, Simon rode away from home one morning in the dead of winter. Whether he informed Catherine of his destination or purpose is unknown, as are the nuances and temperaments at the time of his departure. Also unknown is whether she experienced sorrow or relief at his leaving. In notes written during an interview of Girty's daughter Sarah in 1864, historian Lyman C. Draper wrote:

From Mrs. Sarah Munger; daughter and only surviving child of Simon Girty, interviewed near the town of Harlem in Winnebago County, Illinois, December 15, 1864:

Once, Simon Girty (... Mrs. Munger cannot remember personally about it and only remembers hearing her father narrate it, probably soon after Wayne's Treaty), longed to visit once more his two favorite brothers Thomas Girty and John Turner, at Pittsburgh, and started pursuing the journey on horseback. As he neared the Pittsburgh region he was careful not to reveal his name. At Turner's on Squirrel Hill, a few miles east of Pittsburgh, a strange horse was seen grazing there, and an old man occasionally noticed [by the local residents]. It soon got noised abroad and suspicions whispered around that it was Simon Girty. At this,

a party went to Turner's and Girty, seeing them approaching,
secreted himself in a closet and kept concealed until they went off.
While in the closet he was afraid they would hear the ticking of
his silver watch, and took off his sock and wrapped up the watch
in it to deaden the noise of the ticking, and stuffed it in his pocket.
Then Turner desired that he would not visit him, as he was afraid
that the people's prejudices against Girty in the Crawford matter
might lead them to injure him if they knew that he entertained
Girty—or fire his property.[3]

There are other accounts of this event, suggesting that the incident did indeed occur. If so, Simon's well-meaning visit to his half-brother had very nearly ended in disaster, and he was forced to return at once to Canada. The incident probably deterred any attempt by Simon to make contact with his brother Thomas, who was occupied buying and selling properties and managing a successful farming operation outside Pittsburgh.

Simon's long ride home through the frigid wilderness may have been cathartic, for it appears that he returned to his wife and children in February 1796, and by the end of that month Catherine was again pregnant. A month later, Simon received news that his brother George had died on the 24th of February. The exact circumstances of George's death are unknown, but he was an alcoholic and he died during the worst cold spell of that winter.

For sixteen years Simon had been on the cutting edge of events in the Ohio Country. For a man who sought adventure and challenge, his life had been full. He was admired and respected by his British superiors, as well as by the leaders of the Indian nations, and his influence and scheming were matched by only a handful of men, red or white. Along with everything that the Indians had lost at the Battle of Fallen Timbers, it appears that Simon Girty lost his reason for being. Once he went home to Malden he crossed the line from being honored and needed for who he was, to being someone remembered for whom and what he used to be.

In the spring of 1796, looking out from his riverfront farm, Simon could observe boatload after boatload of equipment and goods being ferried across the Detroit River to Fort Malden. In order to meet the June deadline, by which time Wayne's troops were to occupy Detroit, the British were hurrying their evacuation and transfer. The time was fast approaching when Girty would no longer be able to visit the city that had replaced Pittsburgh as his favorite—a place where many of his best friends resided. The situation gnawed at him.

Following the American possession of Fort Miamis in May 1796, Girty frequently left home to travel by ferry to Detroit. People recalled him remaining astride his big roan mare with her silver mane and tail until the boat landed at a Detroit wharf. Then, according to the stories, he would ride from one tavern to another, drinking with his friends, protesting what was happening and cursing the oncoming Americans. When his money ran out, he would return to the Canadian side of the river. Still drunk, he would trust his horse to find her way home.

By mid-June there were few if any English soldiers left in Detroit, and the city had been emptied of all official property. Of some 2,200 residents, about 1,700 had followed the British garrison across the river to Amherstburg in Essex County, Upper Canada.

On the morning of 7 July, a small force of American troops arrived in the town in two schooners and, after landing and assembling, they smartly marched their way through the town to Fort Lernoult. Lining the streets was a stern, expressionless crowd who neither welcomed nor jeered their presence. Reaching the fort the soldiers found the gates locked. According to Butterfield, the British had left the keys in the possession of an old Negro man who lived close by. Summoned, the old man approached and turned them over to the Americans with a polite smile. Upon entering the fort, the Americans found that virtually every glass window in the place had been broken, the wells had all been filled with stones, and missing doors, shelves, and hardware confirmed that everything of value had been stripped and hauled away.

While the Americans inspected their pillaged fort, Simon was drinking at a nearby tavern close to the river, with his horse tied to a post on the street. Warned by friends that the American troops had arrived, Girty refused to take the early ferry back to the Canadian side. That afternoon a squad of American soldiers, who may have been alerted to his presence, hurried towards the tavern.

According to John McCormick, who was interviewed by Lyman C. Draper in 1863:

After the Americans took possession of Detroit in 1796, Girty was there, and drunk, cursed the Americans for poltroons and cowards, when a file of soldiers undertook to apprehend him and put him in the guardhouse, when he spurred his horse and leaped off the wharf, plunging into the river, and as he rose, he took off his hat and shouted "Hurrah for King George!" and then swam over to the Canada shore . . .[4]

While McCormick's story paints Girty as a carefree cavalier who lingers long enough to curse the Americans before colorfully plunging into the river and swimming to safety, Governor William Walker, Jr., of Kansas, offers a more sedate and credible version of the escape:

WYANDOT GAZETTE, 18 APRIL 1872

In the summer of 1796, the British government surrendered the northern posts to the United States. Girty was at Detroit when the boat laden with the American troops which were to occupy that post hove in sight. He became so alarmed, that he would not wait for the return of the ferry boat, but plunged his horse into the river, at the risk of drowning himself and horse reached the Canadian shore, then pouring out a volley of maledictions upon the U.S., Girty mingled with all the diabolical oaths his imagination could coin.[5]

In contrast to McCormick's plucky image of Girty, Walker portrays Simon in a state of anxiety, like a felon on the lam who bolts into the river and who curses the Americans only when he is safely to the other shore. The truth is, neither McCormick nor Walker witnessed the event. Absent of any "diabolical" curses, the simplest and most reliable account is the one that Amherstburg resident Henry Wright, Sr., claims he was told by Girty himself:

> *He was there one day and got to drinking, and the Americans,*
> *finding out who he was, chased him, when he got on his horse,*
> *plunged into the river, and swam across.*[6]

Whether Girty was terrified or not, all these accounts agree that in order to avoid capture, in a daunting demonstration of horsemanship, Girty had plunged his horse off the wharf and somehow remained in the saddle or clung to the big mare's tail during her long and exhausting swim to the Canadian shore.

A month prior to the American occupation of Detroit, McKee (whom Lord Dorchester had promoted to Deputy Superintendent General and Inspector for Indian Affairs for Upper and Lower Canada at the end of 1794) submitted a proposal calling for the appointment of regional superintendents at Forts Malden, George and St. Joseph. McKee's proposal was accepted in July, and before retiring to his new home on the Thames River, he appointed Matthew Elliott to oversee the office of Indian Affairs at Fort Malden. Once again Simon's boss was one of his long-time friends.

Before 1796 came to an end, Catherine's mother Sarah Malott passed away, the Americans took possession of Fort Mackinac and, on 20 October, Simon's son Bredon Prideaux Girty was born. The boy was named after Lieutenant Prideaux Selby, of the Fifth British Regiment, a good friend of Simon's who was then stationed at Fort Malden. In mid-December, in a mundane and inglorious ending to what had been an explosive and extreme military career, General Anthony Wayne died from gout.

The birth of Prideaux failed to curtail the escalating discord between Simon and Catherine. Early in 1798, having reached the limit of her endurance, Catherine Girty left Simon and went to live with her brother Peter Malott at his home in Gosfield Township (now part of Kingsville, Ontario, about 16 miles from Malden). According to Sarah Girty, who was seven years old when her parents separated, her mother left her father "on account of his drinking and unkindness."

Catherine took her eighteen-month-old infant (Prideaux) with her, leaving Nancy Ann (age twelve), Thomas (age ten), and seven-year-old Sarah with their father.[7]

Writers who later sought to exploit Girty's notorious image made maximum use of his supposed abuse of Catherine. In *History of the Girtys*, Butterfield included a spurious passage from an 1887 letter written to him by William Charles Mickle, Jr., (whose father, in the 1850s, emerged victorious from a lawsuit with Catherine Girty over possession of the Girty homestead). Mickle, Jr. wrote:

There is no one I am acquainted with who knows Mrs. Girty's age, or when she was married. But my mother-in-law, who is one of the oldest women in the county being nearly ninety, says she thinks Girty and his wife were married in Detroit, but she is not sure; as for her (Mrs. Girty's) age she (mother-in-law) does not know anything about it. She was taken prisoner by the Indians during the Revolutionary War; she does not know whether she was a child or a young woman when she was captured. My mother-in-law thinks it would have been as well if she had staid among the Indians instead of marrying Girty, for he used to take his sword and hit her alongside the head just for fun.[8]

When closely examined, Mickles' account is suspect. He could only have been one or two years of age when Simon and Catherine separated, and he pointed out that his mother-in-law was "nearly ninety" at the time he wrote his 1887 letter to Butterfield. Thus the accusation that Simon frequently beat his wife over the head with his sword "for fun," is hearsay or conjecture. However, even if the Mickle story is suspect, it does not prove that Girty was innocent of such accusations; he may indeed have physically abused his wife during their frequent and virulent conflicts. At this stage of his life, Girty's accusers portrayed him in one dimension: that of a violent, irresponsible drunkard. A different perspective can be gleaned from the fact that after Catherine left him, Simon retained possession of their three eldest children. Six years later, still living with their father, all four of his children were apparently happy and healthy. In addition, during the same span of time, Girty satisfactorily fulfilled his responsibilities as an interpreter for the Indian Department.

It is easy and convenient to cast Catherine as the helpless victim. However, when thirty-three year old Catherine left Simon, she had been married to him for fifteen years, and measured by any standard she was a strong-willed, robust young woman. During her life she had faced and overcome the mental and physical duress of capture and long-term captivity by Indians, and had almost single-handedly managed four children and a frontier homestead. What is known is that she did leave Simon, and that within a few years all their children were living with him and not her.

Late in 1798, accused of stealing goods requisitioned by him for the use of Indians, Matthew Elliott was removed from office as Deputy Superintendent of Indian Affairs; and in January 1799, following a siege of illnesses, Alexander McKee, who had been Simon's best friend and principal benefactor, died. McKee's position was soon filled by his son Thomas, under whom Simon continued to serve as an interpreter.

With time, the animosity between Simon and Catherine cooled. Apparently Simon Girty and her brother Peter Malott remained on friendly terms, and perhaps communication between Simon and his estranged wife was reestablished through him.

According to Girty's daughter Sarah (interviewed by Lyman C. Draper in 1864):

About the year 1800, Simon Girty was at Sandwich, going up some outside stairs to a building, with snow on the steps, when his foot slipped. He fell and broke his right ankle, and limped ever after.[9]

Although a differing account claims that Simon broke his leg while crossing a fence behind his house in deep snow, several of the Canadians whom Draper interviewed remembered Girty being lame after an accident. Whichever account is correct, the fifty-nine-year-old white warrior, whom the Indians had called a "Manitou" because of his fleetness, could no longer sprint like a deer. The same hardy man, who had once traversed fifty miles on snowshoes in a single day and night, would never walk again without the aid of a stout, knobby, walking stick. The agile and adroit Girty had no choice but to resign himself to the life of a cripple, and after the accident few people recalled seeing Simon walking. Most everyone remembered him astride a horse.

At this stage of his life Girty was recalled by many as a drunken reprobate: a man who, from horseback, would curse and threaten people with his walking stick; or who, bellowing like a demon, took delight in chasing frightened children from the streets. It should be noted, however, that even his legendary alcoholic exploits are absent of physical violence—there are no reports of him actually striking or harming any adult or child. While many of the storytellers laughed at his drunken exploits, they also portrayed him as a man who tipped his hat and was unfailingly courteous to any women he encountered. The truth is less colorful or tragic. Throughout the early 1800s Girty continued to satisfactorily serve the Indian Department; and from his wages he was able to provide necessities for his children and his farm. While raising his children, he expanded his land holdings by acquiring two valuable 200 acre patents in 1802—one in Gosfield, and another in Colchester, with both parcels fronting on Lake Erie.

In 1803 Girty was visited at Malden by his old friend Solomon McCulloch, who had come all the way from Pittsburgh to see him. During his visit, Simon took McCulloch to a place where hundred of Indians had gathered to perform a ceremonial funeral dance in honor of Alexander McKee, who had died on the same day four years earlier. According to Simon Kenton who related the story to Judge John H. James in 1832:

[The dance] commenced in the morning and continued until next day.

Young McKee, then a Captain in the British Army—a large man about 6 feet 3, with other officers joined in it.

... Girty told McCulloch that as long as he had been with the Indians, this was the third dance of the kind he had witnessed. They are only for men of distinction among them.

> *Girty often talked to him [McCulloch] about his adven-*
> *tures, and the tears would roll down his cheeks and his voice be*
> *choked at a recurrence to some of the events in which he had been*
> *an actor. He had saved the lives of hundreds by diverting and*
> *restraining the Indians.*
> *Girty was anxious to see his brother Thomas who lived near*
> *Pittsburgh. McCulloch proposed to take him in disguise, but the*
> *dread of being hanged restrained him.*[10]

It was also in 1803 that Thomas Girty's wife Ann was shot and killed one night at their Butler County, Pennsylvania home. The murderer was a local named David Kerr, who claimed some right to the Girty land. It may well have been news of Ann Girty's death that prompted Simon to mention his desire to visit his elder brother to Solomon McCulloch.

Despite McCulloch's statement that Simon Girty was afraid of being caught and hung if he went south to visit Thomas, in the spring of 1804, Simon Girty was camped near the banks of the Mississippi with a family of Delaware Indians, not far from Camp River Dubois (present site of Hartford, Illinois) where Captain William Clark and the men of the Lewis and Clark Expedition were spending the winter. Situated on the east bank of the Mississippi River, at the mouth of the River Dubois, some sixty miles north of Kaskaskia, the U.S. expedition had arrived there the preceding November, quickly cutting logs and erecting a military camp comprised of several log cabins and other structures. Notes in Clark's daily journal reveals how he met with Girty on 26 March, and the following day witnessed Girty and his traveling companions canoeing south on the Mississippi, in the direction of St. Louis:

> *Monday the 26th of March 1804, a verry Smokey day I had*
> *Corn parched to make parched meal, workmen all at work pre-*
> *pareing the Boat, I visit the Indian Camps, In one Camp found 3*
> *Squars [Squaws] & 3 young ones, another 1 girl & a boy in a 3rd*
> *Simon Girtey & two other family---- Girtey has the Rhumertism*
> *verry bad*

*Those Indians visit me in their turn, & as usial ask for
Something. I give them flour &c. Several fish Cought today, the
Mississippi R Continu to rise & discharge great quantity of foam
&.*

*Tuesday 27th rain last night verry hard with Thunder, a
Cloudy morning. One man Sick today. All hands parching Corn
etc. Som Delaways pass down to St. Louis (Simon Girty) river
continue to rise, beating at two morters parched Corn. "I am
unwell"*[11]

Captain Clark's notes do not reveal the location of the Indian
camp where he met with Girty. And except for the phrase in his
March 26 note: "...in a 3rd [Indian camp] Simon Girtey and two
other family ..." Clark gives no further description about the people
with whom Girty was traveling, nor does he mention the location of
Girty's camp. When Clark and his men had arrived (the preceding
November), the east bank of the Mississippi River was the western
boundary of U.S. Territory, while the western banks were the eastern
boundary of Upper Louisiana, which, at that time, was under Spanish
control. For diplomatic purposes, the Lewis and Clark expedition
was obliged to remain on the U.S. side, but, in fact, on 9 March, just
17 days prior to Clark's meeting with Girty, Spain had transferred
Upper Louisiana to France, and one day later, France had transferred
the same holdings to the United States. So, technically, no matter
upon which side of the Mississippi River Girty was camped, he was
legally on U.S. soil and subject to arrest.

Clark's notes also omit revealing the reasons why he frequently
traveled outside the protection of Camp River Dubois to visit nearby
villages and Indian camps, but these tours were part of his duties, as
both he and Captain Merriwether Lewis had been tasked by President
Thomas Jefferson to gather as much intelligence as possible about the
peoples and regions through which they journeyed. At Kaskaskia the
preceding fall, in addition to recruiting 12 soldiers from that station, a
half-French, half-Omaha Indian trader named Francois Labiche had
been hired to serve the expedition as an interpreter, a guide and an

expert boatman. It can be reasonably assumed that whenever the co-leader of the Lewis and Clark expedition left the protection of Camp River Dubois to visit nearby Indians, he would have been accompanied by an escort of armed men as well as an interpreter – probably Labiche. So, then, why didn't Clark attempt to capture Girty?

Other than citing Girty's full name, Clark's rudimentary notes do not include any further description. But surely, was this a stranger completely unknown to Clark, it would seem that the explorer would have delineated the white traveler's reason for being there with Delawares – describing him perhaps as a trapper, hunter, Indian trader, etc. The fact that Clark describes him simply as Simon Girty speaks for itself. If we assume Clark knew who Simon Girty was, and we know he made no attempt to capture or kill him, we are left wondering why this was so. The most reasonable explanation is that Clark's responsibility for the safety of his expedition far outweighed any benefits that might have accrued from capturing or killing a sickly, 63-year old man who was greatly respected and admired by the great majority of the Indians of that region.

Whether Girty's real objective was to visit Thomas or John Turner, Jr., and whether he completed that trip, remains unknown, but by the fall of 1804 Girty was home again at his farm in Malden. His connections to the past were being severed one-by-one. Alexander McCormick had died at Colchester in 1803—with Simon Girty still unaware that he had served as an American spy during the Revolutionary War. McCormick's death was followed by that of Peter Drouillard, who died at his farm located between Malden and Sandwich. Sensing the autumn of his own life, on 11 November 1804, Girty dictated the following letter to John Turner:

Dear Brother
   I take this opportunity of writing to you hoping these few lines may find you and family in perfect health as it is with me at present, thanking god for it. Dear Brother I have to inform you that a separation took place about six years back between me and my wife. She remains with her brother, and my children & myself live together, we are all very well and doing as well as the

situation of the country and the times will permit. I have held
some consultations with my children and some of their best friends
of mine in this neighborhood and am advised for Certain reasons
to make a Second will and as I find myself perfect in Bodily
strength and health I have deemed and Ben. Advise prudent,
therefore Dear Brother I hope you will be good enough to send
me the former which remains in your hands. I never received any
letter or letters from you in the one in which you gave your order
to Alex Clark and when you find a conveyance I will be exceed-
ingly obliged to you to send Mr. Clark's obligation for money
together with my will. I have three Deeds at Present on my house
for two hundred acres. Each the grant of his majesty and three
more I shortly expect. My brother James is yet living. I cannot
give any further intelligence concerning the affairs of me and
my family. I will likewise ask you to send me an account of the
times with you or whether I might be safe to go see you or not, as
I should be Quite happy to see You once Before my Departure to
another Region from which no traveler returns. So Dear Brother
I conclude with my Good wishes Toward you and your family and
remain your affectionate
All here remember their Brother
Love to you and their Aunt Simon Girty[12]

In their wills, Simon and John left property to each other and provided for each other's descendants.

By this time, in violation of the Fort Greenville treaties, Americans
were pouring across the Ohio River, invading what few lands had been
set aside for the Western Tribes. The Indians' protests were ignored
and, guided by the Shawnee chief Tecumseh and his brother (known
as "The Prophet"), the tribes began to respond by organizing.

In 1805 Simon's eldest daughter Nancy Ann married Peter
Govereau, who owned an inn and tavern in nearby Amherstburg.
Two years later Sarah Girty married Joseph Munger, leaving only
seventeen-year-old Thomas Girty at home with Simon. "Tommy," as
Girty affectionately called his favorite son, was the focal point of a

letter Girty dictated to John Turner, Jr. on 10 November 1807, which was delivered by an Indian:

Dear Brother

I herewith Send You a Copy of a letter which I wrote you by Mr. Alx. Clarke which he had forgot and left at Mr. Reids what I have now to Say is that my time is but Short and that I have but Six Months more till my Mortgage is out and by you to write me this winter if you will do what I request in my Letter and if you do not write about it this winter I will go and See you this Spring and go by the way of Pres Isle and if I clear my Mortgage I have left in my Will my land to little Tomy. My compliments to My Aunt & remain in expectation of your answer by Old Little Sun.

Your brother James is alive and enough to do.

Your affectionate Brother, Simon X Girty[13]

While Girty fretted over both paying off his mortgage and hoped that one day he would be able to leave debt-free land to his son Thomas, news came that Joseph Brant had died of natural causes at his home on the Grand River, in Burlington, Upper Canada. There can be little doubt that Simon was saddened by this news. At the beginning of the Revolutionary War they had been on opposite sides, but after Simon's defection, the two had fought hard against the Americans. Just before the Battle of Fallen Timbers, Brant had offered a compromise settlement with the Americans which Simon, under McKee, had no choice but to oppose. Reviewing their long and stormy relationship, surely Girty realized that the night the Mohawk had attempted to kill him they had both been drinking hard, and that he had insulted and provoked Brant in front of too many men, red and white. Although their personal relationship never fully recovered from that event, there were many times after the Revolutionary War when Girty and Brant had conspired and worked together in support of causes to which they were mutually dedicated. There should be little question but that at the time of Brant's death, Simon had forgiven him for the wound he had suffered at his hands, even though the physical consequences of that wounding still punished him. In addition to experiencing increasingly severe headaches, Girty had begun to lose his vision. Except for the warm and earnest relationship he had with his son Thomas (the only member of his family who still remained with him at Malden after the others had married and moved away), old Girty might have become a hermit in his declining years.

As tensions between the United States and England escalated towards what would soon become the War of 1812, the vulnerability of Canadian border towns like Amherstburg and Malden was obvious. Thanks to his legendary status and the large rewards still being offered to anyone who brought in his head, there must have been a number of ambitious Americans who lusted for the glory of killing the hated white renegade. Abraham Hull, a Captain in the United States Army, and son of William Hull, Governor of Michigan Territory, confided to Adam Brown, a Wyandot chief, that if war between the United States and England did erupt, 10,000 men from Kentucky would take Amherstburg. If so, Captain Hull boasted, then Simon Girty, Matthew Elliott, Thomas McKee, William Caldwell and all the other members of the British Indian Department would be caught, arrested, and summarily put to death. Adam Brown relayed Hull's threat to Thomas McKee, and there can be little doubt that Girty soon learned of it.

Resigned to the possibility of yet a new war against the Americans, British authorities anxiously sought the support of the Western tribes. Because of his connections and influence, Matthew Elliott was considered the best candidate to lead the effort and, despite his earlier dismissal as Superintendent of Indian Affairs at Fort Malden in June 1808, Governor Francis Gore restored him to his former position. Elliott immediately sent invitations to Tecumseh, his brother The Prophet, and many other chiefs to confer at Amherstburg with the governor. At the same time, there was a rapid, general assessment within the Indian Department to determine who were the most qualified and able agents to pursue the desired alliances. While James Girty was among those recommended and appointed, Simon Girty was passed over. Whether this was due to his drinking or his failing eyesight is unknown, but William Claus, Deputy Superintendent of Indian Affairs at Niagara, wrote Prideaux Selby: "S. Girty is incapable of doing anything."[14]

On 13 June, Tecumseh, his brother, and five other Shawnee leaders met with Matthew Elliott and Governor Gore. The Shawnees advised Gore that the western tribes would tolerate no further encroachment by American settlers. Tecumseh indicated that if the British were determined to fight the Americans, and they committed a large enough force to conduct a serious war against their mutual foe, they could count on having many warriors to fight by their side. Gore requested and received Tecumseh's promise to do all he could to keep the Indians in check and avoid making war upon the Americans until the British were organized and ready.

Although Simon had no part in the pivotal conferences, Tecumseh must have felt that old Girty's input was still valuable. According to Girty's daughter Sarah, the Shawnee leader paid her father several visits at Malden between 1808 and 1812.

In June of 1809 Simon's son Thomas married Monica Evans, a local beauty, who came to live with her husband and his father on the Girty homestead.

An interesting and detailed description of Simon (c. 1810) appears in one of Canada's earliest novels, *The Canadian Brothers* (1840), written by John Richardson. Richardson was raised at Amherstburg and served as a young ensign during the War of 1812. In his novel, Richardson masked Girty as "Sampson Gattrie." Although lengthy, Richardson's rich exposition of Simon is worth scrutiny, because he knew Girty and remembered him with clarity:

JOHN RICHARDSON, *THE CANADIAN BROTHERS*,
MONTREAL, 1840

Nearly midway between Elliott's and Hartley's points, both of which are remarkable for the low and sandy nature of the soil, the land, rising gradually towards the center, assumes a more healthy and arable aspect; and, on its highest elevation, stood a snug, well cultivated, property, called at the period of which we write, Gattrie's farm. From this height, crowned on its extreme summit by a neat and commodious farm-house, the far reaching sands, forming the points above named, are distinctly visible. Immediately in the rear, and commencing beyond the orchard which surrounded the house, stretched forestward, and to a considerable distance, a tract of rich and cultivated soil, separated into strips by zig-zag enclosures, and offering to the eye of the traveler, in appropriate season, the several species of American produce, such as Indian corn, buck wheat, "etc." with here and there a few patches of indifferent tobacco. Thus far of the property, a more minute description of which is unimportant. The proprietors of this neat little place were a father and son, to the latter of whom was consigned, for reasons which will appear presently, the sole management of the farm. Of him we will merely say, that, at the period of which we treat, he was a fine, strapping, dark curly-haired, white-teethed, red-lipped, broad-shouldered, and altogether comely and gentle tempered youth, of about twenty, who had, although unconsciously, monopolized the affections of almost every well favored maiden of his class for miles around him—advantages of nature, from which had resulted a union with one of the prettiest of the fair competitors for connubial happiness [the woman cited here is undoubtedly Monica Evans Girty].

The father we may not dismiss so hastily. He was—but, before attempting the portraiture of his character, we will, to the best of our ability, sketch his person.

Let the reader fancy an old man of about sixty, possessed of that comfortable amplitude of person which is the result rather of a mind at peace with itself, and undisturbed by a worldly care, than of any marked indulgence in indolent habits. Let him next invest this comfortable person in a sort of Oxford gray, coarse capote, or frock, of capacious size, tied closely round the waist with one of those parti-colored worsted sashes, we have, on a former occasion described as peculiar to the bourgeois settlers of the country. Next, suffering his eye to descend on and admire the rotund and fleshy thigh, let it drop gradually to the stout and muscular legs, which he must invest in a pair of closely fitting leathern trousers, the wide-seamed edges of which are slit into innumerable small strips, much after the fashion of the American Indian. When he has completed the survey of the lower extremities,

to which he must not fail to subjoin a foot of proportionate
dimensions, tightly moccasined, and, moreover, furnished with a
pair of old English hunting spurs, the reader must then examine
the head with which this heavy piece of animated machinery is
surmounted. From beneath a coarse felt hat, garnished with an
inch-wide band or ribbon, let him imagine he sees the yet vigorous
grey hair, descending over a forehead not altogether wanting in a
certain dignity of expression, and terminating in a beetling brow,
silvered also with the frost of years, and shadowing a sharp, grey,
intelligent eye, the vivacity of whose expression denotes its possessor
to be far in advance, in spirit, even of his still active and powerful
frame. With these must be connected a snub nose—a double chin,
adorned with grisly honors, which are borne, like the fleece of the
lamb, only occasionally to the shears of the shearer—and a small,
and not unhandsome, mouth, at certain periods pursed into an
expression of irresistible humour, but more frequently express-
ing a sense of lofty independence. The grisly neck, little more or
less bared, as the season may demand—a kerchief loosely tied
around the collar of a checked shirt—and a knotted cudgel in his
hand,—and we think our sketch of Sampson Gattrie is complete.[15]

Clearly, Richardson remembered Simon's eyes as gray, not dark brown or black. According to Simon's daughter-in-law Catherine (wife of Prideaux) her father-in-law began to lose his vision in about 1811, and he was completely blind two years before he died. If Girty was suffering from advanced cataracts, his eyes might indeed have appeared gray—just as Richardson describes. We also note that Richardson's description of Simon, his son Thomas, and Thomas' wife (Monica Evans-Girty) omits any mention of Simon's estranged wife or his other children, which is accurate for the time period, as they were all living in Amherstburg.

Richardson continues:

To one who could ride home at night, as he invariably did, after
some twelve hours of hard and continued drinking, without roll-
ing from his horse, it would not be difficult to enact the sober man

*in its earlier stages. As his intoxication was relative to himself, so
was his sobriety in regard to others—and although, at mid-day,
he might have swallowed sufficient to have caused another man
to bite the dust, he looked and spoke, and acted, as if he had been
a model of temperance. If he passed a lady in the street, or saw
her at her window, Sampson Gattrie's hat was instantly removed
from his venerable head, and his body inclined forward over
his saddle-bow, with all the easy grace of a well-born gentleman,
and one accustomed from infancy to pay deference to women;
nay, this at an hour when he had imbibed enough of his favorite
liquor to have rendered most men insensible even to their presence.
These habits of courtesy, extended moreover to the officers of the
Garrison, and such others among the civilians as Sampson felt to
be worthy of his notice. His tones of salutation, at these moments,
were soft, his manner respectful, even graceful; and while there
was nothing of the abashedness of the inferior, there was also no
offensive familiarity, in the occasional conversations held by him
with the different individuals or groups, who surrounded and
accosted him.*[16]

While tensions rose between the United States and Great Britain, the Girty farm prospered under the diligent care of Thomas and Monica, and served as a warm refuge to Simon. Displaying his affection for his eldest son, in May of 1812, just after Thomas had joined the local militia and when Monica was carrying their first child, Simon sold the northern half of his farm to his eldest son for five shillings. The next month, on 18 June, the United States declared war on Great Britain. William Hull, Governor of Michigan Territory, was handed command of the United States Army on the Detroit frontier; and on 5 July he reinforced Detroit with an army of 2,000 men, whom he brought up from Ohio. After a brief foray across the Canadian border near Fort Malden, Hull withdrew back to Detroit. On 5 August, Canadian forces, strengthened by Tecumseh and twenty-four Shawnee warriors, attacked and defeated an American supply column of 150 Ohio militiamen at Brownstown. Four days later, near the same location, a similar attack took place (the Battle of Monguagon) but this time the Americans prevailed. British and Indian losses were six killed and twenty-one wounded. Apparently, during either the Brownstown or Monguagon fights, Ensign Thomas Girty of the First Regiment of Essex Militia was killed, after serving heroically. In an interview with Sarah Girty Munger in 1864 Lyman C. Draper wrote:

INTERVIEW NOTES, LYMAN DRAPER

His (Simon Girty's) son Thomas was in the skirmish in the War of 1812 nearly opposite Malden. A Canadian officer was wounded and begged young Girty to carry him, and Thomas Girty carried him a long distance on his back. They came to a puddle of water on the way and both drank freely. Girty, from his overexertion, was immediately taken sick with a fever and died, and was buried in his father's orchard ... the officer got well.[17]

In an earlier 1848 interview, Catherine Malott Girty had informed Lyman Draper that her son died on the 21st of September, at which time he was twenty-four years old.

Two months after her husband's death, Thomas's widow gave birth to Simon's granddaughter, whom she named Catherine Cady Girty.

During the months following Thomas's death the tides of war continued to ebb and flow. The Americans crossed the Detroit River and threatened to take Fort Malden, but then prudently withdrew back across the river as General Brock, reinforced by Tecumseh's forces, approached. Pursuing their advantage, the Canadians crossed over and besieged Detroit. During this fighting Simon Girty's recent loss was tragically echoed by that of Matthew Elliott, whose son Alexander was killed on 12 November when captive Indians allied to the United States overpowered their guards. Grief-stricken, Matthew Elliott returned to Amherstburg with the body of his son in mid-December.

In early 1813, Catherine Girty was still living with her daughter Nancy Ann and her son-in-law Peter Govereau at their tavern and inn at Amherstburg. Even though he was almost totally blind now, Simon continued to make frequent visits to the place; his horse evidently knew the way to and from and required little if any guidance. There is nothing to indicate whether Simon and his estranged wife spoke during these visits; but it is likely, for the Govereau home and business was too small to avoid such encounters.

The next major event in Girty's life is gleaned from another statement Girty's daughter Sarah gave to Lyman C. Draper during their 1864 interview. The incident she revealed was preceded by Commodore Oliver H. Perry's 10 September 1813 victory over the British fleet on Lake Erie:

SARAH GIRTY MUNGER

After Perry's victory, and it was evident General Harrison was coming to Malden, Colonel Matthew Elliott went and told Girty that he and all connected with the British Indian Department must be off, as they would most likely be massacred if they should remain and all went to Burlington and stayed till after the close of the contest.[18]

Sarah Munger's recollection was essentially correct. According to William Caldwell, Jr., following Perry's victory, Girty went with many others (perhaps with Matthew Elliott's party) to Burlington for safety. Both Girty and Matthew Elliott spent the remainder of the war among the Mohawks, at or near Joseph Brant's estate on the Grand River. Just before the retreat to Burlington, Elliott ordered the Indians and their families to provision themselves from Girty's cornfields.

Another story associated with this period of Girty's decline claims that, just after the Battle of the Thames, Simon Kenton went to Girty's home at Malden to protect him from American soldiers, and that he arrived there just before, or just after, Girty had departed for Burlington. In one version, Kenton prevents an American patrol from burning Girty's farm (as the Americans had done to Elliott's home). According to Draper's notes from his interview with Sarah Girty Munger:

> *As Harrison's men came to the mouth of the Detroit River below*
> *Malden, they went to Girty's house and asked for him—were*
> *told he had gone down the Lake. "If he were here," said some, "we*
> *would soon fix him so he wouldn't need any more fixing in this*
> *world."*
>
> *"No you wouldn't!" responded some friend of Girtys. (This*
> *was, no doubt Simon Kenton, who was there with the American*
> *army, and who went there to protect his old benefactor: LCD.)*
> *Some of the men threatened to burn the house over Mrs. Girty's*
> *head [this would have been Monica Evans-Girty], but the officers*
> *and Kenton prevented it.*[19]

However, according to Butterfield, Kenton's honorable and heroic intervention does not ring true:

> *Some time after Harrison landed in Canada, Commodore Perry*
> *had occasion to send one hundred Kentucky soldiers to Detroit.*
> *They went on shore on the Canada side of the river, below Malden,*
> *and proceeded thence to their point of destination; but, before*
> *reaching there, the men destroyed the house and furniture of*
> *Elliott (then known in all that region as "Colonel Elliott"), also*
> *ruining his fences, barn, and storehouses.*
>
> *... Doubtless had his [Girty's] property been pointed out to*
> *the Kentucky detachment, it would likewise have been ruined.*
> *There is a current (but erroneous) tradition that his house was*
> *about to be burned when Simon Kenton stept forward and*
> *declared it should not be done; that Girty was his friend who had*
> *once done him a great kindness; and that, thereupon, the soldiers*
> *desisted. But, as we have shown, Kenton was, at this time, with*
> *Harrison, and could not, therefore, have interposed to save the*
> *property of "his friend."*

Apparently, the drama of one of America's greatest, most patriotic frontier heroes interceding to save his old friend (and one of America's greatest enemies) was simply too much for Butterfield to accept.

However, while there is no documentation to support Butterfield's claim that Kenton was somewhere else at the time, there is evidence to support the tale of Kenton's intervention on Girty's behalf, for in notes on this subject by Draper the following appears:

Taken from Simon Kenton's old papers, in possession of his son William M. Kenton, Esq., of Monticello, White County, Indiana, interviewed December 8, 1851 by LCD:

Simon Kenton, when out in 1813 on the Thames Campaign, visited Simon Girty near Malden. They were glad to see each other. Rehearsed over their early history; & Girty observed if he had been treated fairly, he no doubt would then have been with Kenton, pursuing the retreating British troops.[20]

Additionally, a statement given to Draper by Sarah McCord, Kenton's daughter, corroborates the account, claiming that Kenton crossed over (the Detroit River) to find Girty, and found him after he was already blind, wearing his signature red handkerchief around his head.

There is no question that Kenton crossed into Canada with the initial American invaders, and that he was present later at the Battle of the Thames where, immediately after the conflict, he was summoned to identify Tecumseh's body. Obviously, Kenton's primary commitment was to aid his comrades and the American cause, and surely he did not travel all the way to Canada from Kentucky with the sole intention of saving Girty. Still, understanding the nature of Kenton, there can be little doubt that he bore a debt of honor to the friend who had rescued him so many years before. What remains unclear is whether he reached Girty's farm in time to meet with him there, or whether Kenton got there after Girty had already gone. Either way, the records strongly indicate that Kenton made the effort to find and help his friend, and his gesture speaks eloquently of the depth of affection and honor between these two frontiersmen.

In Burlington, old Girty was taken in by Mohawks, who treated him gently and honored him as a former chief. The friendship, kindness and generosity Simon received from the natives had remained consistent since Simon had first been captured and adopted as a teenager; the Indians were a well from which he had always been able to draw physical, emotional and perhaps even spiritual nourishment. During their winter hunts at Burlington the younger warriors sometimes entertained older men by stationing them at strategic positions where, accompanied by a few capable marksmen, they would wait while the main party of hunters drove game to them through the snow. Girty—who had always lived for the moment—would have come easily to this life, warming to the banter, jokes and camaraderie.

Surprisingly, while Simon was at Burlington, the Missouri Gazette published his obituary:

MISSOURI GAZETTE, 7 MAY 1814

St. Louis, Saturday, 7 May 1814:

Simon was adopted by the Senecas and became as expert in hunting as any of them. His character, as related in Kentucky and Ohio, of being a savage, unrelented monster, is much exaggerated. It is true that he joined the Indians in most of their war parties, and conformed to their mode of warfare, but it is well authenticated that he has saved many prisoners from death. And that he was considered an honest man, paying his debts to the last cent; and it is known that he has sold his only horse to discharge a claim against him. It is true that he was a perfect Indian in his manners, that his utmost felicity was centered in a keg of rum, and that he was abusive to all around him, even to his best friends. Yet we must recollect that his education was barbarous, and that mankind are more apt to sink into barbarism than he is to acquire the habits of a civilized life. For the last ten years he had been crippled by rheumatism, yet he rode to his hunting spirit in the midst of bodily pain, and would often exclaim: "May I breathe my last on a field of battle!" In this wish Simon has been gratified, for in the battle of the Moravian Towns, on the River Thames, he was cut to pieces by Colonel Johnson's mounted men.[21]

Although it is unlikely Simon was ever made aware of this untimely obituary, his dramatic death as depicted in the Missouri newspaper would no doubt have brought a raucous belly laugh from the aged, crippled, and nearly blind frontiersman.

On the same day that the *Missouri Gazette* story was published, Matthew Elliott, who had been quartered in Joseph Brant's old mansion, passed away after an illness of three months. Like Alexander McKee, Elliott had also died wealthy, and left large estates and numerous slaves to his family. With his passing, Simon Girty was now the only living member left of the infamous three traitors of McKee, Elliott and Girty who, for over thirty years, had caused the United States immense trouble along the northwest frontier.

Although the War of 1812 was concluded after negotiations, on 24 December 1814, General Prevost, at Quebec, was not officially notified of this event until the next March. Two months later, Girty's name appeared in a letter written by William Claus, the new Superintendent of Indian Affairs in Canada. Simon's name is included in a list of "officers and others whose services, I think, may be dispensed with, and a return of interpreters whose age and infirmities render them unfit for further service."[22]

Returning from Burlington, Simon arrived at Amherstburg early in the summer of 1816. Totally blind, he took up residence at the inn owned by his daughter Nancy and her husband Peter Govereau. Catherine Girty and Simon were once again living under the same roof. Simon had changed considerably since Catherine had last seen him. His spell in the wilderness with the Mohawks had mellowed him, and he was sober. Clearly, for the first time in their relationship, her husband needed her care and companionship, and apparently Catherine's nurturing instincts took over.

At the same time Simon returned from his sojourn among the Mohawks, Monica Evans Girty and her daughter were still living at the Girty homestead in Malden. Soon after Simon's return she remarried, and left with her infant daughter to live at her new husband's home in McComb County, Michigan Territory. Simon and Catherine then returned to their old home in Malden together. Three months later James Girty died, on 17 April 1817, at his home at Gosfield, Essex County. At the time of his death James' hands and wrists were severely deformed and crippled by rheumatism. His Shawnee wife had passed away thirteen years earlier, and his meager estate was left to his son and daughter.

Simon was now the last of the "Injun Girtys." Considering his blindness and his inability to travel on his own, it is not difficult to envision Girty's steady withdrawal from outside events. His wife was now his primary companion, and the meals and conversations they shared were the highlights of his days. There is every reason to believe that until the heavy winter snows of 1817, Simon and Catherine were frequently visited by their son, daughters and in-laws. At his core, Simon Girty had always been a cheerful, lively character, and it is unlikely that he was morose or sullen during his final months.

With the farm buried in deep snow drifts, Simon fell ill on 15 February 1818 and apparently recognized the seriousness of his situation. According to Butterfield, Catherine explained to him how he might still obtain pardon for his sins, and prayed earnestly for him at his bedside.

Girty's entire family was present when, during the morning of 18 February, in the midst of a driving snow storm, the old warrior went "to another region from which no traveler returns." Also in attendance were some elderly Indians (most likely Wyandots) who, trading places with each other, sat or knelt next to his bed, held his hand, and spoke softly to him in their own tongue.[22]

Upon receiving news of Simon's death, the commandant at Fort Malden dispatched a military detail to the Girty home. On 20 February uniformed troopers had to carry Simon's casket over the top of a fence to a grave site about fifty yards west of the house, as the snowdrifts were too high to allow use of the gate. Witnessed by Simon's wife, his children, grandchildren and many friends, an honor guard fired a volley, and Simon was buried in a shallow grave which was to be deepened in the spring, after the ground had thawed. The most notorious character of the early American frontier had survived for seventy-seven years.

"SIMON GIRTY AND HIS BROTHERS," *STANDARD HISTORY OF WILLIAMS COUNTY, OHIO,* 1920

His name is inscribed with that of Brutus, of Benedict Arnold, and of Judas Iscariot.... Of all these known instances of white renegades, none equals the cruelty and absolute baseness of Simon Girty.

EPILOGUE

TWO YEARS AFTER Simon Girty's death Daniel Boone also passed away. During their lifetimes the unrelenting expansion of colonial America steadily accelerated. Both of these frontiersmen witnessed the conflict between the colonists and Natives change from one in which the outcome was unknown to one in which the Indians were doomed. Twenty years after Girty's death, Andrew Jackson's government forced the removal of thousands of Native Americans from east of the Mississippi to the far west—namely, Oklahoma Territory. By the late 1880s, after Custer and Geronimo, all Indians became wards of the federal government.

Simon Kenton died in 1836, some eighteen years after Simon Girty. Catherine Malott Girty never remarried and expired in 1852, thirty-four years after the death of her husband. Simon's elder brother Thomas died in Pennsylvania on 3 November 1820 and John Turner, Jr. died at Squirrel Hill, Pittsburgh, on 20 May 1840.

Because Simon's legend greatly overpowered the truth of his life, many of his descendants on both sides of the Canadian-U.S. border endured the burden of his vilification. Old Dwight Girty told me that when he grew up in Windsor, Ontario, he was taunted for being a descendant of the infamous Simon Girty. As a young man Dwight's grandfather Simon Peter Girty dropped "Simon" from his name. When he passed away, the inscription on his tombstone read "Peter Girty." Years later, while working at a newspaper, Dwight Girty began to seriously research the life of Simon Girty. After years of diligent work, he concluded there was nothing to be ashamed about and he

SIMON GIRTY, U. E.
1741 – 1818

GIRTY'S LIFE CROSSED CULTURAL BOUNDARIES
BETWEEN NATIVE AND WHITE SOCIETIES ON THE
FRONTIER OF AMERICAN SETTLEMENT. IN 1756
HIS FAMILY WAS CAPTURED BY A FRENCH-LED
NATIVE WAR PARTY IN PENNSYLVANIA. SIMON WAS
ADOPTED BY THE SENECA, THEN REPATRIATED IN
1764. AN INTERPRETER AT FORT PITT (PITTSBURGH),
HE BECAME AN INTERMEDIARY WITH NATIVE NATIONS
IN 1778, DISMAYED OVER REBEL POLICY ON THE
NATIVES, GIRTY FLED TO DETROIT. DURING THE
REVOLUTIONARY WAR AND SUBSEQUENT CONFLICTS
IN THE OHIO VALLEY, HE WAS EMPLOYED BY THE
BRITISH INDIAN DEPARTMENT WHILE SERVING NATIVE
NATIONS AS A NEGOTIATOR, SCOUT AND MILITARY
LEADER. ANGRY AT HIS DEFECTION AND FEARFUL OF
HIS INFLUENCE, AMERICANS MADE GIRTY A
SCAPEGOAT FOR FRONTIER ATROCITIES. HE IS
BURIED HERE ON HIS HOMESTEAD.

ERECTED BY THE BICENTENNIAL AND TORONTO BRANCHES,
UNITED EMPIRE LOYALISTS' ASSOCIATION OF CANADA, WITH
ASSISTANCE FROM THE ONTARIO HERITAGE FOUNDATION

replaced the tombstone at his grandfather's grave with a new one that reads: Simon Peter Girty.

As far as I know, all of the Girty descendants in Canada and in the United States lived responsible, productive lives. The ones I met were hospitable, helpful and kind.

In 1838 Simon's son Prideaux served as a Major in the Third Essex Militia Regiment during the Upper Canada Rebellion (Patriot War). In 1844 he was appointed Superintendent of Education for the township of Gosfield. In 1847, he was appointed Justice of the Peace. He also represented Gosfield Township on the District Council. He owned and operated what may have been the first steam-powered grist and sawmill in Essex County. In 1853 he was killed in an industrial accident while inspecting a new type of machinery in Dayton, Ohio.

Prideaux's eldest son Thomas became a doctor who served the communities of Albertville, Union and Ruthven. Dr. Thomas Girty's oldest son was Dwight Girty's grandfather, Simon Peter Girty.

Both the Girtys and the Malotts played significant, productive roles in the settling and development of the Kingsville area, and today these families continue to contribute to their communities.

There are descendants of John Turner Girty and Thomas Girty living in Pennsylvania, and there are Delaware and Shawnee descendants of James and George Girty living in Oklahoma.

Despite what might have been expected by early American historians, my research has failed to reveal a single felon among Girty's descendants.

Pressures from modern historians (including this writer) to tell the true story of Simon Girty brought positive results in 1995, when the United Empire Loyalists of Canada recognized Girty's life and contributions, and a plaque[1] in his honor was erected at the location of his first home site in Malden, Canada. Simon Girty is also honored by the Six Nations, who still remember him as an "Indian Patriot."[2]

Why is it that Boone remains a popular American icon—the greatest pioneer ever—while Girty—America's most notorious renegade—is almost forgotten? It cannot be that heroes have more historic staying power than hooligans, or we wouldn't remember Attila, Genghis Khan, or Vlad the Impaler. As a horrific figure, Hitler will surely be evoked for centuries to come. Maybe Girty has been forgotten because even though most of us celebrate the spirit of our pioneering forefathers, we also know in our hearts that what happened to America's first inhabitants was grossly violent and unspeakably cruel. Girty's legend and his real story both remind us of things we would rather not confront. If Simon had simply defected during the Revolutionary War, and had then served with a regular unit of the British Army, no one would have remembered him. Girty wasn't extraordinary because he was a rogue who changed sides during the American Revolution, but because he saw beyond the distortions of frontier racism and remained true to his convictions, despite the costs. Boone is famous because he helped whites fight Indians. Girty was notorious because he helped Indians fight whites.

THE GIRTYS OF ESSEX COUNTY, ONTARIO

THE GIRTY NAME HAS ALMOST DISAPPEARED from Essex County, Ontario, but Simon Girty's spirit lives on in the lives of his many descendants in both Canada and the United States. The three children who survived after Simon's death in 1818 contributed positively to an emerging British settlement along the Detroit River and Lake Erie's northern shoreline. The Lot 11, Malden farm site, fronting on the Detroit River, where he and Catherine raised their two sons and two daughters, now proudly displays a commemorative historic plaque. Of the original farmstead, only a few unmarked graves remain that bear the remains of the original inhabitants. No Girtys live nearby, although proud descendants frequently return to visit their ancestor's former home.

Thomas Girty, Simon's elder son, perished after serving nobly as ensign with the First Regiment of the Essex Militia during the War of 1812–1814. His only daughter, born two months after Thomas' death, lived most of her youth in Michigan, where she married and died. Little else is known about her.

Much of the Girty legacy lives on through the lives of Simon and Catherine's daughters and their numerous descendants. Their first-born daughter, Nancy Ann Girty, who married the Amherstburg innkeeper and ship carpenter, Peter Geauvreau (Govereau), was the one who gave solace to both her parents when they were estranged. The Geauvreaus' four daughters, Catherine Hayes, Elizabeth McKenzie (second husband Henry Bruner), Nancy Ann Sanford and Caroline (Sara), married into prominent Colchester and Gosfield families. The marriage of the Geauvreau's youngest child and only son, Thomas, linked the family with three of the most prominent and prolific families of Gosfield: Fox, Scratch and Wigle. Many Geauvreau descendants remain in the Harrow and Kingsville areas.

Sarah Girty, who married Joseph Munger in 1807, was the daughter who cared for her mother Catherine in her old age. In fact it was at the Munger home in Colchester where Simon's aging widow died. The Mungers themselves have a colorful past. In 1794, Joseph's father, Charles Munger, was killed at the Battle of Fallen Timbers. When Joseph's mother remarried, taking her daughters with her to Pennsylvania, Joseph remained in Colchester with his uncle William Munger. The Munger name survived in the area due to Joseph and Sarah Munger's thirteen children. Shortly after Catherine Girty died, Sarah and Joseph Munger, along with part of their family, moved to Winnebago County, Illinois. Both died there. Surrounding the Munger farm and family businesses, a new village in Colchester Township developed. It was first dubbed "Munger's Corners" because John Girty Munger, a son of Joseph and Sarah Munger, had a blacksmith shop on the south-east corner of King Street and Given Road (Snake Lane) and across the street was the Joseph Munger farm. By 1854, when the community's first post office was established, the town's name was changed to Harrow. Many Mungers and Munger relatives still reside there.

Simon Girty's son Prideaux Girty, who as a child had come with his mother, Catherine Girty, to stay at his Uncle Peter Malott's farm near present Kingsville, spent much of his life in the Kingsville area. He proved to be a community-minded citizen—a positive force in Gosfield Township's early history. At the age of sixteen, during the War of 1812–14, he became a member of the London Militia, serving as ensign at the Battle of Lundy's Lane. In 1816, he married Catherine McKenzie, sister of the wife of his cousin William Malott. In 1820, he received a 200-acre land grant as a son of a United Empire Loyalist. By 1829, he resided on his town lot in Albertville, about two miles east of present day Kingsville. In 1834, he sold his portion of the Simon Girty farm, the southern portion of Lot 11, Concession 1, Malden Township. At about the same time, Catherine, the daughter of his deceased brother Thomas Girty, sold the northern half of the same farm. So, sixteen years after Simon's death, the tidy little Girty farm was no longer owned by the family. It had existed but fifty years, 1784-1834. In 1838, Prideaux served as Major in the Third Essex Militia Regiment (Colonel John Prince's Regiment) in the Upper Canada Rebellion (Patriot War). In 1844, Prideaux was appointed Superintendent of Education in the Township of Gosfield, which also included the present Kingsville town site. In 1847, he was promoted to the rank of Colonel in the First Essex Militia Regiment. At about the same time, he was also appointed Justice of the Peace. During the following three years, Prideaux Girty represented Gosfield Township in the District Council, which embraced the Counties of Essex, Kent and Lambton. At the same time, he owned and operated a steam-powered grist and sawmill in the hamlet of Albertville (commencing in the mid-1830s). This was thought to be the first steam-powered grist and sawmill in Essex County. He was still in the mill business in 1853, for in that year he was in a Dayton, Ohio gristmill looking over some new type of machinery, when some sort of accident caused his death. So well respected was he that some Gosfield families named their children for him—Prideaux Fox, Prideaux Wigle and Prideaux Malott, to name just a few.

Prideaux's family of six sons and three daughters added to the Girty legacy. We know of daughters who married in the Kingsville area. Four of his sons left for the Washington and Oregon western states, while one left for Peel County, Upper Canada. After he became a medical doctor, Prideaux's oldest son, Thomas, resided in Gosfield Township. He served well the communities of Albertville, Union and Ruthven. Family tradition tells that he made periodic trips to Pelee Island, on one of his cousin William Malott's vessels, in order to care for the sick.

Dr. Thomas Girty's oldest son was named Simon Peter Girty; but by 1871, he had dropped Simon from his name, due to the infamy of his grandfather's name caused by American publications. From then on, he was known as S. Peter Girty or just Peter Girty. All of Peter Girty's family remained in Essex County except his youngest son, George Lawrence, who resided in Blenheim in Kent County, where his descendants remain to this day. One of Peter Girty's sons was

Edsel Girty, well-remembered for delivering mail by horse and buggy. Later in his life, he sold insurance and issued drivers' licenses.

Of Edsel Girty's family of six, only one son, Dwight Girty, and two daughters, Lorraine Olsen and Lucille Simpson, have survived and at this date, still live in Essex County. The Girty name will live on in Essex through Dwight Girty's son, David, and through his children. It was Dwight Girty who worked diligently to obtain accurate data to build respect and appreciation for his ancestor, Simon Girty.

Surely, old Simon would sit back and smile if he were to know of the accomplishments of his many descendants. (Since this was written, Dwight and Lucille have died.)

THE MALOTTS

Part of Simon's legacy may be attributed to his dutiful wife, Catherine Malott. She not only performed the tasks of a farm wife but also managed the Girty farm. While her husband Simon Girty was wandering forest trails, attending tribal conferences and meeting with associates in the British Indian Department at the Council House, she was performing farm chores, overseeing the planting and harvesting of crops, and in the meanwhile caring for her children. It was she who created a stable environment for their enlarging family.

Ultimately, when the demands of such a trying life became intolerable for her, she left her husband. She hurried down to her brother Peter Malott at his Lot 4, Gosfield Township home on the outskirts of present Kingsville, Ontario. She brought her eighteen-month old son Prideaux with her. If her other older children were with her some of the time during her separation from Simon, we do not know, although we do know that all her children demonstrated loyalty to her at different times. Catherine felt close to her brother, Peter Malott, her nearest sibling.

In 1780, when they were about fifteen and sixteen, Catherine and Peter, as well as their mother Sarah Malott and several other Malott children, were captured by a group of mixed tribes on the Ohio River (at a site now known as Powhatan Point), not far south of present day Wheeling, West Virginia. Their father, on another boat in the small flotilla, escaped, and thinking them all dead, returned to his former home in Washington County, Maryland. Within a year, Sarah Malott and all of her children, except for Catherine, had been turned in at Detroit for a ransom. The British merchant William Macomb likely paid the ransom as he did for so many other Indian prisoners. In 1784, it was Simon Girty who lured Catherine away from the Shawnees along the Mad River. He brought her to Detroit, married her, and, with her, made their home on his British Land Grant, Lot 11, Concession 1, Malden Township.

British merchant William Macomb, who had purchased Grosse Ile, (downriver from Detroit), from the Potowatomi Indians, devised a plan for settling ransomed prisoners on his island. Among the first tenant farmers placed there were Sarah Malott and her family. This was about the time when Catherine and Simon had come to their Malden farm across the Detroit River from Grosse Ile. Catherine's brother Peter remained on Grosse Ile, farming and earning money from other jobs. There he married Mary (Polly) Jones, another ransomed prisoner of the Indians, who had formerly lived in West Virginia. William Macomb had employed her as a household servant. While on Grosse Ile, Peter and Mary's first son Joseph was born. Ambitious and enterprising, Peter Malott made several formal requests to the British Land Board in Detroit for free lands in the new Gosfield settlement on the north shore of Lake Erie. In 1792, he received Lot 4, a farm of 200 acres in Gosfield Township. Family tradition tells that he forfeited one milk cow as payment to a soldier who held the original certificate for the lot.

Quickly moving to Gosfield, Peter, his wife, and young son Joseph, were well established by the time that Catherine Girty came to stay with them in their fine, black walnut log cabin (by then, Mary had given birth to two daughters, only one of whom survived). How long Catherine remained at Peter's Gosfield home before returning to Amherstburg and Malden, we do not know. In 1804, Peter seems to have been on good terms with his brother-in-law Simon Girty, for when Peter and Mary's last child was born on March 13, 1804, he was named Peter Girty Malott. On July 1, 1805, Peter bought Lot 7, W.D. Gosfield, comprising 200 acres, from Simon Girty for 37 pounds, 12 shillings and 6 pence. Peter continued to acquire adjoining land, and by the time of his death in 1815, he owned 714 acres of prime land on the western edge of the present town of Kingsville, which he bequeathed to his two sons, Joseph and Peter G., and his two living daughters, Mary Wilkinson and Ann Williams. On a December day when he was boiling down cider for winter use, he was scalded so severely that he didn't survive. His widow Mary lived on in the cabin with her son Peter Girty Malott and his family until her death in 1845.

Joseph Malott married Mary McKenzie, whose sister Catherine would later marry his cousin Prideaux Girty. They settled on the Lot 7 portion of his father's holdings, now part of Linden Beach. He became well-known as a farmer and Methodist Lay Preacher. His two sons John (Jack) and William became prominent lake captains. The brothers built a wharf in front of their Linden Beach home in the 1860s for shipping grain to the Northern armies during the American Civil War. For a short time afterward, they shipped grain directly to England. Captain William Malott built four sailing vessels, the *Wave,* the *Eureka,* the *Alzora* and the *Antelope,* and sailed as master of these for several years. In his mid-life, William built a large frame home in Kingsville on a hilltop in front of which, in 1877, he built a dock that early maps label as Malotte's Dock. The Canadian government bought his dock in 1883 and Captain Malott was named Harbour Master. With subsequent changes and improvements, the dock remains as Kingsville's Federal Dock.

Peter Girty Malott (he was known simply as Peter G.) spent his whole life on his father's homestead, farming the large acreage that the family had cleared. He also served as a captain of the local militia. After he and his wife Julianna Wigle raised nine children in the original log cabin, they built a substantial frame home on the same property with the assistance of Skedaddlers, men who came into the area as draft dodgers during the American Civil War. The house remains today in good condition. Julianna became the area midwife between 1857 and 1885, and delivered 726 of the township's babies, including her own grandchildren. Family tradition tells that she charged two dollars for boys and one dollar for girls.

Peter G. Malott's sons were John, Ezra and Leonard. All three were involved in community affairs, and all were farmers and landowners. John grew fruit and grain and for a time, and advertised that he was a grape grower and winemaker. Leonard lived in town most of his life while his sons farmed his acreage. He was a builder and owned a sash and door factory. All the nine sons and daughters of Peter G. and Julianna Malott lived out their lives in the Kingsville area, just as most of the next generation would do. James Malott, a Kingsville pharmacist, has his home near Lake Erie on his great-great-great-grandfather's original Land Grant, Lot 4, W.D. of Gosfield, almost abutting the site of the original log cabin. Like the Girtys, the Malott blood flows through much of the fabric of the Kingsville area.

Madeline Hilborn Malott [1]

LIST OF PRINCIPAL CHARACTERS

Lt. Colonel John Armstrong—British colonial officer, commanding British forces west of Susquehanna River, based at Carlisle, Pennsylvania.

Captain Henry Bird—British officer SECOND in command at Detroit under Major Lernoult. His arrogant attitude caused him to be disliked by Indians, who often refused to follow him or accept his commands.

Blue Jacket—Powerful Shawnee war chief, friend of Simon Girty during Indian wars.

Daniel Boone—Influential and popular American pioneer, frontiersman and militia officer.

Colonel Henry Bouquet—Swiss mercenary in command of English forces against Indians in 1760s. Achieved surrender of western tribes in 1763-64.

General Edward Braddock—Sent by King George II to invade and conquer Indians of Ohio Country. His primary objective was the reclaiming of former Fort Pitt (then Fort Duquesne) from French control. Defeated by Indians ten miles from Fort Duquesne in July 1755, he died shortly thereafter as a result of his wounds.

Samuel Brady—Important U.S. frontiersman, militia officer and Indian fighter.

Chief Joseph Brant—Powerful, influential Mohawk war chief, also a captain in British Army. Played an important role in organizing confederation of western and northern tribes at onset of the Indian Wars. Nearly killed Simon Girty in drunken attack with a sword during Revolutionary War, but worked with Girty during the Indian Wars that follow.

COLONEL DANIEL BRODHEAD—U.S. Army officer, one time commander of Fort Pitt during the Revolutionary War.

BULL—Delaware chief, brother to Pipe, pro-American, shot down during Squaw Campaign by militia under command of Edward Hand. William Crawford present during attack on Bull's village.

COLONEL JOHN BUTLER—British commander at Niagara during Revolutionary War.

RICHARD BUTLER—Influential Indian trader, Westmoreland supporter, opposed to Dunmore, Connolly, and Girty, among others. Later a U.S. general with St. Clair. Killed at defeat of St Clair's army in Battle of Wabash. Killed in front of Girty.

CAPTAIN WILLIAM CALDWELL—Member of the British army, based at Detroit. During Revolutionary War commands two companies of Butler's Rangers. Good friend of Girty.

GOVERNOR GENERAL SIR GUY CARLETON A.K.A. LORD DORCHESTER—c. 1790. In command of British government in Upper Canada.

LT. ABRAHAM CHAPLINE—U.S. officer, captured by Shawnees, escapes to warn Kentucky of forthcoming British attack.

GEORGE ROGERS CLARK—Frontiersman, soldier, surveyor. Top frontier general on American side during the Revolutionary War. Effective Indian fighter.

DR. JOHN CONNOLLY—Irish businessman and Loyalist, aid to Lord Dunmore, successful land dealer, and entrepreneur. Politically savvy, based at Pittsburgh.

CORNSTALK—Principal Shawnee war chief. Commands Shawnees at Battle of Point Pleasant.

GENERAL CHARLES CORNWALLIS—Surrendered large British army at Yorktown, 1781, in effect signaling the end of the Revolutionary War.

WILLIAM CRAWFORD—Surveyor and close friend to George Washington. Influential businessman, Justice of the Peace, militia officer, later a colonel in U.S. army.

MICHAEL CRESAP—Operated trading post at Redstone, Pennsylvania.

GEORGE CROGHAN—Influential and wealthy Indian trader and land dealer, based near Lancaster, Pennsylvania; also British Deputy Superintendent of Indian Affairs, at Fort Pitt. Later replaced by Alexander McKee.

MAJOR ARENT SHUYLER DE PEYSTER—British commander at Fort Detroit during Indian Wars.

CAPTAIN COULON DE VILLIERS—French officer in command of Shawnees and Delawares who attack and capture Fort Granville in 1755.

GOVERNOR ROBERT DINWIDDIE—Governor of Virginia, shareholder in Ohio Company.

MAJOR EPHRAIM DOUGLAS—U.S. emissary sent to British authorities in Canada following Revolutionary War, seeking to advise Indians to vacate their lands which were now owned by the U.S. British authorities did not allow Douglas to meet with Indians, and he abandoned his mission within a few months.

PIERRE DROUILLARD—Indian trader, British Indian Agent in Ohio Country during Revolutionary War. Friend of Simon Girty, who saved Simon Kenton from burning by Shawnees.

DAVID DUNCAN—Popular Pittsburgh tavern owner, he and his wife were good friends of Simon Girty, Jr.

MATTHEW ELLIOTT—Indian trader, British Indian agent, friend of Simon Girty, Jr. Eventually appointed British Superintendent of Indian Affairs, based in Malden, Ontario, taking over after death of Alexander McKee.

BENJAMIN FRANKLIN—Influential printer, politician, businessman, inventor, diplomat and land dealer.

GEORGE GIBSON—Brother of John Gibson, dies from wounds received in defeat of St. Clair's army.

JOHN GIBSON—U.S. militia officer, Indian trader, later U.S. Army Colonel commanding Fort Laurens, a pre-war rival of Girty.

MONICA EVANS GIRTY—Wife of Thomas Girty who is youngest son of Simon Girty, Jr.

PRIDEAUX GIRTY—Son of Simon Girty, Jr.

SIMON, JR., THOMAS, GEORGE AND JAMES GIRTY—Four sons of Simon, Sr. and Mary [Newton] Girty.

SIMON GIRTY, SR.—Indian trader, husband of Mary Newton, father to Simon, Jr., Thomas, James and George Girty.

THOMAS GIRTY—Youngest son of Simon Girty, Jr.

DANIEL GREATHOUSE—Led Americans who murdered Logan's family at Yellow Creek.

GUYASUTA—Principal war chief of Western Senecas or "Mingoes." Shares leadership with Pontiac in war against British colonial forces, 1761—62. Patron of Simon Girty, Jr.

GENERAL SIR FREDERICK HALDIMAND—British commander of Canada, Governor General of British North America.

HALF KING A.K.A. POMOACAN—Important Wyandot war chief and close friend of Girty.

LT. GOVERNOR HENRY HAMILTON—British governor of Canada and commander of the frontier war, based at Detroit.

BRIGADIER GENERAL EDWARD HAND—Continental Army commander at Fort Pitt during first half of Revolutionary War. In command of disastrous Squaw Campaign.

LT. COLONEL JOSIAH HARMAR—U.S. commander of 1st American Regiment at Fort Pitt, 1785. In command of badly defeated American army in Indian Wars, just prior to defeat of St. Clair.

LT. GOVERNOR JEHU HAY—Following Indian Wars, was appointed to command at Detroit by British authorities. Influential Indian trader.

REVEREND JOHN HECKEWELDER—Important Moravian missionary, close associate and friend to David Zeisberger. Also clandestinely provided intelligence helpful to Americans while claiming to British authorities that he and his church were neutral.

PATRICK HENRY—Wealthy land dealer, businessman and influential politician.

WILLIAM HULL—Governor of Michigan and commanding U.S. army on Detroit frontier during Indian Wars.

ABNER HUNT—American surveyor captured by Indians in 1791 and tortured to death. Girty was blamed for not preventing Hunt's death.

GENERAL WILLIAM IRVINE—U.S. officer who replaced John Gibson as commander of western war at Fort Pitt. Gibson was in temporary command at Fort Pitt following transfer or removal of Brodhead.

SIR JOHN JOHNSON—British Superintendent of Indian Affairs, son of Sir William Johnson.

SIR WILLIAM JOHNSON—New York based British Superintendent of Indian Affairs. Adopted Mohawk, influential with Iroquois Confederation.

KAYINGWAURTO A.K.A. OLD SMOKE—Principal war chief of Eastern Senecas.

SIMON KENTON (A.K.A SIMON BUTLER)—Outstanding frontiersman, hunter, Indian fighter, scout, and close friend of Simon Girty; an American hero during Revolutionary War.

DR. JOHN KNIGHT—U.S. surgeon with Crawford's militia army at Battle of Sandusky. Captured with Crawford, but later escaped.

HENRY KNOX—First U.S. Secretary of War.

MAJOR RICHARD BERRINGER LERNOULT—British commander, 8th King's Regiment at Detroit. One-time commander of Fort Detroit.

COLONEL ANDREW LEWIS—Wealthy land dealer and Virginia militia officer who commands Virginia army at Battle of Point Pleasant against Cornstalk and Shawnees.

BENJAMIN LINCOLN—Retired U.S. general sent to negotiate treaty with Indians just prior to Fallen Timbers.

LITTLE TURTLE—Brilliant Miami War Chief, a great tactician and combat leader.

COLONEL ARCHIBALD LOCHRY—American officer killed in British-Indian river ambush.

JOHN LOGAN—Mingo war chief. The murder of his family by whites starts Dunmore's War against the Shawnees.

ELIZABETH LOWREY—Girty's girlfriend at Fort Pitt in the 1760s and early 70s.

GENERAL ALLAN MACLEAN—British commander at Niagara after Revolutionary War.

PETER MALOTT—Brother of Catherine, Canadian resident near Amherstberg.

SARAH MALOTT—Mother of Catherine (Girty's wife).

ALEXANDER MCCORMICK—American spy posing as British Indian trader in Ohio Country during Revolutionary War.

MAJOR HUGH MCGARY—Hot-headed U.S. militia officer who rejected Daniel Boone's warning not to proceed across Blue Licks River, and led Kentuckians into a disastrous ambush.

BRIGADIER GENERAL LACHLAN MCINTOSH—U.S. commander at Fort Pitt during Revolutionary War, replaced the disgraced General Edward Hand.

THOMAS MCKEE—Important and influential Indian trader in Lancaster County, father of Alexander McKee.

GEORGE MORGAN (AKA TAMANEND, "PEACEMAKER")—Successful, influential merchant, Indian trader, commissioner of Indian Affairs for rebel American government during Revolutionary War.

GOVERNOR LEWIS MORRIS—Governor of New Jersey at time of French and Indian War.

SARAH GIRTY MUNGER—Daughter of Simon Girty, Jr. Married Joseph Munger.

JOHN MURRAY, FOURTH EARL OF DUNMORE (A.K.A LORD DUNMORE)—Governor of pre-Revolutionary Virginia, shareholder in Ohio Company. Strong Loyalist.

CAPTAIN PIPE—Pro-peace Delaware chief, who later turns against Americans. His brother Bull was murdered by American militia during Squaw Campaign.

JOSEPH NICHOLSON—American frontiersman, scout, spy.

TIMOTHY PICKERING—Postmaster General, sent to negotiate treaty with Lincoln and Randolph.

CAPTAIN CHARLES POLKE—U.S. officer who went to Canada seeking to retrieve his family, who had been captured by Indians and were at Detroit.

PONTIAC—Ottawa chief who, with Guyasuta, leads confederation of western tribes against British Colonial authorities (Pontiac-Guyasuta War).

BEVERLY RANDOLPH—One time governor of Virginia, also sent to negotiate treaty with Indians prior to Fallen Timbers.

COLONEL DAVID ROGERS—American officer in command of U.S. supply boats; killed in river ambush by Girty and Indians during Revolutionary War.

NANCY ANN GIRTY SANFORD—married daughter of Simon Girty, Jr.

GOVERNOR JOHN GRAVES SIMCOE—First governor of Upper Canada.

ARTHUR ST. CLAIR—Served in French and Indian War under General Jeffrey Amherst. Was largest landowner in western Pennsylvania. In 1787 appointed by Washington as first governor of Northwest Territory. In 1791 led American army that suffered greatest defeat ever by Indians.

GENERAL JOHN SULLIVAN—U.S. Army officer, a commander in frontier war. Led a successful destructive campaign against Iroquois tribes and Shawnees during Revolutionary War.

TECUMSEH—Great Shawnee chief and advocate for Indian unification during Indian Wars. Killed in battle against Americans during War of 1812.

COLONEL JOHN TODD—Militia officer who led avenging volunteers to Blue Licks following terrible American defeat there by British-Indian forces (among them Simon Girty).

TOWEAH (A.K.A CHIEF JACOBS)—Delaware war chief who rules at Kittanning, participates in trial and execution of John Turner, Sr.

JOHN TURNER, SR.—Married widow Mary Girty.

JOHN TURNER, JR. (A.K.A JOHN GIRTY)—Son of John Turner, Sr. and Mary Girty Turner, half-brother to Simon, Jr., Thomas, James and George Girty.

LT. EDWARD WARD—British colonial officer in command of Fort Granville at time it was captured.

GEORGE WASHINGTON—Wealthy and influential land dealer, principal shareholder of Ohio Company, later leader of American military forces during War for Independence, and eventually first President of the United States.

GENERAL ANTHONY WAYNE, A.K.A. MAD ANTHONY—American Army general who defeated Indian confederation in critical battle at Fallen Timbers in 1794—bringing an end to the "Indian Wars."

CONRAD WEISER—An important trader-supplier and civic leader, often used by British Indian Department in Lancaster County. Multi-lingual and well-liked by Indians, he was a wholesale supplier to Simon Girty, Sr.

WHITE EYES—Important Delaware chief, friendly to Americans.

WHITE MINGO—Minor Seneca Chief.

COLONEL DAVID WILLIAMSON—U.S. militia commander, ordered slaughter of ninety-six Delaware Moravian converts at Gnadenhutten. Commanded 1st Moravian Expedition which preceded 2nd Moravian Expedition which resulted in American defeat at Battle of Sandusky. This was followed by execution of William Crawford, who was burned to death by Indians in revenge for deaths of Delaware innocents in Gnadenhutten massacre.

CAPTAIN JAMES WILLING—U.S. Marine commander of gunboat *Rattletrap*, in which George Girty served as a lieutenant.

WILLIAM WILSON—American frontiersman, scout and spy.

WINGENUND—Important Delaware chief, friendly to Americans; confidant and close friend to Reverend John Heckewelder.

CAPTAIN JAMES WOOD—Intrepid Virginia officer of militia, sent on diplomatic mission to western and northern tribes at beginning of Revolutionary War.

JONATHAN ZANE—Notable American frontiersman, one of famous "Zane brothers," and an old friend of Simon Girty, Jr.

REVEREND DAVID ZEISBERGER—Leader of Moravian church-missions in Pennsylvania and Ohio. Proclaimed he and his fellow Moravian missionaries were neutral during the Revolutionary War, while in fact were providing secret intelligence about British-Indian movements and actions to American commander at Fort Pitt.

ACKNOWLEDGMENTS

MY DEEPEST THANKS AND APPRECIATION TO MY LATE WIFE PHYLLIS, to my Sioux brother Chaske Bad Bear Wicks, and to Simon Girty's 3rd great grandson, Dwight Girty of Windsor, Ontario, all of whom supported this work and "went west" during the nineteen years it took to research and write Girty's story. I miss them terribly.

Thanks to my new wife, Mary Ann, who tolerates me, brightens my mornings and sweetens my nights.

Thanks to authors Allan W. Eckert, Tim Truman, Larry Nelson, Ed Butts, Colin G. Calloway, film producer Randy Wilkins, the librarians at The Huntington Library, and all the other writers, librarians and research specialists who so graciously gave me their time and help.

Thanks to Mark A. Baker for his help and expertise on colonial woodsman skills, and to Aaron Tobul for his friendship, suggestions, and great assistance with the manuscript. Thanks to Lewis and Clark re-enactor Bob Shannon Anderson, of Marysville, Ohio, for bringing to my attention an 1804 meeting between Girty and William Clark (Bob is a direct descendant of Lewis and Clark member George Shannon).

Thanks to David E. Kane, my publisher and fiddler friend, and to Barbara Lehmann, President, Simon Kenton Historic Corridor, for her help and friendship. Author/historian John Mack Faragher will always have my gratitude for his remarkable editorial insight.

I'm grateful also to my fellow historian, the late Madeline Malott of Kingsville, Ontario, Canada for all her kindness, expertise and friendship.

Finally, I nod to Consul Wilshire Butterfield who, although he certainly didn't mean to, showed me exactly where to look for the truth about Simon Girty.

PHILLIP W. HOFFMAN
Pace, Florida
April 2008

NOTES AND SOURCES

PROLOGUE [PAGES VII-XI]

1. "The instrument": quote of Daniel Boone from John Shaw's recollection of an earlier interview he had with Boone, in *Lyman Draper Manuscripts,* microfilm, 16C67.

2. "His Shawnee captors . . .": quote of John Mack Faragher, in his: *Daniel Boone: The Life and Legend of an American Pioneer,* Owl Books, New York, 1993, p. 300.

3. "I am very sorry to say": quote of Bettie T. Bryan to Lyman Copeland Draper, August 18, 1884, in: *Lyman Draper Manuscripts,* microfilm, 22C25.

CHAPTER ONE [PAGES 1-44]

1. "Killed a stier," and "5 shillings worth": quotes of Conrad Weiser, from his journal, in: Paul A.W. Wallace, *Conrad Weiser,* University of Pennsylvania Press, 1945, p. 186.

2. Killackchckr's name appears on a list of Indian hostages prepared by Alexander McKee (Thomas' son), on November 10, 1764. For more about these Indian hostages, *See: Lyman Draper Mss.* 10-E-144, and Library and Archives Canada/RG10/reel C-1222/P. 237: *List of Indian Hostages* prepared by Alexander McKee. The list includes "Killackchckr or Simon Girty," and "Katepacomen or Jos. Compass," and "Moondealicker or Wm. Davis" and others. Apparently C.W. Butterfield misread the document, for in his *History of the Girtys,* 1890, he claimed on p. 19 that Simon Jr. was given the Delaware

name "Katepacomen." But, as the list shows, Joseph Compass was Katepacomen. At the date of the list—1764—none of the Delaware hostages were likely to have had any prior contact with Simon Girty, Jr., who had been living among the Senecas of Western New York for eight years. It was Girty, Sr. who had long traded among the Delawares, and no doubt it was he whom Killackchckr had honored by taking his name.

3. Information about the baptism of George Girty came from *The Lutheran Brothers Congregation and the Belonging Society in Lancaster, started in 1743,* by Laurence Thorstannson Nyborg, Pastor. Dwight Girty of Windsor, Ontario, provided the author with a photocopy from this book, whose "Entry #42" reads: "March 8, 1746–Simon Girty and son George. Godfather And. Sanderson & upon Yr. Oct 11, 1746." The latter date is the date of George Girty's baptism. *Note:* Document text is in German.

For the Girty's acquisition of their indentured servant Honour Edwards see *Pennsylvania Magazine of History and Biography*, v.3, (1907) pp. 356–357 "Account of Servants bound and assigned before James Hamilton, Mayor of Philadelphia."

4. "[Simon Sr.] had a difficulty": quote from an 1847 letter by Joseph Munger, Jr. to Lyman Draper, in *Lyman Draper Mss.*, microfilm, 10 E-144. Munger, born more than fifty years after the death of his grandfather, was recalling family hearsay.

5. "Was killed in fighting a duel": quote of Nancy Ann Sanford, taken from: *Affidavit of Nancy Ann Sanford, daughter of Nancy Ann Geauvereau, wife of Peter Geauvereau, and daughter of Simon Girty Jr.,* dated 5 September 1893, at Gosfield, North Ontario, Canada, a copy of which was sent to the author by Mr. Dwight Girty of Windsor, Ontario. The document states:

> I Nancy Ann Sanford make oath to say that Simon Girty (senior) emigrated to this colony of Pennsylvania about the year 1740 AD. He married an English lady by the name of Mary Newton by whom he had four sons, Thomas, Simon, George and James. Simon Girty Sr. was killed in fighting a duel with a British officer.

6. This story came to light after Canadian writer-historian Ed

Butts (Harold Horwood, Edward Butts, *Pirates and Other Outlaws of Canada,* Doubleday, Canada, 1984) sent the author a photocopy of a document in possession of the State Historical Society of Pennsylvania, Harrisburg. As is evident by the text, the law concerning such matters required a full year's wait by applicants before any of a deceased's property could be seized, and during this period of time, the administrators were required to compile a true and complete list of all the deceased's assets and liabilities. During the waiting period, the Registrar of Probate would accept any claims by others against the estate, and at the conclusion of the one year term all legitimate claims could be settled. McKee and Gibson had no intention of waiting a full year, nor did they intend to share anything with other claimants. The document shows an application date of February 9, 1750, which was several months prior to Girty, Sr.'s death. The document also shows an activation date of February 9, 1751. In 1763, without opposition, McKee was awarded ownership of Girty's property on the Susquehanna River.

7. "fifty feet square" and "fifteen miles northeast": quotes from Governor Morris to General William Shirley, February 1756, in William A. Hunter, *Forts on the Pennsylvania Frontier,* Pennsylvania Historical and Museum Commission, Harrisburg, 1960, p. 383.

8. "Captain Ward Marched": news article in *Pennsylvania Gazette,* August 19, 1756, Carnegie Library, Pittsburgh.

9. "He had dried wood": quote of Captain de Villiers' report, taken from: William A. Hunter, *Forts on the Pennsylvania Frontier,* 1960 pp. 393–394. *Note:* the original source of the story is: *Rapport de l'archiviste de la province de Quebec,* v. 1931–32, p.43. *See also: Library and Archives Canada/MG18/reel J9/vol. 2/pp.38–39.*

10. "After ascertaining": from Armstrong's report on his attack on Kittanning, taken from: C. Hale Sipe, *Indian Wars of Pennsylvania,* Harrisburg, Pennsylvania, 1929, p. 306.

11. "One of the Indian fellows": quote from Armstrong's report on his attack on Kittanning, Ibid., p. 307.

12. "After the English had withdrawn": report of Barbara Leininger, and Marie Le Roy, Ibid., p. 313.

13. "The day after my arrival": James Smith quote from John

Bradford, *Scoowa: James Smith's Indian Captivity Narrative,* 1799, reprint Ohio Historical Society, Cleveland, 1899, pp. 28–29.

14. "We continued": quote of Isaac Webster, from: *A Narrative of the Captivity of Isaac Webster,* 1808, reprint Ye Galleon Press, Fairfield, Wa., 1988, pp. 4–6.

15. "At the time appointed": quote of Lewis Henry Morgan, in his: *League of the Iroquois,* N.Y. 1851, reprint, Citadel Press, New Jersey, 1962, p. 314.

16. "Their houses," Ibid., pp. 327–328.

17. "The chief or warrior," Ibid., pp. 107–108.

18. "Thus, it often happened," Ibid., p. 324.

19. "Some time in July," quote of James Smith in: Bradford, John. *Scoowa: James Smith's Indian Captivity Narrative,* Ohio, 1799, reprint Ohio Historical Society, Cleveland, 1899, p. 116.

20. "They met his army," James Smith quote taken from C. Hale Sipe's *Indian Wars of Pennsylvania,* 1929, pp. 372–372.

21. "Which may interfere" and "the ministry": quotes of Randolph C. Downes, in his: *Council Fires on the Ohio,* University of Pittsburgh Press, 1940, p. 189.

22. For detailed information on land speculators like Washington, *See:* Thomas P. Abernethy, *Western Lands and the American Revolution,* Virginia, University of Virginia Press, 1937.

23. "According to the nature": quote of Wills De Haas, *History and Indian Wars of West Virginia,* 1851, reprint 1989 McClain Printing Co., Parsons, W. Va., pp. 131–132.

24. "All prisoners": treaty terms from: Wills De Haas, Ibid., p. 132.

25. "If we choose": quote of Henry Bouquet, in: Walter O'Meara, *Guns at the Forks,* New Jersey 1965, pp. 247–248.

26. "No pen can describe": quote of C. Hale Sipe, from his: *Indian Wars of Pennsylvania,* Harrisburg, Pa. 1929, pp. 481–482.

27. "Simon" and "Jammy": entries on captive list, 14 November 1764, prepared by Alexander McKee in: *Library and Archives Canada/ RG10/reel C-1222/P. 237: List of Indian Hostages.*

28. For Simon's appearance the author uses the one given by Girty's daughter, Sarah Girty Munger, from Lyman Draper's notes of his interview with her in 1864, in: *Lyman Draper Mss.* 20-S-208,

2-S-30. *See also: Amherstburg Echo,* Nov. 21, 1884 "Life of Simon Girty." There are many variations of Simon's appearance in both American and Canadian literature, but the description provided by his daughter Mrs. Sarah Munger to historian Lyman C. Draper, stands as the most credible account. Furthermore, her description of Simon was corroborated elsewhere, as I have shown here. In the text, James' description is taken from the same interview of Sarah Munger by Draper.

CHAPTER TWO [PAGES 45-64]

1. Thomas Girty apprenticeship: *Western Pennsylvania Historical Magazine,* v. 7, 1924, *"Early Settlers in the 15th Ward of Pittsburgh,* by Mrs. S. Kussart, p. 191.

2. "Theecheapei": In *Western Pennsylvania Historical Magazine* v. 39, 1956, pp. 187–203, the article "Indian Captives Released by Colonel Bouquet" by William Ewing, lists the names of virtually all the captives returned by the Indians to Colonel Bouquet in 1764 and 1765. List G records the names of 44 captives who were returned by the Shawnees on May 10, 1765 (the original lists are part of the Gage Papers, Clements Library, University of Michigan). The format of the list, in columns from left to right, shows the listing number that was assigned to each captive, and their "English or Indian Names," "age Yrs.", "From where taken", "What [length of time] time prisoners." Born in February 1755, John Turner, Jr. was ten years of age at the time this list was created. He had been in captivity with the Indians since the fall of 1756, or almost nine years. Included on "List G" are eleven males believed to be between the ages of nine and twelve. Of these, five have English names, and Turner is not mentioned. Of the remaining six, all of whom are approximately the right age and who bear only Indian names, only two are shown who were thought to have been captive for more than eight years: No. 14, Neculissika, ten years old, ten years a captive, and No. 20, Theecheapei, eleven years old, ten years a captive. Neculisska is listed as having been taken at "Jameses river, Virginia." Since he is the only male captive shown to have been taken from Pennsylvania rather than Virginia, Theecheapei is John Turner, Jr. According to the list, he was taken at "Cove, Pennsylvania." In

Thomas Francis Gordon's *Pennsylvania Gazetteer,* Philadelphia, 1832, are lists on page 121 showing several locations with the word "Cove" as part of their name, including "Cove Mountain, Rye Township, Perry Co." Assuming this is the "Cove, Pennsylvania" referred to on the above captive list, it puts Theecheapei in the same general region which included Fort Granville. In *Simon Kenton, His life and Period,* 1930, Edna Kenton wrote on p.56 that in 1832, during an interview with Judge John H. James, on the subject of the capture of Simon Girty and his family (including John Turner, Jr.,) the then seventy-seven-year-old Simon Kenton stated: "Simon Girty was taken prisoner at Little Cove . . ."

As cited elsewhere, there are numerous articles showing Turner, Jr.'s return in May of 1765. The list we cite above is the only list of captives being returned in that month. There can be little doubt that John Turner, Jr., was the Theecheapei who appears on the list.

3. "Dissatisfaction with the Proclamation line": *Note:* Broad popular dissatisfaction with English rule, i.e. the Stamp Act, taxation without representation, the right of British soldiers to invade and search private homes and seize private property, etc., was the result of masterful public relations efforts by conspiring rebel leaders (many of whom were successful businessmen). Men like Patrick Henry and Benjamin Franklin had been activated by the King's Proclamation of 1763, a decade before the actual War for American Independence began. Commanding his own media empire, Benjamin Franklin was the most successful printer in Colonial America and published its largest newspaper, *The Pennsylvania Gazette.* Most of the people living in Britain's American colonies were unaware of the grave injustices of English rule until such actions were brought to their attention by those who had a rationale for wanting them to know.

"From a sudden hint": extracted quotes, George Washington to William Crawford, September 21, 1767, taken from: Consul Wilshire Butterfield, *Washington–Crawford Letters,* also known as *Washington Crawford Correspondence,* Cincinnati, 1877, pp. 1–4.

4. "I was going": Morgan to his partners, July 20, 1768, taken from: Alvord & Carter, eds., *Trade and Politics in the Illinois Country,* Illinois Historical Society, Springfield, (1921), pp. 354–355.

5. For the story of these Girty land claims *See: Western Pennsylvania Historical Magazine* v. 12, 1929, "*Squirrel Hill*," by Margaret A. Frew, pp. 242–257.

6. "commanding": man, from Lyman Draper's notes, *See: Draper Manuscripts,* microfilm, 2-S-30.

7. "Under cover," Baynton to Croghan, January 10, 1770, *Baynton, Wharton & Morgan Papers,* microfilm, Commonwealth of Pennsylvania, Division of Archives, Harrisburg, Pennsylvania, MG 19, Reel 1, Frame 66.

8. "was afraid": quote of Reverend David McClure, D.D., from his diary. *See: Old Westmoreland Magazine,* "The Diary of Reverend David McClure, D.D." v. II, no.1, August 1981, p. 42.

CHAPTER THREE [PAGES 65-82]

1. "He saw one of the crowd": quote of Samuel St. Clair from his 1774 deposition, in: *Pennsylvania Archives,* 1774, Old Series 4 (1853) pp. 565–566. St. Clair reported exactly what he saw at the time of the event. The blow that Girty blocked was that of a rifle barrel and not a saber, as legendary versions of the story proclaim. Numerous renditions of Girty's life portray him as an abuser of women, yet his actions here strongly conflict with such critiques. Indeed, up to this stage of his life there are no incidents of him abusing a woman.

2. "war is inevitable": from Virgil A. Lewis, *History of the Battle of Point Pleasant,* Charleston, Va., 1909, p. 16.

3. "Only he had not": quote by Edna Kenton, in her: *Simon Kenton,* New York, 1930, p. 10.

4. "One of the three best friends": quote of Simon Kenton, in: Edna Kenton, *Simon Kenton,* p. 56.

5. "raised up in his place": quote of writer Wills De Haas, from his: *History and Indian Wars of West Virginia,* W. Virginia, 1851, reprint, McClain Printing, Parsons, W. Va., 1989, p. 150.

6. "if he was, was not Simon Girty": quotes of Joseph Nicholson, in: Thwaites & Kellogg, *Dunmore's War,* Wisconsin Historical Society, 1905, p. 151. *Note:* The Shawnee inquiry if Nicholson was Simon Girty indicates that the Shawnees knew that Girty was supporting the

Virginians.

7. *Note:* According to Mr. Phillip Anderson, Hydraulic Engineer, U.S. Army Corps of Engineers, Huntington District, Huntington, W. Va., his estimate of the 1774 current of the Ohio River for this stretch of the stream, is 3 feet per second (about 2 m.p.h.). Mr. Anderson believes that three men paddling hard in a canoe should have been able to make perhaps five to seven miles per hour. At this rate, Girty, Kenton and Parchment could have covered the distance from the mouth of the Little Kanawha to the "Big" Kanawha in 12–14 hours. Mr. Anderson also points out that the current was slow enough that it would have been practical to paddle a canoe back upstream. He thinks that if the paddlers were fresh, a return trip from Big Kanawha to Little Kanawha would take only two to four hours more than the downstream leg.

8. "the Indian had been hit": quote of William Murphy, in notes of Lyman Draper from an interview with Murphy, *See: Lyman Draper MSS*, microfilm, 3-S-11.

9. "And then": quote of Matthew Elliot, in: Alexander Scott Withers, *Chronicles of Border Warfare*, Cincinnati 1895, reprint McClain Printing Co., Parsons, W. Va., 1989, p. 182.

10. "I appeal to any white man": quote of Chief John Logan, from: C. Hale Sipe, *Indian Wars of Pennsylvania*, p. 500. *Note:* In 1775, Captain James Woods (who was on a tour of the western tribes with Girty as his guide) met with Logan and noted in his journal: "Logan repeated in plain English the Manner in which the people of Virginia had killed his mother, Sister, and all his Relations during which he wept and Sung Alternately and concluded with telling me the Revenge he had taken . . ." *See:* Thwaites and Kellogg, *Revolution on the Upper Ohio,* 1908, p. 49.

CHAPTER FOUR [PAGES 83-122]

1. "Who we are confident" and "Their devotion": quotes from Officer's Resolution, in: Richard Orr Curry, *"Lord Dunmore and the West: A Re-evaluation"*, in *West Virginia History Quarterly Magazine,* Vol. XIX, July 1958, no. 4, p. 238.

2. Extract from Sheriff Whiteside's deposition, quoted from

William Henry Smith ed. *The St. Clair Papers,* v.1, Newport Rhode Island, 1788, reprint, De Capo Press, New York, 1971, p. 351.

3. "At Fort Pitt": quote of list prepared by Lord Dunmore, February, 1775, in: Butterfield, *History of the Girtys,* p. 32.

4. "Brethren": quote from speech by Indian delegate, taken from: *Virginia Magazine of History and Biography,* v. 14 (1906), p. 67.

5. "Brothers, the Delawares": speech of James Wood, from his journal: Thwaites, *Revolution on the Upper Ohio,* Wisconsin, 1908, p. 46.

6. "Brothers, the Big Knife": King Newcomer quote from: James Wood's report to Virginia commissioners, in Thwaites, *Revolution on the Upper Ohio,* Wisconsin, 1908, p. 47.

7. "We were": , Ibid., p. 50.

8. "We rode fast": Ibid., p. 50.

9. "War Post said" "Did not stand" and "In this conversation": Ibid., p. 52.

10. Ibid.

11. "They might rest assured": quote of James Wood, Ibid., p. 53.

12. "To be a place": Ibid., p. 54.

13. "When we arrived": Ibid., p. 56.

14. "Were all determined": Ibid., pp.57–58.

15. "I explained": Ibid., p. 58.

16. "In all of which": Ibid., p. 60.

17. "From every discovery": Ibid., pp. 66–67.

18. "Required to reveal": quote from: *Pennsylvania Magazine of History and Biography,* v. 58, 1934, pp. 32–33. *Note:* The Indian Agent at Fort Pitt at this time was Richard Butler.

19. "I Alexander McKee": document from: *Pennsylvania Magazine of History and Biography,* v. 58, 1934, pp. 32–33.

20. "To prevent impositions": quote of Morgan's instructions from: Gregory Shaaf, *Wampum Belts and Peace Trees,* Fulcrum Press, Golden, Colorado, 1990, p. 21.

21. "To Simon Girty": contract Morgan to Simon Girty, May 1, 1776, from: *George Morgan Letter Book* (microfilm), 1776, reel 32.

22. "Your Father": quote of Colonel John Butler, from his speech at Niagara, in: Barbara Graymont, *The Iroquois in the American*

Revolution, Syracuse University Press, 1972, p. 97.

23. "You know": June 1776 peace message to George Morgan from Six Nations, taken from: Ibid., p. 97.

24. "Brothers and nephews": quote from peace message of Six Nations directed at southern tribes, taken from: Ibid., p. 100.

25. "That these": quote from U.S. Declaration of Independence.

26. "had discharged": quote from Morgan's journal, taken from: *Lyman Draper MSS.,* Microfilm 12-U-45(3). *See also:* Butterfield, *History of the Girtys* p. 38.

27. "Brothers the Big Knife": address of White Mingo to George Morgan and others at Fort Pitt, August 26, 1776, from: *George Morgan Letterbooks,* microfilm, v. II pp. 13–15 University Microfilms International, Ann Arbor, Michigan.

28. "Parties of white men": Morgan to Congress, from: Max Savelle, *George Morgan Colony Builder,* Columbia University Press, New York, 1932, p. 143.

29. Quote, John Gibson to Edward Hand, December 10, 1777, from Thwaites and Kellogg, *Frontier Defense on the Upper Ohio,* pp. 179–181.

30. *Author's Note:* For more information on these events, *See:* William H. Darlington, *Christopher Gist's Journals,* Pittsburgh, 1893, reprint Argonaut Press Ltd., New York, 1966, pp. 214–215, and Thwaites and Kellogg, *Frontier Defense on the Upper Ohio,* pp. 179–181. Although he apparently told Gibson nothing about the British depot at Cuyahoga, Girty later dictated a written report of his mission that was sent to George Morgan. Appearing in *Christopher Gists Journals,* the report is lengthy, intelligent, highly detailed, and includes Girty's interpretations, comments and observations. Most likely, Girty dictated the written report at the request of General Hand. There is no question that Girty's news about the British supply dump at Cuyahoga was the basis for General Hand's later expedition against that target, which became the infamous "Squaw Campaign."

31. "a citizen not without": quote of Butterfield from his: *History of the Girtys,* 1890, p. 47.

32. "As I am credibly informed": Hand to Crawford, February 5, 1778, from: Thwaites & Kellogg, *Frontier Defense,* pp. 201–202.

CHAPTER FIVE [PAGES 123-140]

1. I have been unable to find any biographical information about William Brady, but he was not related to the famous frontiersman Samuel Brady. Why General Hand entrusted his expedition to Brady's navigational skills, rather than Girty's, remains a mystery.

2. "According to Samuel Murphy" and "She fell partly": quotes of Lyman Draper from notes of his interview with Murphy, in: *Lyman Draper Manuscripts,* microfilm, 3-S 13–14.

3. "Several men" and "in favor of Connell": quotes of Samuel Murphy from Lyman Draper's notes of his interview with Murphy, in: *Lyman Draper Manuscripts,* microfilm, S-5–13.

4. "He could no longer stay": hearsay quote of Major John Finley's son, from notes of an interview of David Finley by Lyman Draper. Taken from *Lyman Draper Manuscripts,* microfilm, 21-S-216–217. *Note:* Finley's son David related this material to Lyman Draper during an interview at Tilton, Fleming County, Kentucky in 1866. John Finley had been a partner of David Duncan and his son married one of Duncan's daughters. David Finley told Draper that his father "spoke well of Girty."

5. "There is some evidence": quote of Edna Kenton from her: *Simon Kenton,* New York, 1930, p. 54.

6. "Girty and I": quote of Simon Kenton, Ibid., p. 55.

7. "A hint": quote of Edgar W. Hassler, from his: *Old Westmoreland,* Pittsburgh, 1900, p. 46.

8. "You will no doubt": Hand to Crawford, March 30, 1778, in: Thwaites & Kellogg, *Frontier Defense on the Upper Ohio,* pp. 249–254.

9. "The elopement": George Morgan to Henry Laurens, March 30, 1778, Ibid., pp. 254–255.

10. "As we drew near": quote of John Heckewelder, in his: *Narrative of the Missions of the United Brethern,* 1828, Philadelphia, reprint, Arno Press, New York, 1971, pp. 149–176. *See also:* Butterfield, *History of the Girtys,* pp. 52–53, and Edmond De Schweinitz, *Life and Times of David Zeisberger,* 1871, Philadelphia, p. 463.

11. "The fugitives told": quote of John Heckewelder, in his: *Narrative of the Missions of the United Brethern,* p. 171.

12. "Returned to his countrymen": quote of Butterfield, from his: *History of the Girtys,* 1890, pp. 61–62.

13. "By your own showing": Leatherlips quote as written by Butterfield, in his: *Crawford's Expedition Against Sandusky,* Cincinnati 1873, p. 186.

14. "I cannot but praise": quote of Henry Hamilton taken from: Kelsay, *Joseph Brant Man of Two Worlds,* Syracuse University Press, 1984, p. 303.

CHAPTER SIX [PAGES 141-154]

1. "Someone who had": quote of a Henry Hamilton address to Indians assembled at Detroit, April 1778, in: *Simon Girty Interpreter and Intermediary,* by Colin G. Calloway, in James Clifton, ed., *Being and Becoming Indian,* Chicago, Dorsey Press, 1989, p. 46. *See also:* Michigan Pioneer and Historical Collections, 9:442–444 (1886).

2. "Knowingly and willingly": quote of Supreme Executive Council of Pennsylvania, taken from: Butterfield, *History of the Girtys,* p. 65.

3. "A party of 80 Wyandots": Zeisberger to George Morgan, July 19, 1778, taken from Louise Phelps Kellogg, *Frontier Advance on the Upper Ohio,* Wisconsin Historical Society, 1916, p. 119.

4. "Attend to the behaviour": Henry Hamilton orders to agents, taken from John D. Barnhart, ed., *Henry Hamilton and George Rogers Clark in the American Revolution, with the Unpublished Journal of Lt. Gov. Henry Hamilton,* Crawfordsville, Ind. 1951, p. 34.

5. "Girty went to him": quotes of Edna Kenton, *Simon Kenton,* New York, 1930, pp. 120–122 *Note:* Although there are several accounts of this incident, Edna Kenton's is probably the most accurate and it agrees with the other renditions on the major issues.

6. "[There] . . . then ensued": Ibid., p. 123.

7. "They say when a man comes": Ibid.

8. "This form of adoption": quote of Simon Kenton, from: Edna Kenton, *Simon Kenton,* p. 124. Kenton's Indian name Great White Wolf was provided to the author by Barbara S. Lehmann, President, Simon Kenton Historic Corridor, Urbana, Ohio.

9. "On the third date": quote taken from Edna Kenton, *Simon*

Kenton, p. 133.

10. "The governor had sent": quote of Drouillard, Ibid., p. 133. Other sources on this incident: *Michigan Pioneer Historical Collection*, 9:470 (1886), *Lyman Draper Manuscripts* 8-S-65–66, Thwaites, *Revolution on the Upper Ohio*, p. 128, Note 24. The earliest accounts of this incident seem to agree that Girty went to Logan's winter camp to seek his assistance in saving Kenton, and that Girty met with the Mingo chief long before Kenton and his guards reached that point in their journey to Sandusky. The path between Wapatomica and Logan's hunting camp is the same path that leads to Upper Sandusky. Obviously, after securing Logan's support, Girty hurried on to Sandusky, where he met with Drouillard. Girty had a superb grasp of the situation and, after having exhausted his own powers, he went to Logan and Drouillard for help.

CHAPTER SEVEN [PAGES 155-170]

1. "That thirteen days ago"" Zeisberger to Gibson, January 19, 1779, in: Butterfield, *History of the Girtys*, p. 88.

2. "46 suits of clothing": Ibid, pp. 88–89.

3. "Was coming after him": Gibson to George Morgan, January 22, 1779, excerpt taken from Ibid., p. 88.

4. "Summary, Colonel John Gibson to General McIntosh": January 22, 1779, taken from: Kellogg, *Frontier Advance on the Upper Ohio*, Wisconsin Historical Society, 1916, pp. 205–206.

5. "Had little expectation": quote of Butterfield, from Butterfield, *History of the Girtys*, p. 92.

6. "Begging and Praying": quote of Butterfield, Ibid., p. 93.

7. "Despite the fair promises": Bird to Mason Bolton, May 14, 1779, in: *Michigan Pioneer Historical Collection*, 19:413, (1892).

8. "Girty told": Richard Conner quote, by John Heckewelder, from: Butterfield, *History of the Girtys*, p. 100.

CHAPTER EIGHT [PAGES 171-182]

1. "Following a brief interrogation": quote of Consul Wilshire Butterfield, from his: George *Rogers Clark's Conquest of the Illinois*,

Columbus, Ohio, 1904, p. 467. *See also:* Butterfield: *History of the Girtys,* p. 105.

2. "I take the liberty": Girty to Lernoult, September 6, 1779, quoted from *Haldimand Papers,* MG 21, Additional Mss. 21760, British Library, also James A. Clifton, ed., *Being and Becoming Indian,* Chicago, 1989, p. 47, and Butterfield, *History of the Girtys,* p. 113.

3. "He killed Rogers": quote of Jacob Drennon, from: *Lyman Draper Manuscripts,* microfilm, Wisconsin Historical Society, 12-CC 237–238.

4. "I have the pleasure": De Peyster to Haldimand, November 1, 1779, in: Butterfield, *History of the Girtys,* p. 111.

CHAPTER NINE [PAGES 183-194]

1. "I had before that day": quote from Bird to De Peyster, July 1, 1780, *Register of the Kentucky Historical Society,* v. 54, p. 325.

2. "Hinkson was very supple and active": quote of Simon Girty in *Lyman Draper Manuscripts,* microfilm, 20-S-200, 3-S 98–99. *See also:* Burch, *A Family Record,* p. 21, Register of the Kentucky Historical Society, v.54, October 1956, p. 315. *Note:* In December 1864, Lyman Draper interviewed Girty's daughter Sarah Munger, near Harlem, Illinois. Draper's notes (3S 98–99) include: "The then seventy-three-year-old woman stated 'Girty was on Bird's expedition in the summer of 1780 against Kentucky—got to a fort and Girty was the flagbearer, white flag—and when he went in, he said hundreds of rifles were pointed at him; he told them if they did not surrender they would all be killed, as the Indians were so angry and he could not save them. They surrendered, and Girty said he had hard work afterwards to save them from the Indians. Heard him speak of Hinkson whom, very likely, from old acquaintance in Pittsburgh country, he helped to escape—and also how he frequently managed to get prisoners away.'"

3. "McKee and Elliott's slaves": quote of Margaret Paulee taken from: Milo M. Quaife, ed., *When Detroit Invaded Kentucky,* pp. 23. *See also:* Horsman, *Matthew Elliott,* pp. 29–30. *Note:* American captive Margaret Paulee, who was living at that time at the Shawnee Towns on the Scioto, stated the following in her narrative:

The Indians thought a great deal of McKee and Girty. There was an Indian chief named Blue Pocket [Blue Jacket] who had married a half-French woman of Detroit, who lived in great style, had curtained beds and silver spoons. I was fond of visiting this house, they always seemed kind and desirous of giving me tea, & c. He had his Negro slaves, so had McKee. (West Virginia History Quarterly, v. 23, No. 4, 1961, pp. 290–291.)

4. "Charles Gatliff and myself": quote of Simon Kenton, taken from Edna Kenton, *Simon Kenton*, p. 153. *Note:* Differing with Bird's account, Kenton's story tends to agree with Butterfield's conclusion that several Americans were killed after their surrender of the two stations. It should be realized however, that fighting had taken place prior to the surrenders at Ruddle's and Martin's Stations, and some of the dead and scalped bodies Kenton saw may well have been those of men who had been killed before the attacking Indians entered the stockades.

5. "We pursued to a place": Simon Kenton quote taken from: Edna Kenton, *Simon Kenton*, pp. 154–155.

6. Source: *Clark's Shawnee Campaign of 1780*, Clark County Historical Society, Springfield, Ohio, 1980, p. 10.

CHAPTER TEN [PAGES 195-204]

1. "Brother": Brodhead to Delaware, December 2, 1789, from: Louise Phelps Kellogg, *Frontier Retreat on the Upper Ohio*, 1917, p. 289.

2. "Indians of Coshocton": quote of Simon Girty delivering De Peyster's speech, taken from: Butterfield, *History of the Girtys*, p. 125.

3. "We sent to Coshocton": Girty to De Peyster, May 4, 1781, taken from: Michigan Pioneer Historical Collection 10:478–479 (1886).

4. "How many prisoners": Joseph Brant quote taken from Butterfield, *History of the Girtys*, pp. 130–131, which was based on notes of Lyman Draper, from his interview of Sarah Girty Munger, *Lyman Draper Manuscripts*, microfilm, 20-S-196–197. There are many accounts of this event, most of which agree that Brant was bragging, that Girty insulted him, and that Brant struck Girty over the head

with his sword, either from the side or from behind. In his interview notes (20-S-198–199), Draper wrote that Catherine Girty (Simon's wife) had told him that Simon "received a severe sword cut at the hands of Brant, across the head, very much as Mrs. Munger (Sarah Girty Munger) describes it."

5. "Brain-beating" and McKee's "I'll have you hung": quotes taken from interview notes of Lyman Draper, *Lyman Draper Mss.* 20-S-197.

6. "Brant shed tears": quote also from notes of Lyman Draper. *See:* Lyman Draper Manuscripts, microfilm, 10-E-146–147.

CHAPTER ELEVEN [PAGES 205-222]

1. "The cold during the night": Heckewelder from his *Narratives of the Missions of the United Brethren,* taken from Butterfield, *History of the Girtys,* 1890, pp. 136–137.

2. "Does anyone here know me": Simon Girty's quote from Lyman Draper's notes of an interview with Samuel Murphy, *Lyman Draper Manuscripts*, microfilm, 3-S-21–22.

3. "The missionaries at this time": Heckewelder quote from Butterfield, *History of the Girtys,* 1890, pp. 136–137.

4. "Go out in the snow": Heckewelder quote and story from: Heckewelder, *Narrative of the Missions of the United Brethren,* reprint 1971, Arno Press, New York, p. 301.

5. "Told him they were Moravian Indians": John Carpenter quote taken from C. Hale Sipe, *Indian Wars of Pennsylvania,* 1929, p. 647.

6. "Uneasy in his mind": Half King to De Peyster, February 1781, taken from Butterfield, *History of the Girtys,* 1890, p. 138.

7. "He told us": Heckewelder quote taken from Ibid., p. 140. *Note:* Butterfield states (in *History of the Girtys*) on p.144: "It is altogether probable that Le Villier told the missionaries what was not true as to Girty having ordered him to drive them like cattle to Detroit. Between this Frenchman and Girty there was no good feeling."

8. Girty to De Peyster, 12 April, 1782, taken from Ibid., pp. 159–160.

9. "He did return": Heckewelder journal passage taken from Ibid., pp. 147–148. *Note:* Butterfield wrote: "Both the missionaries

were unduly frightened at the boisterous behavior of Girty. Had he broken in upon them, the result would have been, beyond a doubt, only more swearing and threatening; for the renegade stood in too much fear of De Peyster to have harmed them, drunk as he was." (p. 148). Zeisberger later claimed that Girty drank and raved at them the whole night through, but the next morning, their tormenter was sober enough to ride a horse and make his way back to Upper Sandusky, which he reached late that afternoon.

10. "That's not it": quote of Christian Fast's recollection of Girty taken from Ibid., p. 152.

11. "The object of your command": Irvine quote taken from Butterfield, *An Historical Account of the Expedition Against Sandusky,* 1873, pp. 69–73.

12. *Note:* Regarding Crawford's age, most sources claim he was born in 1732. But in 1969, Grace U. Emahiser published an official Crawford family genealogy entitled: *From River Clyde to Tymochtee and Col. William Crawford,* Gray Printing Co, Fostoria, Ohio. The author referred to an old family bible that included the birth date of William Crawford, stating it to be 1722. Accordingly, Crawford would have been 60-years old at the time of the Battle of Sandusky.

13. Sources: Heckewelder, *Narrative,* 1828, reprint 1971, p. 342, Blanco *The American Revolution,* vol.1, p. 417, De Schweinitz, *Life and Times of David Zeisberger,* J. B. Lippincott, & Co., 1871, p. 563.

14. "All in the army were cut to pieces": quote taken from *Lyman Draper Manuscripts,* microfilm, 4-S-137.

15. "Talked of taking": quote of Baron Rosenthal, from his *Journal of a Volunteer Expedition to Sandusky, Pa.,* 1894, reprint, Arno Press, New York, 1969, p. 151.

CHAPTER TWELVE [PAGES 223-236]

1. *Author's Note:* For details on this matter *see: Western Pennsylvania Magazine* v.70, no. 1, January 1987, pp. 53–67 "Accuracy of the Knight Narrative," by Parker B. Brown. *See also:* Wyandotte Gazette, April 18, 1872, interview of William Walker by M. B. Newman, and Butterfield, *History of the Girtys,* 1890, pp. 173, 183, and *Crawford's*

Expedition Against Sandusky, 1870, p. 333.

2. "Seemed disheartened": quote of Elizabeth McCormick from notes by Lyman Draper of his interview with her son, John McCormick, in 1863, in *Lyman Draper Manuscripts,* microfilm, 17-S-204 *Note:* The two principal sources for the story that Girty suggested an escape plan to Crawford were Girty himself and Elizabeth Turner McCormick. *See also: Lyman Draper Manuscripts,* microfilm, 17-S-191, where, following an interview with Catherine Girty, widow of Colonel Prideaux Girty (Simon's son), Draper wrote in his notes: "The day before Crawford was burned, Girty told him that if he could, in any way, manage to get loose that night, that he, Girty would have his negro (sic) man at a given place with a horse for Crawford to escape. But Crawford seemed unwilling to make an attempt. These facts were repeatedly told by Girty himself, corroborated by Mrs. Elizabeth McCormick, the latter the widow of Alexander McCormick, an early Indian trader who settled in Canada."

Allegedly, Girty's black slave at this time was a man named Sam Wells.

Whether or not these are the actual details of an escape plan that Girty presented to Crawford, both Simon Girty and Mrs. McCormick repeated the identical story for years. In support of the story, the road to Detroit was less than four miles west of McCormick's Place and Girty knew there was little chance of saving Crawford as long as he remained in the hands of Delawares. Indeed, Crawford's only chance was to escape.

3. "Girty had promised": quote of William Crawford as told by Dr. Knight, appearing in: Brackenridge, ed., *Indian Atrocities,* Philadelphia, 1783, reprint, Ye Galleon Press, Washington, 1983, p. 20.

4. "These Indians": Wingenund quote written by Heckewelder, from his: *Narrative of the Missions of the United Brethern,* Philadelphia 1838, reprint Arno Press, New York, 1971, p. 341.

5. "Very much favored": quote of William Crawford as told by Thomas Silk to Lyman Draper during an 1850 interview, from Draper's notes, in: *Lyman Draper Manuscripts,* microfilm, 4-S-185. *Note:* This quote is from Mr. Thomas Silk, an old acquaintance who

visited Simon Girty at his home near Malden in 1799, and who was interviewed by Lyman Draper at Uniontown, Pennsylvania, in 1850. Considering that Mr. Silk was attempting to remember what was said during a visit with Girty that had occurred fifty years earlier, the informant's memory was remarkably clear. The details concerning the death and the name of the Indian killed during the American assault on the Kuskuskee Town on the Shenango River during the Squaw Campaign, could only have come from someone like Girty, who would have known such particulars. According to Silk, Girty stated that "both McKee & himself had interfered to save Colonel Crawford."

While it is well established that Girty and Matthew Elliott attempted to save Crawford, this is the first time that any informant told Draper that McKee was also actively involved in the effort. Although absent from the scene of the action, McKee surely had been sent messages by Girty and Elliott, and he may well have been working behind the scenes on Crawford's behalf.

6. "Girty said he had interceded": quote of Joseph Jackson, in: *Lyman Draper Manuscripts,* microfilm, 11-C-6233.

7. "He offered": Elizabeth McCormick quote from Ibid., 12-U-45.

8. "Offering for his ransom": quote of Sarah Girty Munger, taken from: Lyman Draper's notes of his interview with Mrs. Munger, in Ibid., 20-S-200. *See also:* Butterfield, *Crawford's Expedition Against Sandusky,* pp. 174–175, 380.

9. "If he was the doctor": quote of Simon Girty taken from Brackenridge, ed., *Indian Atrocities,* 1783, Philadelphia, reprint Ye Galleon Press, Washington, 1983, pp. 21–23.

10. "Yes," and "A rascal": quotes of Dr. Knight, Ibid.

11. "He would take it all": quote of William Crawford as recalled by Dr. Knight, Ibid.

12. "Talked much God": Scotash quote taken from: "Accuracy of the Knight Narrative," by Parker S. Brown, *Western Pennsylvania Magazine,* v. 70, no. 1, January 1987, p. 62.

13. "Girty shed tears": quote of Elizabeth Turner-McCormick, from Lyman Draper's notes of his interview with her son John McCormick in 1863. Taken from *Lyman Draper Manuscripts,* microfilm, 17-S-205.

14. "While Crawford was being burned": quote of Sarah Girty Munger, from notes of Lyman Draper's interview of her son Joseph Munger Jr. from: *Lyman Draper Manuscripts,* microfilm, 20-S-200.

15. Irvine to George Washington, July 11, 1782. Quote taken from: Butterfield, *Washington Irvine Correspondence,* p. 126.

16. Caldwell letter to De Peyster, June 13, 1782, quote taken from: Butterfield, *History of the Girtys,* p. 183. *Note:* Crawford's cruel death was deplored by the highest English authorities, including General Haldimand. Investigating the incident, De Peyster quickly established the roles of everyone involved: Caldwell, McKee, Elliott and Girty. The tone of Caldwell's words recounting Girty's report to De Peyster, speaks eloquently of Girty's demeanor: "Crawford died like a hero," etc. These are hardly the sentiments of someone who enjoyed watching a man being tortured to death, which was what Butterfield wrote in his *History of the Girtys.* The subsequent American damnation of Girty was primarily based upon Butterfield's statements in his *History of the Girtys*—that Girty laughed when Crawford begged him to shoot him, and that Girty enjoyed the spectacle of Crawford's burning. Butterfield based his account on Knight's story edited by Brackenridge, in the latter's 1783 book, *Indian Atrocities.*

17. Verse from folk song from: J.H. Newton, C.G. Nichols, A.G. Sprankle, *History of the Panhandle of West Virginia,* p. 123, credited to Frank Cowen, Esq., of Greensburgh, Pa., 1879, reprint, Heritage Books, Maryland, 1990.

18. "These men talk like fools": Wingenund quote taken from: Charles McKnight, *Simon Girty: The White Savage,* Philadelphia 1880, p. 339.

19. De Peyster to Thomas Brown, July 18, 1782, De Peyster quote taken from: Butterfield, *History of the Girtys,* pp. 365–366.

20. Jonathan Alder story and quote taken from: Henry Howe, *Historical Collections of Ohio,* 1847, v. II, pp. 168–173.

21. "With a train": quote from Butterfield, *History of the Girtys,* pp. 192–193.

22. "Girty recited": Girty speech summary from: J.H. Newton, C.G. Nichols, A.G. Sprankle, eds., *History of the Pan Handle, Historical Collections of the Counties of Ohio, Brook, Marshall and Hancock, West*

Virginia, 1879, reprint, Heritage books, Maryland, 1990, p. 125.

23. McKee to De Peyster, July 22, 1782 taken from: Butterfield, *History of the Girtys,* pp. 192–193.

CHAPTER THIRTEEN [PAGES 237-244]

1. "When a sufficiency": quote from Alexander Scott Withers, *Chronicles of Border Warfare,* 1895, reprint, McClain Printing Co., Parsons, W. Va., 1989, pp. 348–349.

2. "Those on foot": quote from Butterfield, *History of the Girtys,* p. 195.

3. "In the twilight": Girty and Reynolds quotes taken from: Blanco, *The American Revolution,* p. 191. *See also:* Withers, *Chronicles of Border Warfare,* pp. 350–351, and Butterfield, *History of the Girtys,* pp. 196–197.

4. "On the morning": John Todd account from: Good, James E. ed., *Calendar of Virginia State Papers,* v. III (1883), pp. 330–338.

5. "From the situation": Benjamin Logan report excerpt, quoted from: Good, James E. ed., *Calendar of Virginia State Papers* v. III (1883) pp. 280–282.

6. "Being reinforced": Boone quote from: Richard L. Blanco, ed., *The American Revolution,* v. I, pp. 135–136.

7. "Disappointed": Colonel Arthur Campbell to Colonel Wm. Davies, October 3, 1782, quote from: Butterfield, *History of the Girtys,* p. 199.

CHAPTER FOURTEEN [PAGES 245-262]

1. "They discovered": quote of George Rogers Clark taken from: Butterfield, *Washington Irvine Correspondence,* p. 400. *See also:* William Albert Galloway, *Old Chillicothe,* Xenia, Ohio, 1934, pp. 85–86.

2. "Having received": quote from letter of De Peyster to McKee, taken from *Michigan Pioneer and Historical Collections,* 11:340–341 (1887).

3. *Author's Note:* Although he served as an agent of the British Indian Department, Girty received the pay of an English captain, was provided an officer's uniform, and was referred to in letters by Colonel De Peyster, as "Captain Girty." *See: Michigan Pioneer and Historical*

Collection, 11:344 (1887).

4. "Caressed him": Lyon quote from: C. Hale Sipe, *Indian Wars,* p. 658.

5. "Intelligent spy": Haldimand to De Peyster, spring 1783, *See: Michigan Pioneer and Historical Collections,* 11:350–351 (1887).

6. "Of necessity, not choice": quote of John Turner, Jr. from Butterfield, *History of the Girtys,* p. 210.

7. "About 1783": quote of James Blashford, from Lyman Draper's notes of his 1846 interview with Blashford, in *Lyman Draper Manuscripts,* microfilm, 3-S-126–127.

8. "Father": quote of Half King from minutes of council meeting, June 14, 1783 in: Library and Archives Canada/RG10/Vol. 10, p. 208.

9. "Had been compelled": quote of Ephraim Douglas from: C. Hale Sipe, *Indian Wars,* p. 681.

10. "Simon Girty ... a principal evidence": quote from De Peyster to MacLean, July 7, 1783, in: *Michigan Pioneer and Historical Collection,* 20:136 (1892). *See also:* C. Hale Sipe, *Indian Wars,* pp. 682–683.

11. "Girty brought two pistols": quote of Sarah (Girty) Munger, in Lyman Draper notes of his interview with her, *Lyman Draper Manuscripts,* microfilm, 20 S 196–197.

12. "I have delivered": quote of De Peyster from De Peyster to MacClean, August 11, 1783, *See: Michigan Pioneer and Historical Collection,* 20:170.

13. "Of their willingness": quotes from councils at Lower Sandusky, from *Michigan Pioneer and Historical Collections,* 20:174–175.

14. "The King still considers": McKee speech taken from: Ibid., p. 176.

15. "Brothers": quote of Joseph Brant, from: Ibid., pp. 178–180.

16. "Father Listen": Half King quote from: Ibid., pp. 181–182.

17. "Doing right": quote of McKee from: Ibid., pp. 181.

CHAPTER FIFTEEN [PAGES 263-284]

1. "The Indians were about": Simon Girty quote from: *Indiana Magazine of History,* v. IX (1913) *"Indian Captives in Early Indiana,"* by Logan Esarey, p. 110. *Author's Note:* The Polkes' return journey was

uneventful and they safely reached Louisville, Kentucky, on the 24th of December, 1783.

2. "for as our settlements approach": Philip Schuyler quote taken from: John Ingram, *Simon Girty: Degeneration through Violence,* Master of Arts Thesis, 1981 Graduate College of Bowling Green University, p. 92.

3. "In short": John Ingram quote taken from: Ibid. *See also:* Reginald Horsman, *Expansion and American Indian Policy, 1783–1812,* Michigan State University Press, 1992, pp. 6–7.

4. "To preserve": George Washington quote from: Ingram, *Simon Girty: Degeneration through Violence,* p. 92.

5. "One of the captives": quote of Charles McKnight, taken from his: *Our Western Border,* Philadelphia, 1875, p. 423.

6. Picture No. 32 quote from: The Henry Hotel Booklet, which can be found at: Carnegie Library, Pittsburgh, File #P2858, pp. 57–58, r640.24 P67. The booklet includes an engraving of the Catherine Malott painting.

7. "fell hard": quote of Catherine Girty (widow of Simon Jr.'s son Prideaux), from notes of Lyman Draper's interview with her. *Lyman Draper Manuscripts,* microfilm, 17-S-163. *See also:* McKnight, *Our Western Border,* Philadelphia 1875, p. 423.

8. "We were nine days": John Crawford quote taken from: *Lyman Draper Manuscripts,* microfilm, 12-CC-159–161.

9. "You know brethren": Captain Johnny speech taken from: Library and Archives Canada/MG19/F35, v. 2, pp. 1–4.

10. Josiah Harmar to Secretary of War, May 29, 1785, from: William Henry Smith, ed., *The St. Clair Papers,* v. II, pp. 6–7.

11. "October 8. Was informed": Daniel Elliott quote from: *Lyman Draper Manuscripts,* microfilm, 14-S-196–201.

12. "God gave us this country": quote of Shawnee Chief Kekewepellethe from: Bil Gilbert, *God Gave Us This Country,* Anchor Books, Doubleday, New York, 1990, p. 115.

13. "We plainly tell you": quote of Richard Butler from: Horsman, *Expansion and American Indian Policy,* p. 22.

14. "The Shawnees could choose": quote of Richard Butler, from: Ibid., p. 22.

15. "Brethren, our people": quote of Kekewepellethy, taken from Ibid., p. 23.

16. Ibid.

17. "The deponent saith": quote of William Doleman, taken from Notes of Lyman Draper, *Lyman Draper Manuscripts,* microfilm, 14-S-216–217.

18. Girty to McKee, 11 October 1786, from: Library National Archives of Canada, microfilm, MG19 F35, Series 2, CO 42/87, folio 314–314v, and docket on 315v.

19. McKee to Sir John Johnson, November 12, 1786, from: Library National Archives of Canada, microfilm, MG19, F35, v.4, Dossier 646, Series 2, pp. 1–4.

CHAPTER SIXTEEN [PAGES 285-300]

1. "At this council": quote of Butterfield from his: *History of the Girtys,* p. 229. *See also:* Horsman, *Matthew Elliott,* p. 57.

2. "No white man": quote of Butterfield, from his: *History of the Girtys,* p. 240.

3. "The flag of the United States": message to the Northern tribes by St. Clair, from: Wiley Sword, *President Washington's Indian War,* University of Oklahoma Press, 1985, p. 63.

4. "Mr. John Van Meter": quote of Joseph Doddridge, from his *Notes on the Settlement and Indian Wars,* 1824, Akron, reprint 1989, McClain Printing, Parsons, W. Va., p. 282.

5. "John Quick": quote of Alex McCormick, Jr., from Lyman Draper's Notes, in: *Lyman Draper Manuscripts,* microfilm, 17-S-207–208.

6. Lt. Kingsbury to General Harmar, 12 January, 1791, taken from: *Lyman Draper Manuscripts,* microfilm, 2-W-385–387.

7. "Baker's Station": quote of A.B. Tomlinson, in *"First Settlement of Grave Creek,"* pp. 352–353, in *American Pioneer,* v.2, pp. 347–358, Cincinnati, 1843. *See also:* Butterfield, *History of the Girtys,* p .249.

8. "The information of Simon Girty": Lord Dorchester to Mr. Grenville No.79, of 23 January 1791, in *Michigan Historical and Pioneer*

Collection, 24:138 (1895).

CHAPTER SEVENTEEN [PAGES 301-322]

1. "Planting soon": quote of Butterfield from: *History of the Girtys,* p. 259.

2. "That on Sunday": quote of George Setchelstiel from: Milo M. Quaife, ed., *The John Askin Papers,* 2 vols., Detroit Library Commission, 1928–1931, v.i, p. 385.

3. "This is to let you know": quote, Girty to McKee, October 28, 1791 from: *Michigan Pioneer Historical Collection,* 24:329–330 (1895). *See also:* Wiley Sword, *President Washington's Indian War,* 1985, pp. 160–165.

4. "Richard Butler": quote of Wiley Sword from his: *President Washington's Indian War,* 1985, pp. 187–188.

5. "To be divided": Ibid., p. 187.

6. "Girty inquired": Thomas Silk quote from Lyman Draper's notes of his 1850 interview with Silk. *See: Lyman Draper Manuscripts,* microfilm, 4-S-185.

7. "To the great relief": quote of Butterfield from his: *History of the Girtys,* p. 264.

8. "Congress offered": quote of W. Curry Jr., to Rev. Shane, taken from: *Lyman Draper Manuscripts,* microfilm, 13-CC-167.

9. "The American Army": quotes from an anonymous letter presented in: Robert S. Allen, *His Majesty's Indian Allies,* 1992, Dundern Press, Toronto and Oxford, pp. 75–76. Mr. Allen cited: NAC, MG11, co 42, vol.88, A Letter from Niagara, 24 November 1791–News From Detroit.

10. "A staggering sum": quote of Wiley Sword from his: *President Washington's Indian War,* p. 204.

11. "Personally appeared before me": quote of General Anthony Wayne, taken from: United States Congress, *American State Papers, Indian Affairs,* v.i, (1830) p. 243.

12. "On the day of their visit": quote of Butterfield, about Oliver Spencer's meeting with Simon Girty, from: Butterfield, *History of the*

Girtys, pp. 269–270.

13. "Girty said he was disguised": quote of Thomas Silk, in an interview in 1850 with Lyman Draper. From Draper's notes: *Lyman Draper Manuscripts,* microfilm, Wisconsin Historical Society, 4-S-185–186.

14. "Apparently": Anthony Wayne to Secretary Henry Knox, 14 December, 1792, quoted from: Richard C. Knoph, *Anthony Wayne A Name in Arms,* pp. 97–98.

15. "The place where": quote of Butterfield, from his: *History of the Girtys,* pp. 273–274.

16. "Besides the papers transmitted": quote, Henry Knox to President George Washington, 6 December, 1792, from: *American State Papers, Indian Affairs,* v.1, (1830) p. 322.

CHAPTER EIGHTEEN [PAGES 323-350]

1. "Would commence hostilities": quote of Wiley Sword, from his: *President Washington's Indian War,* p. 241.

2. "properly authorized": quote of Joseph Brant, from: Kelsay, *Joseph Brant Man of Two Worlds,* 1984, p. 496.

3. "Supported his insolence": Heckewelder quote, from: John Heckewelder, *A Narrative of the Missions of the United Brethren among the Delaware and Mohegan Indians,* Philadelphia 1820, pp. 402–403.

4. "The rejoinder": quote of Butterfield from his: *History of the Girtys,* p. 277.

5. "This side of the Ohio is ours": quote of So-wagh-da-wunk from: Sword, *President Washington's Indian War,* p. 244.

6. "Instead of going home": Simon Girty quote, from: Butterfield, *History of the Girtys,* p. 277.

7. "The vessel called Detroit": quote of William Savery, from his journal, taken from: Butterfield, *History of the Girtys,* p. 279.

8. "You agreed to do us justice": quote of Indian declaration presented American delegation, taken from: Gilbert, *God Gave us This Country,* 1989, p. 168.

9. "We did not effect a peace": Thomas Pickering and Beverly

Lincoln to General Anthony Wayne, August 15, 1793, taken from: Sword, *President Washington's Indian War*, p. 246.

10. "Our negotiations": Jefferson to Charles Pinckney, November 27, 1793, Washington, ed., *Writings of Jefferson, IV*, pp. 85–86 taken from: Horsman, *Expansion and American Indian Policy, 1783–1812*, 1967, Oklahoma University Press, p. 98.

11. "Sent off Simon Girty": quote from Alexander McKee's journal, 15 December 1793, taken from: *Michigan Pioneer Historical Collection*, (1887) 12:108.

12. "One thousand acres": quote of Colin G. Calloway, from his: *Simon Girty Interpreter*, in *Being and Becoming Indian*, edited by James A. Clifton, Dorsey Press, Chicago, 1989, p. 51.

13. "One day": quote of Butterfield from his: *History of the Girtys*, pp. 281–282.

14. "I shall not be surprised": quote of Lord Dorchester speaking to Indians at Quebec, from Cruikshank, ed., *Simcoe Papers*, 2:149–150, in Allen, *His Majesty's Indian Allies*, Dundern Press, Toronto, 1992, p. 82.

15. "Sir, at Seven o'clock in the morning": quote, Wayne to Knox, 7 July 1794, in: Knopf, *Anthony Wayne a Name In Arms*, pp. 345–349.

16. "These Indians all insist": quote, Wayne to Knox, 7 July 1794 from: Knopf, *Anthony Wayne*, p. 348.

17. "We have beaten the enemy twice": Little Turtle quote from: Bert Anson, *The Miami Indians*, in Gilbert, *God Gave Us This Country*, 1989, paperback edition, Anchor Books, Doubleday, New York, pp. 177–178.

CHAPTER NINETEEN [PAGES 351-382]

1. "Sir- I take the liberty": quote, Girty to McKee, 10 November, 1795: Michigan Pioneer Historical Collection, 12:186 (1887).

2. "additional interpreter": quote, Alexander McKee to Joseph Chew, 19 April, 1796, in Michigan Pioneer and Historical Collection, (1892) 20:440–41. For Girty's daily rate of pay. *See: Lyman Draper Manuscripts*, microfilm, Wisconsin Historical Society, 17-S-198.

3. "From Mrs. Sarah Munger": notes of Lyman Draper, from his

interview with Mrs. Munger in 1864, in: *Lyman Draper Manuscripts,* microfilm, 20-S-201–202.

4. "After the Americans": quote of John McCormick, in Lyman Draper's notes, *See: Lyman Draper Manuscripts,* microfilm, 17-S-211.

5. "In the summer of 1796": quote of William Walker, Jr. from: *Wyandot Gazette* (Kansas), April 18, 1872, *"Interesting Correspondence, A Chapter of Early History, Recollections of Simon Girty, the Renegade",* author unknown.

6. "He was there": quote of Henry Wright, Sr. from: *Michigan Pioneer Historical Collection,* (1870) 7:126.

7. "On account of his drinking and unkindness": quote of Sarah Munger, from an interview with her in 1864, in Lyman Draper's notes, *See: Lyman Draper Manuscripts,* microfilm, 20-S-213. Regarding the separation of Simon and Catherine Girty, Girty referred to it in an 1804 letter to John Turner, Jr., *See:* Lyman Draper Manuscripts, microfilm, Simon Girty to John Turner, 12-U-16.

For Catherine taking infant Prideaux Girty with her, but leaving her other children with Simon at Malden when she walked out, I rely upon the following: First, Simon's mention of his separation in an 1804 letter to John Turner, Jr. (Draper 12-U-16), in which Simon states that he and his wife separated six years earlier, and went on to add: "my children and myself live together, we are all very well . . ." etc. Secondly, there is a story written by a reporter named MacLeod, published in the *Amherstburg Echo,* November 21, 1884, the subject of which was Simon Girty, as remembered by a Mrs. McCormick (widow of Alexander McCormick Jr.), who at the time of her interview, was 93-years-of-age; making her seven-years-old at the time of Simon and Catherine Girty's separation. The following questions and answers appear in the article:

Q: Did you personally know Simon Girty of Amherstburg, and had he any children?.

A: I knew him very well. I used to see him every day when I was a child attending school in Amherstburg. He used to go to Fort Malden as Indian interpreter, under the employ of the government. He was a rough but kindhearted man. He had three children, two daughters and a son whose name was

Thomas . . .

. . . Simon Girty's wife was Catherine Malott, but they did not live together many years.

Mrs. McCormick remembered three children living with their father when she was a school girl. Thirdly: Girty descendents in Kingsville and Windsor, Ontario (including the reputable, published historian Mrs. Madeline Malott, and Girty patriarch Dwight Girty, of Windsor), also claim that Catherine took Prideaux (who must have been about eighteen months old) with her when she went to live with her brother.

8. "There is no one": quote from William Mickle, Jr. to C. W. Butterfield, 1 January 1887, taken from: Butterfield, *History of the Girtys*, p. 393.

9. "About the year": Sarah Girty Munger quote from notes of Lyman Draper's 1864 interview with her: *Lyman Draper Manuscripts*, microfilm, 20-S-208, Wisconsin Historical Society.

10. "[the dance] commenced": quote of Solomon McCulloch, as told to Judge John H. James by Simon Kenton: from Edna Kenton, *Simon Kenton, His Life and Period*, New York, 1930, reprint: Ayer Co., Salem, N. H., 1989, pp. 57–58. *Note:* Relating his story to Simon Kenton, McCulloch thought it was 1800 when he was in Upper Canada with Simon Girty at the McKee funeral dance, and he remembered that McKee had died "about three years before." But McKee had actually died in 1799, and the dance honoring him must therefore have taken place in late 1803 or early 1804. McCulloch also told Kenton that when he visited Girty at Malden, Simon had a daughter of 18 and a son of 14 living with him. Nancy Ann Girty was 18 in 1804.

11. "a very Smokey day," and "rain last night verry hard" quotes of William Clark from: *The Journals of the Lewis and Clark Expedition*, vol. II, reprint, University of Nebraska Press, 1986, Gary E. Moulton, ed., p. 181

12. "Dear Brother": Simon Girty to John Turner, Jr., 11 November, 1804 from: *Lyman Draper Manuscripts*, microfilm, 12-U-13.

13. "Dear Brother": Simon Girty to John Turner, Jr., 10 November 1807, from: *Lyman Draper Manuscripts*, microfilm, 12-U-14.

14. "S. Girty is incapable": quote William Claus to Prideaux Selby,

1804, quote taken from: Colin G. Calloway, *Simon Girty: Interpreter and Intermediary,* p. 54, in: James A Clifton, ed., *Being and Becoming Indian,* Chicago, 1989.

15. "Nearly halfway": quote of author John Richardson, from his: *The Canadian Brothers,* Montreal, 1840, reprint, University of Toronto Press, 1976, pp. 99–101. *See:* introduction by editor Karl Klinck who clarifies that the character Sampson Gattrie was based upon Simon Girty.

16. "To one": quote of John Richardson, from his: *The Canadian Brothers,* Montreal, 1840, reprint, University of Toronto Press, 1976, pp. 105–106.

17. "His son Thomas": Sarah Girty Munger quote, in Lyman Draper's notes of his interview with her in 1864, from: *Lyman Draper Manuscripts,* microfilm, 20-S-204. For information on Simon selling land to his son *See:* Butterfield, *History of the Girtys,* p. 307.

18. "After Perry's victory": quote of Sarah Munger written in Lyman Draper's notes of an 1864 interview with her, *See: Lyman Draper Manuscripts,* microfilm, 20-S-203.

19. "As Harrison's men": quote: Ibid., 20-S-203, 204.

20. "Taken from": quote of Simon Kenton, from papers of Simon Kenton, in Lyman Draper's notes, *See: Lyman Draper Manuscripts,* microfilm, 5-S-127.

21. "Simon was adopted": quote from Missouri Gazette, May 7, 1814, taken from *Lyman Draper Manuscripts,* microfilm, 26-S-146–148.

22. "Officers and others": quote William May to unknown, March 1815, from: *Michigan Pioneer Historical Collection,* 1895, 23:109–Indian Pension List.

23. "He went to that region": quote of Simon Girty from his 11 November 1807 letter to his half-brother John Turner, Jr. cited again by Butterfield in his: *History of the Girtys,* p. 328.

EPILOGUE [PAGES 383-386]

1. The historic plaque erected at the Girty farm site on the Detroit River, 8 July 1995, reads:

SIMON GIRTY U.E.

1741–1818.

GIRTY'S LIFE CROSSED CULTURAL BOUNDARIES.

BETWEEN NATIVE AND WHITE SOCIETIES ON THE.

FRONTIER OF AMERICAN SETTLEMENT. IN 1756.

HIS FAMILY WAS CAPTURED BY A FRENCH-LED.

NATIVE WAR PARTY IN PENNSYLVANIA. SIMON WAS.

ADOPTED BY THE SENECA, THEN REPATRIATED IN.

1764. AN INTERPRETER AT FORT PITT (PITTSBURGH),.

HE BECAME AN INTERMEDIARY WITH NATIVE NATIONS.

IN 1778, DISMAYED OVER REBEL POLICY ON THE.

NATIVES, GIRTY FLED TO DETROIT. DURING THE.

REVOLUTIONARY WAR AND SUBSEQUENT CONFLICTS.

IN THE OHIO VALLEY, HE WAS EMPLOYED BY THE.

BRITISH INDIAN DEPARTMENT WHILE SERVING NATIVE.

NATIONS AS A NEGOTIATOR, SCOUT AND MILITARY.

LEADER. ANGRY AT HIS DEFECTION AND FEARFUL.

OF HIS INFLUENCE, AMERICANS MADE GIRTY A.

SCAPEGOAT FOR FRONTIER ATROCITIES. HE IS.

BURIED HERE ON HIS HOMESTEAD.

ERECTED BY THE BICENTENNIAL AND TORONTO BRANCHES,.

UNITED EMPIRE LOYALISTS' ASSOCIATION OF CANADA, WITH.

ASSISTANCE FROM THE ONTARIO HERITAGE FOUNDATION.

2. For Girty being an "Indian Patriot," this statement was told to the author by the late John Mohawk, Professor, Native American Studies, SUNY Buffalo. Mohawk, a Seneca, was a member of the Grand Council of the Iroquois.

APPENDIX [PAGES 387-394]

1. For the family history of the Girtys and Malotts in Canada after Simon Girty, I am deeply indebted to Canadian historian Madeline Hilborn Malott, of Kingsville, Ontario (her husband is Hazen Malott, a direct descendant of Peter Malott—Catherine Girty's brother). Among Mrs. Malott's published works are: *Simon, Peter and Polly: A Chronology of Malott and Girty families,* 1994, Madeline Hilborn Malott, Speedprint Inc., Leamington, Ontario, also: co-writer: *Kingsville 1790—2000: A Stroll Through Time,* two volume set, Kingsville-Gosfield Heritage Society, Windsor, Ontario, 2003.

BIBLIOGRAPHY

PRINCIPAL SOURCES

Abernethy, Thomas P. *Western Lands and the American Revolution.* Virginia: University of Virginia, 1937, reprint ed. New York: Russell and Russell, 1959. Tracing the land dealings and investments of leading colonial politicians and businessmen, including those of George Washington, Benjamin Franklin, George Morgan and other notables, this book provides outstanding perspectives of political and commercial actions involving land acquisition through the colonial and revolutionary periods.

Baynton, Wharton & Morgan Papers. Harrisburg, Pa.: Microfilm collection, Commonwealth of Pennsylvania, Division of Archives, MG19, reel 1. Provides superb detail of George Morgan's interests during the colonial and Revolutionary War periods, with several references to the Girtys.

Butterfield, Consul Wilshire. *History of the Girtys.* Cincinnati: Robert Clarke & Co., 1890. Although slanted against Girty, this work is nevertheless the most thorough history of Girty's activities prior to his defection. Luckily, Butterfield cited his sources, and these citations lead to a great deal of interesting and little known information on Girty and the period.

_____. *An Historical Account of the Expedition against Sandusky.* Cincinnati: Robert Clarke & Co., 1873. Preceding the author's biography of the Girtys by seventeen years, his account of Simon Girty in this work is by far the most accurate. In his 1890 book, he discounts facts he presented in this work. Provides an excellent perspective of the doomed Crawford expedition and Girty's alleged role in these events.

_____. *Washington–Crawford Letters,* also known as *Washington Crawford Correspondence.* Cincinnati: Robert Clarke & Co., 1877. Mainly comprised of letters between George Washington and his surveyor-friend William Crawford, this work exposes Washington's preoccupation with land acquisition prior to the Revolutionary War, and clearly reveals his hatred for the King's Proclamation of 1763, prohibiting direct acquisition of Indian lands by British subjects, except through sanction of the king.

_____. *Washington Irvine Correspondence.* Madison, Wis.: David Atwood, 1882. Provides important insights into dynamics of the frontier war, with strong detail of development of Pittsburgh commercial trade.

Draper, Lyman C. *Lyman Draper Manuscripts Collection.* Madison, Wis.: Wisconsin Historical Society microfilm. An invaluable resource, particularly the S, SS, U, C and E series of the collection, 1830 thru 1880. Comprised of letters, journals, newspaper articles, and notes by Lyman Draper based on interviews that he conducted over a 40-year span while researching material on the early American frontier (colonial and revolutionary periods), this collection was also the principal source used by Butterfield for his biography *History of the Girtys.*

Michigan Pioneer and Historical Collections. Lansing, Mich.: Vols. 1- 40, (1876–1929). Containing numerous documents and passages about Simon Girty, including excerpts from British military records, letters and other materials, this collection was an excellent source, particularly concerning Girty's activities after his defection in 1778. Refer to specific citations in *Notes and Sources.*

Morgan, George. *George Morgan Letterbooks.* Ann Arbor, Mich.: University Microfilms, International. for years 1775–1776, and 1778–1779. Contains numerous references to Simon and James Girty, and is particularly helpful in understanding commercial dynamics and Indian relations.

National Archives of Canada. Ottawa: Microfilm Collections, MG 10, 18, 19, 21. A generally important and informative source for information about the British Indian Department, as well as English military and political affairs, from 1730 through 1820. The *Haldimand Papers, Sir William Johnson Correspondence* were an especially useful and valuable source.

SECONDARY SOURCES

Allen, Robert S. *The British Indian Department and the Frontier in North America, 1755–1830*. Ottawa: Canadian Historic Sites No. 14, Indian and Northern Affairs, 1975.
_____. *His Majesty's Indian Allies–British Indian Policy in the Defence of Canada 1774–1815*. Toronto: Dundurn Press, Ltd., 1992.
Alvord, Clarence W. and Carter, C.C., eds. *Trade and Politics in the Illinois Country*. Springfield: Illinois Historical Society, 1921.
Arnow, Harriette Simpson. *Seedtime on the Cumberland*. New York: Macmillan, 1960.
Baldwin, Leland D. *Pittsburgh–The Story of a City*. Pittsburgh: University of Pittsburgh Press, 1938.
Barnhart, John D, ed. *Henry Hamilton and George Rogers Clark in the American Revolution, with the Unpublished Journal of Lt. Gov. Henry Hamilton*. Crawfordsville, Ind.: R. E. Banta, 1951.
Blanco, Richard L., ed. *The American Revolution 1775–1783, an Encyclopedia*. Two volumes, New York: Garland Publishing, 1993.
Botsford, C. M. *At The End of the Trail*. Windsor, Ontario: Windsor Print & Litho Ltd., limited edition, 1985.
Brackenridge, Hugh Henry, ed. *Indian Atrocities, Narratives of Dr. Knight & John Slover*. Philadelphia: 1783; reprint ed. Fairfield, Wash.: Ye Galleon Press, 1983.
Bradford, John. *Scoouwa: James Smith's Indian Captivity Narrative*. Lexington, Kentucky, 1799; reprint ed. Cleveland: Ohio Historical Society, 1899.
Brown, Mary S. "In Memory of the Early Settlers of Squirrel Hill and Their Descendants." booklet, Pittsburgh: Mary S. Brown Memorial Methodist Episcopal Church of Pittsburgh, c. 1905.
Brown, Parker B. "The Battle of Sandusky." *Western Pennsylvania*

Historical Magazine (April 1982).

_____. "Accuracy of the Knight Narrative." *Western Pennsylvania Historical Magazine* (January 1987).

_____. "Fate of the Crawford Volunteers." *Western Pennsylvania Historical Magazine* (October 1982).

Buck, Solon J. *The Planting of Civilization in Western Pennsylvania.* Pittsburgh: University of Pittsburgh Press, 1939.

Burch, Mary J. *A Family Record, Embracing a Sketch of the History of the Scratch, Wigle, Fox, Frioend, Wilkinson, Shepley, McCormick, Malotte, Coatsworth, Iler Families.* Windsor, Ontario: The "Review" Steam Printing House, 1850.

Burton, Clarence Munroe. "John Connolly a Tory of the Revolution." *Proceedings of the American Antiquarian Society,* Annual Meeting, v. XX, Worcester: Published by The Society, 1909.

Butterfield, Consul Wilshire. *History of George Rogers Clark's Conquest of the Illinois and the Wabash Towns 1778 and 1779.* Columbus: Fred J. Heer, 1904.

Calloway, Colin G. *Crown and Calumet.* Norman: University of Oklahoma Press, 1987.

Calloway, Colin G. "Simon Girty, Interpreter and Intermediary." in Clifton, James A. ed. *Being and Becoming Indian: Biographical Studies of North American Frontiers.* Chicago: Dorsey Press, 1989.

Carter, Clarence Edwin. *The Illinois Country, 1763–1774.* Washington, D.C.: The American Historical Association, 1910.

Curry, Richard Orr. "Lord Dunmore and the West, A Re-Evaluation." *West Virginia History Quarterly Magazine,* v. XIX (July 1958).

Darlington, William H. *Christopher Gist's Journals.* Pittsburgh: J.R. Weldin & Co., 1893; reprint ed. New York: Argonaut Press Ltd., 1966.

De Haas, Wills. *History and Indian Wars of West Virginia.* Wheeling, W. Va.: H. Hoblitzell, 1851; reprint ed. Parsons, W.Va.: McClain Printing, 1989.

De Schweinitz, Edmund. *Life and Times of David Zeisberger.* Philadelphia: J. B. Lippencott & Co., 1871.

Division of Archives, Land Records Section, Land Warrants, document 1763 No. 852, Harrisburg, Pennsylvania.

Doddridge, Joseph. *Notes on the Settlement and Indian Wars.* Wellsburgh, Va.: Printed at the office of the Gazette for the author, 1824; reprint ed. Parsons, W. Va.: McClain Printing Co., 1994.

Donehoo, George P. *Pennsylvania, a History.* New York: Lewis Historical Publishing Co., 1926.

Downes, Randolph C. *Council Fires on the Ohio.* Pittsburgh: University of Pittsburgh Press, 1940.

Esarey, Logan. "Indian Captives in Early Indiana." *Indiana Magazine of History, v.* 9 (1913).

Ewing, William. "Indian Captives Released by Colonel Bouquet." *Western Pennsylvania Historical Magazine,* v. 39 (1956).

Faragher, John Mack. *Daniel Boone: The Life and Legend of an American Pioneer.* New York: Henry Holt and Company, 1992.

Fenton, William N. *The Great Law and the Longhouse.* Norman: University of Oklahoma Press, 1998.

Flexner, James Thomas. *Mohawk Baronet.* Syracuse: Syracuse University Press, 1989.

Frew, Margaret A. "Squirrel Hill." *Western Pennsylvania Historical Magazine,* v. 12 (1929).

Gilbert, Bil. *God Gave Us This Country.* New York: Anchor Books, 1990.

Girty, Catherine. *"Deposition of Catherine Girty, Widow of Simon Girty." May 19, 1832,* Certificate of marriage, Sandwich, Ontario: Clerk of the Peace's Office, October 17, 1838.

Gordon, Thomas F. *History of Pennsylvania from Discovery to 1776.* Philadelphia: Carey, Lea & Carey, 1829.

Graymont, Barbara. *The Iroquois in the American Revolution.* Syracuse: Syracuse University Press, 1972.

Harper, Eugene R. *The Transformation of Western Pennsylvania 1770–1800.* Pittsburgh: University of Pittsburgh Press, 1991.

Hassler, Edgar W. *Old Westmoreland: A History of Western Pennsylvania During the Revolution.* Pittsburgh: J.B. Weldin, 1900.

Hazard, Samuel, ed. *Pennsylvania Archives, Old Series.* Philadelphia: Joseph Severns & Co., 1854.

Heckewelder, John. *History, Manners and Customs of the Indian Nations Who Once Inhabited Pennsylvania and the Neighboring*

States. Philadelphia: Historical Society of Pennsylvania, revised 1876; reprint ed. Bowie: Md.: Heritage Books, 1990.

_____. *Narrative of the Missions of the United Brethren Among the Delaware and Mohegan Indians from its commencement, in the year 1740, to the close of the year 1808*. Philadelphia: McCarty and Davis, 1820; reprint ed. New York: Arno Press, 1971.

"Henry Hotel Booklet." containing an engraving of Catherine Malott, Pittsburgh: Carnegie Library, File # P2858, r640.24.

Hoberg, Walter R. "Early History of Colonel Alexander McKee." *Pennsylvania Magazine of History and Biography*, v. 58, 1934.

Horsman, Reginald. *Matthew Elliott, British Indian Agent*. Detroit: Wayne State University Press, 1964.

_____. *The Frontier in the Formative Years, 1783–1815*. New York: Holt, Rinehart and Winston, 1970.

_____. *Expansion and American Indian Policy, 1783–1812*. E. Lansing: Michigan State University Press, 1967.

Howe, Henry, ed. *Historical Collections of Ohio in Two Volumes*. Cincinatti: Derby, Bradley & Co., 1848; reprint ed. Cincinnati: C. J. Krehbiel & Co, 1908.

Hunter, William A. *Forts on the Pennsylvania Frontier 1753–1758*. Harrisburg: Pennsylvania Historical and Museum Commission, 1960.

Ingram, John. *Simon Girty: Degeneration through Violence.*, Master of Arts Thesis, Ohio: Graduate College of Bowling Green University, 1981.

"Interesting Correspondence, A Chapter of Early History, Recollections of Simon Girty, the Renegade." writer unknown, Wyandotte, Kan.: *Wyandotte Gazette,* April 18, 1872.

Jaebker, Orville John, Ph. D. *Henry Hamilton: British Soldier and Colonial Governor*. unpublished Ph.D. dissertation, Bloomington: Indiana University, 1954.

Jacob, John L. *A Biographical Sketch of the Life of the Late Captain Michael Cresap*. Cumberland, Md.: 1826; reprint ed. New York: Arno Press, 1971.

Jennings, Francis. *Empire of Fortune*. New York: W. W. Norton & Co., Inc., 1988.

Johnson, Patricia G. *General Andrew Lewis of Roanoke and Greenbrier.* Charlottesville: University of Virginia, 1980.

Jones, David (Rev.). *A Journal of Two Visits Made to Some Nations of Indians on the West Side of the River, Ohio, in the years 1772 and 1773.* New York: J. Sabin 1865; reprint ed. Fairfield, Wash.: Ye Galleon Press, 1973.

Jones, Uriah J. *History of the Juniata Valley.* Harrisburg: Harrisburg Publishing Co., 1889.

_____. *Simon Girty, The Outlaw.* Philadelphia: G. B. Zeiber, 1846, reprint ed. Harrisburg: The Aurand Press, 1931.

Kellogg, Louise Phelps. *Frontier Advance on the Upper Ohio.* Madison: Wisconsin Historical Society, 1916.

_____. *Frontier Retreat on the Upper Ohio.* Madison: Wisconsin Historical Society, 1917.

Kelsay, Isabel Thompson. *Joseph Brant 1743–1807- Man of Two Worlds.* Syracuse: Syracuse University Press, 1984.

Kenton, Edna. *Simon Kenton: His Life and Period.* New York: Doubleday, Doran & Co., Inc., 1930.

Knopf, Richard C., ed. *Anthony Wayne: A Name In Arms.* Pittsburgh: University of Pittsburgh Press, 1960.

Lafferty, Maude Ward. "Destruction of Ruddle's and Martin's Forts in the Revolutionary War." *Register of the Kentucky Historical Society,* v. 54, no. 189 (October 1956).

"Life of Simon Girty." Amherstburg, Ontario: *Amherstburg Echo,* (November 21, 1884).

Lewis, Virgil A. *History of the Battle of Point Pleasant.* Charleston, W. Va.: The Tribune Printing Company, 1909.

Lorant, Stefan. *Pittsburgh, the Story of an American City.* New York: Doubleday & Co., 1964.

Lough, Glen D. *Now and Long Ago: A History of the Marion County Area.* Morgantown, W. Va.: Morgantown Printing and Binding Co., 1969; reprint ed. Parsons, W. Va.: McClain Printing Co. 1994.

MacLean, J. P. *Journal of Michael Walters.* Cleveland: Western Reserve Historical Society, tract no. 89, v. IV 1899.

MacLeod, _____. "Simon Girty as Remembered by Mrs. McCormick." *Amherstburg Echo,* November 21, 1884.

McClure, David. "The Diary of David McClure D.D." *Old Westmoreland Magazine*, v. II, no. 1 (August 1981).

McCutchen, Joseph. "Simon Girty." *American Pioneer*, v. II, no. VI, 1843.

McKee, Raymond W. *The Book of McKee*. Dublin, Ireland: Hodges, Figgis & Co. 1959.

McKnight, Charles. *Our Western Border*. Philadelphia: J. C. McCurdy & Co., 1875.

_____. *Simon Girty the White Savage, A Romance of the Border*. Philadelphia: J. C. McCurdy & Co., 1880.

Moore, John H. "A Captive of the Shawnees." *West Virginia History Magazine*, v. 23, no. 4 (July 1962).

Morgan, Lewis Henry. *League of the Iroquois*. Rochester, N.Y.: Sage & Brothers, 1851; reprint ed. Secaucus, N.J.: Citadel Press, 1962.

Neible,, George W. "Account of Servants bound and Assigned before James Hamilton, Mayor of Philadelphia." *Pennsylvania Magazine of History and Biography*, v. 31, 1907.

Nelson, Larry L. *A Man of Distinction Among Them*. Kent, Ohio: Kent State University Press, 1999.

_____. *Cultural Mediation on the Great Lakes Frontier; Alexander McKee and Anglo-American Indian Affairs 1754–1799*. Ph.D. dissertation, Ohio: Bowling Green State University, May 1994.

Newman, M. B. "Interview of William Walker." *Wyandotte Gazette*, April 18, 1872.

Newton, J. .H., C.G. Nichols, A.G. Sprankle, eds. *History of the Pan Handle of West Virginia*. Wheeling, W. Va.: J.A. Caldwell, 1879; reprint ed. Bowie, Md.: Heritage Books, 1990.

Norton, A. Banning, ed. *A History of Knox County, Ohio, From 1779 to 1862*. Columbus: Richard Nevins, 1862.

O'Brien, Maire and Conor Cruise. *Concise History of Ireland*. New York: Thames & Hudson Ltd., 1972.

Olmstead, Earl P. *Blackcoats Among the Delawares*. Kent, Ohio: Kent State University Press, 1991.

O'Meara, Walter. *Guns at the Forks*. Englewood Cliffs, N.J.: Prentice Hall Inc, 1965.

Palmer, William P., ed. *Calendar of Virginia State Papers from January 1, 1782 to December 31, 1784.* v. III. Richmond: James E. Goode, 1883.

"Peck's Life of Boone." Thomas Girty obituary, from *Niles' Weekly Register,* v. IX, December 16, 1820, in *Sparks' Library of American Biography,* 2nd Series, v. III, Boston: Charles C. Little and James Brown, 1847.

Pennsylvania, Allegheny County, *Thomas Girty-Jacob Caselman deed.* Recorder of Deeds, Allegheny County, Pennsylvania, Deed Book 10, p. 381 (October 23, 1801).

Pieper, Thomas I. and James B. Gidney. *Fort Laurens, 1778–79, The Revolutionary War in Ohio.* Ohio: Kent State University Press, 1976.

Quaife, Milo M. *Fort Laurens, 1778–79.* Detroit: Burton Historical Collection leaflet, November 1925.

_____. ed. *The John Askin Papers,* two volumes, Detroit: Detroit Library Commission, 1928–1931.

Richards, James K. "A Clash of Cultures: Simon Girty and the Struggle for the Frontier." *Timeline,* Ohio Historical Society, v. 2 (July 1985).

Richardson, John. *The Canadian Brothers.* Montreal: A.H. Armour & H. Ramsay, 1840; reprint ed. Toronto: University of Toronto Press, 1976.

Rogers, T. L. "Earliest Settlements in the Fifteenth Ward of the City of Pittsburgh." *Western Pennsylvania Historical Magazine,* v. 7 (1924).

_____. "Simon Girty and Some of his Contemporaries." *Western Pennsylvania Historical Magazine,* v. 8 (1924).

Rosenthal, Baron Gustavus De. "Journal of a Volunteer Expedition to Sandusky." *The Pennsylvania Magazine of History and Biography,* v. XVIII, no. 2 (July and October 1894); reprint ed. New York: Arno Press, 1969.

Savelle, Max. *George Morgan Colony Builder.* New York: Columbia University Press, 1932

Seaver, James Everett. *A Narrative of the Life of Mary Jemison, the*

White Woman of the Genesee. Canandaigua, N.Y.: J. D. Bemis & Co., 1824.

Shaaf, Gregory. *Wampum Belts & Peace Trees: George Morgan, Native Americans, and Revolutionary Diplomacy.* Golden, Colo.: Fulcrum Press, 1990.

Sipe, C. Hale. *Indian Wars of Pennsylvania.* Harrisburg: Telegraph Press, 1929.

_____. *The Indian Chiefs of Pennsylvania.* Butler, Pa.: Ziegler Printing Co., 1927.

Slocum, Charles Elihu. *History of the Maumee River Basin.* Defiance, Ohio: Bowen & Slocum, 1905.

Smith, William Henry, ed. *The St. Clair Papers.* Cincinatti: Robert Clarke & Co., 1882; reprint ed. New York: De Capo Press, 1971.

Spencer, O.M. *Indian Captivity of O.M. Spencer.* New York: Carlton & Lanahan, 1834, reprint ed. New York: R. R. Donnelly & Sons, 1917.

St. Clair Clarke, Matthew and Peter Force, eds. *A Documentary History of the English Colonies in North America.* American Archives, 4th Series. Washington, D.C.: 1837–1846.

Stagg, Jack. *Anglo-Indian Relations in North America of 1763.* Ottawa: Indian and Northern Affairs Ministry of Canada, 1981.

Sullivan, James., ed. *Papers: Sir William Johnson.* 14 volumes, Albany: The University of the State of New York Press, 1911.

Superintendent's Correspondence. Microfilm, Ottawa: National Archives of Canada, RG 10, reel C.1222.

Sword, Wiley. *President Washington's Indian War.* Norman: University of Oklahoma Press, 1985.

Tanner, Helen Hornbeck. *Atlas of Great Lakes Indian History.* Norman: University of Oklahoma Press, 1986.

Thomson, Charles. *An Enquiry into the Causes of the Alienation of the Delaware and Shawanese Indians from the British Interest and into the measures Taken for recovering Their Friendship, etc.* London: 1759.

Thwaites, Reuben Gold and Louise Phelps Kellogg, eds. *Dunmore's War.* Madison: Wisconsin Historical Society, 1905.

_____. *Frontier Defense on the Upper Ohio.* Madison: Wisconsin

Historical Society, 1912.

Thwaites, Reuben Gold. *The Revolution on the Upper Ohio 1775–1777*. Madison: Wisconsin Historical Society, 1908.

Tomlinson, A. B. "First Settlement of Grave Creek." by A. B. Tomlinson, *American Pioneer*, v. II, Cincinnati: John S. Williams, 1843.

United States Congress. *American State Papers, Indian Affairs*. v. 1, Washington, D.C.: 1830.

Volwiler, Albert T. *George Croghan and the Western Movement 1741– 1782*. New York: AMS Press, 1971.

Walker, Hon. Charles I. *Annual Address Before the State Historical Society of Wisconsin*. Madison: 1871.

Wallace, Anthony F.C. *The Death and Rebirth of the Seneca*. New York: Vintage Books, 1972.

Wallace, Paul A.W. *Conrad Weiser 1696–1760 Friend of Colonist and Mohawk*. Philadelphia: University of Pennsylvania Press, 1945.

_____. *Indians in Pennsylvania*. Harrisburg: Pennsylvania Historical and Museum, 1989.

_____. *The Travels of John Heckewelder in Frontier America*. Pittsburgh: University of Pittsburgh Press, 1985.

Webster, Isaac. *A Narrative of the Captivity of Isaac Webster*. Ohio, 1808, reprint ed. Fairfield, Wash.: Ye Galleon Press, 1988.

West, J. Martin, ed. *Clark's Shawnee Campaign of 1780*. Springfield, Ohio: Clark County Historical Society, 1980.

White, Richard. *The Middle Ground: Indians, Empires, and Republics in the Great Lakes Region, 1650–1815*. New York: Cambridge University Press, 1991.

Withers, Alexander Scott. *Chronicles of Border Warfare*, Cincinnati: The Robert Clarke Company, 1895; reprint ed. Parsons, W. Va.: McClain Printing Co., 1989.

INDEX

—H—

—I—

Ross, Alexander, 85
Royal Proclamation [*see* Kingís
    Proclamation]
Ruddle, Captain Isaac, 186–89
Ruddle's Station, 188–90, 240
    description of, 185–86
    attack on, 187

—S—

Sakayengwalaghton [*see*
    Kayingwautro]
Salt Lick Town, 127
Sanderson, Andrew, 8
Sandusky Towns [*see* Upper
    Sandusky Towns]
Sandusky, meeting at, 320,
    323–24, 328
Sanford, Nancy Ann, 11
Saunders [Sanders], Samuel, 10–11
Savery, William, journal of, 331
Sawaghdawunk, 330
Schmidt, Rev. Johann, 99
Schuyler, General Philip, 267–68
Scioto River, 21, 48, 73, 77, 96, 120,
    130, 135, 196, 200, 202, 209,
    274, 292
Scipio, 191
Scippo Creek, 78, 80
Scotash, 209–11, 214, 227
Scots-Irish traders, 3, 21
Scott, Captain David, 126
Scott, General Charles
    attacks Scioto Indians, 292
Seekonk, 96
Selby, Lieutenant Prideaux, 361,
    371

Semple's Tavern, 61
Seneca Indians [*see* Western
    Seneca Indians]
Seneca Lake, 25
Setchelstiel, George
    files complaint against SG,
    302–03
Settlers
    attitude toward Indians, 6
Seven Nations of Canada, 319, 329
Shade, The, 98
    death of, 282
Shawnee Indians, 4, 40–41, 45–47,
    53, 55–56, 83, 98, 102–112, 119,
    130, 146, 149, 153–54, 165–66,
    169, 173, 175, 180–82, 187,
    192, 193, 200, 208, 216, 220,
    223, 226, 233–35, 245–48, 259,
    272–74, 276, 278–79, 285,
    289–291, 294–95, 302, 306,
    319–320, 323, 325–26, 329–33,
    368, 371, 375, 381, 385
    ties with French, 5–6
    transport Mary Girty 18,
    20–21
    at Squirrel Hill, 38
    and Dunmore's War, 64–68,
    70, 72–73, 76–79, 81, 88
    towns destroyed, 72, 281
    Girty and Wood's visit to, 96
    ambush Kenton and Boone,
    150
    cede land to Americans, 353
Shebosh, John, 135–36
Sherman Creek, 9–10
Sherman's Valley, 9, 13

—T—

Phil Hoffman is a screenwriter who scripted shows for Combat! and other dramatic TV series. Working under the late Jay Silverheels (Tonto in the Lone Ranger TV series), Hoffman taught a writing class for nine years at the Native American Actor's Workshop in Los Angeles. He also ran his own ad agency for thirty years, and is an award winning, world–renowned cutlery designer whose original Lakota knives were accepted into the Permanent Design Collection of the Museum of Modern Art in New York City. A serious student of the history of North America's Woodland Indians, Hoffman spent nineteen years researching Simon Girty's life. He lives with his wife and two Labrador Retrievers near Pensacola, Florida.

Breinigsville, PA USA
16 March 2011
257787BV00002B/25/P